Joyce's Allmaziful Plurabilities

The Florida James Joyce Series

UNIVERSITY PRESS OF FLORIDA

Florida A&M University, Tallahassee
Florida Atlantic University, Boca Raton
Florida Gulf Coast University, Ft. Myers
Florida International University, Miami
Florida State University, Tallahassee
New College of Florida, Sarasota
University of Central Florida, Orlando
University of Florida, Gainesville
University of North Florida, Jacksonville
University of South Florida, Tampa
University of West Florida, Pensacola

JOYCE'S
Allmaziful Plurabilities

Polyvocal Explorations of *Finnegans Wake*

Edited by Kimberly J. Devlin and Christine Smedley

FOREWORD BY SEBASTIAN D. G. KNOWLES

UNIVERSITY PRESS OF FLORIDA

Gainesville / Tallahassee / Tampa / Boca Raton
Pensacola / Orlando / Miami / Jacksonville / Ft. Myers / Sarasota

Copyright 2015 by Kimberly J. Devlin and Christine Smedley
All rights reserved
Printed in the United States of America on acid-free paper

This book may be available in an electronic edition.

First cloth printing, 2015
First paperback printing, 2018

23 22 21 20 19 18   6 5 4 3 2 1

Library of Congress Cataloging-in-Publication Data
Joyce's allmaziful plurabilities : polyvocal explorations of Finnegans Wake / edited by Kimberly J. Devlin and Christine Smedley ; foreword by Sebastian D. G. Knowles.
    pages cm—(Florida James Joyce series)
Includes index.
ISBN 978-0-8130-6154-2 (cloth)
ISBN 978-0-8130-6481-9 (pbk.)
1. Joyce, James, 1882–1941. Finnegans wake. 2. Joyce, James, 1882–1941—Criticism and interpretation. I. Devlin, Kimberly J., 1957– editor. II. Smedley, Christine, editor. III. Knowles, Sebastian D. G. (Sebastian David Guy), author of introduction, etc. IV. Series: Florida James Joyce series.
PR6019.O9F593553 2015
823'.912—dc23   2015019370

The University Press of Florida is the scholarly publishing agency for the State University System of Florida, comprising Florida A&M University, Florida Atlantic University, Florida Gulf Coast University, Florida International University, Florida State University, New College of Florida, University of Central Florida, University of Florida, University of North Florida, University of South Florida, and University of West Florida.

University Press of Florida
15 Northwest 15th Street
Gainesville, FL 32611-2079
http://upress.ufl.edu

Contents

Foreword: Polyvocal Explorations of *Finnegans Wake* vii
List of Abbreviations xi

Introduction: The Prodigal Text 1
   Kimberly J. Devlin and Christine Smedley

1. The "gift of seek on site": The Subject of Prophecy in I.1 14
   John Terrill

2. "Here Comes Everybody": HCE and the Existence of Others in I.2 29
   Jim LeBlanc

3. Weathering the Text: Barometric Readings of I.3 44
   Tim Conley

4. Habeas Corpus Epiphany in I.4 59
   Mia L. McIver

5. Joyce's Common Reader: A Primer for Sensory Consciousness in I.5 75
   Colleen Jaurretche

6. Playful Reading: I.6 and Game Theory 90
   Sean Latham

7. Shem's "strabismal apologia": The Split Vision of the Famine in I.7 114
   Christine Smedley

8. Fluid Figures in "Anna Livia Plurabelle": An Ecocritical Exploration of I.8 133
   Margot Norris

9. Moveable Types: The Character System in "The Mime of Mick, Nick and the Maggies" in II.1   149
   Carol Loeb Shloss

10. "MUTUOMORPHOMUTATION": Horus and Set as Principles of the Digital and Analog in II.2   169
    Jeffrey Drouin

11. Irish History and Modern Media: Generating Courage in II.3   186
    Enda Duffy

12. Joyce's Countergospel in II.4   201
    David Spurr

13. Salvation, Salves, Saving, and Salvage: The Linguistic Underpinnings of III.1   220
    Kimberly J. Devlin

14. Jaunty Jaun's Brokerly Advice in III.2   239
    Patrick A. McCarthy

15. The Daughter in the Father: The Revolutionary Aspect of III.3   255
    Sheldon Brivic

16. The Porters, Polypragmatic Paradigms, and Pseudoselves in III.4   272
    Richard Brown

17. "Ricorso": The Flaming Door of IV   290
    Vicki Mahaffey

List of Contributors   307
Index   311

Foreword

Polyvocal Explorations of *Finnegans Wake*

Thomas Tallis's great 40-voice motet *Spem in Alium* is a masterwork of Renaissance polyphony; *Finnegans Wake*, by contrast, is perhaps best understood as a claustrafork of Mishrashnist preverbosity. In the Tallis motet, each part requires utter and complete concentration in itself, and only by putting the sum of its parts together can the motet speak in all its exquisite cross-relations. *Finnegans Wake* also requires utter concentration on a single line, whose meaning is made manifest only when taken as part of a chorus of plurabilities. Each chapter of *Finnegans Wake*, as Kimberly Devlin and Christine Smedley clearly establish, requires a separate voice to sing in its own register, and only by joining all 17 chapters into a polyvocal whole can the text resonate in all its confounding glory.

And what voices they are! Enda Duffy sounds a trumpet, making a clarion call to action by interpreting the book's title as an imperative ("Finnegans Wake!") in his reading of the politics of II.3. David Spurr argues as sinuously and subversively as a clarinet in his serpentine reading of the countergospel in II.4. Margot Norris has such a gift for intonation in her reading of the "Anna Livia" section of I.8 that all her sentences sound perfectly in tune, like three French horns. Sean Latham's switched-on study of game theory for the question time in I.6 sounds for all the world like a virtuoso synthesizer playing Bach. Vicki Mahaffey brings the book to a beautiful close with her reading of the Ricorso in IV, where the final lines of her essay sound like the singing line of a cello, bowing up and down across the string. The 17 writers in this volume have been perfectly chosen for their command of the material, yes, but also for their particular timbre, their particular approach and style. This is what made "Our Exagmination . . ." such an ideal introduction to "Work in Progress," and what makes *Joyce's Allmaziful Plurabilities* such an ideal introduction to *Finnegans Wake*: each approach is discrete and singular, allowing the eager but baffled member of the Wakean audience to discover several different ways into the music of the text. Each author has found a perfect pitch, and the whole glorious chord now sings together.

Finnegans Wake is, according to this book:

a. a node or vortex from which and through which and into which ideas are constantly rushing
b. a circular dance for narrative power in the style of Jane Austen
c. a game that teaches you how to play itself as you proceed level by level
d. a gathering of the limbs of Osiris
e. a set of Russian dolls in which character is nested within character
f. all of the above and more

The answer, of course, is "f." These 17 gifted critics have "come to give you metaphors" for *Finnegans Wake*, to borrow Yeats's immortal phrase from his introduction to *A Vision*. There is the metaphor of the relay, which turns out to be the perfect approach for what Devlin and Smedley in their introduction call "The Prodigal Text." For Sean Latham, the book is in pieces and is best learned through "chunking"; Tim Conley's reading of the atmospherics in I.3 suggests that any slice of *Finnegans Wake* will reveal by synecdoche the greater whole, in the manner of a Mandelbrot set. *Joyce's Allmaziful Plurabilities* gives us the source code, to use Latham's helpful analogy, for each chapter, the core data from which we can all build our own varying and contradicting readings. The relay metaphor gives us a further way in. There is a word relay in I.6 that takes us from birth to death, letter by letter (*FW* 142.35–143.01):

as BORN for
LORN in
LORE of
LOVE to
LIVE and
WIVE by
WILE and
RILE by
RULE of
RUSE 'reathed
ROSE and
HOSE

But then the path bifurcates, giving us two separate outcomes:

HOLE/HOME

One way leads to death, the place of our beginning, and the other leads to life and all the comforts of an abode of bliss. Like Milton Bradley's *Game of Life* (and you will see that both "LIKE" and "LIFE" were possibilities in the word ladder), *Finnegans Wake* can lead us to the Poor Farm or to Millionaire Acres, to "HOLE," which completes a circular trajectory from birth to the grave, or to "HOME," completing a separate circuit from birth to marriage and return. Joyce characteristically gives us both answers: "by rule of ruse 'reathed rose and hose hol'd home" (*FW* 142.36–143.01). Through this allmaziful book, we reach the wreath and the rose, finding both hole and home. *Spem in alium*: there is, after all, hope in others.

Sebastian D. G. Knowles
Series Editor

Abbreviations

All citations from *Finnegans Wake* are included in parentheses in the text without a preceding symbol. We have used the most recent edition (Oxford: Oxford University Press, 2012), edited by Robbert-Jan Henkes, Erik Bindervoet, and Finn Fordham. Citations are to page and line numbers. The following additional abbreviations are used in parentheses:

        CW   James Joyce. *The Critical Writings of James Joyce*, ed. Ellsworth Mason and Richard Ellmann. New York: Viking Press, 1959.

        D   James Joyce. *Dubliners* / Text, criticism and notes, ed. Robert Scholes and A. Walton Litz. New York: Viking Press, 1969.

        JJII   Richard Ellmann. *James Joyce*. New York: Oxford University Press, 1982.

        JJA   *The James Joyce Archive*, ed. Michael Groden et al. New York: Garland, 1977–79. The last two pages of issues of the *James Joyce Quarterly* provide a guide to the volumes referred to.

    LettersI, II, III   Joyce, James. *Letters of James Joyce*. Vol. I, ed. Stuart Gilbert. New York: Viking Press, 1957; reissued with corrections 1966. Vols. II and III, ed. Richard Ellmann. New York: Viking Press, 1966.

        P   James Joyce. *A Portrait of the Artist as a Young Man* / Text, criticism and notes, ed. Chester G. Anderson. New York: Penguin, 1977.

        SH   James Joyce. *Stephen Hero*, ed. Theodore Spencer, John J. Slocum, and Herbert Cahoon. New York: New Directions, 1963.

SL James Joyce. *Selected Letters of James Joyce,* ed. Richard Ellmann. New York: Viking Press, 1975.
U   James Joyce. *Ulysses*, ed. Hans Walter Gabler et al. New York: Vintage, 1986.

Introduction

The Prodigal Text

KIMBERLY J. DEVLIN AND CHRISTINE SMEDLEY

The completion of this volume last year corresponds with the seventy-fifth anniversary of the publication of *Finnegans Wake*; the serialization of Joyce's *Work in Progress* culminated in book form in May 1939. In 2015, it seems timely to reflect on the *Wake*'s changing fortunes in the interval of these years and to reaffirm the book's enduring significance in an increasingly plural, polyglot, and global culture. Many critics take note of the book's early negative reviews and then proceed to remark on its later canonization, as epitomized by Harold Bloom's designation of the *Wake* as the twentieth century's highest aesthetic achievement.[1] In 1998, the Modern Library ranked *Finnegans Wake* 77th on its list of the 100 best English-language novels of the century. Yet the notion of the *Wake* as a curiosity for the academic elite, a largely esoteric and acquired taste, is evidenced by the book's thumbnail description on Amazon as "largely unread by the general public." Many critics of the 1940s saw Joyce's last work as an elaborate hoax, and this sentiment still endures as evidenced by a recent satirical article in the *Guardian* announcing, "World Exclusive! *Finnegans Wake* Nonsense!"[2]

Much of the resistance to *Finnegans Wake* centers on the excesses it generates—the excess of time it took Joyce to produce his final work and the excessive expenditure of effort required to appreciate its multiplicities of meanings. Joyce himself alluded to the text's linguistic prodigality by referring to his writing as a "splurge on the vellum" (179.30–31). Such excesses consequently provoked exasperated responses to the book, even among his friends, including Ezra Pound's infamous conclusion that "Nothing, so far as I can make out, nothing short of divine vision or a new cure for the clapp [sic] can possibly be worth all the circumambient peripherization" (*LettersIII* 145). Harriet Shaw Weaver wrote with concern to Joyce in 1927, critiquing "the darknesses and unintelligibilities of your deliberately entangled language system. It seems to me you are wasting your genius" (*JJII* 590). Joyce may have parodied these anxieties when he wrote, "where in the waste is the wisdom?" (114.20).

This sense of Joyce's extravagant waste of time, to say nothing of his material expenditures of ink and paper, transfers from the artist to readers, who may spend countless hours tracking down intertextual allusions or etymological derivations. The process of reading the *Wake* may produce a feeling of being trapped in an "Allmaziful" structure (104.01)—an amazing maze of textuality, but one with no center and no clear way out once one has entered. Seventy-five years later, readers may justifiably ask whether the continuing "splurges" of time and energy seemingly demanded by the labyrinth of *Finnegans Wake* are defensible. Our response to the question is obviously affirmative, but it does require a certain mind-set: one must recall the positive meaning of *prodigal* as "giving or given in abundance; lavish or profuse."[3] *Finnegans Wake*, in this sense of the word, is indeed a prodigal text.

Critiques of the *Wake* that explore its prodigal experimentalism may provide more helpful entrances to the text than earlier models, by exposing the futility of a potential mastery of its mysteries, instead underscoring an unlimited and unruly proliferation of meanings—what Joyce called "Plurabilities" (104.02). One of our aims is to celebrate the verbal richness and excesses that the text generates. But *Finnegans Wake* is not nonsense, nor is it a system of clever but self-indulgent word play. Rather Joyce's linguistic prodigality produces semantic excesses—pluralities of possibilities, in terms of meanings—that veer off in multiple, nonexclusive directions. These claims are not to deny the book's notorious difficulty. Indeed, the *Wake* requires an appreciation of what W. B. Yeats lamented as "The Fascination of What's Difficult." Enda Duffy argues in his essay in this volume that the text also requires "courage" to read some of its sections. Such reading, however, amply rewards those who would undertake the challenge—the text's neologisms and haunting resonances may intrude upon what Joyce calls our "wideawake language" (*LettersIII* 146) and permeate the dreams of even the most recalcitrant of Joycean insomniacs. Its radical re-visioning of absolutes may inspire alternative imaginings of entrenched political, linguistic, historical, and religious forms. Far from being apolitical, the *Wake* has been described by Phillippe Sollers as "the most formidably anti-fascist book produced between the wars."⁴ In her contribution, Vicki Mahaffey suggests, "The revolution that is *Finnegans Wake* frees and constrains readers to experience revolutions of their own: upheavals that are at the same time historical returns." The text is, in addition, potentially addictive: I (KJD) have had periods throughout my life when it is difficult to make it through the day without a sampling of zany Wakean language. Before he published his indispensable book of annotations to the *Wake*, Roland McHugh made a related claim about its strange readerly affect: "We never really understand what [ALP] is saying but the power in the words satisfies something and we continue resolute. Eventually [the *Wake*] can make all other reading feel inadequate. And it never runs out"⁵—one more testament to the work's positive prodigality.

The experimental dimensions of the *Wake* are beyond enumeration, although several will be explored by our contributors. We choose to focus briefly here on the one innovation that is used consistently in every chapter, on literally every page of the book: readers variously identify it as a technique within the tradition of Lewis Carroll's portmanteaux words or of Sigmund Freud's dream condensations. Thus, for example, when an unusual aroma is noted by an anonymous voice in III.1, it is described as "sharming" (427.14)—at once charming and shaming. One effect of such compacting of meaning is the expression and intensification of emotional ambivalence: condensations can paradoxically produce excess and brevity at the same time. "[E]vesdripping" (89.01) may conjure up the nosy practice of "eavesdropping," but in the context of the *Wake* it may also refer to the titillating urination of temptresses, avatars of Eve. Portmanteaux often reveal coded references to the taboo. This simultaneous destabilization and profusion of meanings create what Margot Norris calls "double-talk," although the implied limit to duality is slightly misleading.⁶ Another effect of portmanteaux is polyvocality: each of the many voices in the *Wake* frequently sounds as if it is speaking in tongues, producing triple talk, quadruple talk, quintuple talk—and even more plural evocations of layered diction. The term *polyvocal* is usually defined in terms of music, but in *Finnegans Wake* it is certainly applicable to writing and speech.

Joyce's technique of the multilayering and compression of meanings in individual words may be conceptualized as an experimental revision of figures of speech. Derek Attridge persuasively points out that one should reconsider "the traditional analysis of metaphor and allegory as a relation between a 'literal,' 'superficial' meaning and a 'figurative,' 'deep,' 'true' meaning. The portmanteau word, and *Finnegans Wake* as a whole, refuses to establish such a hierarchical opposition, for anything that appears to be a metaphor is capable of reversal, the tenor becoming the vehicle, and vice versa."[7] One can even argue that the *Wake* has *only* figurative language, with no "literal" or stable identifiable ground. We (and other Wakeans), for instance, often refer to HCE as a "he" and agree that the acronym sounds like the initials of an unknown human name—unknown on account of their pluralities in the text. But HCE has so many nonhuman forms, sometimes dissolving into funny linguistic phrases ("Haveyou-caught-emerod's" [63.18–19]), that his renderings deconstruct the technique known as "personification," with its anthropomorphizing bias. "Heinz cans everywhere" (581.05) emphasizes HCE's materiality—in addition to providing an uncanny proleptic vision of Andy Warhol's art. More accurately and more neutralizing, HCE should technically be referred to as "they"—as his identification as "Here Comes Everybody" suggests, with the "body" taking relentlessly protean shapes (32.18–19).

Joyce implicitly addresses the central demand of his experimentalism in a phrase from the text's opening chapter: "every word will be bound over to carry three score and ten toptypsical readings throughout the book of Doublends Jined" (20.14–16). This statement is hyperbolic, insofar as no word in the text carries, as a figurative load, seventy ways to read it, including even the lengthy thunderwords (which sometimes string together multiple synonyms for a single word in different languages). But words within words will pile up, as a brief look at *toptypsical* illustrates: one may see and/or hear in it *top, topped, typical, topical, tipsy,* and—given its immediate context of writing and drinking—*type, typo,* and *tope*. In his *Annotations to "Finnegans Wake,"* McHugh adds *topsy-turvy*.[8] We wonder if *toptypsical* echoes the last part of *hierarchitectitiptitoploftical* (5.01–02), *toploftical* meaning "haughty." Do readings, as productions of interpretive meanings, prove to be an imperious enterprise, as architectural building can be? (One need only to think of the raising of the Tower of Babel, an ongoing Wakean motif.) Or do they, like architectural structures themselves, provide and raise the foundations for multicultural existence? The mythic fall of the Tower of Babel produced the diversity of tongues that fascinated Joyce. Even though the word we just cited implies "hierarchies" and higher and lower positions within, such structures are difficult to establish in *Finnegans Wake* when reading its languages (as Attridge suggests). In the first passage above in this paragraph, which word within *toptypsical* modifies the word "readings"? Technically, we would argue, all of them: the phrase proves its point about overburdened signifiers and demonstrates that none of the possible modifiers are hierarchically privileged. It also generates polyvocal mysteries: what are "typical" readings? Or "typo" readings? Or "tipsy" readings? (to ask only three of the questions implied).

The distaste for Joyce's excesses sometimes correlates with a larger aversion to radical linguistic innovation itself; but the experimentalism in the *Wake*, of course, is a crucial part of its originality, ingenuity, and humor—as well as its seductive potential. Who can resist the compact and poetic charm of this philosophical insight: "First we feel. Then we fall" (627.11)? Joyce's experimentalism represents a reinvention of ambiguity and, at its extreme, indeterminacy. The "fall" in the *Wake*, for instance, may be moral, economic, social, emotional, gravitational, and/or atmospheric; it may be caused by guilty deeds, financial disaster, loss of class status, disappointments in feeling, physical unsteadiness, and/or changes in the weather. For those who are resistant to the strange and excessive, *Finnegans Wake* can still have appeal: the key may be a focus on those lines, phrases, or words that one initially digests and appreciates and delights in—a focus we both deployed on early readings of the text. Even though there are many parts that stubbornly continue to elude the reader, every time we open the *Wake*—and read a paragraph, a few pages, or an entire chapter—we usually learn, hear, or see something new and interesting. Additionally, the sections of the text that we do understand—or can at least venture an interpretation of—are engaging, witty, and/or (even) moving. Readers may also find points of access by availing themselves of some of the invaluable guides to *Finnegans Wake*.

One major problem with some of the available handbooks to the *Wake*, however, is that they tend to "level" the text, that is, to take the work's polyvocal languages and make them univocal, in the interest of making the work more accessible. No one would deny that these guides are useful—Joseph Campbell and Henry Morton Robinson's pioneering attempt to provide *A Skeleton Key to "Finnegans Wake"* comes to mind, as does Danis Rose and John O'Hanlon's more recent *Understanding "Finnegans Wake."*[9] But they do, in their linear narrative orientations, tend to diminish the richness and play of the *Wake*'s polysemous nature. We are told of the elusive letter—a synecdoche for *Finnegans Wake* as a whole—"The proteiform graph itself is a polyhedron of scripture" (107.08). It is not only protean in form but also a three-dimensional structure, a polyhedron being an object with many faces—not simply two, like an ordinary sheet of paper. *Finnegans Wake* is similarly multidimensional, as Joyce moves away from the horizontal pull of discourse with his vertical layerings. If one imagines the text in both spatial and temporal terms, one can almost visualize the language rising off the page as it produces strata of meanings. The letter is also described as "the strangewrote anaglyptics of those shemletters patent" (419.19–20), evoking again a three-dimensional object: McHugh glosses *anaglyptic* as "pertaining to carving in low relief." In *Finnegans Wake*, we are invited not only to see and hear but also to feel the depth of its texture.

Another volume with an author for (almost) every chapter is Michael Begnal and Fritz Senn's *Conceptual Guide to "Finnegans Wake."* It remains very helpful, but the *Wake*'s multiplicities are not the main focus, as its title indicates. The most recent volume with a similar structure, *How Joyce Wrote "Finnegans Wake": A Chapter-by-Chapter Genetic Guide*,[10] contains fascinating research in uncovering the process of the text's nonlinear evolution. However, that volume's goals, offered by genetic criticism, clearly differ from ours. Some of our contributors to this volume do helpfully employ genetic techniques in parts, but we hoped for, and fortunately received, a variety of critical approaches geared toward teasing out the "darknesses and unintelligibilities" of Joyce's multilayered language system.

Given this state of available critical entries to *Finnegans Wake*, we are attempting to create something different—a chapter-by-chapter guide with other aims. First, because each chapter has its own peculiar structure and focus, we have asked our contributors to capture some of the uniqueness of their selected section. Second, we have requested that each of them "raise" the text by including close readings of parts of each chapter to emphasize its vertical dimensions: the Wake was written partially with a focus on increased layerings, as *How Joyce Wrote "Finnegans Wake"* demonstrates. It ultimately emerged, however, as a forward-moving series of chapters, and on the most general level—in terms of presenting each individual contribution—we will follow that horizontal presentation.

We have also encouraged the deployment of multiple methodologies, by deliberately inviting Joyceans who have used different approaches, who come from varied backgrounds, and from different stages of the so-called "Joyce industry." As the essays in this volume show, the *Wake* may mean different things to many people; the diversity of perspectives and contrasting interpretations in this volume exemplify a Joycean "collideorscape" (143.28)—colliding meanings (which interpreters may only try to escape) and a kaleidoscope of visually verbal constellations. These formations and reformations in the *Wake* produce in generation after generation continuing reinterpretations of the text: the "seim anew" (215.23–24). The contributors to this volume provide readers with both familiar and novel frameworks for engaging the *Wake*, including myth, feminism, psychoanalysis, philosophy, game theory, homophonies, ecocriticism, historicism, atmosphere, and/or contextual criticism. Such frameworks open up the pluralities of meaning inherent in Joyce's text, unlocking new and illuminating readings of the *Wake*. The following paragraphs offer summaries of each chapter, especially helpful, we hope, for those who want to start with their personal portal of entry to this maze of a book.

Chapter I.1 is often viewed as introductory to the whole, and John Terrill outlines one central ongoing concern: the *Wake* as impossible detective fiction, with its proposed ciphers remaining beyond readerly solution. He connects these mysteries to biblical prophecy, the book of Daniel in particular—an important pretext to I.1 that has been glossed in annotation but never explained. Terrill proceeds then to delineate the ambiguous status of several male prophets: their roles as creative and sexualized beings, as slavish translators of pre-authorized meanings, or as privileged amanuenses to higher sources of knowledge. In the second half of his essay, he turns to the possible function and place of women in these largely androcentric hierarchies of linguistic transmission. Focusing on Kate and ALP, Terrill illustrates how women on occasion escape the position of passive repository of the *logos*, by creating eclectic and restive semantic systems, in female voices or writings. His essay effectively deploys contextual criticism in its use of the Bible, with feminist and psychoanalytic theories as additional tools.

Jim LeBlanc provides us with an excellent introduction to the proliferative motif of "the sin in the park" and its metaphysical implications as they emerge most clearly in I.2. He uses a philosophical framework provided by Jean-Paul Sartre: the famous *Being and Nothingness* postdated the writing of *Finnegans Wake*, but its arguments bear uncanny resonances when placed in the context of Joycean themes. LeBlanc focuses in particular on two early contrasting versions of "the sin": the first involves an alleged peeping tom, while the second consists of the protagonist's encounter with "the cad" in Phoenix Park. Through close readings of these scenes, LeBlanc emphasizes the *Wake*'s representation of being as inevitably splintered and self-alienated, stolen by the Other's gaze, temporality, and language.

Tim Conley opens by discussing the problematic—and increasingly passé —study of atmosphere in literary criticism. But because I.3 contains references to atmosphere—as weather, climate, environment, and mood—he proceeds to use it as a helpful approach to *Finnegans Wake*: in the face of the disappearance of the conventions of plot, character, setting, and even symbols, the phenomena of external and internal sensory flux prove oddly relevant as a way of sensing—as feeling, hearing, and seeing—the text's language. Paradoxically, the *Wake* becomes at many junctures a clearly cloudy book. Conley demonstrates that the relationship between the human and its environs is much more complicated than personification and that the work is stunningly successful in its resistance to portraying nature as a mere fixed object. Through its poetics of ambience, the *Wake*'s atmosphere emerges as composite and changeable, creating its unique "dynamic ecosystem."

The demand of the crowd in the trial of I.4—to produce the body—introduces a thematic of *habeas corpus*. Mia L. McIver proceeds to emphasize the recurrently ambiguous status of the body or corpus in the *Wake*: present as referent, but absent to sight, perhaps hidden or in hiding, or in disguise, a starving form, but expanding through self-cannibalization. The odd nature of the corpus in I.4 leaves a residue of the flesh, the body reduced to relics or traces. The absurdity of the trial lies, in part, in the problem of trying to "try" a body that has gone astray, an evasion adumbrated in its endlessly mutating identities (as a female pig, Festy King, Crowbar, and Parnell, to name a few). The remainder of the flesh in I.4, McIver suggests, is unruly, an excess, a restlessness, a disturbance, far from dead or inert.

Colleen Jaurretche's interpretation of I.5 examines the common reader in both usages of the phrase: a book that teaches us how to read, and a person primed for the perception of meaning. The essay begins by asking what happens if we take literally the book's conceit of letters as both characters on a page and personalities in a story. Looking at the alphabet through Vico's lens, Jaurretche suggests why Joyce was fascinated with *The Book of Kells*—one of the books he regarded as central to the inception of *Finnegans Wake*—and how etymologies of writing inform reading the *Wake* and reading more generally. In her analysis, reading becomes an act that brings together sense and cognition to serve as a central trope of *Finnegans Wake*: the amalgamation of word and image.

Sean Latham opens up I.6 through contemporary game theory. He argues that this chapter of questions and elaborate answers involves the interplay of constraint and creativity, much as most games do. He focuses on I.6—and by extension, the *Wake* itself as a whole—as a play of "emergence" (in contrast to that of "progression"). The text implicitly evokes rules within which lie possibilities for actions and interpretations rather than stabilized meaning. The *Wake* becomes an interactive structure, pushing readers away from expectations of narratology to the enriching surprises of ludology.

Christine Smedley's essay interrogates I.7 as a "strabismal apologia" (189.08), a description of the chapter that suggests "strabismus," a doubled or cross-eyed vision, and "abysmal," a woefully inadequate confession. She contends that such splitting informs and explains the chapter's entire narrative mode: an ironic apologia of Shem/Joyce voiced through his rival split self, Shaun/Stanislaus. Such irreconcilability of vision functions on multiple levels: personal, national, and textual. Most centrally, it suggests a new way to envision a foundational event in Irish memory, the Famine, where the apology of Shem the Celt materializes only in a moment of fractured, disunited disclosure, seeing conflicting versions of the historical trauma at once and suggesting a mutual disinheritance. Beneath the ironic excesses of Shaun's attack, Joyce articulates the failure of the artist to give voice to the Famine dead, a concern which scholars are only recently uncovering in the Joycean oeuvre.

In her innovative ecocritical approach to I.8, Margot Norris explores the inseparability of river and women through the "figure" of ALP: the constrained but lively and liquid Liffey and the oppressed but strong and evolving female being. Norris calls for a more nuanced reading of ecocriticism that is attuned not just to nature in the raw, so to speak, but those aspects of nature overlaid with culture so as to be unrecognizable—the urban environment and the modern body. Despite being an urban writer, Joyce tries to restore and make us alive to the natural world even if it is mediated by the voices of the washerwomen. But the washerwomen themselves have a natural materiality—as seen in their bodily ailments—even as they are marked by cultural codings (such as class and age). The essay demonstrates the way the human can destroy and pollute the earthly world, but with the latter never succumbing to dominance. Joyce simultaneously emphasizes that the "figure" of ALP is fluid and mutating: exploring the plurabilities of her form and image, Norris demonstrates how he avoids representing nature through an essentializing lens.

In her provocative interpretation of "The Mime of Nick, Mick and the Maggies" in II.1, Carol Loeb Shloss reads the chapter's game as courtship ritual, but one that is disturbing in its allocation of narrative space. The interiority of Izod, she notes, is only followed sporadically, and when exposed often reveals dysphoria. At the center of II.1 is the issue of "those first girly stirs" (222.33)—or the representation of female desires. Izod and the flower girls are set up as "the one" and "the many": her eventual rejoining of the troupe signifies sexual rejection, an unwelcome retreat from not being the chosen, the special object of desire. The problem lies in the troupe's specific position as objects, as beautiful dancing females, engulfed in a language of "showing off." This tale of confused courtship, Shloss suggests, demonstrates how "those first girly stirs" are viewed conventionally and lasciviously as external self-display, at the expense of being occasions for internal expressions of elided female desires—sexual feelings and emotions.

Jeffrey Drouin argues that II.2 is polyvocal in a different way through its visual graphics and narrative format: it separates some of the multilayered voices of the Earwicker family members into spatial regions of the page. In this chapter, during the geometry lesson, Shaun makes the two-part "grand discobely" (294.12–13) of sexual knowledge and rational analysis that unites him and Shem into the adult male who in II.3 will lead Issy in an attack against their father. Drouin suggests that this overtly Oedipal process entails much more than the development of the complete human male and the overturning of the generational cycle. Shaun and Shem, in their association with contrary parts of the body, represent the senses of vision and hearing which, respectively, operate upon digital and analog information signals. The uneasy collusion of discretely segmented and continuous information streams has a basis in the new media of magazines, cinema, radio, and television of Joyce's day. Moreover, these binaries are cast as a retelling of the contendings of Horus and Set from Egyptian mythology, which, Drouin points out, is an underexplored area in *Wake* scholarship. II.2 also embodies a parallel media revolution in which the old linear forms of print give way to modern forms that feature a variety of simultaneous information streams, a brand of modernism that is brought to life in the polyvocal communications that appear in the margins, footers, and body of the page.

Enda Duffy characterizes II.3 as the wild, bellicose center of the *Wake*. Its clashings are multidimensional: in personal battles, in diverse and conflicting media, in more generalized historic warfare, and in tensions between affective states—courage and cowardice, drunkenness and sobriety, seeing and hearing, reality and phantasmagoria. More than any other section of the text, II.3 is steeped in references to major Irish historical conflicts, as Duffy traces in countless political allusions and themes. He makes clear throughout that *Finnegans Wake* is a revolutionary challenge, not just stylistically but also in its vision of the socius as a work in progress (in every sense of the phrase), and in its "new light"—its allowance that "a radical version of the Irish worker will at last come into being in the narratives of Ireland."

David Spurr's analysis of II.4 focuses on the "joysis crisis" (395.32) at its center—the moment when Tristan French-kisses Isolde. The kiss evokes others in the fictions of Joyce (Mulvey and Molly, Molly and Bloom) and those of his predecessors, Richard Wagner and Dion Boucicault. The presentation of it in the *Wake*, as in his literary pretexts, foregrounds the double function of the tongue as sexual organ and organ of speech, as desire and signification are united. The amorous encounter is given the magnitude of a religious epiphany, bringing together—but without prioritizing—body and spirit, flesh and word. The *jouissance* of the kiss signals both liberation from the *logos* of the law and a new relation to language. Joyce's mixing of the sacred and the profane produces a heretical but celebratory "countergospel," in his ongoing recasting of the traditional New Testament Gospel throughout II.4. A variant of this mixing is also seen throughout the *Wake*'s polyphonic language, which foregrounds both physical sounds and proliferative meanings.

Kimberly J. Devlin explores the homophonic underpinnings of III.1 by looking at examples of salvation, salves, saving, and salvage. She enumerates the Shaun-figure's profusion of identities, for instance, as a supposed source of salvation when he takes shape as a pseudo-Christ or an obese fallen priest. He is a devotee to salves in his self-representation as the Ondt, who is also a saver in his accrual of worldly goods. Literary salvage is ultimately associated with his brother Shem, who—like Joyce himself—creates art from litter, in an act of ecological literary recycling.

Patrick A. McCarthy's treatment of III.2 offers on one level genetic criticism, comparing passages as they initially appeared in *transition* with their final published form. He also provides deep readings of Jaun's language throughout, exploring the logic of puns and distortions, in numerous passages that decidedly "raise" the text. McCarthy revisits the allusions to Lord Byron and his works, for instance, to note the way Joyce interconnects the personal and the historical: the poet's scandalous brother-sister incest becomes analogous to political movements such as Sinn Fein, which encouraged dangerous isolationism and alliances with only "kin" (in a subtle foreshadowing of Hitler's racism). In his other discussion of important authors alluded to in III.2, McCarthy provides us with original information on yet another "Finn" in the *Wake*: Francis J. Finn, S.J. The references to his novels for juveniles are glossed for their aptness and humor. He closes with an analysis of the figure of Dave the Dancekerl, often aligned with Shem but here also merging with Jaun, in part through a confusion of pronouns. The chapter satirizes the strange mixture of Jaun's hypocritical piety, its brotherly advice repeatedly lapsing into sexual innuendo.

In his analysis of III.3, Sheldon Brivic explains the chapter's confusing multivocal interrogations through a structure of nesting: the daughter is nested in the father, who is nested in the son Shaun, who is nested in his mother. Positing a dream that, at its deepest level, contains myriad identities, Brivic demonstrates that the dialogue can simultaneously voice the desires of the abusive father, the daughter's painful protests, and the mother's search for freedom. The maternal internal voice sees injustice as the basis of paternal authority and power. According to Brivic, the interior conflict and division of the seemingly isolated singular subject is dramatized most prominently throughout III.3 in its proliferation of polyvocal internalized personalities.

Richard Brown's study of III.4 raises the question of mimesis in *Finnegans Wake*: the chapter draws attention to the problem of what exactly is being represented, of what is its elusive subject matter. The ostensible topic of the Porter family leads to a profusion of intertextual points of contact, many of which serve to foreground systems of representation. The focus on watching produces mimetic paradigms from theater, film, pictorial arts, sports reporting, sex manuals, and photography. The residues of realism in III.4, which may remind us of other bedroom scenes from Joyce's other works, are ultimately dissipated by the chapter's self-conscious references to performativity and by its ongoing polyvocality.

Using Egyptian mythology as her contextual backdrop, Vicki Mahaffey addresses the themes of fire and water, the twin principles of creation in book IV. The "Ricorso" explores how the world is regenerated through the diurnal reappearance of the light and heat of the sun, replicated in man's self-renewal through his "son" and through the washing and cleansing of water by rain and baptism—the liquid being the element gendered in the *Wake* as female. One lover of water and of the mother ALP is Kevin/Shaun, who is also misogynistic in his desire for a phobic chastity. The argument between saint and sage—Muta and Juva—focuses (as a complement to hydrophilia) on light, colors, and the visual world. Mahaffey's discussion of ALP's letter and monologue suggests that in closing, the maternal figure grows younger and younger as she passes out and away into her "salvocean" (623.29), in which she will simultaneously die and begin again.

The goal of this volume is not to "convert" people to read *Finnegans Wake*. As many who have taught the text probably know from experience, this is a futile enterprise: some students will revel in the opportunity to read such intriguing writing, while others will flat out reject it. We hope instead that this volume will assist both those open to new forms of discourse and those "already converted," who are looking for new points of textual entry to Joyce's allmaziful work.

In closing, we would like to thank Patrick A. McCarthy and Margot Norris for ongoing advice on this volume as it progressed. We would also like to acknowledge Pat as the final editor of one of the essays when we were trying to trim a considerably longer version of our text. Garry Leonard, Tony

Thwaites, and Sebastian Knowles gave appreciated suggestions for revisions in the final review of our manuscript. We are also very much indebted to the expertise of Shannon McCarthy, the acquisitions editor at the University Press of Florida, who patiently helped us to complete the various steps toward publication. And one final thanks to Enda Duffy for this book's inception: during a conference he organized for the Southern California Irish Studies Colloquium at the University of California, Santa Barbara in February 2011, the three of us agreed that new chapter-by-chapter readings by a polyvocality of Joyceans would be a timely and useful venture.

Notes

1. Harold Bloom, *The Western Canon* (New York: Harcourt Brace, 1994), 422.
2. Darragh McManus, "World Exclusive! *Finnegans Wake* Nonsense!" *Guardian*. Web. 9 March 2010.
3. *The American Heritage Dictionary* (Boston: Houghton Mifflin, 1992), 1445, s.v. "prodigal."
4. Phillippe Sollers, "Joyce & Co.," in *In the Wake of the Wake*, ed. David Hayman and Elliott Anderson (Madison: University of Wisconsin Press, 1978), 109.
5. Roland McHugh, "Recipis for the Price of the Coffin," in *A Conceptual Guide to "Finnegans Wake,"* ed. Michael H. Begnal and Fritz Senn (University Park: Pennsylvania State University Press, 1974), 31.
6. Margot Norris, *The Decentered Universe of "Finnegans Wake"* (Baltimore: Johns Hopkins University Press, 1974), 103.
7. Derek Attridge, *Peculiar Language: Literature as Difference from the Renaissance to James Joyce* (New York: Cornell University Press, 1988), 207.
8. Roland McHugh, *Annotations to "Finnegans Wake,"* 3rd ed. (Baltimore: Johns Hopkins University Press, 2006), 5.
9. Joseph Campbell and Henry Morton Robinson, *A Skeleton Key to "Finnegans Wake"* (New York: Penguin, 1980); Danis Rose and John O'Hanlon, *Understanding "Finnegans Wake"* (New York: Garland, 1982).
10. *How Joyce Wrote "Finnegans Wake,"* ed. Luca Crispi and Sam Slote (Madison: University of Wisconsin Press, 2007).

1

The "gift of seek on site"

The Subject of Prophecy in I.1

JOHN TERRILL

The first chapter of *Finnegans Wake* has a great deal of work to perform, not the least of which is a project of confusion and dislocation. The reader immediately finds herself in a watery element where she is at once entering the book "mid-stream" ("riverrun"), only to find herself entirely "at sea" ("fr'over the short sea") (3.01, .04). If this first page introduces the reader to anything resembling a story, it has something to do with a fall, be it "Eve and Adam's" famous *felix culpa* or the ostensibly deadly tumble of Tim Finnegan, protagonist of the irreverent drinking song "Finnegan's Wake" (3.01, .19). The fall is thus already twin, preparing us for a veritable flurry of pairings, contrasts, and "doublin" in even the first handful of lines of the book (3.08): Eve and Adam (3.01), Swift and Sterne (3.12), father and son(s) (3.13), sea and shore (3.01, .04), Europe and America (3.05–06), and Catholic green and Protestant orange (3.23–24). This text is a world seemingly composed of concatenating signifiers, of "both/and" not "either/or," of series that resolve themselves, in good dialectical tradition, in syntheses. Hence Joyce makes "twone" (3.12): meaning is "twinned," and binary terms resolve into a final unity.

And yet the curious reader may find such conjoinings suspect from the outset. That the recirculating riverrun of signification has an origin seems rather odd (does a circle have a starting point?), and "Howth Castle and Environs" is hardly a stable locus, as the castle spreads out over the countryside in yet another conjunction (3.03). As presented in the opening of the *Wake*, there is no stable source from which the river springs. Despite the narrator's invocation of the cliché that there are two sides to every story or "two sights for ever a picture," this tale is not one that can be captured in the deployment and subsequent collapsing of binary terms (11.36). Indeed, the saying itself, in its transformation into a visual register, already broadens its range of meaning. It comes as no surprise, then, that the *Wake* begins to expand its claims about its scope of signification. The singular story that encompasses just two readings or perspectives explodes into Shahrazad's interminable narrative sequence when the narrator touches on the circumstances surrounding Finnegan's death: "There extand by now one thousand and one stories, all told, of the same" (5.28-29). *Finnegans Wake,* then, purports to offer an event narrated in many ways, all of which are told in the text. Throughout I.1, this polyvocality is ostensibly delivered through the agency of the prophet, who rereads the text as a way of glossing it, but who thus enters into the problematics of interpretation as flattening of meaning. The tension between the prophet as creative force and as slavish transmitter of authorized meaning is thrown into relief when the chapter makes rare allusion to women who, like Shahrazad, compose the text but who are also associated with the "prophetic" mode of interpreting the text's significance.

Detective Fiction

The first chapter of the *Wake* sets up the destabilizing mission of the larger text, which refuses to pursue a straightforward plot and which employs language that is a sort of panglossic hash of what Lewis Carroll calls "portmanteau" words. This is, of course, part of Joyce's stated project of "working in layers" in order to create a "writing of the night" and an "esthetic of the dream" (*JJII* 546). The subject of the text is thrown into radical ambiguity, and I mean "subject" in its many valences: the topic of the book, the book's "protagonist," the reader as agent of interpretation, and even the syntactical subject. At stake in each of these, though, is the subject of utterance or the semiotic signifier. Hence chapter I.1 describes attempts to resolve these categories in relation to language by positioning HCE as prophet who foretells the events of the text and the reader as detective who plumbs its mysteries. Each of these postures fails to be revelatory, though, through their ignorance that the drama of language—of its origins, its transformations, its sexual signification, and its existential power—is itself the central mystery of the chapter. The seer and the investigator both miss the mark when they seek out narrativized knowledge and meaning, for the language of the *Wake* is insistently paradoxical and resistant to narrative. It is elusively corporeal and impotently sexual.

The *Wake* then posits a tension: on the one hand, between always collapsing meaning whereby signifiers deployed in couplets combine synthetically to point toward an originary locus ("seek on site" [5.25] is rooted in "second sight"), and on the other hand, between increasingly proliferating meanings that expand through allusive chains. It is in this latter mode that the narrator enjoins the reader, "if you are abcedminded, to this claybook, what curios of signs (please stoop), in this allaphbed! Can you rede (since We and Thou had it out already) its world? It is the same told of all. Many. Miscegenations on miscegenations. Tieckle. They lived und laughed ant loved end left. Forsin" (18.17–21). Here Joyce, in a typically metafictional gesture, begins to address the reader's consumption of the text and foregrounds textual reflexivity by forecasting rhythmically the last line of the book ("A way a lone a last a loved a long the") as well as the tale of the Ondt and the Gracehoper ("andt, and andt, / *He larved ond he larved*") (628.15–16, 418.09–10). The *Wake* is rendered as a "claybook," punning on the French *clef* (key), as if the text could be unlocked or were itself the solution to an extraordinary enigma.

As I will discuss in greater detail shortly, this riddle is also prophetic, citing as it does the writing on the wall at Belshazzar's feast: "And this is the writing that was written, *Mene, Mene, Tekel, Upharsin*" (Daniel 5:25).[1] In this well-known biblical episode, a ghostly hand writes these words on the wall to the horror of the Babylonian regent's dinner guests. Belshazzar calls on the prophet Daniel to interpret the mysterious text, and Daniel divines that God is warning the ruler that his reign has been numbered, weighed, and divided (Daniel 5:26–28). That very night, the Persian army conquers Babylon by surprise and massacres the court. It is from this Old Testament episode that we derive the idiom "the writing is on the wall." In other words, this passage is a delightful invitation to decode the *Wake* by focusing on the sign, the word, and even the letter, be the alphabet Roman or Hebrew.

The injunction to read investigatively resumes when Joyce, as Roland McHugh notes, wittily encodes the ancient inscriptional practice of *boustrophēdon*, which is bidirectional text wherein each line is written alternately left-to-right and right-to-left.[2] Joyce cites the components of the Greek portmanteau word (*bous*, ox; *strophē*, turn) when he writes, "furrowards, bagawards, like yoxen at the turnpaht" (18.32). He then offers a few examples of aural boustrophedon, beginning with "Here say figurines billycoose arming and mounting. Mounting and arming bellicose figurines see here" (18.33–34). The reader is enjoined, then, to read for patterns and ciphers, as the text suggests that it is aware of and can reproduce structures that are rhetorically carefully parallel or isomorphic. And Joyce, of course, was deeply influenced by Giambattista Vico's 1725 treatise *Scienza Nuovo* (which Joseph Campbell calls "the philosophical loom on which Joyce weaves his historical allegory"), and the Viconian model is heavily invested in cyclical time, patterns of repetition and variation, and recurring episodes, though they may return inverted or deformed.³ The *Wake* thus encourages the reader-detective to decipher the text: to unpack its language and to retrieve the logic of its submerged structures.

Of course, the project of decryption unravels even before it begins, preventing the reader from serving as a latter-day Daniel who can crack the code and reveal the divine condemnation. First, possible allusions and provisional readings simply accrete. The aforementioned "allaphbed" is "alphabet," "aleph, beth," "Allah," "ALP's bed," and so on. Second, the text points both forward to later scenes in the *Wake*, as we have noted, and back to earlier episodes, such as the way that "(please stoop)" evokes mistress Kathe's solicitous warning that we "[m]ind [our] hats goan in" to the Museyroom, a site that is cluttered with curios (8.09). We might even detect an echo of *Ulysses*—that is, a much earlier episode still—if the "word/world" confusion recalls Martha's typo in her letter to "Henry Flower," in a line that is very much on Bloom's mind: "I do not like that other world" (*U* 5.245, 6.1002, 8.328). The implicit claim, then, that the *Wake* is a cipher is entirely misleading. There is no *passe-partout* that opens the text's many doors, nor a Kabbalistic numerology that solves its mathematics, nor indeed a cryptogram that makes sense of Joyce's alphabets. The word is never a simple and straightforward affair in the *Wake*. It is polyvalent and polyvocal, so that to take the readerly posture of detective in the *Wake* is to enter into an elusive and ultimately interminable project.

Reading the Writing on the Wall

It is significant that the aforementioned passage cites the book of Daniel, for this introduces a pattern of association between HCE and prophets in general or Daniel in particular. Of course, HCE is also equated to a godhead, when, for instance, we read of "the days when Head-in-Clouds walked the earth," which is presumably "Inn the Byggning," when God declared "[f]iat-fuit," or, as Genesis would have it in Ecclesiastical Latin, "*fiat lux et lux fuit*" (18.23–24, 17.22, .32, Genesis 1:3). Or more frequently, HCE is the deity in his Christ-like aspect, which is fitting for a book that ostensibly treats the death and resurrection of Tim Finnegan. It is in just such a context that Christ is the subject of comical apostrophe: "Hohohoho, Mister Finn, you're going to be Mister Finnagain! Comeday morm and, O, you're vine! Sendday's eve and, ah, you're vinegar!" (5.09–11). Of course, HCE performs rather miserably in these roles as divine father or son. As God he is absent (no longer walking the earth); foul ("Load Allmarshy": the Lord Almighty is heavy and mired); and an "abramanation": as author of the covenant promising that Abraham would be the "father of nations," he is an abomination (17.08, 26.19–20, Genesis 12:2). As Christ, HCE as a paschal sacrifice is the butt of jokes: his resurrection is dubious if he turns into "vinegar" and is "going to be fined again"; he is doubtless soused as "he seesaw[s] by neatlight of the liquor"; and his skill in performing miracles is sorely wanting (5.12, 4.33–34). After all, the wedding at Cana would have soured quickly had Jesus presented the party with vinegar rather than wine (John 2:1–11).

HCE fits uncomfortably as a deity, and the narration tends to position him more commonly as a prophet. In the Muslim tradition, Christ is typically understood to be a prophet, and indeed the *Wake* alludes to Muhammad as well as to Buddha and Confucius, if we stretch the point and gloss all these men as prophets (19.35–20.17, 18.24–29, 19.22–25). "Bygmester Finnegan" is also an original and ironic seer when we learn that "one yeastyday he sternely struxk his tete in a tub for to watsch the future of his fates," but what visions he might have are surely the figments of alcoholic hallucination, for "by the might of moses, the very water was eviparated and all the guenneses had met their exodus" (4.18, .21–22, .23–24).

But to return to the prophet of the writing on the wall, Joyce has, in Daniel, found a fitting avatar for HCE in a number of senses. Daniel serves foreign and conquering kings, Nebuchadnezzar and Darius, with different religious practices than his own: these facts fit neatly with the religio-colonial struggles of Ireland that are staged in Joyce's work (though granted HCE is often placed on the side of the colonizer, as in the case of the Norwegian captain, the Duke of Wellington, or King William I).[4] As a prototype for Christ, Daniel is thrown into the sealed lion's den and then exits the cave safely, much as his priestly Judean companions, Shadrach, Meshach, and Abednego, emerge unsinged from the fiery furnace (Daniel 3:14–27, 6: 16–23). Furthermore, the book of Daniel is famously structured around a chiasm, "[a] formal patterning of a literary or rhetorical unit that preserves symmetry while reversing the order of the terms, to produce the sequence ABBA," and some critics argue that the book even has a double chiastic structure—all of which may remind us of the lessons of the boustrophedon.[5]

Above all, though, the prophet Daniel is the interpreter of dreams. Daniel gets his professional start when he reveals the sacred meaning of Nebuchadnezzar's dream of the giant statue with the golden head and the clay feet (from which we derive the idiom "to have feet of clay"), which is destroyed by a stone hurled at its weakest point (Daniel 2:1–49).[6] The dream, as Daniel divines, foreshadows a nearly Viconian cycle of epochs: ages of gold, silver, brass, iron, and clay, the last of which will be swept away in a cleansing messianic gesture that will herald a return to prelapsarian paradise (Daniel 2:37–45). That Joyce has this episode in mind as a pretext for I.1 becomes clearer when we consider the mention of Nebuchadnezzar in the guise of "Nobucketnozzler" (24.35). Moreover, we even find allusion to the fallen statue of the king's dream: "His clay feet, swarded in verdigrass, stick up starck where he last fellonem, by the mund of the magazine wall" (7.30–32).

But more than being an interpreter of dreams about empire or of writing on the wall, Daniel is the enunciator of the dream itself. The king craftily demands of his court magicians, "If ye will not make known unto me the dream, with the interpretation thereof, ye shall be cut in pieces, and your houses shall be made a dunghill" (Daniel 2:5). Daniel must therefore first demonstrate his divine insight by sketching the king's unknown dream; only then may he proceed to illuminate it. This is a first suggestion, then, that in the Wakean mode, prophecy is more than the revelation of a deterministic future: it is a creative act as well, which (re)produces the object of its own analysis.

This turn to the creative aspect of the prophet is extended in further Old Testament allusions. A citation of the book of Habakkuk explicitly moves the prophet into the realm of textual production: "He who runes may rede it on all fours" (18.05–06). This line's "runes" may contain residues of Daniel's ghostly *Mene Tekel* glyphs, but here the inscriptive hand is firmly embodied in the one who "writes" (inscribes "runes") and "reads" alike.[7] The immediate source of this line, though, is Habakkuk 2:2: "And the Lord answered me, and said, Write the vision, and make it plain upon tables, that he may run that readeth it." The work of the prophet is once again the reproduction of a text, which is to be glossed and here fixed in material language on "tables."[8] It is important to note, then, that association of HCE with the figure of the seer makes him the force that creates the object to be interpreted, whether that object be a dream, clay tablets, or the text of the *Wake*. The prophet is both reader and author, though notably he is author in only the most limited sense. In other words, he is amanuensis at once to God and to king.[9]

We see that in these passages, language is substantial; it may be mysterious, but it is not abstract. If we understand "claybook" in the most straightforward fashion, it is something material, perhaps evoking a cuneiform tablet, Habakkuk's "tables," or even the Mosaic code as "inscribed by the finger of God" (Exodus 31:18). Later in the chapter, this reading is reinforced when the narrator as mourner at the wake or as Egyptian funerary priest enjoins the dead man to rest "aisy," for his family is doing fine; the twins Kevin and Jerry are attending school and "turning out tables by mudapplication" (24.16, 26.35–36). Notice that while again the subject is the agent of inscription (applying mud to be written on), he is not the origin of the text, as the line evokes the scribe's work of copying (by multiplying), much like the boys' other occupation in school, "spelling beesknees," which implies rote recitation (26.35).

Or as we have mentioned, the book could also be a physical place, such as the Museyroom, if we remark on the coincidence of the former passage's mention of "curios" (the Willingdone Memorial as cabinet of curiosities) and its solicitous warning to "please stoop" (the echo of Mistress Kathe's "Mind your hats goan in!") (18.17–18, 8.09). It is clear that the textual production attains physical texture, and this is reinforced in I.5, when, just after the recitation of the mamafesta's by-names, HCE adopts a heroic-prophetic posture in his investigation of the letter. HCE is here "the hardily curiosing entomophilust" and "the eternal chimerahunter" (107.12–13, .14). The letter or perhaps the *Wake* as a whole is a "proteiform graph," or protean cuneiform writing (Greek: *graphē*). And this writing "itself is a polyhedron of scripture" (107.08). The materiality of the letter and the word is once again emphasized, where here it attains a hard Euclidean texture. Of course, this line also speaks to the polyvocality of the text in the citation of its multifaceted nature.

Indeed, when the prophet-writer enters the scene, he is multiplied through the persons of anonymous novitiates, and much like Daniel or Habukkuk, these writers are transcribers of the word: "There was a time when naif alphabetters would have written it down the tracing of a purely deliquescent recidivist" (107.09–10). The novice acts as recorder, and the text is again substance and medium as the object of tracing or indeed as the trace. This passage resonates, too, with an earlier apology for a recorded history's holes: "Somewhere, parently, in the ginnandgo gap between antediluvious and annadominant the copyist must have fled with his scroll" (14.16–18). Here, the prophet model is shown to be a radical failure, as the letter is never delivered; the divine history of HCE is erased.

Stewing the Word in the Womb

The psychical ramifications of casting the prophet as a productive force but one whose creativity, suitability, and agency are repeatedly undercut become clearer when we begin to focus on writing's sexual dimension as articulated in I.1. After all, the *Wake* as a "polyhedron of scripture" is "a very sexmosaic" (107.13). And as we remember from the "claybook" passage, language is a (sexual) admixture of elements, "miscegenations on miscegenations" (18.20). Here we begin to understand the ways that the *Wake*'s posited materiality of language frames and is extended by its application in a sexual context.

Hence when the narrator theorizes in passing on the development of written language, the genesis is coyly physical: "When a part so ptee does duty for the holos we soon grow to use of an allforabit" (18.36–19.02). On the most obvious level, the text posits synecdoche, whether *pars pro toto* or *totum pro parte*, as the essential condition of language. But the sentence also invokes sexual intercourse: a presumptively male body part—a *petit*, though growing, penis—performs for a presumptively female hole. Indeed, read in this light, the birth of the alphabet becomes a play of synecdochic sexual organs. One of the principal inducements to language, then, is the promise of phallic ability. As the mourners say rather plaintively at the wake, "If you only were there to explain the meaning, best of men, and talk to her nice of guldenselver. The lips would moisten once again" (28.10–12). The word is that which must be offered to the woman to entice her. Moreover, the word is analytical or exegetical; it delivers "meaning," which we have seen associated with the prophet. The mourners also suggest somewhat snidely that some talk of hard currency is in order, but notice that "guldenselver" also evokes "good and evil"—the sacred tree of Eden, the divine knowledge of God. Thus it is the transmission of the divine word or of special knowledge that authorizes sexuality. This is not an unfamiliar notion in the Judeo-Christian creation myth: though here the fall is a potential one (in contradistinction to its typical status as always already having transpired), it is certainly a *"felix" culpa*, and it is initiated by the Adamic figure rather than woman or serpent. It also may be a repletion, as the "once again" suggests. This passage neatly bundles up language with sexual knowledge and potency in one brief, sacrilegious fable.

If the word attains a phallic power, then the place of femininity within this system begs to be considered. In the line above, the fiction of the narrative makes the woman the sought-after object rather than an expressly desiring subject, and it makes her sexual availability automatic or algorithmic. That is, when one inputs the correct sequence (insert a coin or say the magic word), the woman will become wet. The prophet-type is thus similar to the museum-goer whose characteristic inquisitiveness turns the cultural excursion into a sexually domineering endeavor involving "[p]enetrators" entering a "museomound" (8.05). This puts femininity on the side of the object of analysis or of the receptacle of signs and curios.

The "ivargraine jadesses with a message in their mouths" are perfect examples of this impulse (19.23–24). They themselves presumably do not speak, as their mouths are full; they do not have language but instead hold it in trust. Given that McHugh observes that Arthur Pendragon's mother Igraine is alluded to here, as well as a legend that Confucius's mother spied a beast bearing in its mouth a jade tablet that prophesied the sage's birth, we might imagine this as a secular Annunciation scene that makes the woman the matrix for the creative power of the word. In late medieval and Renaissance painterly tradition, Mary is "impregnated" by rays of gold leaf emanating from the dove as symbolic realization of the Holy Spirit (and it is precisely this image that motivates the Parisian joke that Stephen recalls about Mary's charmingly naïve response to Joseph's angry question about Jesus's paternity: "*C'est le pigeon, Joseph*" [*U* 3.162]). The medium of transmission is more properly the word, however, and hence the episode is called the Annunciation rather than the Illumination or the Pigeonification.

This transformational power of the word is further underscored by Joyce here in that "ivargraine" should also be understood to refer to the Parable of the Wheat and Tares of Matthew 13:24–30, which is called in French "*le bon grain et l'ivraie*." The expression "to separate the wheat from the chaff" derives from this episode, but more important to our analysis, this is the occasion on which the disciples ask their master why he preaches in parable. Christ responds, "Because it is given unto you to know the mysteries of the kingdom of heaven, but to them it is not given," implying that the mysteries of the real are accessible only through cypher, performance, and allusion (Matthew 13:11). Hence Christ transmits God's knowledge entirely in this encoded fashion, as we learn in another prettily chiastic line: "All these things spake Jesus unto the multitude in parables; and without a parable spake he not unto them" (Matthew 1:34). When Joyce cites this episode, though, he makes Christ into the ambiguously feminine aspect of "jadesses," as we have seen, and he renders the Word as enciphered in a particularly physical fashion on a jade stone, which is delivered, though not authored, in their mouths.

Woman continues to be associated with the receptacle of the Word elsewhere in the chapter. In one example, the text of the *Wake* is first described in terms of its eclectic component media: "[a] bone, a pebble, a ramskin" (20.05). This passage cites the tradition that the Quran was written on "pieces of parchment or papyrus, flat stones, palm leaves, shoulderblades and ribs of animals, pieces of leather, and wooden boards."[10] This sacred text, which is again rendered as a material reality, as a sort of figurative polyhedron in its heterogeneity, and as an ad hoc ordering, is a collection that the prophet must leave "to terracook in the muttheringpot" (20.06–07).[11] The line has uterine echoes, when we recall that *Mutter* is German for mother. It may imaginatively silence this feminine aspect as well, if we take *mutter* as the English verb that denotes indistinct murmuring.

This motif of the Word in the womb occurs still more explicitly among Stephen's progressively more inebriated ruminations in the "Oxen of the Sun" episode of *Ulysses*: "In woman's womb word is made flesh but in the spirit of the maker all flesh that passes becomes the word that shall not pass away" (*U* 14.292–94). Stephen posits a gendered and hierarchized creative opposition that makes the woman productive of the material through the intercession of the logos. The masculine, "properly" creative aspect, though, refines the material and makes of it rarefied, immortal form. As Ewa Ziarek glosses this passage, "The flesh is recuperated back into a position of the living speech—the paternal logos." Stephen's odd line makes the woman the medium of creation, in the sense of the stratum in which the logos as seed is implanted, but she is further injured when her passive creativity is glossed as the inverse of the more desirable creative mode that produces the masculine word. "[T]he maternal body," Ziarek writes, "is also an obverse coin of artistic production, its indispensable, negative, blind, and mute side."[12] It is seemingly precisely this tradition that the *Wake* leans on here when the idiotically muttering woman is but the matrix for the genesis of the sacred text. Nevertheless, there is a contrary tendency at play throughout I.1 that makes the feminine principle more creatively successful and even agential than she might first appear.

Production and the Prophetess

Chapter I.1 introduces the reader quite early to Mistress Kathe, who is presumably an aspect of Kate, the family housecleaner. One is exhorted to apply "to the janitrix, the mistress Kathe," for "her passkey" to the Willingdone Museyroom (8.08). Thus Kathe is "janitor" in the sense of one who cleans, but she is also presumably "janitor" in the etymological sense of guardian of the door or liminus, as well as "genetrix," or mother. Her association with the womb becomes still stronger when we recall that Kathe brackets her tour with the admonitions to "Mind your hats goan in" and "Mind your boots goan out" (8.09, 10.22), which for Tindall "make the episode seem the begetting and birth of a child and the nine tips the customary months of gestation."[13] "What a warm time we were in there," we are told, as we quit the Museyroom (10.25).

This narrative of the womblike Kathe, whose "museomound" is subject to "penetrators" (despite this supposed *mons veneris* being located ironically at the site of the perfectly phallic Wellington Monument in Phoenix Park), is undercut by the tour that she takes us on of the museum. That is, Kathe is not the passive flesh in which the word is incubated. Rather, Kathe, like Stephen's "maker," gathers up that which is material in the form of artifacts of battle, and she produces them as logos in the text of her speech. She acts very much as interpreter or, indeed, as prophet in the mode of Daniel, in whom we have seen this chapter take such an interest—that is, the Daniel who interprets dreams and the Daniel who orders and enunciates the writing on the wall. For Kathe goes further than simply pointing out physical objects in the museum, such as the "the flag of the Prooshious" and the "triplewon hat of Lipoleum" (8.11–12, .15–16). Kathe also renders or at least repeats the word in the form of the battle cry, which one presumes must be essentially immaterial, not an object or artifact, residing as it does in the realm of the performative utterance: "This is the Willingdone cry. Brum! Brum! Cumbrum! This is jinnies cry. Underwetter!" (9.26–27). Of course, it remains true that Kathe, like Daniel, reproduces a text that is already given, but also like the prophet, she gives meaning to otherwise enigmatic utterances in her narrativization of them, which situates them in a context and which ultimately heralds the spectacular death of the leader in question.

Understood in this creative context, Kathe is reminiscent of ALP as the hen, or "gnarlybird," who constructs the letter from the detritus, "all spoiled goods" surrounding her (10.32, 11.18–19). And indeed, one of the lessons of the "middenhide hoard of objects" that appears a bit later in I.1 is that language is fundamentally material (19.08). "Olives, beets, kimmells, dollies, alfrids, beatties, cormacks, and daltons" are, of course, a translinguistic, Babelesque alphabet: aleph, beth, gimel, daleth, alpha, beta, gamma, delta (19.08–09). This coincidence of "real" object and alphabetic signifier may ultimately be positioned as mythological here, an artifact of paradise before the fall, if we take "middenhide" to evoke "maidenhead," as shorthand for the presexual, in addition to the more obvious "middenheap." And the alphabetic play ends just a few lines later upon the arrival of the Satanic snake on the scene ("See the snake wurrums everyside!"), who introduces the "prohibitive pomefructs" (19.12, .15, *pomme*: French for apple; *fructus*: Latin for fruit).

Language, then, moves from the ideogrammatic, where the sign "coincides" with the object that it represents (such that an aleph "is" an olive), to the contingent and the abstract (the alphabetic character or the word as unmoored from its "real" antecedent) in a sort of fall and through the intercession of some feminine principle. The hen participates in this becoming-symbolic as she gathers up the items of rubbish haphazardly, piecing together and creating the meaningful in the form of the letter apparently at random. Margot Norris calls ALP's method "unsystematic and anarchic": "She selects bits of rubble randomly; the nature of her gifts is arbitrary, and her mode of distribution, indiscriminate."[14]

ALP and Kathe both engage with a material system out of which they create a symbolic structure that, while meaningful, is ultimately contingent. It is in this spirit that Norris maintains that ALP "does not arrange, regulate, designate, or judge, but merely gathers together," so that her actions create as a sort of parable of language, but one that eschews "the semantic function of language" in favor of spectacularizing "the potentiality of language for an infinite number of combinations within a finite system."[15] It is with this in mind that we should read the claim in I.1 that ALP is a prophet: "She has a gift of seek on site" (5.24–25).[16] Our other models of the (masculine) prophet begin with the ready-made sign, such as the manifest content of the dream or the literal glyph on the wall, and of these they make meaning, which tends to fix and flatten—a totalizing gesture that is authorized through recourse to the ultimate authority, God. For the prophet as ALP, the "sight" of the sign inspires search and collection rather than unifying explication. She moves from the material to the symbolic, which is contingent and performatively narrativized, as in the case of Kathe's rendition of the distorted Battle of Waterloo or ALP's letter as an exculpation or reclamation of her husband.

The most legible form of the prophet in I.1 is HCE as Daniel or Habakkuk, who acts as God's amanuensis or translator of authorized and univocal meaning. By contrast, it is the submerged figure of woman as prophetess who ultimately appears as the cause of the proliferation of meaning, which is a position that seems more attuned to the *Wake's* project of polysemy. This is part of Shari Benstock's point when she insists on the importance of ALP's and Issy's writing in the book, which she opposes to HCE's interpretive acts: "When man has tried to read the riddle, he has stripped woman of her complexity, emptied her of significance." In this respect, the reader, the critic, HCE, and the prophet all share in a tyranny of impositional meaning or even epistemic violence: "Critics have silenced whole portions of *Wake* language in the denial of the link between woman and writing. The reader's effort is similar to Earwicker's: to possess knowledge (of his sin) by limiting that knowledge."[17]

As Norris reads ALP's last lines of the book, "Lps. The keys to. Given!" (628.15), this image "resonat[es] against the New Testament's 'Power of the Keys' by which the Son of God empowered man with his authority," such that ALP's keys "will open not the kingdom of Heaven, but the free 'chaosmos' that is *Finnegans Wake*."[18] The prophetess as seeker and seer does not reveal or promise a synthetic *telos*, a Heaven in which God's message always arrives clear and free of error and always has meaning that is singular and true; she points instead toward pluralities and concatenations of signification. ALP is the appropriate interpreter of the *Wake*, who rejects Habakkuk's injunction, "the Lord is in his holy temple: let all the earth keep silence before him" (Habakkuk 2:20). That is, the feminine aspect of the prophet does not accede to mute passivity when the reifying logos takes root in its material home—in the womb of the earth, of Eve, or of Mary. She takes instead the material of the middenheap and the matter of the text, and of them she creates a rowdy and restive language, signifying variously, even if her voice is sometimes reduced to a mutter.

Notes

1. All references to the Bible use the King James Version.
2. Roland McHugh, *Annotations to "Finnegans Wake,"* 3rd ed. (Baltimore: Johns Hopkins University Press, 2006), 18.
3. Joseph Campbell and Henry Morton Robinson, *A Skeleton Key to "Finnegans Wake"* (Novato, Calif.: New World Library, 2005), 5. For a brief and useful primer on Joyce's Viconian structures, see William York Tindall, *A Reader's Guide to "Finnegans Wake"* (Syracuse: Syracuse University Press, 1996), 8–11.
4. I do not forget the fact that Arthur Wellesley, 1st Duke of Wellington, was, in fact, Anglo-Irish. As Vincent Cheng adeptly reads 10.17, "Willingdone as 'bornstable ghentleman' refers directly to Wellington's famous answer (so much like Cain's) when asked if he were Irish: 'If a gentleman should be born in a stable, it does not follow that he should be called a horse.' ... In denying his own Irishness, Wellington was—like Cain—trying to deny the humanity and allhorseness in all of us." See Vincent J. Cheng, *Joyce, Race, and Empire* (Cambridge: Cambridge University Press, 1995), 272.

5. Robert Alter and Frank Kermode, eds. *The Literary Guide to the Bible* (Cambridge: Belknap-Harvard University Press, 1987), 668, 343–45, 347–49.

6. Thus Nebuchadnezzar becomes a type of Finn MacCool, the giant that is the landscape of Dublin ("the brontoichthyan form outlined aslumbered"), who is asleep and likely to wake one day as the myth would have it, but who is in I.1 dead and mourned, like Nebuchadnezzar's statue: "Macool, Maccool, orra whyi deed ye diie?" (7.20–21, 6.13).

7. A biblical connection between Habakkuk and Daniel exists as well. In the deuterocanonical "Bel and the Dragon" episode, which appears as Daniel 14 in Roman Catholic and Eastern Orthodox Bibles but has been rejected by most Protestant denominations, God spirits Habakkuk out of a field, where he has just made some stew, and drops him in the lion's den, commanding that he give his dinner to Daniel. Daniel eats the stranger's food, praises the Lord, and then God returns Habakkuk to the Judean pasture.

8. The book of Habakkuk, like that of Daniel, famously has a macro-chiastic organization across and within its three chapters. Alter and Kermode further argue that Habakkuk revolves around productive lacunae and destabilized narrative logic: "[Habakkuk's] suggestiveness depends largely on the dramatic inconsistencies which result from the composite structure. Scholars have tried to construct a unified scenario for the section, but it is precisely the disjunctions . . . that account for its resonance. . . . For all of its surprising shifts and sublimations, the dialogue manages to generate a logic of its own, or to goad us into constructing one" (219). In a way, Habakkuk is spiritual kin to the *Wake* through its deployment and subsequent dismantling of complex, leveled structures in a way that demands epiphanic work of the reader.

9. The Hebrew word for prophet, *navi*, means "spokesperson," which underlines the fact that the prophet's primary charge is to be the transparent mouthpiece of God. This stricture is made quite forcefully in Deuteronomy: "I . . . will put my words in his mouth; and he shall speak unto them all that I shall command him. . . . But the prophet, which shall presume to speak a word in my name, which I have not commanded him to speak, or that shall speak in the name of other gods, even that prophet shall die" (Deuteronomy 18:18–20).

10. Norman O. Brown, *Apocalypse and/or Metamorphosis* (Berkeley: University of California Press, 1991), 90.

11. Brown describes the Quran as a "collage," citing "the beautiful inconsequentiality of the arrangement of the suras [chapters]: from the longest to the shortest" (90). According to this view, the Quran, while an eminently "meaningful" text, does not attain its meaning through systematic structure. What Joyce focuses on here are the both random and organic aspects of its production, and in this way Joyce deploys once more the tension between structure and its absence or its incongruities.

12. Ewa Ziarek, "'Circe': Joyce's *Argumentum ad Feminam*," in *Gender in Joyce*, ed. Jolanta W. Wawrzycka and Marlena G. Corcoran (Gainesville: University Press of Florida, 1997), 154.

13. Tindall, *Reader's Guide*, 36.

14. Margot Norris, *The Decentered Universe of "Finnegans Wake"* (Baltimore: Johns Hopkins University Press, 1976), 68.

15. Ibid., 69.

16. It would be disingenuous to claim that ALP is represented unproblematically as a creative, authorial, or prophetic force here, for as McHugh notices, this passage is littered with references to Muhammad's camel. These allusions may attempt chauvinistically to recuperate ALP as only a helpmeet for HCE, as the beast of burden that patiently transmits the "proper" prophet. ALP need not be understood in this analysis to be a redemptive and affirmational figure who is an authentic artist. She may be a figure whose agency is suppressed or denied in the narration, or she may be one who is less a prophet of life or resurrection than she is a prophet of dire premonition or of accusation and condemnation.

17. Shari Benstock, "Nightletters: Woman's Writing in the *Wake*," in *Critical Essays on James Joyce*, ed. Bernard Benstock (Boston: G. K. Hall, 1985), 230.

18. Norris, *Universe*, 72.

2

"Here Comes Everybody"

HCE and the Existence of Others in I.2

JIM LEBLANC

> Many of the issues raised in *Finnegans Wake* ... are finally metaphysical rather than psychological or social. The subject of guilt in particular is most profitably pursued as an ontological problem. In other words, events in *Finnegans Wake* elucidate the human condition, particularly the relationship of self and other, in an abstract and timeless way.
>
> Margot Norris, *The Decentered Universe of "Finnegans Wake"*

In part 3 of *Being and Nothingness*, in a chapter devoted to "The Existence of Others," Jean-Paul Sartre introduces his notion of *le regard*, or "the gaze."[1] To set the stage for his presentation of this concept, Sartre describes an encounter between his prototypical subject and a man in a public park to illustrate concretely that "through the mere appearance of others, I am put in the position of passing judgment on myself as on an object, for it is as an object that I appear to others" (266). The existence of others, as exemplified by this encounter with the man in the park, is "first the permanent flight of things towards an end that I grasp at one and the same time as an object at a certain distance from me and one that escapes me insofar as it unfolds around itself its own distances.... Thus all of a sudden an object has appeared that has stolen the world from me" (301). This phenomenon is not restricted, of course, to the actual appearance of others in the subject's world. The existence of others, once revealed, is internalized and becomes a "concrete, everyday relation that I experience at each instant: at each instant, the Other looks at me" (303). This fundamental aspect of the relationship between self and other constitutes the dynamic of the gaze, and the ontological importance of this dynamic cannot be overstressed, for, as Sartre remarks, "I recognize that I am as others see me" (266).[2]

The apperception, or sudden recognition of this existential truth, is realized through shame—specifically, "shame *of myself before the Other*" (266). This awareness of myself in a world where there are others, who bestow upon me a being that appears for the Other but resides in me, is vividly illustrated in Sartre's text through another concrete, everyday example. "Let's imagine," writes Sartre, "that for reasons of jealousy, curiosity, or vice I have just stuck my ear against a door and looked through the keyhole. . . . But suddenly I hear footsteps in the hall: someone is looking at me" (305–6). It is this look—or merely the sound of the footsteps that herald the look—that leads me to recognize the ontological dependency of my self on the existence of others. This is an alienated self, to be sure, for through the gaze I come to realize that the meaning of the situation in which I find myself always eludes me to some extent, is always "stolen" from me, and the truth of the world is always otherwise than it appears to me. Moreover, this sense of self as alienated identity never fully dissipates in the absence of the concrete look of another person, for this look is internalized as the gaze of the Other. The sense of shame associated with the gaze of the Other—this ontological dimension that is propped on the originary and repeated revelation of one's being-in-the-world where there are others—is, according to Sartre, not a "sense of being this or that guilty object, but in general of being *an* object; that is, of *recognizing* myself in this debased, dependent, and fixed being that I am for others" (336). Further, Sartre depicts shame as that sentiment of "an *original fall*, not because of the fact that I have committed this or that particular fault, but simply because of the fact that I have fallen into the world, in the midst of things, and that I need the mediation of others to be what I am" (336). Thus "original sin is my upsurge in a world where there are others and, whatever my further relations with others, they will only be variations on the original theme of my guilt" (461).

An encounter with a man in a park, a peeping tom, a fall, and a subject suffering from a chronic sense of guilt: these themes are central to the leitmotific "plot" of *Finnegans Wake*, and they are introduced in what is perhaps their least obscure context in set pieces occurring in I.2 of Joyce's work, the chapter christened by Campbell and Robinson as "HCE—His Agnomen and

Reputation."[3] Considered by some to be one of the most accessible parts of the *Wake*,[4] partly because of its somewhat straightforward story as well as its relative linguistic clarity, chapter I.2 relates the events through which the very identity of HCE, the composite older male avatar in the book, is revealed while at the same time it is put into question—a narrative sleight of hand that is emblematic of the entire discursive enterprise of the text. Who is HCE, and how do we know? How does *he* know who he is, and what does the staging of this fundamental existential question within the mind of the dreaming subject of *Finnegans Wake* and in the language of the book's discourse add to our understanding of what is at stake in this timeless query: who am I? It is definitely not my aim to try to prove some kind of influence of Joyce (and certainly not of *Finnegans Wake*) on Sartre. Nor will I argue a case for influence of the French philosopher on Joyce, whose *Finnegans Wake* preceded the publication of *L'être et le néant* by some four years. I do find it striking, however, that both writers employ similar scenarios to tell us something about the consequences for the subject of his/her prototypical encounter with the Other, especially, in Joyce's case, in a book in which one of the leading characters is known, among other things, as "Here Comes Everybody" (32.18–19). It is thus my intent to read Joyce against Sartre to determine what the latter's existential phenomenology tells us about Joyce's project.

The overriding concern of *Finnegans Wake* I.2 is the "quest for the identity of HCE, at once the one and the many."[5] In other words, the chapter sheds light on the quest(ion) of identity both for individuals and for all, a universalization of the problem of identity that can be understood as a hallmark of the human condition. We read straightaway in the chapter's opening lines that this episode of the *Wake* will concern itself with "the genesis of Harold or Humphrey Chimpden's occupational agnomen" (30.02–03). An agnomen is a moniker bestowed on a person to reflect something that the individual has famously or infamously done, often an exploit of some sort. In other words, it is a name that associates the subject with an act, a name that others use to describe the subject and that freezes, as it were, the subject's identity in a past accomplishment or activity and objectifies that subject in a role that he/she may or may no longer choose to assume. In HCE's case, the agnomen is conferred upon him by no less than a "king" (31.11). The look and opinion of this royal other is archetypally symbolic of the internalized gaze of the Other that looks at me "at each instant" and before whom I recognize myself as an object in shame or guilt, as Adam and Eve did before God in their famous Fall. As the tale is told in Joyce's work, the king and his foxhunting party come across HCE at a time of "prefall paradise peace" (30.15), before the Fall, before Adam and Eve realized in shame before God that they were naked, before "Gob scene you in the narked place" (34.10; God saw you obscenely naked in the park or marketplace). HCE's agnomen, which is not plainly voiced until many lines later in the text as "Earwicker" (33.30 and 34.14), stems from the king's first glimpse of HCE "bearing aloft . . . a high perch atop of which a flowerpot was fixed earthside" (31.01–03), which he uses to catch, as he himself puts it, "thon bluggy earwuggers" (31.10–11). At this the king remarks that "we have for surtrusty bailiwick a turnpiker who is by turns a pikebailer no seldomer than an earwigger!" (31.26–28). This regal christening portends the gossip that will further define HCE as the chapter and, in fact, the entire book progress, for HCE, in his mythic origins, already seems to be fighting a losing battle against those bloody, buggy earwigs—both the insect (Forficula auricularia, so called from the belief that these creatures bore into one's head through the ear) and, in the word's figurative sense, those garrulous rumormongers who, as others, steal the world from him and give rise to his alienated identity through words whispered from ear to ear.[6]

Of course, the identity of HCE, as readers of *Finnegans Wake* quickly perceive, is not that simple. The king's quip portrays HCE and his "surtrusty" (sure, as in secure and well guarded, as well as extremely trusted or true) "bailiwick" (the space over which one holds official authority, as well as the figurative sphere of one's work and aptitude) as a "turnpiker," as well as both an "earwigger" and a "pikebailer." We know that HCE, at this particular moment in the *Wake*'s narrative, appears as a turnpike keeper, for he uses his "turnpike keys" to allow "his majesty" and the "hunting party" (31.01–03) to pass through or into his "surtrusty bailiwick." But the king also refers to him as a "pikebailer no seldomer than an earwigger," suggesting that HCE—who is identified from the very beginning of the *Wake* as a fallen "oldparr" (3.17; a young fish or "parr," grown old), whose form is "brontoichthyan" (7.20; like that of a thunderous fish, from the Greek *brontē* [thunder] and *icthys* [fish]), whose breath is "sardinish" (35.35), and who appears regularly, in fact, throughout *Finnegans Wake* as a fish—is also a fisherman: one who bails "pike" (traps or scoops these fish out of an inundated boat, for instance), bears a "perch" aloft when he first meets "his majesty," and is asked by the king for tips on what bait to use for "lobstertrapping" (31.08).[7] Thus HCE's reputation as an "earwigger" is only one among many sources for potential agnominal nicknames, all of which, in themselves, merely supplement the many other forenames and family names by which HCE is known and are, consequently, as Kimberly J. Devlin observes, "a linguistic excess working against nominal containment."[8] Not only, then, are HCE's forenames ("Harold or Humphrey" and countless other variations throughout the text), as well as what might be construed as his family name ("Chimpden" or "Chivychas" [30.14]), in question within the first two pages of this chapter alone but his agnomen seems to have been somewhat arbitrarily chosen to boot.

The mythic origin of HCE's shifty aliases is no less in dispute: "Comes the question are these the facts of his nomengentilisation" (31.33–34, are these the facts concerning the origin of his "clan name" or *nomen gentile*)? "No dung on the road" (31.36–32.01, no bullshit?). We read that it may not have been "the king kingself but his inseparable sisters, uncontrollable nighttalkers, Skertsiraizde with Donyahzade who came down into the world" (32.07–10) to tell the story of HCE, bestowing on the *Wake*'s archetypal male figure an origin that is only as truthful as the tales spun by Shahrazad to save her own life in the *Arabian Nights*. And as we later read in book I, chapter 3, "in this scherzarade of one's thousand one nightinesses that sword of certainty which would indentifide the body never falls" (51.04–06). In fact, the "body" (HCE as the waked corpse or sleeping human form of the *Wake*) is impossible to "indentifide" (identify faithfully—note the way that the Latin *fides*, meaning faith or trust, is embedded in this word), because he is a universal figure, an "imposing everybody he always indeed looked . . . and magnificently well worthy of any and all universalization" (32.19–21); at the same time, he is representative of the prototypical alienated individual subject, one whose being is splintered by the Other, who steals the world from him through the gaze and through subsequent loquacious, uncontrollable "stolentelling" (424.35, both storytelling and stories that steal). HCE is thus the "soul of everyelsesbody rolled into its olesoleself" (329.18–19), hence his particularly appropriate and descriptive appellation "Here Comes Everybody" (32.18–19). At the same time he is the singular "'Thom' or 'Thim' [Finnegan] of the fishy stare who . . . is not all there and is all the more himself since he is not so" (507.01–04), whose "fluctuating identity," in Devlin's words, "is a function of its mediated status,"[9] founded by the appearance of others in the world who look at him.

HCE's original fall or sin ("this municipal sin business" [5.14]), the source of his chronic shame and guilt, is articulated, more or less, in the next several lines of I.2, although like most events in the *Wake* this transgression is repeated in numerous and often contradictory iterations throughout the text. First, "Skertsiraizde" and "Donyahzade" morph into two music hall girls, "Rosa and Lily Miskinguette" (32.11), who perform for HCE in the guise of "good Dook Umphrey" (32.15, good Duke Humphrey). The description of this affair soon gives way, however, to more serious and sober remarks about how a "baser meaning has been read into these characters the literal sense of which decency can safely scarcely hint" (33.14–15). Through rumor, which "has been blurtingly bruited [*bruit*: rumor in French] by certain wisecrackers" (33.15–16), along with insinuation (33.25), "ludicrous imputation" (33.26), implication (33.34), "blondy" (white bloody) lies (34.09–10), and "slander" (34.12), HCE is accused by three apparently drunk "regarders" (or watchers [34.16]—recall here the French term for the gaze, *le regard*) of "having behaved with ongentilmensky immodus opposite a pair of dainty maidservants in the swoolth of the rushy hollow whither, or the two gown and pinners pleaded, dame nature in all innocency had spontaneously and about the same hour of the eventide sent them both" (34.18–22). The ungentlemanly immodesty with which HCE is charged seems to entail not only looking at the two "dainty maidservants" answering the call of nature (later described as "two madges on the makewater" [420.07]), but also an "incautious . . . partial exposure" (34.26–27) on his own part. Thus HCE's sin, as recalled at this moment of the *Wake*, involves two young girls peeing, while HCE, as voyeur (literally, one who sees or looks), in turn exposes himself to the girls who are looking back at him. In the continually shifting manner of all Wakean discourse, this scene seems to have evolved out of the preceding vignette with the two music hall girls, whose surname is "Miskinguette." This surname evokes Mistinguette (the stage moniker of a French cabaret diva and silent film star), but also serves as a portmanteau containing *miss* (or young lady), *guette* (French for "watching for," in the sense of lying in wait for), and *king*. The "king" in question here is no longer the royal personage whom HCE encounters in the opening sequence of this chapter, but HCE himself, now as the "good Dook Umphrey," a royal figure whose confidence is at least temporarily secure (he is an "imposing everybody" and "magnificently well worthy" [32.20–22]) and whose sense of self is not immediately threatened by the unwelcome look of others, whom he perceives, at the current instant, as admiring.[10] Thus it is not clear whether it is the two misses who lie in wait for the "king," or vice versa—if, indeed, either party is actually lying in wait for the other or merely watching.

But the "bushes have eyes, don't forget" (522.12–13) and there "were treefellers in the shrubrubs" (420.08, on one level, three fellows in the shrubs), who were "watching the watched watching" (509.02–03). Although HCE is apparently unaware of the presence of these three "annoying Welsh fusiliers" (33.26–27) at the time of his alleged transgressions, they will ultimately reveal themselves among HCE's accusers: "Hay, hay, hay! Hoq, hoq, hoq! Faun and Flora [the two girls] on the lea love that little old joq [HCE as an aged shameful joke]" (33.27–28)—the phrase echoes the American drinking song, "Little Brown Jug." The three drunken soldiers (who also "love that little [brown jug]") are witnesses to HCE's act and thus evoke those "footsteps in the hall" that alert the Sartrean subject, kneeling at the door and looking through the keyhole, to the fact that he has been seen and suddenly and undeniably objectified by the gaze of an other who has stolen from him an important facet of his subjective world as voyeur and revealed to him his objectness in shame and guilt. Given that this scene includes one individual who is both watching and watched by two others and who are all three in turn watched by three more, it vividly illustrates a kind of tangled, multilayered existential phenomenological dynamic between self and other, powered by the gaze. The original sin in *Finnegans Wake* is thus the upsurge of "Everybody" (HCE) in a world where the subject sees and is seen by others who bestow upon him an alienated identity, which he continually internalizes and, in a word, becomes.

This realization of HCE's objectness in shame and guilt is restaged in the next scene in chapter I.2. Up until this point, we only know about what is alleged to have taken place in the "rushy hollow" (an allusion to the "Hollow," an area in Dublin's Phoenix Park) through rumor, insinuation, and the "stolentelling" of the "gossipocracy" (476.04) of others. "Whatever it was they threed to make out he thried to two in the Fiendish park" (196.09–11), the "unfacts, did we possess them, are too imprecisely few to warrant our certitude" (57.16–17). However, HCE himself reveals his feelings of guilt for "this or that particular fault" in another timeless mythic tale, in which he appears "billowing across the wide expanse of our greatest park" (Phoenix Park), "ages and ages after the alleged misdemeanor" (35.05–08). He encounters a man in the park, a "cad with a pipe" (35.11). Not surprisingly, given this sudden revelation of the Other at the scene of his original sin or crime (which was witnessed by the "annoying Welsh fusiliers in the people's park" [33.26–27]), HCE sees the cad who "accosted him" (35.15) as a threat, even though this man in the park does little more than greet HCE with a "nice how-do-you-do in Poolblack" (or in the language of Dublin, the Irish name of which meant "black pool" [35.16–17]) and ask him the time ("how much a clock it was" [35.18]).[11] In a phenomenological sense, though, this question is not immaterial to the existential effect of the encounter with the Other, for the gaze reveals my objectness not only in space but also in time. "The appearance of the look of others," writes Sartre, manifests itself to me through an *Erlebnis* [a mental experience] that was, in principle, impossible for me to acquire in solitude: that of simultaneity.... The look of others, in so far as I apprehend it, gives my time a new dimension. As a present apprehended by others as my present, my presence has an outside: this presence, which becomes a present for me, is alienated for me as a present to which others make themselves present.[12]

In other words, just as the appearance of others through the gaze reveals an unfolding of spatial distances around (conscious) objects that are not me, my recognition of the other's look also unveils a temporal dimension of my being that, at least in part, always eludes me. Thus the cad's seemingly innocuous question about the time emphasizes for HCE another dimension of his being-for-others, an identity that is alienated and "stolen" from him in time as well as in space, a chronic shame engendered by a sense of always being in the wrong place at the wrong time or at least in a place and time that is never completely his own.

The "Earwicker of the spurring instant, realizing . . . the supreme importance, nexally and noxally, of physical life" (35.21–23)—the narration here hinting at Hegel's famous formulation of the "life-and-death struggle" between self and other[13]—answers the cad's question about the time, but immediately offers a stuttering denial of the "hakusay accusation againstm" (36.04, "accusa-, accusation against him," the voicing of which also intones the Japanese *haku*, or "say," creating a kind of double bilingual stammer), while in the same stroke identifying himself as the accused (*accusé*: the one accused in French) through his telltale stuttering. What accusation, readers may ask? HCE's stammering continues: "for the honours of our mewmew mutual daughters" (the two girls, but also Everybody's daughters), "I am woowoo willing to take my stand, sir, upon the monument" (the "duc de Fer's overgrown milestone" or the Wellington Monument in Phoenix Park) "that there is not one tittle of truth" (a stuttering slip of sexual innuendo) "in that purest of fibfib fabrications" (36.18–34, although he may well be fibbing about the fabrications). HCE guiltily denies an "accusation againstm" that is never actually verbalized by the cad, whose literal question to HCE seems innocent enough. But like the peeping tom discovered with his eye to the keyhole, the subject who perceives himself "caught in the act" (of being) by the gaze of the Other is always "put in the position of passing judgment on [himself] as an object" and realizes his objectness in shame. Thus HCE, in a kind of preemptive effort to reassert his subjectivity, tries to disavow the "original sin" that is his "upsurge in a world where there are others," which in *Finnegans Wake* manifests itself as the "municipal sin business": HCE's rumored "incautious . . . partial exposure" to the "pair of dainty maidservants" whom he spies answering the call of "dame nature" in the "rushy hollow" of the same "people's park" where he subsequently encounters the cad who, as the Other, steals the world from HCE through the former's look or gaze.

It is important to remember, however, as John Bishop observes, that "everybody in the world ['Here Comes Everybody'] has dreamed of perpetrating some nasty public indiscretion, but having dreamed of such an offense hardly means that one really committed it."[14] HCE makes his own claim to this effect later in the *Wake* when, in response to reiterated "hakusay accusation[s] againstm"—this time in the form of a lengthy list of derogatory names—he affirms that "he was not guilphy but . . . reconnoitring through his semisubconscious the seriousness of what he might have done had he really polished off his terrible intentions" (72.28–31). In other words, even as he reasserts his innocence, HCE cannot help but confess "his terrible intentions," which he entertained at least "semisubconscious[ly]," though as always the slipperiness of the *Wake*'s discourse renders the truth of this disclaimer difficult to establish. What we do know is that HCE, as sleeper, dreams of a particular sin, a forbidden wish-to-be-fulfilled involving two girls, his daughter(s) perhaps, in a kind of "I'll-show-you-mine-if-you'll-show-me-yours" vignette: "to peekaboo durk the thicket of slumbwhere" (580.14–15, to peek through [*durch* in German] the dark thicket of slumber somewhere). But this "humphriad of the fall and rise while daisy winks at her pinker sister among the tussocks" (53.09–10) is universalized, becomes the dream of "everybody in the world," in the encounter between HCE and the "cad with a pipe." For in its emblematic function as the prototypical encounter between Self and Other, this scene reenacts the originary guilt of the human condition—to wit, being-in-the-world where there are others—as does the subject's encounter with the man in the park in Sartre's philosophical text. As William York Tindall suggests, HCE's sin "remains indefinite" and therefore may be "any sin of every man or every sin of any man."[15] Thus the sin in the park, or the "municipal sin business," becomes generalized, becomes any and all crimes perpetrated—or even conceived—by "Here Comes Everybody," rather than "this or that particular fault," for the incident transcends the murky facts of its proliferation as a "blurtingly bruited" tale of exhibitionism and voyeurism in the "hollow" of Phoenix Park.

It is not surprising, then, that this universalized sin is one involving nude exposure before others, given the traditional association of this act with the story of Adam and Eve ("Gob scene you in the narked place") and Freud's observation that dreams of being naked—in which the dreamer feels "shame and embarrassment and tries to escape or hide"—are not only typical (in other words, common to many) but related to the myth of the Fall.[16] Nor is it surprising that HCE's encounter with the Other involves a "cad with a pipe," a scenario based on Joyce's father's account of being robbed one night by "some sort of ne'er-do-well" in Phoenix Park.[17] The inclusion and elaboration of this sort of biographical detail are common to Joyce's approach to all his works, and in this case, it provided him with a "blurtingly bruited" real-life crime in Phoenix Park (an incident that may or may not have actually taken place, given John Joyce's penchant for storytelling and embellishing the truth) on which to layer the many aspects of HCE's "guilphy" reputation. As an element of HCE's dream, this event functions as a kind of "day's residue"—those seemingly indifferent wakeful impressions which, according to Freud, supply the dreamer with a "necessary point of attachment" for more troubling latent dream thoughts to slip into the dream.[18] In this case, John Joyce's putative encounter with the thief in the park serves as a useful narrative screen for the more disturbing thought of the inevitable and inescapable contingency of the human condition, whereby we have fallen into a world where there are others who rob that world from us and alienate us in our own being.

Among the layers of polyvalent, overdetermined narrative that occur at this point in *Finnegans Wake*, readers may also detect subtle allusions to the 1882 Phoenix Park murders, one of the most celebrated crimes of Joyce's early youth and another example of a contemporary event that provides a "point of attachment" for the more distressful and latent ontological implications of HCE's encounter with the cad. HCE's stuttering, for instance, in addition to signaling his sense of guilt, recalls that of Lord Frederick Cavendish, the newly appointed British chief secretary for Ireland and one of the victims in this infamous event who, like many of HCE's multiple manifestations, represents one in a long line of foreign invaders of Ireland. And like the rumor and hearsay surrounding HCE's transgression, Senan Molony writes that "thousands of snippets of pure gossip" spread across Dublin during the first few days following the Phoenix Park slayings of Cavendish and Thomas Henry Burke (the permanent undersecretary for Ireland and second victim)—as happens following the commission of any scandalous crime that captures the public's imagination.[19] Among these rumors and specious accusations was one initiated by a certain Reverend Hogg, who told the police that he believed a man named Patrick "Bird" Finnegan was involved in the affair,[20] a name that resonates in the cad's parting remark to HCE (Finnegan): "I have met with you, bird, too late" (37.13). Further, Timothy Kelly, one of the defendants at the Phoenix Park murder proceedings, who was eventually convicted and hanged, is reputed to have placed a bet on a horse during the trial and to have sung ballads in his cell on the eve of his execution—among them Michael Balfe's "I Dreamt I Dwelt in Marble Halls" from his opera *The Bohemian Girl*. These two bits of gossip about the case surface in *Finnegans Wake* I.2, particularly in the rapidly spreading chatter about HCE's alleged transgression from the cad to his wife ("Our cad's bit of strife" [38.09]), who in turn relays the story to her kids ("a hundred and eleven others" [38.13]) and to "her particular reverend" (38.18), who passes it on while placing "safe and sane bets" (39.01) at a racetrack. Eventually, the story ends up in the mouth of a certain Hosty, who pens "The Ballad of Persse O'Reilly" (44.24–45.30, *perce-oreille*: earwig in French) about HCE's alleged crime. Balfe's opera appears in chapter I.2 as well, just before the introduction of HCE's "ongentilmensky" behavior, when HCE as "good Dook Umphrey" attends a performance that includes "selections from The Bo' Girl" (32.35). Finally, we note that the cad's watch was "bradys" (35.20), both slow (from the Greek, *bradus*) and belonging to (Joseph) Brady, the Irish "Invincible" who knifed both Burke and Cavendish, according to the testimony presented at the trial. Brady and his accomplices were found guilty on April 13, 1883—that is, on the same day of the year that HCE encounters the "cad with a pipe," at least in this particular staging of that event in chapter I.2, on "one happygogusty Ides-of-April morning" (35.03). These allusions to the Phoenix Park murders are somewhat fleeting. In later iterations, for example, HCE's encounter with the cad takes place on a "hoppy-go-jumpy January [both June and January] morn" (332.24–25) and on the "hydes of March" (603.15, the Ides of March, or March 15). They do, however, help both to elucidate and to further adumbrate the imprecise and shadowy nature of HCE's "elusive transgression that flickers across the surface of the dream in an endless array of forms."[21]

Thus the particular sin or crime attributed to HCE in *Finnegans Wake* is necessarily obscure, given his totalizing manifestation as "Here Comes Everybody." As this universalized somebody, HCE bears the existential burden of both original sin (our fall into the world where there are others who mediate our identity and reveal to us our objectness) and guilt for all crimes perpetuated by everybody. Hence Joyce's use of Adam and Eve's originary crime, his father's story about his putative mugging in Phoenix Park, the famous Phoenix Park murder case that occurred in the year of Joyce's birth, and the sexual fantasies involving an older man and young girls in an incestuous context—crimes general and personal, mythic and real, and mingled and mangled—in the "nat language" (at once "night language," "knot language," and "not language") of the *Wake*'s discourse, in which the author stages the dream of his fictional character and universal avatar.

If it is through the look or gaze (*le regard*) of the Other that I come to recognize the ontological dependency of my self on the existence of others, it is through language that I come to recognize that the meaning of my existence is "stolen" from me by the Other. "We are resigned to seeing ourselves through the eyes of the Other," writes Sartre; "this means that we strive to apprehend our being through the revelations of language."[22] Moreover, language is not, for Sartre, some kind of supplementary attribute or phenomenon associated with our being-for-others. Rather, language *is* this being. It is thus inherently fundamental and even gives rise to the human condition [*la réalité humaine*] in so far as "the appearance of the Other confronting me through the gaze causes language to arise as the condition of my being."[23]

What better forum, then, to present the prototypical encounter of the Self with the Other than a text in which the identity of a character is stolen and shaped by others and described in a language, the full meaning of which escapes not only the subject within but the reader outside the text. The crime that defines HCE's reputation (that aspect of his being-for-others that is to a great extent out of his control) is related repeatedly over time through a slippery and endlessly signifying series of tales and anecdotes, like some universal game of telephone. The identity of HCE, the meaning of which is revealed to him by others through language, becomes muddled and impossible to verify or even stabilize. Again in the words of Sartre: "the 'meaning' of my expressions always escapes me; I never know exactly if I am signifying what I want to signify, nor if I'm signifying at all."[24] This effect is dramatically illustrated in the *Wake* through the "stolentelling" of HCE's life, the rumors that define his reputation both as a continually morphing individual and as the universalized figure of "Everybody," and through HCE's repeatedly failed attempts to clarify matters and clear his name.

It is important to note that I have restricted my analysis in the foregoing pages to what might be considered the primary but by no means only description of HCE's elusive, alleged transgression and his encounter with the other as man/cad in the park in *Finnegans Wake*. As both universal event and as repeated narrative motif throughout the *Wake*, these events and "the amount of all those sort of things which has been going on onceaday in and twiceaday out every other nachtistag [*Nacht*: night, and *Tag*: day in German] among all kinds of promiscious individuals at all ages . . . and allover all and elsewhere" (66.02–06) pervade Joyce's text. HCE's fall and the guilt associated with it are both timeless and ubiquitous, and the archetypal nature of this event is well reflected in the polylingual and polyvocal dream discourse that Joyce deploys to relate it. This "nat language at any sinse of the world" is not/night language signifying in any sense of the word any sins of the world (83.12), and it is the "nat language" of everybody. Hence we have the relevance of the scenes in the park with the girls and the cad and their archetypal representation of the encounter with the Other for everyone, everywhere.

As avatar for "everybody" in the dream text that is *Finnegans Wake*, HCE comes to know that dimension of his being-in-the-world that is out of his control, that is "stolen" from him by the Other—through a sense of guilt associated not only with his alleged perverse activity with the two girls in the shadows of the "rushy hollow" but with all crimes: this self-conscious self-alienation is our original sin or fall. Chapter I.2, with its focus on the question of HCE's identity, contains emblematic representations of alienated human subjectivity as informing incidents for the *Wake*'s oneiric narrative, in which the dream-work portrays the revelation of the Other through an encounter with a man in a park and a peeping tom caught in the act. The power of these stories—presented not only in the "stolentelling" of the *Wake*'s narrative but in the many layers of its discourse—is reaffirmed and reinforced by Sartre's use of the same narrative examples in his magnum opus on the phenomenology of being. The story of "Here Comes Everybody," at its most basic level, thus relates what it means *to be* human in a world where the meaning of our existence, and even that of our names, often escapes us, while at the same time, in the look and language of the Other, it tells us who we are.

Notes

1. Jean-Paul Sartre, *L'être et le néant: essai d'ontologie phénoménologique* (Paris: Gallimard, 1943), 298–349. All translations are mine. According to Tilottama Rajan, it is Sartre's introduction of the existential phenomenological principle of *le regard* that gave rise to the subsequent Lacanian and poststructuralist use of the concept. See Tilottama Rajan, *Deconstruction and the Remainders of Phenomenology* (Stanford: Stanford University Press, 2002), 156. Lacan, himself no fan of Sartre's later humanistic existentialism, praised Sartre's analysis of the gaze of the Other as "one of the most brilliant passages" in the philosopher's work. See Jacques Lacan, *The Four Fundamental Concepts of Psycho-Analysis*, ed. Jacques-Alain Miller, trans. Alan Sheridan (New York: Norton, 1978), 84.

2. Sartre's English translator, Hazel E. Barnes, renders the French term *le regard* as "the look." Although Lacan and his French readers understood very well the

connection between this aspect of Lacanian theory and Sartre's earlier presentation of the concept, the difference between the English terms *look* and *gaze*, though representing the same French term, may have obscured this relation for English readers over the years.

3. Joseph Campbell and Henry Morton Robinson, *A Skeleton Key to "Finnegans Wake"* (New York: Penguin, 1977), 16.

4. See, for instance, William York Tindall, *A Reader's Guide to "Finnegans Wake"* (Syracuse: Syracuse University Press, 1969), 56–57, and Bill Cole Cliett, *Riverrun to Livvy: Lots of Fun Reading the First Page of James Joyce's "Finnegans Wake"* (privately published, 2011), 259.

5. Eric McLuhan, *The Role of Thunder in "Finnegans Wake"* (Toronto: University of Toronto Press, 1997), 80.

6. In addition to its primary entomological denotation and its figurative sense of a whispering gossiper, the word *earwig* is also Dublin slang for a gossipy barfly—a usage that is particularly relevant in *Finnegans Wake* with its twelve pub patrons. See Edmund Epstein, *A Guide through "Finnegans Wake"* (Gainesville: University Press of Florida, 2009), 37.

7. I am indebted to Roland McHugh's *Annotations to "Finnegans Wake,"* 3rd ed. (Baltimore: Johns Hopkins University Press, 2006). I draw here and throughout this essay on his useful line-by-line, phrase-by-phrase, word-by-word glossing of Joyce's text.

8. Kimberly J. Devlin, *Wandering and Return in "Finnegans Wake"* (Princeton: Princeton University Press, 1991), 68.

9. Ibid., 123.

10. Sartre notes that pride, or vanity, arises from the same existential structure as that of shame, although in pride I recognize a responsibility for the objectness [*l'objectité*] conferred on me by others and embrace that alienating identity willingly through a denial of my subjective freedom. See Sartre, *L'être et le néant*, 337.

11. The minatory nature of this encounter is further reinforced, however, later in the *Wake* when the "unknowable assailant" appears with a "revolver" rather than a pipe (62.31–33).

12. Sartre, *L'être et le néant*, 313.

13. G.W.F. Hegel, *The Phenomenology of Mind*, trans. J. B. Baillie (New York: Harper & Row, 1967), 232.

14. John Bishop, *Joyce's Book of the Dark: "Finnegans Wake"* (Madison: University of Wisconsin Press, 1986), 166.

15. Tindall, *Reader's Guide*, 58.

16. Sigmund Freud, *The Interpretation of Dreams*, in *The Standard Edition of the Complete Psychological Works of Sigmund Freud*, vol. 4–5, trans. James Strachey (London: Hogarth, 1958), 242–45.

17. John Wyse Jackson and Peter Costello, *John Stanislaus Joyce: The Voluminous Life and Genius of James Joyce's Father* (New York: St. Martin's Press, 1998), 141.

18. Freud, *Interpretation of Dreams*, 564.

19. Senan Molony, *The Phoenix Park Murders: Conspiracy, Betrayal & Retribution* (Douglas Village, Cork: Mercier Press, 2006), 58.

20. Ibid., 78.

21. Devlin, *Wandering and Return*, 118. For more on the many possible allusions to the Phoenix Park murders of 1882 in *Finnegans Wake* and elsewhere in Joyce's works, see Edward A. Kopper Jr., "Some Elements of the Phoenix Park Murders in *Finnegans Wake*," *A Wake Newslitter* 6 (1967): 115–19, and Patrick A. McCarthy, Morris Beja, and Mel Seesholtz, "James Joyce and the Phoenix Park Murders: A Forum," *Irish Renaissance Annual* 4 (1983): 76–93.

22. Sartre, *L'être et le néant*, 404.

23. Ibid., 422. Bernard-Henri Lévy has recently characterized Sartre's take on language as "no longer a 'tool' but the element of Being, its dwelling, my dwelling, the fabric of which I am made as well as that from which all things are woven." See Bernard-Henri Lévy, *Sartre: The Philosopher of the Twentieth Century*, trans. Andrew Brown (Cambridge: Polity Press, 2003), 154.

24. Sartre, *L'être et le néant*, 423.

3

Weathering the Text

Barometric Readings of I.3

TIM CONLEY

Atmosphere as a literary or aesthetic term appears to have fallen out of usage. It is much less likely to be employed now in, say, a serious discussion of poetry than it is in a restaurant review. Yet the term still has a home in the ninth edition of *A Glossary of Literary Terms* (2009), though its definition is brief: "the emotional tone pervading a section or whole of a literary work, which fosters in the reader expectations as to the course of events." If this begs the question of what distinction there might be between *atmosphere* and *tone*, synonymy further obscures, dilutes, and perhaps even empties the term's value when *mood* and *ambiance* are proffered as "alternative terms frequently used."[1] The *OED* categorizes such usage as merely "figurative," not specific to any particular discourse: "Mental or moral environment; a pervading tone or mood; associations, effects, sounds, etc. evoking a characteristic mood."

The apparent obsolescence of *atmosphere* has, I think, a network of interconnected causes. In part, it is the term's ineluctable uncertainty, imprecision, and slipperiness that make it weak and impractical. In addition to the variety of synonyms clustered around it, *atmosphere* is so often combined or connected with other formal elements—setting, theme, character—as to make it almost inseparable from them. This is most dramatically the case with genre, some kinds of which are wholly enveloped by an "atmosphere" because those genres are themselves committed to establishing and strictly maintaining a particular "mental or moral environment." Such popular genres extend from the gothic to *World of Warcraft*. The tough guy poise of a Sam Spade or the acumen of a Philip Marlow requires just the right admixture of cigarette smoke and perfume and would be abruptly snuffed out by the introduction of fluorescent office lighting or a few choice notes from a harpsichord: the saturation is total but precarious and must be carefully preserved as atmosphere and style become one. The paradox is that "atmosphere" is essential to more or less fixed genres which try to limit the variability or, in Umberto Eco's vision of the "open work,"[2] close a given text (it is uphill work to read *The Monk* as not horrific or to demonstrate that Sherlock Holmes has, at a story's end, sent a guiltless party to prison). But the term's usefulness seems to have diminished for discussions that try to resist absolute, oppressive interpretations.

There is, too, something rather mawkish about *atmosphere*. Not only is it technically imprecise or at any rate vague; it implies an emotional response within the reader, one which can more or less safely be generalized. Again, critical trends have moved away from what are seen as unnecessarily constraining interpretations. Yet for all that, the purposes of *atmosphere* have in some respects been usurped by the now de rigueur (though perhaps no less slippery) term *affect*. Whatever the comparative strengths or weaknesses of *affect*, it most distinctly lacks the environmental connotations of *atmosphere*. While this takes a step away from the pitfalls of pathetic fallacy often inherent if perhaps not unavoidable in the use of *atmosphere*, the preference for *affect* may represent a most literal displacement, a removal of the contingencies of place from considerations of readerly response.

After Derrida, the containment of the text implied by a differentiation of an "atmosphere" within a work from an indistinct other or even a vacuum without lacks feasibility: literature without air locks. Thus talk of atmosphere may well seem to smack of a fogeyish criticism, hermetically sealing off the world of the text from the world of the reader, with all the attendant depoliticizing effects such a gesture has by design.

Yet these tangled problems with talking about the atmosphere of a literary work—its unquantifiable and affective vagueness and its implied hermeneutics of separation and closure—make it tantalizing to reassess for studies of *Finnegans Wake*, a book that infamously troubles the very tools and terminology on which literary criticism so often relies. As readers have over the decades had cause to marvel and moan, the *Wake*'s counter-teleological distortions of time and space prohibit a delineation of causality integral to "plot" as such; these same distortions as well as those to language make "setting" an effectively indeterminable variable, and the ways in which speakers and subjects keep collapsing into one another reduce "character" to a cluster of attributes that occasionally align into a recognizable pattern, such as the initials HCE and ALP. Given the book's volatile, persistent mutability (of character, language, and so on), might not the nebulous concept of "atmosphere," with a refreshed understanding of the world's atmosphere as itself a mutable phenomenon, turn out to be more useful in considerations of the *Wake* than these other, typically more stable ones have been?

Finnegans Wake is a very cloudy book, but this essay will concentrate its meteorological survey on the third chapter, which, as Roland McHugh has observed, begins with a fog ("you spoof of visibility in a freakfog" [48.01–02]) and ends with rain, though it is ambiguous whether the rain has begun or is abating: "Rain. When we sleep. Drops. But wait until our sleeping. Drain. Sdops" (74.18–19). McHugh remarks that the whole of the chapter "is embraced by the Irish climate" (and I'll return to this rather odd phrasing later).[3] This strategy of focusing on this one chapter in order to test a kind of reading approach for the book does not imply that the *Wake* is neatly or usefully divisible into coherent, independent parts, and yet neither is Joyce's book a cohesive, syncretic whole that can be safely summarized.[4] This paradox also highlights how serviceable the contemplation of "atmosphere" is to our appreciation of the *Wake*, for the discussion of—indeed, the very concept of—climate and environment necessitates both an understanding of the phenomenon as local and relative and an acceptance of the provisionality and the erroneousness of its study.

The weather is the universal subject of conversation *par excellence*. It allows for amicable oscillation between the particular and the general, and everyone is entitled to and usually has an opinion. It is also, for these reasons, often viewed as a harmless, even pacifying subject. The newspaper's phrase "Snow is general all over Ireland," which haunts Gabriel Conroy (and the reader) at the conclusion of "The Dead," is first voiced by Mary Jane as a polite way of moving the conversation away from the rudeness of Bartell D'Arcy. It is a means of moving from the uncomfortably specific to what seems an inoffensively general scale of things:

—It's the weather, said Aunt Julia, after a pause.
—Yes, everybody has colds, said Aunt Kate readily, everybody.
—They say, said Mary Jane, that we haven't had snow like this for thirty years; and I read this morning in the newspapers that the snow is general all over Ireland. (*D* 211)

Watch the pronouns here, for Joyce neatly captures the irregular way that they tend to be employed in what seem like banal, innocuous conversations.

It would seem, if very indirectly, to refer to the cause of D'Arcy's hoarseness (if not his coarseness), but *it* could mean just about anything, just as the *it* habitually used in an utterance like Lily's "Is it snowing again, Mr Conroy?" (*D* 177) has no definite referent. (What snows? It.) *Everybody* is repeated to remove all doubt, but the assertion is factually incorrect, an exaggeration. *They* is the abstract authority behind every weather report.

All of this becomes valuable for readers of *Finnegans Wake* when we recall that it is a book composed, as Finn Fordham has it, of "unravelling universals."[5] After the snow that "is general all over Ireland" has fallen, "by now one hears turtlings all over Doveland" (61.02). Unique wordflakes are everywhere, and every possible weather system is likewise lexicalized. The *Wake's* various voices are often an indistinct *they* full of contradictory reports, dubious prophecies of a future hopelessly jumbled with the past, all "falsetissues, antilibellous, and nonactionable" (48.18), none of which inspire confidence: "Thus the unfacts, did we possess them, are too imprecisely few to warrant our certitude" (57.16–17). Similar pronoun trouble, of course, plagues the reader on every page, if not in every sentence. In this chapter, it is variants of *he* and *his* that make for an unfixed subject, and *he* begins as a singer, "quite a musical genius in a small way and the owner of an exceedingly niced ear, with tenorist voice to match" (48.20–21)—like Bartell D'Arcy or the other legendary singers reverentially recalled in "The Dead." Whatever he is—for he is or may also be (or was or may have been) in the course of this chapter, an actor, a fisherman, a dustman, a tailor, a photographer, and a giant, among other things, and at the chapter's end is a list of "abusive names he was called" (71.05–06)—he emerges from "a poisoning volume of cloud barrage indeed" (48.05). He materializes from the air itself.

The connections between character and atmosphere discernible in the *Wake* are radical versions of the notions that Bloom entertains in *Ulysses* about how climate shapes temperament, how one can see more clearly after a rainfall, and so on. (Joyce himself expresses such sentiments from time to time in his correspondence, complaining of the adverse effect a "bad climate" has on him and his work [*LettersI* 116]). In a book whose characters are topographies (a masculine mountain and a feminine river, for example), the properties of a geographical region and the qualities of a person are so effectively indistinguishable as to efface the neat causality of such ideas as Bloom's about the Cinghalese made lethargic and lazy by the "[s]leeping sickness in the air" (*U* 5.36) and the Mediterranean's heating of its people's blood and passion. Here is one of the countless versions of the creation of the world given in the *Wake*:

> Before he fell hill he filled heaven: a stream, alplapping streamlet, coyly coiled um, cool of her curls: We were but thermites then, wee, wee. Our antheap we sensed as a Hill of Allen, the Barrow for an People, one Jotnursfjaell: and it was a grummelung amung the porktroop that wonderstruck us a thunder, yunder. (57.10–15)

Some exegetical notes are due here, scattered as they must be. God created heaven before He fell ill, or before Jack fell down the hill, and some time just before Satan had his fall, God opened an empty hell to catch him. Eve was made of Adam and was herself a kind of improvement of paradise. The emergence of mountains shapes the paths of rivers, which can then be said to be lapping the Alps. The German word *um* is "of," in the sense that here is being spoken what things are made "of," and is incidentally the prefix for *Umwelt*, "environment." Termites, "wee" as they are, build tall mounds, just as ants build antheaps and humans misguided towers, meant to unify. To speak of when we were "but . . . wee" is a remembrance of childhood, and termites predate human beings on the earth by many millions of years. In physics, a therm is a specific measure of heat or energy; in antiquity, it is a public bath or hot spring. To thermalize is to bring something into or to attain equilibrium with the surrounding environment, and the formation of the earth's landscapes was a gradual cooling process. And then of course there is thunder, never long unheard in the *Wake*, the sound of a god, in Vico's thinking the inspiration for human speech, wondrous grumbling, which changed isolated hermits (also in "thermites") into communities. Those communities in turn tell the story of how the world and they were formed.

The creator is his creation; character is not only place but the formation of place. Joyce does not fetishize "nature" as an object but instead conceives of it, like his own writing, as a process. This significantly disrupts the conditions for pathetic fallacy. When, say, the name of Count Dracula is uttered, or the detective announces to the gathered suspects that the murderer is among them, the lightning flashes, the thunder crashes—these atmospheric phenomena are symbols, which is to say that they possess an equivalence with something other than themselves. With its functional, changeable language of rain, wind, and thunder, the *Wake* presents the reader with the unsettling possibility that, in addition to the dissolution of such reliable traits and bellwethers as plot, character, and setting, the concept of "symbols" may have little value for the study of this book, that there is no symbolization as such in *Finnegans Wake*.[6] The climate may be connected with or comparable to many different and disparate things, but there is no definite equivalence. The "everintermutuomergent" principle of *Finnegans Wake* (55.11–12), according to which all twains are always meeting (or always about to meet), depends on *a priori* difference, just as there can be no reconciliation if there has not been a sundering: "the coincidance of their contraries reamalgamerge in that indentity of indiscernibles" (49.36–50.01).

Why does McHugh say that "the whole of I.3 is embraced by the Irish climate" rather than that the Irish climate is embraced by the text? Both are quite abstract assertions, but one does not seem more probable than the other. "I have called the weather 'uncaring,'" writes McHugh, "but at some levels it is obviously personified."[7] That "obviously" is undone by the phrase preceding it, which is another way of saying that at some levels McHugh is obviously incorrect, for the problem with personification is that it puts the man-made cart before the natural horse. For some reason, we do not speak of Earwicker the publican as an instance of "mountainfication." It is understood that the "natural world" is a projection screen. But as I have said, the *Wake* does not operate under this assumption. Much of I.3 is concerned with how to identify the multiform "he" who emerges from its opening miasma, and the problem is that, to borrow the terms of Marshall McLuhan, the figure cannot be made out from the ground, nor portrait from landscape:

> It is nebuless an autodidact fact of the commonest that the shape of the average human cloudyphiz, whereas sallow has long daze faded, frequently altered its ego with the possing of the showers (Not original!). Whence it is a slopperish matter, given the wet and low visibility (since in this scherzarade of one's thousand one nightinesses that sword of certainty which would identifide the body never falls) to indendifine the individuone (50.35–51.06)

What does "he" look like? Like the "commonest" and "average" man: "Come on, ordinary man with that large big nonobli head, and that blanko berbecked fischial ekksprezzion" (64.30–31). To make matters worse, his appearance changes with the weather. Not only can he not be absolutely identified for the "wet and low visibility" of a downpour (the Irish regularity of such occasions is why he carries "the state slate umbrella" [52.26–27]), he also assumes new identities, alter egos, with each precipitation, and there may be no "original" or bonafide (in "identifide") identity for him anywhere.

Our indeterminable hero is also the cause of the weather that causes him. The dainty fog or "little cloud" of "nebuless" presages the vision of "Nuvoletta in her nightdress" in I.6 (157.08–159.18) and the "little cloud, a nibulissa" alternately weeping and laughing in II.1 (256.33). At the end of I.3, she mourns him and dissolves into rain, but she also looks forward to the day when he returns, gathering "nubilettes to cumule" (73.35) and flashing his "lightning lancer" (73.36). The cloud will become the river, and the daughter will become her mother when her father awakes after the one thousand and one nights. This parent-child confusion, part of the understanding of nature as a process of transition and recurrence, is why the questions "what formal cause made a smile of *that* tothink? Who was he to whom? . . . Whose are the placewheres?" (56.31–33, my italics) remain unanswerable. The phrase "windy Nous blowing . . . through the hat" (56.29–30) blends *nous* (thought) with *pneu* (air) to make a perverse sort of reference to the inspiration celebrated by Shelley: "the mind in creation is as a fading coal, which some invisible influence, like an inconstant wind, awakens to transitory brightness."[8] Joyce unites the consciousness of character and/or narrative with the wind, so that mood and setting and character all "reamalgamerge" to form what might well be called "atmosphere." This effect is significantly more complex than personification.[9]

Written while "Work in Progress" was just a few years away from becoming *Finnegans Wake*, William Empson's *Seven Types of Ambiguity* wrestles with the problem of "atmospheres." "Interest in 'atmospheres' is a critical attitude designed for, and particularly suited to, the poets of the nineteenth century," Empson observes.[10] But he also conjectures that "the belief in Atmosphere"—notably capitalized—may be a product of "the belief in Pure Sound":

> Critics often say or imply casually that some poetic effect conveys a direct "physical" quality, something mysteriously intimate, something which it is strange that a poet could convey, something like a sensation that is not attached to any of the senses. . . . It can be either felt or thought; the two are similar but different; and it requires practice to do both at once. Or the statement might, one cannot deny, mean that there has been some confusion of the senses. But it may mean something more important, involving a distinction between "sensation" and "feeling"; that what the poet has conveyed is no assembly of grammatical meanings, capable of analysis, but a "mood," an "atmosphere," a "personality," an attitude to life, an undifferentiated mode of being.[11]

The apparent strangeness of Empson's declining even to mention Joyce in *Seven Types*, though he does discuss Proust and T. S. Eliot (we can hear the influence of Eliot in the word *personality* and what follows it), might be explained by the apprehension shown about this potential "confusion of the senses." Empson's last sentence quoted above could be applied to the *Wake*, which certainly "is no assembly of grammatical meanings" as such, may or may not be "capable of analysis" (Empson surely means "capable of being analyzed," but the ambiguity is entertaining), and does seem to enjoy "an undifferentiated mode of being." Discomfited by the notion that the sounds of words are themselves the meaning of poetry—which discomfort allows the critic to ignore Joyce and the entire body of avant-garde poetry produced in the twenty years prior to his book—Empson is resigned to the position that "atmosphere is conveyed in some unknown and fundamental way as a by-product of meaning" and "is the consciousness of what is implied by the meaning."[12]

Finnegans Wake revels in this "confusion of the senses," which Empson sees as an effect of atmosphere (or Atmosphere), which is itself linked to the conception of a language that can mean what it says, if not say what it means. Examples of synaesthesia in I.3 are not hard to find: there is "the touching seene" (52.36), conflating touch and sight, or "some seem on some dimb Arras, dumb as Mum's mutyness . . . odable to os across the wineless Ere" (53.02–04), a parody of Joyce's own earlier prose that muddles together at least three and perhaps four of the senses (sight, hearing, smell, and taste). The deprivation of the senses, and the alleged augmentation of compensations of others, is a paradoxically apocalyptic theme: "The mouth that tells not will ever attract the unthinking tongue and so long as the obseen draws theirs which hear not so long till allearth's dumbnation shall the blind lead the deaf" (68.32–34). In the *Wake*, the primary revelation is also the ultimate revelation: that we cannot comprehend what is revealed.

Take this confusing cataclysm, for example:

> he dreamed that he'd wealthes in mormon halls when wokenp by a fourth loud snore out of his land of byelo while hickstrey's maws was grazing in the moonlight by hearing hammering on the pandywhank scale emanating from the blind pig and anything like it (oonagh! oonagh!) in the whole history of the Mullingcan Inn he never. This battering babel allower the door and sideposts, he always said, was not in the very remotest like the belzey babble of a bottle of boose which would not rouse him out o' slumber deep but reminded him loads more of the martiallawsey marses of foreign musikants' instrumongs or the overthrewer to the third last days of Pompery, if anything. And that after

> this most nooningless knockturn the young reine came down . . . ruinating all the bouchers' schurtes and the backers' wischandtugs so that be the chandeleure of the Rejaneyjailey they were all night wasching the walters of, the weltering walters off. Whyte. (64.04–21)

The dreamer wakes to a "hammering" and "battering" reminiscent of a volcanic explosion (the last days of Pompeii), followed by a drenching rain, or perhaps the queenly wife of the man who "dreamt that he dwelt in marble halls" angrily comes downstairs and lets fly with all her devastating wrath. On the one hand, this all seems the stuff of fable, tall tale, and nursery rhyme, with the proverbial blind pig, references to the Tower of Babel and the fantasia of a nocturne, and even, for good measure, the butcher, the baker, and the candlestick maker. Yet there is a real account of a store's caretaker, the very Maurice Behan named in the text (63.35), startled from his bed one night by the sound of three men trying to break into the store or, in their version of events given at their trial, "only trying to open a bottle of stout by hammering it against the gate."[13] The end of this passage anticipates the last lines of I.8 (216.04–05), which recurrence might signal an operatic sort of leitmotif, though the ruinously bleaching "Whyte" becomes "Night!" leaving readers unable to establish a definite, revelatory last word or note to this repeated but varied apocalyptic scenario and rhythm. This passage's comparison of this tempest to "foreign musikants' instrumongs," prompting the reader to consider that what seems like incomprehensible babble might be music produced by an uncommon means, can be juxtaposed with a 1928 letter that Joyce wrote to Harriet Shaw Weaver:

> We had some dreadful wind storms here [in Paris], one when we were out in the clinic which threw my wife back a little, accompanied by some unseemly remarks by the Reverend Mr Thor. . . . The groaning of the lift mingling with the howling of the blast and shrieking of the trees and the cannonading of the hailstorms making anti-music with the frenzied shouts of the French staff, causing the rubber carpeting sound proofed edifice to form a pandemoniacal box for the wren-like twittering of my nerves. (*LettersI* 277–78)

Joyce's "anti-music," an arresting concatenation of independent noises (emulated by the string of gerunds, a frequent device in the *Wake*), is an ambient effect. Whereas music proper is produced by musicians, "anti-music"—here heard in, of all places, an elevator—is produced by the environment. Perhaps Empson's worried characterization of a belief in "Pure Sound" is a little off the mark here, for it might be more apt to call the *Wake*'s ambient soundscape of noise, which is reminiscent of but not synonymous with music, "Impure Sound," in keeping with the text's mongrel hybridizations of languages and cultures, figure and ground.

Useful insights are to be discovered in more recent "ecocritical" debates. Timothy Morton argues for the production and appreciation of an "ambient poetics" which

> interferes with attempts to set up a unified, transcendent nature that could become a symptomatic fantasy thing. Critical close reading elicits the inconsistent properties of this ambient poetics. Ambience compromises ecomimesis because the very processes that try to convey the illusion of immediacy and naturalness keep dispelling it from within.[14]

I have already pointed out that *Finnegans Wake* resists conceiving of or representing nature as an object, and in I.3 the fog, wind, rain, and thunder are subjects in the fullest possible sense—articulate, doubtful, and self-doubting subjects—but subjects always in progress (the weather is never certain at any given moment). Since honest readers of the *Wake* can attest that the more they read of the book, the less rather than more certain they become about how to read it, such "inconsistent properties" that simultaneously frustrate and enliven close readings might persuade us to think of the *Wake*'s ambient poetics. "Ambient poetics," Morton writes, "is about making the imperceptible perceptible, while retaining the form of its imperceptibility—to make the invisible visible, the inaudible audible."[15] This formulation accepts the *Wake*'s synaesthesia as a means for developing a sensorial matrix (in the most primal connotation, an *aesthetic*) with which to perceive the elements of the world otherwise unknown to us, though all around us.

Again, take the world's atmosphere. What is it that we are breathing?

> We might leave that nitrience of oxagiants to take its free of the air and just analectralyse that very chymerical combination, the gasbag where the warderworks. And try to pour somour heiterscene up thealmostfere. (67.07–10)

Here the invisible elements are literally elements: the nitrogen, oxygen, and hydrogen of which air is made (helium appears in the next sentence). Moreover, the thunderstorm, the ur-signifier, is itself being submitted to analysis, so as to better understand how wind ("gasbag" recalls the "Aeolus" episode of *Ulysses*), rain ("warderworks" as waterworks), and lightning (the electrical in "analectralyse") combine to make the ineffable, "Him Which Thundereth

From On High" (62.14). Between the sublime and the banality of chemistry lies "thealmostfere" (almost fear, or fear of the almost).

The natural and the supernatural are not distinct categories in the *Wake*'s ambient poetics because both nitrogen atoms and Zeus elude the deadened or habituated senses (those possessed by that "ordinary man" [64.30] or "the common or ere-in-garden castaway" [62.19]). This is not entirely surprising, for where else would one expect to find the ethereal but in the ether? Marina Warner notes: "Air, clouds, vapour, smoke, foam, froth, steam, and their spiritous, sublimed counterparts among airy and even gaseous substances (as Joyce noticed) have served to make manifest the invisible, supernatural, imponderable, and ineffable according to the promptings of belief and fantasy."[16] The legend of the "humphriad" (53.09) variously recounted and recanted in I.3 depends upon a nebulous conjoining of the air of plausible history and the mist of myth—a constant production, in other words, of an "aerily perennious" atmosphere (57.22).

A number of abrupt transitions between paragraphs in this chapter smack of an ostentatiously procedural performance, such as that of an investigation, a legal case (either a contract or a hearing), or a lecture: "But resuming inquiries" (66.10); "To proceed" (67.07); "Now to the obverse" (67.28). Such rhetoric so smacks of officialdom that it seems to constitute what would typically be called an atmosphere, such as that of a boardroom or courtroom. Accordingly, there is "Sylvia Silence, the girl detective" (61.01) leaning back "in her really truly easy chair" (61.05), puzzling over the clues in the obscure mystery, and concluding with Holmesian deductions such as "by the siege of his trousers there was someone else behind it" (61.25–26). But such overtones are overruled, the classic atmosphere of detective fiction permitted to be sensed only to be contradicted—for example, when Sylvia breaks her silence (just as the "cloudletlitter silent" [73.29] will later burst) to speak with the voice of Elmer Fudd. The reader is told that "Your machelar's mutton leg's getting musclebound from being too pulled" (64.32–33), and sylvan mystery is supplanted by floral factuality:

> There are 29 sweet reasons why blossomtime's the best. Elders fall for green almonds when they're raised on bruised stone root ginger though it winters on their heads as if auctumned round their waistbands. (64.35–65.02)

Gardening tips, fashion notes, or courtship advice? The heady fragrance of the romance novelette is also scented in I.3: tales of "rushy hollow heroines in their skirtsleeves" (67.31) either ruining their reputations or doing away with themselves. Genres and their respective atmospheres clash and commingle, allowing the reader to perceive how those genres function, just as spectroscopic study of gaseous interactions divulge the constituent properties of the respective elements.

Recall the inevitable precariousness of a unified (essentially noncontradictory) atmosphere and how easily the (actually aberrant) consistency of that atmosphere can be sabotaged by the introduction of an uncalled-for element or the wrong proportion of necessary elements. This observation makes for an entertaining thought experiment: calculate with what minimal change to a recognizably "atmospheric" work one can wreak the maximum damage to that atmosphere (and thus to the affect) of a work. The languorous ache of a scene in a soap opera could be devastated with one strategic dialogue change or even a slight change in tempo. Now try to imagine sabotaging the "atmosphere" of *Finnegans Wake*—and despair. The utter inconsistency of tone, idiom, mood, temporality, and so on give the text an impressive integrity. Yet this integrity is not a form of purity, not the effect of a profound circumscription, a containment that readers cannot spoil because they cannot penetrate. On the contrary, the impurity of the *Wake* contaminates and is in turn willingly permeated by the corrupting "atmosphere" in which the reader reads. The reader cannot but bring his or her idioms, moods, and setting into play trying to read a text whose often alien-seeming but tantalizingly familiar language invites and passively accepts the reader's impressions and projections. If "atmosphere" is imagined to be a pure and undiluted phenomenon, the way that Mikel Dufrenne does in contending that "the unity of an atmosphere is thus the unity of a *Weltanschauung*; its coherence is the coherence of a characteristic or quality,"[17] then it might be said that the slasher film *Saw IV* has an atmosphere but *Finnegans Wake* does not; but if "atmosphere" is acknowledged to be composite and changeable, then the *Wake* is a dynamic ecosystem and *Saw IV* is a bottled, inert sample on some laboratory shelf.

Responding to the work of Gernot Böhme,[18] Morton points out that atmosphere is "inevitably not only spatial but also temporal":

> A shower of rain is atmospherically different if you stand in it for two hours, as opposed to five minutes. The "same" atmosphere is never the "same" as itself.
>
> This is a matter not of ontological nicety, but of political urgency. The notion of atmosphere needs to expand to include temporality. *Climate* (as in climate change) is a vector field that describes the momentum of the atmosphere—the rate at which the atmosphere keeps changing. A map of

atmospheric momentum would exist in a phase space with many dimensions. The neglect of temporality in thinking about the weather is why it is practically impossible to explain to people that global warming might result in pockets of cool weather.[19]

This neglect also happens to be why "maps" and "outlines" of *Finnegans Wake* founder: they are the equivalent of the chain of curly lines meant to represent clouds, which serve well enough for the most rudimentary sort of abstraction but offer little insight into the composition and none into the motion and effects of gaseous phenomena. Such schemes make stable and timeless what is—conceptually, at any rate—continuously in flux, and I wonder how much more satisfyingly the cartographic problem of the *Wake* might be dealt with using animated maps, something akin to the satellite imaging seen in televised and online weather reports, that allow a representation of, say, the transformation of a Kevin into a Shaun and then into an Ondt, or one version of a phrase into another over the course of the book—the very "everintermutuomergent" principle I underscored earlier in this essay. As Morton instructively writes, "atmosphere is subject to the same paradox as identity—it does for the weather what identity does for idea of self."[20]

In a condemnation of Heidegger (made all the more caustic by the omission of Heidegger's name), Adorno declares, "Wherever philosophy imagines that by borrowing from literature it can abolish objectified thought and its history—what is commonly termed the antithesis of subject and object—and even hopes that Being itself will speak, in a poésie concocted out of Parmenides and Jungnickel, it starts to turn into a washed-out cultural babble."[21] If we leave aside the proscription regarding philosophy and recognize the scornful final phrase ("ausgelaugten Kulturgeschwätz") as a plausibly fair assessment of *Finnegans Wake*, we can tunnel backwards through Adorno's statement and acknowledge that Joyce's book is an effort both to coax "Being itself" to "speak" and to elide "the antithesis of subject and object." This we have seen in the foregoing, localized meteorological survey of the *Wake*'s ambient poetics (which could readily be extended beyond the environs of I.3). Thus the *Wake* might be philosophy turning into literature, or in Adorno's stricter terms, philosophy imagining itself as literature—and given how the *Wake*'s mutations are always reversible, also literature imagining itself as philosophy. Against Adorno on this score is Arthur C. Danto: "When art internalizes its own history, when it becomes self-conscious of its history as it has come to be in our time, so that its consciousness of its history forms a part of its nature, it is perhaps unavoidable that it should turn into philosophy at last."[22] Given the interesting (and unusual) juxtaposition of the terms *history* and *nature* here, I think we might draw upon this suggestion to shape a new definition of atmosphere: the degree or tendency to which (or even, in the most interesting cases, the fluctuations with which) a literary text's or work of art's consciousness of its history threatens to make it "philosophy at last."

Words, Joyce reminds us in *Finnegans Wake*, are air, the seemingly insubstantial stuff without which there would be no sound, no philosophy, no life. "Words weigh no more to him than raindrips to Rethfernhim," the text boasts, adding: "Which we all like. Rain" (74.16–18). The book is raining words: we see, hear, and feel them falling. Besides being a ritual for the dead, a *wake* is a disturbance of water, a phenomenon of air turbulence, even an open hole in ice. "Finnegan's wake" is his movement through the elements, his figuration of and within the environment. Reading *Finnegans Wake*, in which we move through the obscurity and precipitation, shaping the ambient "anti-music" as much as we hear it, makes for unique disruptions of atmosphere, wakes of our own.

Notes

1. M. H. Abrams and Geoffrey Galt Harpham, *A Glossary of Literary Terms*, 9th ed. (Boston: Wadsworth Cengage Learning, 2009), 17–18.

2. Umberto Eco, *The Open Work*, trans. Anna Cancogni (Cambridge: Harvard University Press, 1989).

3. Roland McHugh, "Recipis for the Price of the Coffin," in *A Conceptual Guide to "Finnegans Wake*,*"* ed. Michael H. Begnal and Fritz Senn (University Park: Pennsylvania State University Press, 1974), 30.

4. See Tim Conley, "'Whole Only Holes Tied Together': Joyce and the Paradox of Summary," *James Joyce Quarterly* 47 (Winter 2010): 231–45.

5. Finn Fordham, *Lots of Fun at "Finnegans Wake": Unravelling Universals* (Oxford: Oxford University Press, 2007).

6. Whether or not he was the first to have his idea, Clive Hart's expression of it is probably the most forceful and succinct: "Our lives are full of fucking symbols: we don't need them in our reading matter as well." See Roland McHugh, *The "Finnegans Wake" Experience* (Berkeley: University of California Press, 1981), 46.

7. McHugh, "Recipis," 30.

8. Percy Bysshe Shelley, "A Defence of Poetry," in *The Selected Poetry and Prose of Percy Bysshe Shelley*, ed. Carlos Baker (New York: Modern Library, 1951), 517.

9. HCE is also undone by the atmosphere or (at least in one incarnation, like

Muhammad lifted into heaven) vanishes into it: he "disappeared . . . from the sourface of this earth, that austral plain he had transmaried himself to, so entirely spoorlessly (the mother of the book with a dustwhisk tabularasing his obliteration done upon her involucrum) as to tickle the speculative to all but opine . . . that the hobo . . . had transtuled his funster's latitat to its finsterest interrimost" (50.08–17).

10. William Empson, *Seven Types of Ambiguity* (New York: New Directions, 1966), 20.

11. Ibid., 16–17.

12. Ibid., 17, 18.

13. Bill Cadbury, "'The March of a Maker': Chapters I.2–4," in *How Joyce Wrote "Finnegans Wake": A Chapter-by-Chapter Genetic Guide*, ed. Luca Crispi and Sam Slote (Madison: University of Wisconsin Press, 2007), 92n14.

14. Timothy Morton, *Ecology without Nature: Rethinking Environmental Aesthetics* (Cambridge: Harvard University Press, 2007), 77.

15. Ibid., 96.

16. Marina Warner, *Phantasmagoria: Spirit Visions, Metaphors, and Media into the Twenty-First Century* (Oxford: Oxford University Press, 2006), 79–80.

17. Mikel Dufrenne, *The Phenomenology of Aesthetic Experience*, trans. Edward S. Casey et al. (Evanston: Northwestern University Press, 1973), 177.

18. Gernot Böhme, *Atmosphäre: Essays zur neuen Ästhetik* (Frankfurt am Main: Suhrkamp, 1995).

19. Morton, *Ecology without Nature*, 166.

20. Ibid.

21. Theodor W. Adorno, *Notes to Literature*, vol. 1, trans. Shierry Weber Nicholsen (New York: Columbia University Press, 1991), 6.

22. Arthur C. Danto, *The Philosophical Disenfranchisement of Art* (New York: Columbia University Press, 1986), 16.

4

Habeas Corpus Epiphany in I.4

MIA L. MCIVER

Here comes every one, every single, last body in *Finnegans Wake*. They are notoriously difficult to keep track of. Tim Finnegan's body is dead until it revives. Finn MacCool's sleeping body lies beneath Ireland, generating the island's topography and keeping us in suspense about whether and when he will grumble awake. Humpty Dumpty's eggshell body has shattered and can't be put back together again. And HCE, the paterfamilias who unites all of the above and more, has committed obscure crimes against the bodies of others, even as his own body has been repeatedly injured.

Habeas corpus names one way to approach the intractable bodies of *Finnegans Wake*. Latin for "that you may have the body" or, more colloquially and imperatively, "produce the body," habeas corpus collects the dislocations strewn across the novel. In legal terms, a writ of habeas corpus requires that the body of a prisoner be brought into the physical presence of the court in order that a magistrate may decide whether there is sufficient justification for continued incarceration. The writ is a remedy for indefinite detention without trial, a procedural device that is supposed to ensure that the wheels of justice turn apace. As David Spurr observes elsewhere in this volume, *Finnegans Wake*'s central problem is the relationship between word and flesh. Habeas corpus mediates the language of the law and the fleshly bodies that are its objects. Using habeas corpus as an entry into thinking about *Finnegans Wake* brings out the politico-legal dimensions of that mediation.

Finnegans Wake discloses affinities between habeas corpus and the old Joycean chestnut of epiphany. Both are reliquaries for a fleshly excess left over from our forms of political representation. As John Bishop reminds us, "All things in the *Wake* start here, 'in the flesh.'"[1] The *Wake* thematizes and dramatizes an uncanny remainder of political theology that formerly justified sovereign power. This excessive residue manifests in some unlikely textual sites: pig imagery that shudders with meatiness; Charles Stewart Parnell's reputation for duplicity; doorways and thresholds that lead through the Roman god Janus to the Feast of the Epiphany on January 6. The polymorphic bodies in *Finnegans Wake* that exist in a dream state somewhere between life and death leave habeas corpus on shaky ground, and this shakiness itself, which also characterizes a Wakean epiphany, punctures tightly held fantasies about justice and interpretation.

As a trope, habeas corpus encompasses more than just legal procedure. In *Finnegans Wake*, it refers us to the circulations of incarnation, resurrection, and transubstantiation, the creation and dissolution of the body politic, and the embodiment of language through sound and through the materiality of permuted letters and words. Reading the *Wake* aloud, for example, reveals sonorous dimensions of rhythm and sense that can only be understood somatically. And yet the evanescence of sound that vanishes into thin air means that such embodiment is momentary and fleeting. Similarly, the figure of habeas corpus sends tremors through the epistemological ground it is supposed to stabilize.

So it is for the shifting, turning, ephemeral figures of the *Wake*: ALP flowing, Issy dancing, Shem fleeing, Shaun wandering. Having the body equates to the body's escaping. This problem of simultaneous appearance and disappearance, arrest and evasion, lies at the heart of chapter I.4. The section presents a case of royal remains, dramatizing the decomposition of a sovereign body after a "real murder, of the rayheallach royghal raxacraxian variety," the really royal murder of O'Reilly/HCE (99.27–28).[2]

Eric Santner theorizes the royal remains as the manifestation of a decomposed sovereignty that lurks behind in modernity.[3] Santner proposes that, although we have passed from monarchical to popular sovereignty, modernity remains haunted by the afterlife of the quandaries of royal representation. In the premodern era, medieval jurists developed a political theology to deal with the question of sovereignty, tying sovereign representation to Christ's two-in-one persona as fully human and fully divine. The king represented two bodies as well, one his own mortal body, the other the abstract body politic.[4]

Once parliamentary democracy had deposed monarchy, the body politic assumed in a distributed form the rights and obligations of governance that the sovereign had formerly monopolized. Santner wonders what happens to the legacy of the sovereign's physical body, which had provided such a singularly compact package for the representation of multiple subjects, a burden of representation that must now be shared. His answer is that, in being dismembered and spread across citizens, the royal body, like HCE's body which "still persisted" (76.20) after having been long buried, persists as an undead remainder, an excess that makes us shiver psychologically and politically. Santner calls this remainder the flesh: neither purely corporeal nor purely imaginary, the flesh is an element that disturbs, animates, and unsettles modern bodies, modern psyches, and the modern body politic. The flesh manifests as a "surplus of immanence" wherever humans feel unfit in the world, the sovereign's divine transcendence having been internalized within individual and collective bodies, which now carry more than they are equipped to carry.[5] Fleshly anxieties emerge when the excess of the sovereign remainder deforms the natural or organic suitedness that might otherwise allow us to move at ease through *unheimlich* settings.

During the mock trial in the middle of chapter I.4, we hear a demand for habeas corpus that illustrates the law's fleshliness. The "macdublins" in the courtroom cry out for the body of an alleged assassin: "Prodooce O'Donner. Ay! Exhibit his relics!" (87.31–32). Figuring the accused as a saint whose remains can be displayed for veneration, the clamor rises on the theological currents that still waft through the secular courtroom. The gallery calls enthusiastically for the martyrdom that it considers a foregone conclusion. The lusty shout for exposure has decidedly profane undertones to it, since "rub of the relic" is an Irish slang term for sex. At once sacred and salacious, habeas corpus here fetishizes a fraction of a corpse to compensate for the assassin's live body, whose movements the court inquiry cannot ultimately determine. The only body that can be produced is a shriveled and shrunken remainder, mere flesh.

Structured in three parts like a "tripiezite suet," a three-piece suit made out of tripe and fat (86.02), and framed by brief introductory and concluding scenes, the chapter asks whether we can ever produce or have a body. As the chapter opens, HCE is dreaming and scheming. He prays anxiously like King William III after the Battle of the Boyne. He channels other sovereigns regal and holy: Attila, Julius Caesar, the pope, and "Foughtarundser," Our Father who ought to be in heaven but is in fact fighting under water (78.16). The first main section concerns his burial at sea, or "burral of the seas" (85.02). There's just one problem: he's not quite dead. Emaciated soldiers spread rumors during a battle that a plump HCE has been roving about in the flesh.

At the end of chapter I.4, similar rumors swirl again, this time about an HCE who has taken on the attributes of Charles Stewart Parnell, leader of the Irish nationalist cause in the second half of the nineteenth century.

The chapter's intervening narrative recounts the backstory of how HCE arrived in his underwater casket. HCE is out for a walk when he is "mistakenly ambushed" (85.03) by an "attackler" (81.18). HCE pleads somewhat unconvincingly that he did nothing to provoke the altercation, but he is tried by proxy anyway through the character of Festy King, a poor, Irish-speaking fellow who shares the traits of HCE and his son Shem the Penman. The mock trial of Festy King makes up the second main section of chapter I.4.

In the chapter's third section, the aftermath of the trial, the judges gossip mildly among themselves and the public gossips wildly about Festy/HCE/Shem/Parnell's whereabouts. Hounded by shame as Parnell was after a divorce scandal forced him from power, HCE still has the last laugh: he is comfortably ensconced in his deep-sea coffin, "under leagues of it in deep Bartholoman's Deep" (100.03–04). The chapter closes with a lyrical transition to ALP singing by the "waters of babalong" (103.12).

The tissue of this narrative is woven from legal discourse, scripture, Roman myth, Irish folktale, memories of Parnell, and newspaper reporting. The chapter is "pigstickularly"—particularly, especially—rich with allusions to pigs and all things porcine (87.09). Festy King has "ellegedly" (the allegations, if proven, could be his elegy) disguised himself and carried "a pedigree pig (unlicensed)" to a fair for the "Irish muck" (86.14, .21, *muc*: pig in Irish), where the beast "ate some of the doorweg" (86.26), the wooden doorway of its sty. The pig's gender is tricky: it is both a "gentleman" and a "sister," a gender instability triggered by a chain of translation linking the Urdu *suar* for pig to the phonetically similar French *soeur*, to the English translation "sister" (86.27). "*Qui Sta Troia*," the narrator interjects at the fair, blaming the pig for its perverse voracity: the phrase combines "Some Sow!" "What a Slut!" and "Here Stands Troy" (86.29).[6] The justification for the gender shift and resulting denunciation lies in the cultural disposition to identify women with, in the words of Simone de Beauvoir, "flesh, life, immanence": the pig is the paramount symbol of fleshliness.[7] Similar markers of repulsively feminine flesh appear in the thunder word for the chapter, which strings together translations of the word *whore* from many languages. That the pig eats its own threshold makes sense given that it is "a creature of the threshold," sacred and profane, desired as a sign of bounty and reviled as ceaselessly appetitive.[8] Pigs do the double work of representing the human capacity for pleasure and reminding us of how close the pursuit of pleasure brings us into the animal world. If, according to de Beauvoir, to be embodied is to be a woman, the *Wake*'s gender-bending pig helps show that the flesh is gendered female as well.

Pigs are an essential link to the story of Parnell's ignominious contact with a female body. Joyce turns Richard Pigott's forgeries, used to implicate Parnell in the Phoenix Park murders of 1882, into "pigottry" (99.19). Parnell escaped blame in that case when the forgeries were discovered because Pigott misspelled *hesitancy* as "hesitency" (82.30), but when he was convicted of adultery in the O'Shea divorce trial in 1890, he was "sacrificed by Irishmen on the altar of English liberalism."[9] In I.4, the prosecution of Festy King, a.k.a. Pegger Festy, "the senior king of all" (90.36–91.01), is compared to the sacrificial bleeding of a stuck pig, or "stuccko-muck" (91.01–02). Pegger Festy recovers sufficiently to mount a self-defense, however, and is likened to a boy, eaten by a pig, whom St. Patrick revives. Just as St. Patrick collects the boy's bones, and just as Isis searches for parts of Osiris's body to reconstitute them, the sovereign body dismembered by the law must be made whole.

A dialectic of having and not having a body, producing and dissolving a corpus, describes the materiality of the bodies in the *Wake*. During his long rest in his tomb, HCE survives immured "by suckage feeding off his own misplaced fat" (79.12–13). By piggishly suckling on his own bodily reserves while he is interred, HCE self-cannibalizes. In Joyce's earlier novels, the nation of Ireland is figured as a cannibal, an "old sow that eats her farrow" (*P* 203, *U* 15.4582–83). In the *Wake*, this theme is shattered and scattered but still discernible. HCE is corpulent (or "Carpulenta" [99.09]) and porculent, because he has been eating "cracklings," fried pig skin (99.04). Pigs, flesh, and the surplus identities are constellated together when HCE and his attacker "pause for refleshmeant" and "a different and younger him of the same ham" strikes up a conversation (82.10–11). Pigs are so prevalent here because they are implicated in the bizarre dimension of HCE's flesh, which grows as he consumes it. He has his body and eats it, too.

The pigs of I.4 themselves undergo a curious transformation not unlike HCE's. In another essay in this collection, Christine Smedley documents the novel's profusions of famine imagery, in which gluttony and abstemiousness are laden with historical significance. Pigs and potatoes are equated in their famine failure by a ferryman in Connemara interviewed by John Millington Synge in the summer of 1905. The ferryman describes his home on Dinish Island as "this bit of rock that a dog wouldn't look at, where the pigs die and the spuds die."[10] The pig Festy carries to the fair is at first a "gentleman ratepayer" (86.27), a fat beast who generates income and wealth. Later in I.4, instead of paying the rent, the pig is "just a gent who prayed his lent" (89.15). In this punning the pig changes from an animal signifying excess to one who solemnly sacrifices, as Catholics traditionally abstain from eating meat during the Lenten fast. The famine ended such voluntary abstention, since if there was no food for people, there was certainly no food for pigs. The body of the pig has changed from a plump one that consumes voraciously to one that is austere and withdrawn. Not only has the "pedigree pig" changed into a "pederast prig" (89.15) but it has also wasted away.

Festy King sells the animal at the fair with difficulty, but it must be done "in order to pay off . . . six doubloons fifteen arrears of his . . . rent" (86.29–31). That he is behind on his rent suggests that he is under a certain amount of stress as a tenant, and therefore his situation is one that land reform in Ireland was intended to remedy. Thirty years after the Great Famine of 1945–52, potato crops failed again, and landlords again refused to reduce rents or otherwise assuage the suffering of hundreds of thousands of their tenant farmers. Against the backdrop of the ensuing Land War occurred the Maamtrasna murders of 1882, in which Myles Joyce and others were wrongfully convicted of killing members of their extended family in County Galway. Festy King is a "child of Maam" (85.22–23) and speaks in "Brythonic" (91.03), a Celtic tongue, with an accent so thick that he, like Myles Joyce, needs an interpreter on the stand. A popular theory of the Maamtrasna murders was that the victims were police informants against tenants who were active in the Land War.[11] In response to the Land League's efforts to reduce rents for tenant farmers and enable them to own the land they worked, the British Parliament began to pass the Coercion Acts, which authorized the use of state power to suppress popular movements. In particular, the first of these, the Protection of Person and Property Act of 1881 (also known as the Peace Preservation Act) suspended habeas corpus, which led to Parnell's arrest and imprisonment in Kilmainham jail, where he remained for more than six months without coming to trial. However, the action designed to isolate Parnell's body from his supporters failed. He was vaulted to heroic status,[12] as the act "caused outrage and substantially fueled the Parnellite cause."[13] The law's refusal to produce the body for trial produced a body that laid a more persuasive claim to representative legitimacy than that made by the law itself.

Parnell haunts the *Wake* as the uncrowned king of Ireland, the epithet given to him by Timothy Michael Healy before they fell out over Parnell's relationship with the married Katharine O'Shea. After the rift, Parnell referred to Healy contemptuously as a chimney sweep in a letter read at the O'Shea divorce trial. Festy King plays the roles of both Parnell and Healy, of the redeemer robbed of his crown on the one hand and of the betrayer-robber on the other. One of his aliases is "Meleky," a bastardization of Malachi, high king of Ireland, and he is caught "impersonating a climbing boy" (86.08), or chimney sweep. As an uncrowned king, Festy is a monarch who, like King Mark in the Tristan and Isolde story, has missed his mark; like Parnell, he has been deprived of the ability to legitimately represent the people. His law is the law of his aliases, an "*elois*" that keeps displacing his personhood onto other identities like "Crowbar" and permuting his names into "Rabworc" and "Tykingfest" (86.07–13). Late in chapter I.4, HCE is known by the name Reynard (97.28), a translation of "Mr. Fox," Parnell's alias that eerily prefigured the way the uncrowned king was chased into the grave.

Festy King wears a Parnellian "fight shirt" (85.34), which recalls the night shirt, or "natshirt," associated with Parnell's "fairescapading" (388.03)—escaping in an escapade down the O'Sheas' rope ladder fire escape. One of the images that most gripped the public imagination during the divorce trial of Captain William Henry and Katharine O'Shea came out in the testimony of Mrs. Caroline Pethers, the O'Sheas' cook and caretaker. She told of the lovers repeatedly being surprised trysting in an upstairs drawing room of the O'Shea home at 8 Medina Terrace, West Brighton, by Captain O'Shea's arrival. Parnell, Mrs. Pethers testifies, fled out the window to the balcony, slid down the fire escape, and a few minutes later knocked on the front door of the house as if he had just arrived.

In the courtroom, the presiding magistrate used this set piece in his summary of the evidence, implying to the jury that it provided significant evidence both of the adultery itself and of Captain O'Shea's lack of connivance in it. "He said that they were all placed in some difficulty by reason of the fact that they had only heard one side, neither the respondent [Katharine O'Shea] nor the co-respondent [Parnell] having thought fit to appear."[14] The law catches the defendants in a double bind in which the absence of their bodies from the witness box is as damning as a confession of their physical desire. This time, the lack of a body on which to act will serve the law's interest, not Parnell's. Having denied the law's desire for a body, his punishment will be even more severe. Ireland's sacrificial mania for its greatest champion was fulfilled, and the unruly bodies of the *Wake* continually thumb their nose (and worse) at the hypocritical public morality that ensnared Parnell.

His charade at the door demonstrates what an ambiguous location the threshold can be. Many references to doors and windows are knotted together in chapter I.4. Interwoven with allusions to "solstitial" winter holidays (82.10), this bundle points toward epiphany as a feast day in the month named for Janus, the god of doorways. In the chapter's opening paragraph, "we habben to upseek a bitty door" (75.11–12): we must search for a way into the story. It might not last long: Festy's pig, the troublesome, supplemental flesh whose unwanted weight he struggles with, is "portavorous" (89.16). Although there is no shared etymology between "portal" and "porcine" (which derive from the classical Latin *porta* and *porcus*, respectively), pigs and doors (and the carrying or portage that goes on through doors) merge in the exploitation of their phonetic similarities in words like "portrifaction," which HCE undergoes while lying in his "watery grave" (78.19–21). The single word "portrifaction" encapsulates the bodily dilemmas of habeas corpus. In its portmanteau, it carries putrification and decay; portliness and enfattening; and different factions at the door seeking to harm the unnaturally obese body. Janus, the Roman god of thresholds, boundaries, and new beginnings, is perceptible in these doorways. His two-facedness makes him kin to the doorkeepers of Irish myth, Camel and Gamal, who appear here as "Camellus" and "Gemellus," the "parfaitly" matched twins (90.18–19).

This imagery carries us across the threshold of the year from Christmas in December to Epiphany in January. Festy is accused of disguising himself by smearing black peat over his face, a self-doubling like that of the twin doorkeepers. His first words after he removes the muck from his face in court are "mhuith peisth mhuise as fearra bheura muirre hriosmas," or "with best wishes for a very merry Christmas," in what might be called pig Gaelic (91.04–05).[15] January used to be called "later Yule" in Old English, and references to "Yuletide" (82.36) or "Juletide" (97.03) cluster near the account of the trial. For example, HCE fattens up on "creamclotted sherriness of cinnamon syllabub" (97.16–17), a seasonal treat at Christmas. Festy King's trial begins "on the calends of Mars" (85.27), New Year's Day in ancient Rome. And, as Adaline Glasheen noted long ago, the name "Festy" puts us in the midst of *Twelfth Night* revels to celebrate a carnivalesque Epiphany (Shakespeare's play includes a character named Feste).[16] Many of these words are collocated once again in a comic scene in chapter III.3, when one speaker exclaims to the other, "How culious an epiphany!" occurred on "the twelfth day," and "*Yule Remember*," when "Toucher, a Methodist," drunkenly loses his pants and exposes his *cul* (ass). What at first seems to be a shocking revelation of Toucher's body turns out to be a repetition of "another good button gone wrong" (507.33–508.23). As we will see shortly, the difference between revelation and repetition is crucial to the type of epiphany proposed by *Finnegans Wake*.

In a theological flourish of habeas corpus, Epiphany produces Christ's body for the Gentiles. Paired with Christmas, it completes in a short time the same movement that later will bring God's covenant to an even greater fulfillment, when the crucifixion again puts Christ's body on display. The word *epiphany* derives from φαίνειν the Greek for "shine," "show," or "bring to light."[17] What is the status of epiphany, then, in a book of the dark? Has Joyce left behind his juvenilia, the early notebooks containing fragments of recorded life he called "epiphanies"? Or is *Finnegans Wake* a "panepiphanal world," replete with revelations (611.13)?

In Joyce's unpublished early work *Stephen Hero*, epiphany is famously defined as "a sudden spiritual manifestation, whether in the vulgarity of speech or of gesture or in a memorable phase of the mind itself" (*SH* 211). Epiphanies are explicitly the experiences of a moment; in fact, they "are the most delicate and evanescent of moments" (*SH* 211). Stephen originally insists on this temporality. Even though the moment may contain a densely compressed history, even though it may provide access to an elongated and intensified present, even if it looks forward eschatologically to "the night of the Apophanypes" (epiphany and apocalypse collapsed, 626.04–05), it is still a moment in which an object's "soul, its whatness, leaps to us. . . . The soul of the commonest object . . . seems to us radiant. The object achieves its epiphany" (*SH* 213). Although secularized in its focus on language, gesture, and objects rather than divine knowledge, Stephen's definition retains the theological quality of revelation, particularly in the way that the epiphany distills the object, not the observer.[18] In *A Portrait of the Artist as a Young Man*, the antithesis of epiphany is a pig, an animal so grossly earthbound that it has no hope of becoming a transcendent object. Stephen becomes frustrated with his friends when they change the subject from aesthetic philosophy to "Wicklow bacon" made out of "flaming fat devils of pigs" (*P* 207). However sublime Wicklow bacon may be, Stephen finds it too devilishly fleshly to be properly epiphanic. The pigs in and around the Festy King trial, then, obstruct the divinely illuminated flashes of truth that Stephen longs for. Ultimately, the verdict is pronounced as an ambivalent "Nolans Brumans" (93.01). Festy is pronounced guilty like the heretic Giordano Bruno of Nola whether he likes it or not (*nolens volens*: willing or unwilling in Latin), but since this guilt is unexceptional, it is nullified, Bruno's conviction is overturned, and Festy is simultaneously acquitted and "scotfree" (93.03).

The flesh that prevents epiphanic revelation emerges through repetitions whose management, Santner argues, is the biopolitical project.[19] Chapter I.4's opening vignette dramatizes in the blink of an eye the transition from sovereignty to biopower. The narrator likens HCE to King Billy, William III of Orange, whose invasion of England resulted in the Glorious Revolution, restricting monarchical power and transferring it to Parliament, and whose defeat of James at the Battle of Boyne reasserted Protestant power over Ireland. HCE hatches a scheme, however, that is reminiscent of a carceral, that is to say, biopolitical regime. He will secure the city by imprisoning all those of the "truly criminal stratum" (76.05). HCE's imagined asylums bear misleadingly bucolic names—"Meadow of Honey," "Mountain of Joy" (76.04–05)—to camouflage the violence that takes place within them. Isolating portions of the population by labeling them criminal, ill, or abnormal would attempt to quell the disturbances of the flesh. Thus HCE would secure obedience at the level of the population through a constant, low-grade anxiety about wellness. Defining the norm by excluding the abnormal, HCE's fantasy aims at "thereby at last eliminating from all classes and masses" the sick and the disobedient, who are declared to be co-equivalent (76.06). A loose translation of Dublin's motto, *Obedientia civium urbis felicitas* enshrines HCE's plan: "the obedience of the citizens elp the ealth of the ole" (76.08–09). The motto, part of Dublin's coat of arms, whispers its quiet reminder nearly everywhere in the city, from the mosaics on the floor of City Hall, to the Lord Mayor's Mansion House in Dawson Street, to the access covers of sidewalk electrical boxes.

Dublin's architecture and infrastructure convey one of the main biopolitical imperatives: to avoid the messiness of punishment, citizens ought to discipline *themselves* by living obedient lives that are salutary to the well-being of the entire population. If we are "changing the venders, from the king's head to the republican's arms" (90.05–06), the republican citizens must be responsible for themselves. They must take up the representation of the head that used to lead them and carry it in their arms, as Festy carries his flesh. The Wakean deformation of the Dublin city motto drops the *H*'s which are so strongly associated in the text with the Hill of Howth, under which lies the "grosskopp," or big head (78.05), of the sleeping giant Finn MacCool. The missing *H*'s thus point to the headlessness of the body politic. In the absence of sovereign representation, obedience elevates the city above strife. Obedience conditions the smooth functioning of its governmental functions. Obedience is in a citizen's best interest, but the ubiquity of the motto reminds citizens of the constant threat of *dis*obedience. Vigilance must be exercised, lest disobedience erupt.

In the preface to *Bodies That Matter*, her study of the materiality and performativity of sex and gender, Judith Butler describes being treated by a colleague as a disobedient child who willfully ignores the conditions of her feminine embodiment.[20] To be obedient is to respect the boundaries of one's embodiment without exceeding them. But HCE in his enfleshment constantly overflows his body. He takes advantage of "the first of the primary and imprescriptible liberties of the pacific subject" to go for a walk in a cemetery (85.06–07). Immediately, he takes down his pants ("bare by Butt's") and, like the Russian general shot by Buckley (whose name peeks through in the warning "beware to baulk a man at his will!"), goes "number two" upon a "public seat" (85.12–15). Abusing his liberty, he rejects the framing of civic participation in terms of self-pacification and hygiene. According to Butler, the performativity that constructs gender has an iterative structure: it is rehearsed over and over again as its effects accrete and crystallize. The performative efficacy of the law likewise requires an iterative structure, and the habeas corpus that materializes the law is the vessel for the law's reiteration. When it overflows, unruly flesh behaves unpredictably. Thus the biopolitical imperative of public health breaks down even as we encounter it on the page: the form of the motto degenerates in its shift from official speech to parodic slang. Now that the leading *H* has been dropped, the 'ole is not whole. The whole has a hole in it, the site marking the exclusion of the disobedient.

HCE is a disobedient corpse who repeatedly arises from his grave. The misplaced fat that nourishes him belongs in the category of supplemental flesh along with the somatic grotesqueries that Santner discusses.[21] These royal remains won't stay put: restless, they refuse to be pacified. Like King Hamlet's, the sovereign's ghost paces through the night. In the face of such tenacity, the city motto's meager nudge toward obedience is completely inadequate. Institutional apparatuses cannot manage the tremulous flesh. There must be another solution. We must look elsewhere to the dream.

The dream work possesses special power in Santner's account of the royal remains, its purpose to form a resonance chamber for the vibrations of the flesh.[22] The dream work is the mode through which the anxiety provoked by the disturbances of the flesh can be shaped into something with a discernible form. Rather than the spare, constrictive aesthetics of modernist painting or the insistence on stuckness that we find in Beckett's drama, the excessive, proliferating, kaleidoscopic turnings of the *Wake* offer a nocturnal dream work that gives strange form to the twitches and hiccups of the flesh, thereby testifying to the persistent aftereffects of political theology within an ostensibly secular age, or "secular seekalarum" (81.08).

Epiphany in the *Wake* partakes of these reverberations. It is a matter neither of frozen transcendence nor of prosaic significance but of rhythmic pulsing, closer to music than to architecture, closer to sculpture than to a still life. If Joyce's youthful theory was of a static experience that animates the person who undergoes it, in the *Wake* epiphany is plastic, ever-shifting in the reader's recognition of internally networked connections within the text. Rather than revealing some new, transcendent knowledge, the *Wake* comprises a surplus of immanence within the body of the text, an awareness that there is nothing new under the sun, and that there is far too much of it. What manifests is not a body but the flesh, with which an encounter is always somewhat of a missed encounter. Remember, the call to produce the body of the alleged assassin during Festy King's trial is, in the same breath, a call to produce merely the relics of that body.

The same root from which the word *epiphany* grew underlies the French word for window, *fenêtre*, which also illuminates and shows forth. In Parnell's case it was *de*fenestration that occasioned an ambivalent epiphany: the revelation, both in the moment and in the testimony at the trial, of the shamming, shamed body on the doorstep, of one who is simultaneously betrayer (of marriage, in favor of a stronger affective bond) and redeemer (a failed one, of Ireland). But to describe this as a "revelation" is problematic. Which Parnell was revealed when Mrs. Pethers opened the door a second time, friend or enemy? And what was revealed in court when she testified that day? Parnell and O'Shea's relationship had been an open secret for almost a decade. The gripping quality of this scene depends not on revelation but on repetition: the idea of two Parnells, one dignified, one ridiculous, and, in Mrs. Pethers's testimony, the idea that the dignified and ridiculous changed places multiple times.

Finnegans Wake challenges the notion, inherent in Joyce's youthful epiphanies, that the temporality of epiphany is momentary or that its crowning characteristic is singularity. Stephen's epiphany begins as a theory of the quantitatively, atomically singular—the object "is that thing which it is and no other thing" (*P* 213)—but even among the extant epiphanies, a quiet but consistent counterpoint of *ecstasis* is discernible if we read backward, seeing *Portrait* through the *Wake*: self-duplication, hearing one's voice outside one's own body, the extraction of innards and the escaping of spirit, looking outward toward the horizon, and breaking free from enclosure are all important recurring motifs. Even the cyclical structure of *Portrait*'s narrative is at odds with a momentary epiphany. Joyce's use of Parnell's self-doubling at the door of the O'Shea house shows us that epiphany is a function of re-presentation, not revelation. Epiphany's temporal dimension oscillates between a body's debut and its subsequent appearances. This focus on repetitive structure—on re-presentation rather than revelation—is what secularizes the theological epiphany, abandoning its content while conserving its form. Joyce recycles his youthful epiphanies in his later, longer works, but the concept of epiphany reaches its apotheosis only in *Finnegans Wake*, in which Vichian time is cyclical and bodies and objects exist fully immersed in iterative histories. *Finnegans Wake* challenges epiphany's autonomous haecceity of self-contained isolation by sending ripples of repetition through the body of the text.

Influenced by Jacques Lacan, Gilles Deleuze is one of the few readers of Joyce to identify epiphany with Wakean processes of repetition. "What takes place in the system between resonating series" of apparent likenesses results in an overwhelming "cosmic extension," he writes, meaning that repetition internal to the text's structure (not collective resemblance to fixed points of reference outside the text) reverberates until it reaches the harmonic amplitude we recognize as epiphany.[23] The elements in the series have no preexisting identity, but their juxtaposition and arrangement make their similarities appear to be "materially effecting the cause" of the linguistic network rather than what they actually are, the effect (76.13). The narrator of I.4 twice asks readers to retreat: to "return to here's here" (76.10), and "to return to the atlantic" (85.20), a double movement of doubling back that seeks but does not find (Where is here? When were we ever in the Atlantic?) a stable body on which to chart a sure narrative path. Such a broken circuit makes of epiphany a delirious disappointment, its brokenness drawing our attention to its status as a textual effect instead of the material cause of a text, in Deleuze's terms. The frame narrative of chapter I.4 is similarly enticing and similarly disappointing: like many frame narratives, it dispenses with communicating *what* happened and promises instead to explain *how* and *why* it happened. The *Wake*, however, denies readers such an epiphanic autopsy of HCE's burial. The chapter finally affirms only "his existence as a tesseract" (100.35), that is, as a four-dimensional figure in non-Euclidean space, difficult to imagine or visualize. Or available only through the extra dimension of another's narration, that of ALP, whose voice picks up on the very next page.

Chapter I.4 is notable for introducing the letter that will be retrieved from the bottom of the midden heap in the next chapter. As the Hen, ALP is responsible for producing the body of the letter, and thereby the letter of the law. But the letter circulates, and the testimony digresses. Like the trial, the letter elicits desire for an epiphanic insight, especially because it seems to have triggered some kind of epiphany for those who have read it. "Ask Kavya for the kay," the key that explains it all, the narrator urges (93.22–23). But the letter and the trial, not to mention the whole of the *Wake*, "[t]reely and rurally" (90.31) frustrate desire for a real and true interpretive revelation.

The fleshless skeleton key of definitive interpretation is the key that would ensure the body of the letter is securely dead; it would open only the certainty that no restless spirits walk the night. The fantasy of Kavya's key is the fantasy of an epiphanic discovery that puts all interpretive doubts to rest. The same desire sustains the genetic fantasy that a perfect reconstruction of the body of the *Finnegans Wake* notebooks and manuscripts will generate self-evident revelation. But the manuscript is the corpse of the living text, the husk it has shed, and all the king's horses and all the king's men can't transmute the cracked materiality of Humpty into a thunderclap again because "Mumpty" and "Rumpty" have taken his place (99.20). Moreover, this is the same fantasy that habeas corpus sustains, a fantasy which is the condition of possibility for justice and also what keeps justice from ever being complete, the fantasy that the body will be the ground for the epiphanic revelation of truth. Even when it is present, the mortal, decomposing, fugitive body is too unreliable to ever realize that fantasy. The textual body of *Finnegans Wake* is always fleeing into its communities of readers.

The call to produce the body resounds in the call to produce the letter. "The letter! The litter! And the soother the bitther!" (93.24). The Middle English *sooth* means truth; if the letter revealed the truth about the crime in question, it would soothe the passions of those involved. Continually associated with litter, however, the letter is trash that decomposes like a human body. Just as the *deuce* in "Prodooce" implies that Hyacinth O'Donnell's redoubled body isn't quite the stable reference that is desired, the letter arrives too late to be introduced into evidence and therefore provides inadequate grounds for judgment. The letter is called for after Festy's trial has concluded; it is not produced for thirteen more chapters.

Habeas corpus and epiphany alike take on the burden of representation in modernity, and both quiver with the excess immanence they inherit thereby. One final passage brings together the hope that a body will prove revelatory and the compensations for the failure of that hope. Summing up the trial and HCE's flight in I.4, the narrator tells us, "Well, even should not the framing up of such figments in the evidential order bring the true truth to light as fortuitously as a dim seer's setting of a starchart might (heaven helping it!) uncover the nakedness of an unknown body in the fields of blue . . . by such playing possum our hagious curious ancestor bestly saved his brush with his posterity" (96.26–35). Don't worry over irrelevant evidence from the witness that bears little or no relation to the trial, the narrator consoles us.

Only fictional figments of the imagination can frame the truth. And even if these figments fail to reveal the true truth, HCE survives by lying low for a while. As indicated by the too-much-protesting "true truth," this passage is drenched in irony. True truth's redundancy is repeated in "uncover the nakedness," while the "dim seer" is an oxymoron. The dim seer is likely Zwierel, an unfortunate Romanian astronomer who reported seeing a new, naked eye nova in 1922. No other observers were able to locate the "nova of the first magnitude," however, because the hapless Zwierel had discovered an already charted star.[24] Like a bumbling magus, the belated Zwierel went in search of an unknown beacon hailing an unknown body, but he failed to produce it. Instead, he ended up with a useless, repetitious superfluity. But it is precisely such an excess, in the form of the flesh, that sustains the shamming HCE in his possum form. Zwierel's inside-out epiphany therefore ironically illuminates the truth of the Wakean epiphany, a structure of immanent repetition that non-produces a non-body that nevertheless survives to rise again and regenerate itself.

Notes

1. John Bishop, *Joyce's Book of the Dark: "Finnegans Wake"* (Madison: University of Wisconsin Press, 1986), 145.

2. The close readings throughout this essay are enabled by Roland McHugh's *Annotations to "Finnegans Wake"* (Baltimore: Johns Hopkins University Press, 1991).

3. Eric Santner, *The Royal Remains: The People's Two Bodies and the Endgames of Sovereignty* (Chicago: University of Chicago Press, 2012), 3–88.

4. See Ernst Kantorowicz, *The King's Two Bodies: A Study in Mediaeval Political Theology* (Princeton: Princeton University Press, 1997).

5. Santer, *Royal Remains*, 27.

6. Women and pigs are linked through the similar sounds in the Greek roots for *pig* (ὗ☒ or *hys-*) and *uterus* (ὑστέρα or *hystero*).

7. Simone de Beauvoir, *The Second Sex*, trans. Constance Borde and Sheila Malovany-Chevallier (New York: Vintage, 2011), 149.

8. Kathryn Conrad and Darryl Wadsworth, "Joyce and the Irish Body Politic: Sexuality and Colonization in *Finnegans Wake*," *James Joyce Quarterly* 31 (Spring 1994): 306. Conrad and Wadsworth draw on Peter Stallybrass and Allon White's Bakhtinian analysis of the pig as carnivalesque in *The Politics and Poetics of Transgression* (Ithaca: Cornell University Press, 1986).

9. Article in the *United Irishman* qtd. in James Lydon, *The Making of Ireland: From Ancient Times to the Present* (London: Routledge, 1998), 318.

10. J. M. Synge, *The Complete Works of J. M. Synge* (Ware: Wordsworth, 2008), 202.

11. James Fairhall, *James Joyce and the Question of History* (Cambridge: Cambridge University Press, 1993), 217.

12. John O'Beirne Ranelagh, *A Short History of Ireland*, 3rd ed. (Cambridge: Cambridge University Press, 2012), 154.

13. Andrew Gibson, "Macropolitics and Micropolitics in 'Wandering Rocks,'" in *Joyce's "Wandering Rocks,"* ed. Andrew Gibson and Steven Morrison (Amsterdam: Rodopi, 2002), 32n11.

14. *O'Shea-Parnell Divorce Case: Full and Complete Proceedings* (Boston: National Publishing Company, n.d.), 25–26.

15. It is thus called by William York Tindall in *A Reader's Guide to "Finnegans Wake"* (Syracuse: Syracuse University Press, 1996), 96. Conrad and Wadsworth also use this term (304).

16. Adaline Glasheen, *A Second Census of "Finnegans Wake"* (Evanston: Northwestern University Press, 1963), 140, 80.

17. See Bishop's "Etymological Chart," a diagram of "The 'funantics' of 'phonemanon,'" 291–93.

18. Hugh Kenner, *Dublin's Joyce* (New York: Columbia University Press, 1987), 145.

19. Santner, *Royal Remains*, 8–10.

20. Judith Butler, *Bodies That Matter: On the Discursive Limits of Sex* (New York: Routledge, 2011), ix.

21. Santner, *Royal Remains*, 188–244.

22. Ibid., 93.

23. Gilles Deleuze, *Difference and Repetition*, trans. Paul Patton (London: Continuum, 2004), 148.

24. Harlow Shapley, "Reported Nova in Lyra," *Harvard College Observatory Bulletin* 780 (December 5, 1922): 2.

5

Joyce's Common Reader

A Primer for Sensory Consciousness in I.5

COLLEEN JAURRETCHE

In the beginning pages of his compendious study of modernism and avant-garde texts, *The Pound Era,* Hugh Kenner observed that the trajectory of modernism ultimately involved the status of image: "A picture is an object in space.... The instinct that[,] as the 19th century progressed[,] drew writing and painting closer and closer together was enacting a massive bafflement at the question, how to go about *meaning* anything. For objects are even more enigmatic than stories." Joseph Conrad aimed "'above all to make you *see'* ... his mind's eye fixed in some ideal space."[1] My goals are to introduce I.5 of *Finnegans Wake* as a chapter that makes us "see" by establishing letter as image, and to place this idea in the context of one of the book's most pervasive linguistic and rhetorical modes, prayer. The shift of meaning from alphabetic character to visual object transforms ideas not only about writing but also readers, ranging from Joyce's famous ideal insomniac (120.13–14) to Kenner's literary seer, and to the common reader in both senses of the phrase: the book as sampler—as a collection of varied discourses—as well as the curious and open-minded person willing to take seriously the *Wake's* integration of language and prayer as well as word and visual image.

Critics have often noted in *Finnegans Wake* an ongoing interplay between letter as visual figure and written missive. Most work on I.5 references its indebtedness to *The Book of Kells,* the remarkably ornate early Irish medieval Gospel manuscript whose facsimile Joyce owned and revered and which dominates the discussions of the alphabet within the chapter.[2] In almost equal amounts, the criticism of I.5 focuses on Joyce's atomization of the alphabet as part of his interest in *Kells* and the practical role the chapter plays in introducing writing as an overt subject.[3] I wish to lay out how Joyce's concept of language relates image to writing, reading, and discernment of meaning inherent in word etymologies. The chapter culminates in his conceptual use of ceremonial elements in *The Book of Kells* in the service of untraditional models of reading and books.

Language possesses vitality, and letters have visual and spatial qualities. In *Finnegans Wake* I.5 Joyce gives us a manifesto about the "writer complexus" (114.33), a phrase that not only alludes to the complex subterranean life from which art emerges and which the book seeks to emulate, but also invokes the concept and reception of writing in Western culture within "active and agitated" minds (114.34). His foremost authority is Giambattista Vico, whose fabular account of writing establishes language's origin in prayer, a word that derives from states of wishing and being. According to Vico, those first states were communicated in gesture (a sort of visual image), which gave way to song, then speech in poetic form. In the strange and wonderful mythology that Vico invents in his idiosyncratic *New Science*, verbal poiesis quite literally makes the world.[4] Joyce loved the creative mythology and willfully crafted etymologies that form Vico's thesis. He was equally enchanted by Vico's notion of letters as figures, springing from a godhead as they do in almost all stories of origins. One adumbration of prayer in *Finnegans Wake* is the book's much-acknowledged indebtedness to *The Book of Kells;* both the ancient text and Joyce's Wakean adoption of it confer the status of art object onto manuscripts in general and writing in particular. *Kells* elevates letters to the status of sacred agents in ways that redefine what we see when we regard a page. Joyce's use of *Kells* thus offers new concepts about storytelling as well as physical books.[5]

The factual basis of Western writing supports Vico's intuition that letter is image.[6] Early communication in pictographic and hieroglyphic form conveyed everything from basic accounting to sentiments about life, death, and the presence of divinity. Our present-day writing is no less an amalgamation of the sublime and the mundane, nor less potentially compelling as image and design. And while ancient pictures may seem inherently more pictorial than modern writing, Vico would likely assert that the printed word is no less an image, one upon which we have superimposed modern habits of seeing and reading, but no less as ambiguous and captivating as its pictogramic ancestor.[7]

Finnegans Wake crossbreeds the tradition of Western writing, from ancient papyri to *The Book of Kells,* with Vico's notion of prayer as the potent verbal force that makes the world. The *Wake*'s notorious obscurity derives from its very simplicity—an almost plotless story in which first and last sentence join, with endlessly repeating characters. That *Finnegans Wake* is the book that few read but many cite as the epitome of literary difficulty makes good sense: it *is* obscure, and at face value rudimentary images are vastly easier to understand. But at least in part *Finnegans Wake*'s obscurity emerges, like Kenner's ideal space, from how it makes us see. This essay will now work through the usual sequential order of the three sections that comprise I.5—the Mamafesta, the interpretation of the letter, and *The Book of Kells*—in order to view *Finnegans Wake* as a primer for seeing and a model for agency of word and image.

Mamafesta

The chapter begins "In the name of Annah the Allmaziful, the Everliving, the Bringer of Plurabilities, haloed be her eve, her singtime sung, her rill be run, unhemmed as it is uneven!" (104.01–03). The opening fuses prayer with the woman-river Annalivia, whose "Mamafesta" fills the first several pages of I.5. *Mamafesta* echoes manifesto and derives from the Indo-European root *man*—to take in hand—from which we get such variations as Latin *manus*, or *manuscript* and *amanuensis*, to the German *munt* for mound and Latin *mundus* for adornment.[8] The second half of *manifesto/Mamafesta* derives from the same root as Latin's lovely *festus* and all the sacred festivities it references.[9] In the context of I.5, with its discovery of a letter buried in a dung, trash, or funereal midden or mound, the manifesto/Mamafesta becomes shorthand for the human and divine handiwork of which the world is composed, and for concepts of internal being and external manifestation, essence and accidence. The "Mamafesta" becomes a manifesto about how to read, one based on the composition, decomposition, and recomposition of words.

Among the "Plurabilities" of the chapter's opening is the Viconian concept of words as originating in "her singtime sung" (104.02). Vico believed human history unfolded in four stages or cycles, roughly corresponding to the seasons or ages of man, as is evidenced by the fourfold organization of the *New Science*. Those correspondences extend to the anthropomorphizing of language whose nascent words emerged as song. Words—whether spoken or printed—are the physical manifestations of an invisible God, one whose trace, for Vico, may be found in the cultural underpinnings of marriage and burial and whose lineaments are revealed in the compounding of root language. Joyce was captivated by Vico's fanciful vision of language and culture for many reasons, not least of which was his preference for the truth of story over literal reality. Vico's formula—*verum factum est*—places truth in narrative. Words become part of the realization of the visible and hence visual universe, an idea incorporated by Joyce in ways ranging from Stephen's desire in "Proteus" to read the physical world inherent in his reference to George Berkeley's "signatures of all things" (*U* 3.2), to the concept of language in *Finnegans Wake*. The subsequent watery river "rill" expands and has a "run" that becomes "unhemmed." Its unraveling plays nakedness against clothing, nature against fabrication, all the while making us think of clingy and/or flowing (rilling) underthings. In Joyce's intellectual garden, propriety is lost, and paradise is found in root origins that reveal the ontological construction of words and narrative.

What ensues is a long dilatory list of songs, headlines, and funny titles, such as *In My Lord's Bed by One Whore Went Through It* (105.34–35), or *A Nibble at Eve Will that Bowal Relieve* (106.29–30). But the section ends with a run-on phrase that comes as close to narrative as any part of the book by invoking the putative sin enacted in the heart of the Wakean garden: "*Naked Truths about a Dear Man . . . and a Pair of Sloppy Sluts plainly Showing all the Unmentionability falsely Accusing about the Raincoats*" (107.04–07). We never do get a clear sense of who did what to whom, and if anything we learn the futility of hoping for simple "*Naked Truths*" as we are guided to the philosophical crux of reading—whether it is a search for information or an exploration of quintessence. A page or two earlier the undergarments that "rill," "run," and become "unhemmed" now appear in an Aristotelian brainteaser where words like "*Unmentionability*" sometimes have straightforward meanings that can be paradoxically mentioned and named; but—as in the implicit pun on underwear—they more often offer teasing, peep-show exhibitions of blurry and allusive reference in the night vision of the *Wake*. In this sense the Mamafesta not only engages gossip surrounding Earwicker's fall but also demonstrates reading as a process of discerning pre-Lapsarian essence—the roots of words and culture—from post-Lapsarian chaos and babble.

The Interpretation of the Letter

The guiding voice of the chapter moves in and out of a lecturing mode as it attempts to isolate the essential qualities of words and their components. We are told that "the proteiform graph itself is a polyhedron of scripture" (107.08), taking us back to the idea of words as divine in origin, but with a sculptural and protein-like twist incarnated in two-dimensional print, a "graph," or in three-dimensional polyhedron shape. *Proteiform* combines *protein* and *protean*, each taken from a different root—one for "first" and the other for "relating to."[10] Since *graph* is taken from "to scratch" or "cut," our word alludes to an original means of inscription: carvings on trees. And, as if matters have not become complicated enough, we are told that there was a time when "naïf alphabetters would have written it down" (107.09): the phrase refers to the Viconian process by which words become things; the record of language transcribed in ancient ways; and the relatively straightforward bit of correspondence, a letter, that will eventually be seen.

The letter is as much a practical document as anything "used by worried business folk who may not have had many momentums to master Kung's doctrine of the meang or the propriety codestruces" (108.10–12). Codestruces are sections of a book, such as a selection of scripture. In this sentence ordinary businesspeople or workers from bygone times ("I am a worker, a tombstone mason" [113.34]) do not possess the skills for exegesis or even necessarily the working out of letters and words; nevertheless, they make sense of images in their environments, such as stained-glass windows, that reflect Gospel truths.[11] Whatever its contents, the letter becomes a statement about alternative forms of literacy that do not depend on high learning, or even logical meaning, but rather, as in Conrad's ideal visual space, work to make us see.

Earwicker, whose eyes are shut in sleep, does not read in the ordinary sense either, but somehow he hears the letter through nocturnal broadcast. For those granted sight, it is an equally untraditional document, one whose "page cannot ever have been a penproduct of a man" (108.31). Its main significance lies not in content but rather, like *The Book of Kells*, in physical apparatus and design. The look of the carapace of the letter occupies the next several paragraphs. We are asked who among us has "ever looked sufficiently longly at a quite everydaylooking stamped addressed envelope?" (109.07–08). The letter's essence is the packaging, where physical appearance and philosophical meaning coincide. Our passage insists that "to concentrate solely on the literal sense or even the psychological content of any document to the sore neglect of the enveloping facts themselves circumstantiating it is just as hurtful to sound sense (and let it be added to the truest taste) as" (109.12–16). As what? In the more obscure learned metaphor the passage offers, as ignoring the accidental in favor of the essential properties of things, or, in its racier interpretation, as neglecting the sex appeal of clothing. Just as Annalivia's "unhemmed" rill, which is literally part of the word *frill*, puts us in mind of adorned underthings, so here too provocation lies in the outer envelope. To dive into the contents is tantamount to envisioning the body under its accoutrements: "straightaway to run off and vision her plump and plain in her natural altogether" (109.19–20). Clothes, it seems, are more than shielding outergarments; like letters and the books that contain them, they are particular objects whose external and internal qualities deserve careful examination. Imagination and fantasy contribute powerfully to the creation of meaning: thus the envelope that encases the letter is "suggestive, too, of so very much more and capable of being stretched . . . [and] of having their surprisingly like coincidental parts separated don't they now, for better survey by the deft hand of an expert, don't you know?" (109.26–30). According to the narrator, one would not want to rush to the contents without first examining the "facts of feminine clothiering" (109.31). So too with reading: in I.5, discernment of meaning begins with actually looking at—maybe even touching—the sensate envelope of the page.

In its idealization of reading and readers, I.5 asks us to imagine what kinds of stories might emerge without benefit of ordinary literacy and applies this question to a putative common reader in the figure of "Belinda of the Dorans" (111.05), a chicken that pecks in the midden of shit, garbage, and writing that is Joyce's imagined barnyard. Biddy's musings conflate highbrow and homespun learning in ways that recall "that original hen" (110.22), Chaucer's Pertelote in *The Nun's Priest's Tale,* who also must discern meaning from the detritus of dreams. Biddy's object in life is replication, preservation, and protection: "she knows, she just feels she was kind of born to lay and love eggs (trust her to propagate the species and hoosh her fluffballs safe through din and danger!)" (112.13–15). What Biddy repeats is the stuff of everyday life: affectionate greetings and closings in the letter, the bringing of young twins into the world, and the "original sin" at the heart of the naughty night dream plaguing Earwicker. One version of her letter reads, "Dear whom it proceded to mention Maggy well & allathome's health . . . & must now close it with fondest to the twoinns with four crosskisses for holy paul . . . pee ess" (111.10–18). The letter is signed with a teastain, an untraditional signature that matches the illiterate, spelled-out "pee ess" saturating the page. Our "original hen" is also our common writer or scribe, literally pecking from the mound a "Mamafesta"—a maternal, festive manifesto—about language and reality. Her uncoverings bring home to roost the wrongness of concentrating on literal sense over "enveloping facts" (109.14); instead, the task of the reader is to discern meaning, however obscurely, from the range of handwriting and scratches that have taken us from images of goats to the abbreviations and expansions of "&" and "pee ess."

Our "lookmelittle" hen (111.33) is a quick reader whose pluckings uncover questions of representation: can we all see the same thing and from the same perspective? Or are we doomed to have some features "palpably nearer your pecker to be swollen up most grossly while the farther back we manage to wiggle the more we need the loan of a lens to see as much as the hen saw" (111.35–112.02). In other words, is a common reader—as both aware intellect and tangible book—even possible in a world, like that of *Ulysses*, of shifting vision and relative understanding? And, lest we think we invented such conundrums, let us recall that interpretive problems begin with earliest questions around the interpretability of images, not letters. The high theology behind concepts of essence and accidence draws from reality conceived as Aristotelian, and our homely hen is no less the peripatetic philosopher and no less driven to shelter herself from the vagaries of Platonic shadows of forms.

About now our narrator, the surrogate common reader, sympathizes with the frustrations of getting through the chapter: "You is feeling like you was lost in the bush, boy? . . . Bethicket me for a stump of a beech if I have the poultriest notions what the farest he all means" (112.03–06). Having recognized that the words on the page are confusing at best, the narrator points out the greatest complication of all. In a pre-Lapsarian state our animal and human friends coexist in some promise of divine dispensation of mutual comprehension, where "the manewanting human lioness with her dishorned discipular manram will lie down together publicly flank upon fleece" (112.21–23). In this fabular garden of delights where the lioness lies down with the manram, it may seem that all stories were straightforward and easy to understand; however, even then the more truthful complexities of art entered human experience, we are told, on "that weird weekday in bleak Janiveer . . . Biddy Doran *looked* at literature" (112.25–27, my italics).

Her perusal and inscription are simultaneous and brief. She aims to tell "the cock's trootabout him," the truth from the perspective of a turkey (*trut*: turkey in German). The "him" is presumably HCE, who "had to see life foully" (113.12–13)—fully, as a fowl, and with the foulness of the possible facts. Because "she is not out to dizzledazzle" with language "the lapins and the grigs" (113.01–02), her original act of writing shuns highfalutin' Latin (*lapin*) and Greek (*grigs*) in favor of barnyard peckings that includes visualization of rabbits (*lapin*: rabbit in French) and short-legged hens (or *grigs*).[12] In so doing she enacts a fantasy of what we all think we want as writers and readers: direct meaning, without ambiguity. She articulates a wish, or entreaty, for clarity, the pragmatics of which take us to the culture's embedded conversations about things in their essence and their complicated relationship to sensory media through which we perceive them. In a larger sense, these questions address the meaning of prayer, whose root word traces back to entreaty, and accompanying states of wishing, feeling, aspiration, and what we desire from the world.[13] An interrogatory voice pipes up with an aviary request to "talk straight turkey" (113.26) about the meaning of Biddy's letter. That "straight" talk involves the garbled question, "*Habes aures et num videbis? Habes oculos ac mannepalpabuat?*" (113.29–30), a distorted adaptation of Psalm 113, "Eyes have they, but they see not. They have ears, but they hear not. . . . They have hands, but they handle not." Through her diggings and rakings, our original hen invokes the epistemological crux of I.5 and the book: all language is filtered through perception, always subject to the senses. Our words, even letters, are sounds and images that permeate us. In the world of the *Wake* there is no mental process that is free of the sensory and tangible world. Hence ALP's mamafesta is likened to a photo negative (111.27); it also takes protean shape as a globe (114.03–05) and a surveyor's diagram with a "geodetic" intention (114.14–15). Like Conrad's attempt to "make us see," the chapter draws from the common midden of memory, sounds, and shapes, and its interpretive challenges are not so much about plot as about what we think reading and art consist of. Let us now heed the directive to the hen, following her through the pages of *The Book of Kells*—"Lead, kindly fowl!" (112.09).

The Book of Kells

In the circular logic and bended time frame of the *Wake*, Biddy's ur-letter both anticipates and fulfills the marks left by the scribes of *The Book of Kells*, Joyce's touchstone for what books are and reading is. Examination of *Kells* gives us the best indication yet of how Joyce saw letters as pictures and imagined them as filled with vitality ordinarily ascribed to living things.

Kells is recognized as the most intricately and beautifully illustrated of all early medieval manuscripts. It is a record of the Gospels, but its illuminations incorporate fabulously elaborated script, images of the Virgin and Child, and recondite pictures of Christ that adumbrate and supersede Gospel narrative: the letters keep supplementing the Gospel story they are intended to tell. Its remarkable look derives from interwoven characters that unfold into figures or images and work back again to join with other letters in the creation of a word. This weaving suggests there is no graphical difference between story and picture.

Joyce compared *Kells* to *Finnegans Wake*, reportedly saying:

> In all the places that I have been to, Rome, Zurich, Trieste, I have taken it about with me, and have pored over its workmanship for hours. It is the most purely Irish thing we have and some of the big initial letters which swing right across a page have the essential quality of a chapter of *Ulysses*. Indeed, you can compare much of my work to the intricate illuminations. I would like it to be possible to pick up any page of my book and know at once what book it is. (*JJII* 545)

Joyce owned and traveled with Sir Edward Sullivan's 1914 facsimile edition whose introduction regarded *Kells*'s ornamentation as conceptual as well as aesthetic. For example, Sullivan concluded that the *Kells* artists were not interested in mimetic representation of nature; rather, the goal was a book to be viewed through the cultural context of monasticism, emanating from and created for medieval interpretive sensibility. At the same time, Sullivan tells us that *Kells* is composed of "disnatured anatomies" whose combination of forms amounts to what he called a "miscegenation of letters," all of which serve the purpose of illustrating the Gospels as "prose in action."[14] Contemporary research on *Kells* supports Sullivan's intuitions: scholars' interpretations vary from seeing the manuscript as pure visual amusement,[15] as "paradigms of the process by which . . . truth was seen and passed on,"[16] or for its potential ceremonial use. According to this last reading, *Kells* possibly grew from the ancient monastic ritual of *Apertio aurium*, the opening of the ears. In this ceremony, intended to prepare catechumens for Easter baptism, four deacons proceeded to the altar, each bearing one of the Gospels decorated with the animal symbol of its apostle. The deacons placed the books on the four corners of the altar, then removed them. The catechumens beheld the bare altar and reflected upon the drama of the incarnation told (as in Viconian myth) in gesture, song, and dramatic action, not verbal explanation.[17] With its multiple uses of fourfold evangelical figures, its emphasis on language whose action rises above the written word, and its astonishing aural properties, *Finnegans Wake* walks in the monastic tradition of *Apertio aurium*, including its attempts to indoctrinate participants in alternative—and inherently communal and exegetical—reading practices.

Direct reference to *Apertio aurium* lies beyond the pages of I.5; moreover, proof of Joyce's knowledge of *Kells*'s actual use in the ritual is beside the point: it was practiced because it enacted views about language and incarnation. In parallel fashion Joyce uses I.5 to point out concepts embedded in *Kells* that inform the use of words in *Finnegans Wake*. The similarities begin with the physically visual decoration of the pages, where the scribes draw up "the highpriest's hieroglyph . . . [of] our hallowed rubric prayer" (122.07–08) with every bit as much joy as Biddy's own barnyard peckings. The words *scribe, scripture,* and *scriptorum* derive from the root for *scratch, cut, pluck, gather,* and *dig*,[18] and resonate not only for our plucky hen but also for the first writers who broke branches from trees and made cuts in bark in an effort to inscribe. From this practice the Latin word for "cut in," *scribere,* came to mean "write." *Scribere* derives from a second, related root that links *cut* to *scrape, separate,* and *discriminate.* Joyce's book imagines the whole relationship of instrument to paper as well as the process of discernment implicit in figuring out the contents of the chapter: we move from Biddy's garbage-midden scratches to the putative crime of our sleeper, to the riddled and curious act of reading, whether of dreams or books.

Kells features alphabet pages, lists of begats, and images of the four Evangelists "for, tiny tot though it looks when schtschupnistling alongside other incunabula, it has its cardinal points for all that" (114.05–07). *Incunabula* refers to early printed texts: in this context *Kells* is cast as "tot" or seedling in the art of making a book, analogous to the earliest origins or development of any and all things. Rubric refers to the letters at the beginning of Gospel verses that were written in red ink. The "highpriest's hieroglyph" is thus both writing and the action of letters that morph into patterns and creatures. The resulting latter-day "proteiform graph" and "polyhedron of scripture" (107.08) is *Finnegans Wake* with its "tenebrous Tunc page of the Book of Kells" (122.22–23). No critic of the chapter has avoided commentary on *Tunc* as an obvious anagram of *cunt,* but none has reflected on its etymological suitability. As a word, *cunt* derives from roots for *knowledge* and *begetting*.[19] Reading and writing is thus a form of carnal knowledge, with resonances of word made flesh that both delighted Joyce and served his purposes very well. The "tenebrous Tunc page of the Book of Kells" models the dynamism of letters and demonstrates why Joyce's book bears (in every sense) the mitochondrial stamp of its illustrated ancestor.

Sullivan's "miscegenation of letters" gets demonstrated when "pees with their caps awry . . . as often as not taken for kews with their tails" (119.35–36) consort with "haughtypitched disdotted aiches" (121.16). In *Finnegans Wake* as in *Kells,* ordinary writing (and conduct) are suspended, and letters set their own quantum rules. These rules are based in a hyper-consciousness of the physical realization of letters, as if taken to the root meaning of *literal*:

a thing that is stamped, or prepared, like the hide upon which images of goats once were imprinted. In such a literal universe, "four shortened ampersands under which we can glypse at and feel for ourselves" somehow rearrange time and sequence so that "the vocative lapse from which it begins" becomes "the accusative hole in which it ends itself" (121.36–122.04). On that medieval Tunc page and in Joyce's modern-day counterpart, randy letters engage in "lubricitous conjugation of the last with the first" (121.30–31), making an alphabetic orgy of both books. In this mélange, to read means to reconcile letter and image in "bi tso fb rok engl a ssan dspl itch ina" (124.07–08) in order to join or restore reality in a self-reflexive visual enactment of the phrase. Language here is tangible and frangible as glass, as fragile and ornate as china. The etymological origins of *reading* encompasses words as seemingly dissimilar as *arranging, fitting, joining,* and *kindred*; at its core, reading is a fundamentally conjoined and communal process of sharing through the medium of language the consciousness of another. Our definition of reading and writing expands from "kakography" (120.22–23), "rude & uncouth Etruscan" handwriting (according to McHugh), to shorthand and Morse code in this "new book of Morses" (123.35). The line "stop, please stop, do please stop, and O do please stop" (124.04–05) suggests the dots used in Morse code. It is both naughty and nice—a coy sexual protest that perhaps protests too much—and echoes the teasing sexuality Joyce deploys as a metaphor for the exchange of letters and words. Reading is complicated and sensual in this chapter, with cognition equated to the fingering of visualized "feminine clothiering" (109.31). In the final paragraph, to write is to "introdùce a notion of time [ùpon à plane (?) sù' fàçè'] by pùnct! ingh oles (sic) in iSpace?!" (124.10–12): Joyce foregrounds and exaggerates the various marks to emphasize their reliance on visual reading (it is difficult to hear physical punctuation marks). To make marks on the page is to punch holes in space; it is an act of demarcation and creation, one that Joyce sees deployed through the inner mechanics of letter and image, essence and accidence, thereby rearranging the universe.

Kells letters are decorative or devotional before they are legible: no one reads it to learn the story of the Crucifixion, just as no one reads *Finnegans Wake* to learn the truth of HCE's transgression or of his possible awakening in the morning. Each work exists in violation of our readerly expectations, so much so that we are hard pressed to call one merely a book or the other merely a novel. The difficulty is tantalizing when we ask what Joyce loved more: the elaborate nature of *Kells*, or the resistance of its words to any conformity? Sullivan's editorial remarks are suggestive as he labels *Kells*'s so-called errors in spelling as evidence of work in progress, Joyce's name for *Finnegans Wake* during the seventeen years of its composition. *Kells*'s designs, Sullivan says, are taken from the earliest proto Indo-European sources, like the word-roots in *Finnegans Wake*.[20] And like Joyce, *Kells*'s artists never intended to show creatures (or letters, for that matter) in their representational state. Instead, elaborateness of form in both works is not merely fanciful but deliberate, suggesting that all books are revealers of ultimate truth through art: we can "[s]ay it with missiles then and thus arabesque the page" (115.03). In other words, like story and myth, our prayer books, artifacts, and adornments allow and entice us to approach meaning. The "innocent exhibitionism of those frank yet caprious underlinings" (121.19–20) implies that graphic marks for emphasis are analogous in their temptations to partially exposed underwear.

Let us return for a moment to our pursuit of who and what the common "reader" is and how Joyce defines the act of reading. In one sense Joyce follows the model of the "oldworld epistola" (117.27) by merging book and person in the concept of "reader," at once invoking the notion of a book as an object (a reader, like a hymnal), and even the particularities of an elaborate book like *Kells*, whose real value may not have been the content of the page but rather its ceremonial presence. Joyce takes literally the hallowed lineage of writers from poets, storytellers, and seers, and understands letters as not only their medium but also autonomous objects imbued with life. Throughout the book "traced words, run, march, halt, walk, stumble at doubtful points" (114.08–09), animating the notion of character in both senses of the word, as a letter and a participant in a story. It is no accident that the origin of the word *letter* also supplies us with *rune* and *magic*. At its core, reading is an act where we "make significant" or "make out a character" and thus magically bring things to life. The *OED* tells us that reading is related to the interpretation of dreams and that to read is to reckon and divine. Seen thus, reading is about irrationality put right. Our projection of meaning on barnyard chicken scratches perfectly reflects a natural desire to make sense of symbols in relation to our lives. The common as well as "ideal" reader is thus a creatively realized book, prefigured by the phantasmagoria of *Kells* and fulfilled in the letters of the *Wake*, as well as in the actively engaged imagination that beholds their pages.

Finnegans Wake reinscribes ancient kinds of image-based literacy that gives meaning to otherwise fragmented and discrete language. The sense of common and communal reader speaks to a primitive kind of writer embodied in the "short pants of the quickscribbler" (122.02–03), the bad-boy twin brother, "Shem the Penman" (125.23), whose self-inscribed excrescences occupy I.7. In its voicing of language as prayer, *Finnegans Wake* is spring and reservoir of all that is present in the modernist imagination, its consciousness and artistic enterprise. Its word and image factory makes common readers of us all in a tenebrous book since whose composition "letters have never been quite their old selves again" (112.24–25) from medieval to modern times.

Notes

1. Hugh Kenner, *The Pound Era* (Berkeley: University of California Press, 1971), 25, 27.

2. Joseph Campbell and Henry Morton Robinson see I.5 as engaged in the humanization of letters, in *A Skeleton Key to "Finnegans Wake"* (New York: Harcourt, Brace, 1944), 103–5. William York Tindall sees the *Wake* as "a thing of words" and insists upon their almost material properties and relevance to meaning, in *A Reader's Guide to "Finnegans Wake"* (New York: Farrar, Straus and Giroux, 1969), 239. He goes on to make basic connections to *Kells*, seeing it as "a thing of beauty," and views I.5 as the easiest of the seventeen chapters of *Finnegans Wake*. Bernard Benstock focuses on the letter as a document rather than characters as alphabet in his overview of I.5—"Concerning Lost Historeve / Book I, chapter v," in *A Conceptual Guide to "Finnegans Wake,"* ed. Michael H. Begnal and Fritz Senn (University Park: Pennsylvania State University Press, 1974), 52. He sees the point of the letter as change, "flux itself." Moreover, he sees *Kells* as representing "*the* literary artifact." In their overview to I.5, Danis Rose and John O'Hanlon lay out the chapter's sequential divisions and recognize that in Joyce's use of *Kells* he is referring to his own process of composition, in *Understanding "Finnegans Wake"* (New York: Garland, 1982), 76.

3. Most notable here is Jed Rasula's examination of the letter in experimental literature. "*Finnegans Wake* and the Character of the Letter," *James Joyce Quarterly* 34 (Summer 1997): 517–30. He makes use of concepts such as Vico's animation of letters and puns on letters as "literal" emblems of how language behaves, right up to the notion of letters as "actants" that would "manifest as a continuum from the morpheme to the somnolent snoozer of the whole." Curiously, commentary on *Kells* is a minor part of his article. He says that Joyce "deviated" from its "precedent by miniaturizing rather than enlarging on the principle of the lively initial." Wilhelm Fuger asserts that "pictorial renderings of the world precede scriptorial ones." "SCRIPTSIGNS: Variants and Cultural Contexts of Iconicity in Joyce," *Joyce Studies Annual* 1997, 60. Here again, though, the role of *Kells* is diminished: "numerous eye-catching M's and W's appear in *Finnegans Wake*, where, after all, *The Book of Kells* is brought into play less for its own sake than as a spectacular case

of another text hard to decipher, that is primarily as an autoreflective device" (78). In another article, Fuger sees ALP's letter as an "allegory of the ur-situation of writing" and as a display of "literature becoming aware of its own existence"—"'Epistlemadethemology' (374.17): ALP's Letter and the Tradition of Interpolated Letters," *James Joyce Quarterly* 19 (Summer 1982): 409, 412.

4. Giambattista Vico, *New Science*, trans. Thomas Goddard Bergin and Max Harold Fisch (Ithaca: Cornell University Press, 1988). Vico's book is a sprawling and intricate work where ideas accrete. It opens with his exegesis of the frontispiece, an engraving of divine illumination that contains written tablets and alphabetic inscription: he sees this image as a device upon which to reflect the mythology of the creation of the universe. His identification of prayer with language is perhaps clearest on 119, where he draws analogies between our first grunts and our divinatory powers. Throughout, Vico's thesis depends on the idea that language is innately divine, evolutionary, and self-replicating.

5. Jean-Michel Rabaté points out that the whole of *Finnegans Wake* opens up an "iconic space of writing, a space which entails a redefinition of reading and writing." He notes the presence of *Kells* as another system, like the sigla, that makes traditional reading problematic—"'Alphabettyformed verbage': The Shape of Sounds and Letters in *Finnegans Wake*," *Word and Image* 2 (July–September 1986): 239.

6. Vico, *New Science*, 14.

7. I am indebted here to Johanna Drucker's foundational study of the esoteric and religious traditions around the alphabet, *The Alphabetic Labyrinth: The Letters in History and Imagination* (London: Thames and Hudson, 1995).

8. In my use of etymologies I am following the precedent set by John Bishop in *Joyce's Book of the Dark: "Finnegans Wake"* (Madison: University of Wisconsin Press, 1986). Whenever possible I will try to give attribution to two remarkable books that have aided me in this work: Carl Darling Buck's *A Dictionary of Selected Synonyms in the Principal Indo-European Languages: A Contribution to the History of Ideas* (Chicago: University of Chicago Press, 1949) and Joseph T. Shipley's *The Origins of English Words: A Discursive Dictionary of Indo-European Roots* (Baltimore: Johns Hopkins University Press, 1984). And of course I must acknowledge the *Oxford English Dictionary*. The particular etymology of *man* is taken from Shipley, 229–88.

9. Shipley, *Origins of English Words*, 69.

10. Ibid., 305, 65.

11. My remark shadows the transformative scholarship of V. A. Kolve, to whom I am always indebted. His pioneering *Chaucer and the Imagery of Narrative: The First Five Canterbury Tales* (Stanford: Stanford University Press, 1984) draws on the entire Western tradition of the perception and interpretation of images and their influence on narrative.

12. See Roland McHugh, *Annotations to "Finnegans Wake,"* 3rd ed. (Baltimore: Johns Hopkins University Press, 2006).

13. Shipley, *Origins of English Words*, 311.

14. See Edward Sullivan, introduction to *The Book of Kells* (London: Studio Editions, 1986), 42, 37, 12.

15. See Etienne Rynne, "Drolleries in *The Book of Kells*," ed. Felicity O'Mahoney, in *The Book of Kells: Proceedings of a Conference at Trinity College Dublin, 6–9 September, 1992* (Scolar Press, 1994), 312.

16. See Carol Farr, "Textual Structure, Decoration, and Interpretive Images in *The Book of Kells*," in *Proceedings*, 349.

17. See Eamonn O Carragain, "'*Traditio evangeliorum*' and '*sustenatio*': The Relevance of Liturgical Ceremonies to the *Book of Kells*," in *Proceedings*, 400–403.

18. Shipley, *Origins of English Words*, 177, 349.

19. Ibid., 129.

20. Sullivan, introduction, 37.

6

Playful Reading

I.6 and Game Theory

SEAN LATHAM

Push Start to Begin

Finnegans Wake took shape around a game. The book itself, of course, did not begin this way: decades of scholarly work have successfully traced its genesis from a small series of unconnected sketches about Irish history written in 1923 through its gradual accretion around a central set of themes, characters, and plots.[1] For much of its early existence, however, Joyce kept the actual title a secret, publishing pieces of it either as "fragments from *Work in Progress*" or as small single volumes with bewildering titles like *Haveth Childers Everywhere*. This process marked a major departure from his strategy for *Ulysses*, which evolved in the pages of the *Little Review* around the resonant name of the Greek hero, giving the still incomplete text a sense of mythic unity. When it came to *Finnegans Wake*, however, Joyce turned the title into a game by dropping enigmatic hints and urging his friends to guess what he had in mind—a procedure that contributed to the sense of confused disappointment that accompanied its serial publication. This game lasted an amazing sixteen years, and like so much else during that period, the guesses offered by various players worked their way into the dense mosaic of the rapidly expanding drafts. Shortly after proposing to Harriet Shaw Weaver that she join in the game following a visit to England in 1927, for example, she responded with what would become the first of many incorrect guesses: "one squared" (*LettersI* 254).[2] In I.6, a chapter that I will argue is all about games, Joyce found a place for this response in one of the questions that encourages his readers to join in the contest as well: "Which title is the true-to-type motto-in-lieu" of the book itself, it asks, before offering a catalogue of incorrect responses including Weaver's own "Wohn Squarr Roomyeck" (139.29, .36).[3] Other guesses proliferated both inside and outside the book before Eugene Jolas actually divined the correct answer in 1938, "thereby winning a wager of 1000 frs" Joyce had "rashly made" (*LettersIII* 427). This guessing game, however, is more than just an amusing anecdote, since gaming as such offers us a new way to understand both I.6 and its larger contribution to the *Wake*. This pivotal chapter turns the book sharply away from the progressive development of plot and toward the emergent potential of play.

Joyce began I.6 in 1927 in an attempt to summarize his work in progress by using the by now familiar device of a catalogue to enumerate its basic narrative elements including character, setting, and plot.[4] The questions and answers in this chapter promise some vision of totality at a moment when Joyce himself seemed unsure about how to fit the pieces of the book together and when some of the strongest supporters of *Ulysses* began to question the wisdom of this new departure. In partial response to this confusion, he thus imagined the chapter as a bridge between two pieces that had already been written: the "mamafesta" (I.5) and "Shem the Penman" (I.7).[5] This chapter was not a narrative bridge, however, since to the degree that the *Wake* has a plot, I.6 clearly stands outside of it, functioning primarily as a kind of narrative caesura akin to the "Wandering Rocks" episode of *Ulysses*.[6] Instead, this section offers a catalogue of the book's central characters and events in a form that has been most often compared to a radio quiz show, oral examination, or questionnaire.

Seeming to address us directly as readers, it begins with a question: "So? Who do you no tonigh, lazy and gentleman?" (126.01–02). In a series of twelve sections the chapter then provides an overview of the book's central elements. HCE, ALP, the city of Dublin, Issy, and the patrons of the bar where a portion of the book is set all receive detailed—if perplexing—descriptions before the questions turn to more general themes such as the fall of man and the cyclic battle between the brothers and their father that drives so much of the book's imagery. In Joyce's drafts, notes, and letters, each of these questions is accompanied by a siglum, a shorthand symbol for each character and for the book itself. He resorted constantly to these sigla (though he called them "signs") as a kind of primitive programming language both in his own writing and in his growing defense of the book's complexity.[7] Like the titles of the Homeric chapters that have become affixed to episodes of *Ulysses*, however, these sigla did not appear in any of the published versions of the chapter. They are instead an extradiegetic addition to the text: a promise preserved in letters and drafts of an underlying structure that is not marked in the book itself. Despite the promise of order, synthesis, and summation, therefore, chapter I.6 ends up leaving us indeed uncertain about just who or what we "no tonigh" [know up to now/tonight].[8]

Failure, however, is often another word for modernism—another way of saying that *Finnegans Wake* at once invokes and rejects summation in order to critique the principles of narrative structure that underwrite the novel as a cultural form. The chapter's final line appears to suggest a last-ditch attempt at synthesis in the phrase "*Semus sumus,*" a strangely corrupted Latinate construction that suggests "we are all Shem" or perhaps "we are all the same" (168.14). Edmund Epstein, in a reading that aims to uncover a consistent structure running through the *Wake*, sees in this passage a moment of radical unification in which Shem and Shaun merge, a symbolic conjunction that aligns the book's vast textual polarities of time and space, mind and body, tree and stone.[9] This kind of grand synthesis, however, misses the point, since in I.6 Joyce's failed summation amounts to a rejection or at least a major reconceptualization of narrative as such. In this chapter, which includes Weaver's guess about the title and which is itself structured around games, quizzes, and other kinds of play, Joyce restructures the *Wake* around the tension between narratology and ludology. Put simply, he stops writing a novel and begins crafting a game. To understand the consequences of treating I.6 as a game, however, we first need to know something about recent developments in game theory as well as Joyce's other experiments with aspects of gaming and play in his earlier works. We will thus have to work our way through some preliminary levels as we learn to play our way through the chapter. These will help us understand how Joyce shifts in I.6 from progression to emergence, from reading to "chunking," from character and plot to affordance and constraint, and finally from fictional world to interactive gamespace.[10]

Tutorial: Joyce and Games

Unfortunately, we know relatively little about the games that Joyce and his children played, though games do figure prominently in his work, from the escapades of the boys in "An Encounter" to the horse race in *Ulysses*.[11] *A Portrait of the Artist as a Young Man*, in fact, begins with a series of games that shape Stephen's development as an artist. The book famously opens with the boy's aesthetic deformation of the "baby tuckoo" rhyme before moving quickly to the description of "wide playgrounds . . . swarming with boys" (*P* 8). The frail young man tries to avoid the rough play on the football pitch, but he excels at another kind of game awaiting him in the classroom: a math lesson cast as a contest between two teams freighted with symbolic names. These opening pages sharpen some of the deep contradictions that structure Stephen's identity, subtly queering his masculinity while at the same time offering a critique of the culture of rough manhood so deeply embedded in the period's elite private schools.[12] But this early vignette also opens up an important distinction between two very different kinds of games, what Jesper Juul calls "games of progression" and "games of emergence."[13] We'll look more closely at emergence in a moment, but put simply, this kind of play is distinguished by its openness and by a relatively simple set of rules that nevertheless lead to radically unpredictable outcomes. The game of football Stephen plays exemplifies this type. From a simple set of initial constraints—stay on a defined field and use any part of your body except your hands to move a ball toward a goal—an infinite set of possible outcomes emerges. The young Stephen, obsessed as he is with rules, order, and structure, thinks the game on the field "useless" in its chaos, and he tries instead to fix the meaning of words like *suck* and *queer* (*P* 11).

In the classroom, however, he clearly enjoys another type of game, the "progressive" match between the York and Lancaster teams. Unlike games of emergence, this sort of game has a single, predetermined path to victory. In this case, one team will win simply by knowing the correct answers to a series of mathematical sums. There is nothing particularly unpredictable about this kind of play, and its rigidity is of a piece with Stephen's larger attempt in this opening chapter to understand the world as a fixed, unchanging place. His famous list drawn on the flyleaf of his geography textbook exemplifies this desire, locating him securely in a divinely ordered space. His climactic trip to the rector's office further intensifies an obsession with strictly governed rules and rigidly predictable outcomes as he seeks relief from Father Dolan's unjust punishment. Stephen here treats justice itself as a kind of progressive game and understands himself as a victor, as his resolution to "not be anyway proud with Father Dolan" suggests (*P* 59). When Stephen emerges from the rector's office, however, he encounters his fellow students once again at play on fields, this time practicing cricket. Although they cheer Stephen's victory in his own game of progression, it is again juxtaposed (in a familiar Joycean chiasmus) with the pleasure they derive from the more open, more chaotic game of emergence. The text, in effect, ironically critiques Stephen's fascination with rules and structure at the expense of open play—a critique that returns even more powerfully in *Ulysses*.

Following Stephen through the early hours of his day, "Nestor" replays the schoolroom scenes from the first chapter of *A Portrait*, this time emphasizing even more clearly the distinction between progression and emergence. Now a teacher, Stephen tries to help Cyril Sargent with his mathematics, sadly realizing that the boy understands the work precisely as a game of progression in which all he has to do is correctly copy out the sums. "Like him was I," Stephen sententiously thinks, "these sloping shoulders, this gracelessness. My childhood bends beside me" (*U* 2.168–69). In a direct echo of *A Portrait*, this strict adherence to rules is juxtaposed with the freedom on the cricket fields, where "sharp voices were in strife" amid the game's uncertain outcome (*U* 2.185). While listening later to Deasy's awful lecture, the game remains present: "From the playfield the boys raised a shout. A whirring whistle: goal" (*U* 2.378). Stephen calls this noise his "God," a "shout in the street" that echoes from the boys' emergent, unpredictable play (*U* 2.386). Here it now evokes clearly a kind of pleasure and unpredictability that stands in stark contrast to the school's rigid rules and Deasy's racist Unionism. By returning to the closing of *A Portrait* and recasting the game Stephen once feared as a site of creative potential, it also points the way toward the importance of such emergent play in *Finnegans Wake*.

As we have seen, the third question of I.6 is structured around the riddling game with the book's title that Joyce played with his friends. Yet it also asks about Dublin's city motto, the response—"Thine obesity, O civilian, hits the felicitude of our orb!"—echoing the actual motto, "Citizens' Obedience is Citizens' Happiness" (140.06–07). The answer to the riddle of the book's title, in other words, points back to the city and through it to Joyce's first published work, *Dubliners*. The question then encodes a number of unexpected allusions to those first stories, especially those built around games. "Which title," it begins, "is the true-to-type motto-in-lieu for that Tick for Teac thatchment painted witt wheth one darkness, where asnake is under clover and birds aprowl are in the rookeries and a magda went to monikshouse?" (139.29–32). The boys in "An Encounter" make a playful journey to see the "Pigeon House," a rookery where the "queer old josser" does indeed seem to be a snake prowling through the clover. And there is an allusion in "magda" to Maria, whose trip from a Magdalen laundry to her brother's house leads to monkey business in the garden. In question three, indeed in I.6 more generally, Joyce casts the *Wake* as a game to be played by the reader, but not a progressive one in which a particular meaning or outcome can be predicted in advance. Instead, Joyce reiterates here the transition that Stephen makes in *A Portrait*: from the rule-bound young man who demands a fixed outcome, to those thundering boys on the pitch in whose shouts he hears the voice of God. As a result, the chapter itself becomes a game of emergence in which small pieces or fragments—like these subtle allusions to *Dubliners*—interact to produce unpredictable outcomes. Such interactions are an essential element of gaming theory, and we can now advance to the next level to see how they operate elsewhere in I.6.

Level One: Chunking

As the very structure of this collection suggests, *Finnegans Wake* is typically treated as a book in pieces, the long debate over its critical history testifying to a general uncertainty about the most effective level of analysis. Indeed, aside from the Bible, perhaps no other work opens itself to readings that can proceed with equal validity by creating, at one end of the spectrum, a mosaic of local phrases drawn from across the book and, at the other end, a totalizing narrative synthesis.[14] As compelling as the promises of unity and coherence might be in works like Campbell and Robinson's *A Skeleton's Key to "Finnegans Wake,"* Gordon's *"Finnegans Wake": A Plot Summary*, and Epstein's *A Guide through "Finnegans Wake,"* it just doesn't make sense to think about the text as somehow primarily about a plot, a cast of characters, or a setting.[15] As Beckett famously put it in his preemptive defense of *Work in Progress*, such "writing is not about something. *It is that something itself.*" Comparing it implicitly to a larger set of avant-garde practices, he argued that the book "is not written at all. It is not to be read. It is to be looked at and listened to."[16] To this list, I want simply to add that it is also to be played: thus one of the first things we must do is decide how the data of the text itself will be sorted, organized, and structured into meaningful units. Though a strange process for reading, this mode of encounter and play has become quite familiar to us in a digital age as we negotiate fragments of data, often supercharged with meaning, that we constantly sort, arrange, and rearrange.[17]

As Lev Manovich argues in *The Language of New Media*, there are a number of striking connections between the avant-garde practices of collage and the digital interfaces we now use to interact with the abstractions of machine-readable data. "New media" objects, he contends, "are rarely created completely from scratch; usually they are assembled from ready-made parts. Put differently, in a computer culture, authentic creation has been replaced by selection from a menu."[18] Digital creation emerges between a set of scripted actions, on the one hand, and a set of transformable, recombinant objects (iterated lines of code, captured images, tables of data), on the other. Digital games, in particular, typically involve players combining procedural actions (a trigger pull, a button click, etc.) with data that has been rendered in abstract ways (as a gun barrel, a door, a monster, or an angry bird). I.6 plays so important a role in *Finnegans Wake*, in large part, because it provides readers with what amounts to a list of the book's core data—what programmers might call an "object library"—on which the book's various processes then operate. Joyce's sigla thus become even more similar to computer code: persistent pieces of data that can be constantly recombined, rewritten, and recirculated. Readers or players of the text succeed by exploring the ways in which they can interact with this data by shaping it into more or less successful interpretive configurations. As a result, the idea of progression and linearity we find in the work of critics like Gordon and Epstein always seems unsatisfactory, becoming more like the sums Cyril Sargent performs than the shout Stephen hears from the fields. Such approaches imagined the text as a fixed, progressive object rather than as an interactive, emergent collection of data. By offering us a look at the book's basic "object library" in its twelve questions, I.6 does not finally offer the kind of synthetic summary Joyce initially imagined. Instead, it models the unpredictable qualities of an emergent game.

To understand how this works, we can look at the ninth question, which Joyce encoded in his drafts with the siglum of a cross enclosed within a circle. For Clive Hart, this particular symbol becomes the centerpiece of the book as a whole, since its "cross of quaternity" condenses so much of Joyce's larger plan in a single image. The four quadrants it creates, he argues, mirror the four parts of *Finnegans Wake*, while the circle itself becomes "the Wheel of Fortune" around which the Viconian cycle of the entire book moves.[19] For Hart, this deep structure appears in the text of the ninth question as well, which asks what a tired suburban reader ("a human being duly fatigued by his dayety in the sooty" [143.04–05]) might make of the *Wake*. In this question, the book appears initially as a telescope that promises to bring the fuzziness of some distantly glimpsed object into clear view. The reader thus becomes a "fargazer" who looks through the glass "with an earsighted view of old hopinhaven" (143.09–10). Like the ordered chain the young Stephen scribbled in his geography book, this figure hopes for a glimpse of heaven and thus some certainty about "the course of his tory" as seen from a single, godlike gaze, what the book calls "the reconjungation of nodebinding ayes" (143.12–14). Object and process, in other words, data and program, appear to become unified in a single eschatological moment where history and all its contradictions coalesce into the numinous mandala Hart identifies. In peering into this "eye of a noodle," in effect, the question invokes a reader who hopes, despite the difficulty of passing through the eye of a needle, to enter into the heaven of a transcendent, telescopic gaze capable of bringing order to the book and its worlds (143.09).

The problem, however, is that this tired reader has grabbed a toy rather than a tool and is thus playing a game. He has picked up a kaleidoscope in which the stability of a single, unified gaze gives way to a pleasurably chaotic recombination of shapes, all bounding and tumbling into unpredictable forms with each turn of the barrel. "Ah how starring!" the "fargazer" gasps, after the cylinder twists and "byhold at ones what is main and why tis twain, how one once meet melts in tother wants poignings" (143.17–26). The course of history—and with it the narrative shape of the book—gives way to a tumble of objects, in which individual pieces suddenly combine into new patterns that stun the viewer. The famous answer to this ninth question calls this toy a "collideorscape," and for many critics this has become a metaphor for the *Wake* itself: a poststructural figure for instability that can never resolve into a single, fixed meaning (143.28). The image within the glass, however, is not entirely chaotic since, as with any kaleidoscope, there are only a fixed number of objects that can actually be recombined. In this passage, for example, Shem, Shaun, and Issy seem to be tumbling about in their father's gaze: "the foles [foals, or children] falling, the nimb now nihilant round the girlyhead so becoming, the wrestless in the womb" (143.19–21). The toy chaotically creates and destroys worlds and people as it turns. As in the *Wake* more generally, however, there is a kind of conservation of plot, setting, and character in which nothing is lost and the same atomistic objects—Shem, Shaun, and Issy in this case—are simply reconfigured in different ways. Thus "Heng's got a bit of Horsa's nose and Jeff's got the signs of Ham round his mouth" before everything tumbles once more (143.22–24).

We can detect the patterns of the brothers and their sister in this passage, because by this point the book has been twisting and turning them through a variety of different plots and passages. As with any kaleidoscope—indeed, with any emergent game—we begin to see patterns and repetitions, familiar shapes and moves that in I.6 materialize in the "object table" from which Joyce consistently draws. In this sense, reading *Finnegans Wake* requires a very specific kind of cognitive activity often associated with gameplay (and other kinds of complex information processing) called "chunking." Put simply, this is a process in which an experienced player combines small elements of a closed system into patterns or objects—chunks—that can be processed more quickly. Here is how Newell and Rosenbloom describe "chunking" as it works in a game of chess: "The master has acquired an immense memory for chess positions, organized as a collection of chunks. His ability for immediate perception and short-term memory of chess positions depends directly on how many chunks are used to encode a position. . . . By implication, master players must spend an immense amount of time within the game, in order to acquire the large number of chunks."[20] Similarly, computer programming depends upon the ability to combine lines of code into chunks or composite objects that can then be assembled and reassembled at a higher level.[21] Something similar happens in the *Wake*. Like chess masters, readers who become familiar with the text learn to assemble chunks of their own that enable them to play more and more skillfully with the text, recognizing, for example, the importance of the letters HCE (even when in different order or when scattered across or between different words). For an adept player of the *Wake*, in other words, the text resolves into something other than a chaotic jumble of words and letters, becoming instead an intricate array of informational chunks that recombine in shifting patterns as the "collideorscape" turns. Thus we see in Heng and Horsa not just an attenuated set of allusions to the sons of Noah and the brothers Hengest and Horsa who led the Saxon invasion of England, but chunks of information about brothers that become part of a more general game being played around (and here even by) Shem and Shaun.

Chunking allows us to link elements of the ninth question to the book as a whole, a move exemplified in the work of readers like Epstein and Hart who argue for this passage's importance. Whereas Hart builds his play through the text around the mandala, Epstein turns instead to the importance of character. He sees in the "fargazer" the figure of "HCE, the Scandanavian fallen sinner who also hopes for his own salvation. He is also the original Adam of the Kabbalah, Adam Kadmon, the gigantic being who was originally coterminus with the universe but 'fell' until he was the size of a man."[22] Here we see a critical chunk actually taking shape, as Epstein becomes less a reader than a player of the *Wake*, linking its smaller elements into larger units that include character, plot, and action. And just as this question invites the process of chunking by invoking the kaleidoscope at the level of the word or sentence, so too does I.6 more generally model this operation at the level of the book. In these twelve questions, after all, Joyce presents the major units of his own work: the object table or programming menu from which he consistently draws the elements upon which his own playful processes go to work. The sigla attached to each question often appear literally in Joyce's drafts and letters as programming tokens—fixed data points that can be joined, recombined, and operated on in a variety of ways, but which nevertheless retain a kind of fixed legibility. The questions of I.6 thus chunk the *Wake* into units, but like the "fargazer" in the ninth question we remain "hapless behind the dreams of accuracy" because simply chunking the book into its pieces is a dull exercise (143.06–07). "Those old diligences," the book reminds us at the end of this chapter, "are quite out of date" (167.26). This diligent and outmoded process is akin to reading the summary of a game of chess rather than actually playing it ourselves. Indeed, when seen merely as chunks, as objects in a table, or entries in a database, the elements of the *Wake* (much like the plot of *Ulysses*) are simply not that interesting: there are belligerent brothers, a befuddled father, a deeply conflicted mother, and a giggling girl, all rising or falling through time and space. This is the stuff of novels, and it is also the stuff Joyce leaves behind, turning his attention from these constitutive elements to the ways in which they can be playfully recombined within a larger interactive system. Understanding why *Finnegans Wake* might be a game rather than just a collection of chunks thus requires us to advance another level. So we'll turn now from the chapter's object library to the dynamic affordances of its rules.

Level Two: Affordance

Theorists have long debated the precise nature of games, and though no single definition exists, there is general agreement that they depend upon a set of fixed and mutually agreed upon rules. This kind of agreement creates what Katie Salen and Eric Zimmerman call the "magic circle" of gamespace, "a shorthand for the idea of a special place in time and space created by the game."[23] Entering such a space requires players to accept arbitrary, often intense constraints on their actions in exchange for the pleasure of gaming. Thus we agree, for example, not to touch a soccer ball with our hands and to stop playing when the ball leaves the field of play. The pleasure of games, in many ways, depends precisely upon the ability of the players to adapt themselves to a highly artificial set of rules, discovering new possibilities for expression within them. The ban against touching a soccer ball, to continue this example, opens up the potential for a player to use her head or the outside of a perfectly positioned foot to make a stylish pass. For the designers and theorists of video games, the artificial impositions of the magic circle are constantly in focus because the rules they encode in programs are themselves governed by the specific tolerances of the hardware and software used to fashion a virtual environment. The system imposes constraints on both the creator and the player so that creativity itself becomes less a Romantic act of pure imaginative invention than a set of dynamic responses to a fixed set of initial rules. Game design, in other words, is as much about constraint as freedom—about discovering the potential for new meaning emerging from the interaction between fixed rules and items listed in an object table.

We will look more closely at emergence in the next section, but first we need to consider the way constraint works in *Finnegans Wake*. Rules and constraints do not necessarily foreclose the possibility of meaningful action or invention; instead, they invite us to discover what the psychologist James Gibson first called the "affordances" of closed systems.[24] Put simply, the "magic circle" created by a set of rules invites us to experiment with the world those rules construct, discovering new possibilities of combination and interaction within a set of constraints. Crucially, such constraints are not simply prescriptive, and thus they create systems that are not predictable. Consider, for example, a video game like *Tetris*, which severely restricts a player's actions: all one can do is rotate six shapes as they appear on the screen. The possible outcomes for any given iteration of the game, however, quickly seem endless as players imagine ever more innovative configurations of very basic geometry. This interplay between constraint and creativity is a crucial component of almost all games, and so it should come as no surprise that Joyce employs it deliberately in I.6.

"And how war yore maggies?" the eighth question asks, in a passage that alludes to an important textual chunk—Issy and the twenty-eight girls who sometimes attend her (142.30). The answer that unfolds is itself a game, or rather a pair of word games that evoke the kind of procedural creativity later developed by the Oulipo group.[25] The first of these emerges in a chain of words in which an adjective at the end of each clause become the verb in the next clause: "They war loving, they love laughing, they laugh weeping, they weep smelling, they smell smiling, they smile hating, they hate thinking, they think feeling, they feel tempting, they tempt daring, they dare waiting, they wait taking, they take thanking, they thank seeking" (142.31–35). The initial part of the answer is thus generated within the narrow affordances of a rule that allows some scope for creativity while nevertheless tightly constraining the possible response. This initial game stretches through fourteen iterations, in which the rules of the game iteratively transform a passive emotional experience into an active engagement with the world. Caught within this game, the girls themselves nevertheless exhibit a wide array of experiences, encompassing love, war, laughter, and thought. The game, in other words, imposes severe restrictions on the text Joyce writes as well as on the characters he fashions, yet a number of creative possibilities for the *Wake* and for the maggies nevertheless emerge. After fourteen rounds of this game, the rules shift and a new, even more restrictive set of constraints are imposed. Modeled on the word ladder game created by Lewis Carroll, each significant word in the sentence now varies by only one letter from the one just before it: "as born for lorn in lore of love to live and wive by wile and rile by rule of ruse 'reathed rose and hose hol'd home" (142.35–143.01). In one sense, this narrowed set of constraints signifies the diminished possibilities for expression the maggies experience as they move from the playfulness of their girlhood to the "hol'd home" of marriage. Formally and thematically, however, the game also emphasizes the importance of improvisation within such constraints, of discovering the affordances of language and marriage alike. Wile and ruse here become strategic modes of play, and the game radically expands when the girls discover a new affordance in the "elope year"—the folkloric practice that gives women the chance to ask men to marry them in a leap year (143.01). In the eighth question, the text as well as its characters become enfolded within a strict set of procedural rules, the marriage plot here unfolding in the same constrained way as the word ladders. Despite their severity, however, these restrictions become the very condition of creativity itself as the rules create a magic circle within the text where the maggies and the reader both can play.

Joyce's experimentation with affordance and constraint—in the generation of text by rule and procedure—is not entirely unique to the *Wake*. Each of the more distinct technics in *Ulysses*, after all, imposes on the writing a series of restrictions, a set of rules within which Joyce then unfolds the events of his fictional world. Thus "Ithaca," for example, explores the expressive potential of the religious catechism while "Sirens" represents Bloom's imagination within the highly restrictive constraints of a *fuga per canonem*. In I.6, however, and particularly in the eighth question, Joyce pursues the consequences of a kind of writing to its extreme by formally incorporating an actual set of games into the text. The characters, the readers, and here even the book itself all remain within a strictly confined magic circle that nevertheless affords numerous creative possibilities. The word chain and word ladder in question 8, therefore, point neither to some deep structure that might be unlocked by a skeleton key nor to the chaos Ezra Pound and others lamented.[26] Instead, they model a game in which narrative fragments are chunked, tested, and reassembled within a set of tight constraints. In advancing to the next level, we'll see how these basic ludic elements contribute to a more general exploration of emergent play in the heavily revised opening of I.6.

Level Three: Emergence

The concept of emergence now has many definitions that extend across fields as diverse as economics, biology, and computer science. Put simply, it describes the patterned yet mathematically unpredictable behaviors that arise from the interaction of elements within a closed system. Like the games of soccer and *Tetris* I have already used as examples, such interactions involve cascading arrays of feedback loops in which very simple rules and objects interact to form increasingly complex outcomes. Crucially, these outcomes are not inherent within any one object or rule and thus only appear (or "emerge") relationally. Here is how N. Katherine Hayles defines the concept in *My Mother Was a Computer*: emergence "is any behavior or property that cannot be found in either a system's individual components or their additive properties, but that arises, often unpredictably, from the *interaction* of a system's components."[27] For Hayles, perhaps our most acute theorist of hypertext fiction, emergence explains the way meaningful patterns develop in contemporary digital literature from the interaction of mobile pieces of text that flicker in and out of existence on a reader's screen. As a literary critical term, emergence describes what Bruce Clarke and Mark Hansen call "the openness-from-closure principle of autopoietic systems"—the unique ability of a closed, rule-bound system to produce a staggering array of different and shifting meanings from the varied interplay of its fixed parts.[28]

As we have already seen, I.6 chunks *Finnegans Wake* into a series of interactive elements that invite and even model the transformation of the text from a book or a novel into a game. In the first question, in particular, what begins as an attempted summation of character quickly gives way to an extended experiment with emergence. As genetic critics have noted, this section of the chapter expanded significantly over the course of Joyce's major revisions, growing from a very short description of HCE in the original 1927 draft to the massive catalogue that grew to astonishing length in 1936.[29] The question's single sentence is essentially unreadable, since its hundreds of independent clauses unfold without subordination or conjunction. It is "a dud letter, a sing a song a sylble; a byword, a sentence with surcease" (129.07–08). This final word captures the dilemma of the entire question, since its ability to describe a single character constantly increases yet constantly stops or ceases in the catalogue of stuttering clauses that unfold around HCE. This chaos initially appears at odds with HCE himself, who is first described as a figure of law, measurement, and control. He is compared to Napoleon, Muhammad, King Arthur, and even Lord Harmsworth, all figures of order, innovation, and control. He "towers, an eddistoon amid the lampless, casting swannbeams on the deep" (127.15–16), promising like Edison or the Eddystone lighthouse to illuminate an otherwise opaque text. As the question unfolds, he becomes closely associated with engineers, builders, and prophets, even becoming a sturdy wall that "forbids us our trespassers as we forgate him" (128.34).

Despite its allusive pleasures, however, this passage also presents a challenge to any reader who might want to compile a single, coherent portrait of HCE. No amount of what question 7 calls "retroratiocination" can resolve this textual Humpty Dumpty (142.17–18). Indeed, the question emphasizes the tension between part and whole, between "Allthing" (everything) and "Eachovos" (each of us), noting that "as far as wind dries and rain eats and sun turns and water bounds he is exalted and depressed, assembled and asundered" (133.35, 136.05–07). The question, in effect, constantly takes HCE apart, puts him together, then takes him apart again in its relentless procession of clauses. Even the brief final answer fails to resolve this problem, since "Finn MacCool" too is only one more temporary assemblage among others (139.14). Unlike the Homeric myth at work in *Ulysses*, there is no shelter here from what Eliot infamously called the "immense panorama of futility and anarchy which is contemporary history."[30] The Irish hero evoked in the answer possessed the magical ability to perceive all things and all time and "could see at one blick a saumon taken with a lance, hunters pursuing a doe, a swallowship in full sail, a whyterobe lifting a host" (139.02–04). This is the same "fargazer" we'll later encounter in the kaleidoscope section, where we discover that there is no transcendent perception, since the barrel can be turned and the pieces rearranged. It is the gaze not of a player who looks for affordances, ruse, and strategies but of the totalizing novelist, imagined here as "that Shedlock Homes person who is out for removing the roofs of our criminal classics," an allusion to Doyle's detective who expressed exactly this desire to peer down into houses and thereby organize all of London within the inescapable logic of his "*deductio ad domunum*" (165.32–34). Taken as a whole, this opening question simultaneously invokes and demolishes the clear resolution of character while reneging on the promise of some deep, mythic order.

This lack of structure, however, can be resolved in a different way if we turn from narratology to ludology, from the "dud letter" of the novel to the emergent potential of the game. As in any emergent system, dynamic interaction becomes more important than a single, static state. Thus rather than understanding this question as a description of HCE or a simple catalogue of his parts, we might instead understand it as another of the *Wake*'s object tables, a collection of units that we chunk according to our own itinerary through the text. He is thus indeed "assembled and assundered" by the operations that readers perform; he himself becomes a game we play. And very early in the passage, in fact, we find a cluster of games that associate HCE with play: "after a good bout at stoolball [he] enjoys Giroflee Giroflaa; what Nevermore missed and Colombo found; believes in every man his own goaldkeeper and in Africa for the fullblacks; the arc of his drive was forty full and his stumps were pulled at eighty" (129.29–33). In one sense, this is just another accretive element in the catalogue as the question for a moment veers into a list of games that includes rugby, soccer, cricket, and even, according to McHugh, a singing game.[31] But these games are themselves part of the emergent play within this question, a question in which individual elements combine unpredictably to produce emergence rather than meaning. Just a few lines above, after all, the book appears to describe both itself and HCE as an object "variously catalogued, regularly regrouped" (129.12). HCE and the question that sets out to inquire about him at the beginning of I.6 both become games—complex systems of interactive elements put in motion within the constraints of a printed text. As players rather than readers, we therefore find ourselves in an emergent system, struggling to catalogue and regroup the elements we encounter, becoming what a later passage calls "latecomers all the year's round by anticipation" (142.16–17), who engage this complex system without the totalizing promise of a key, a schema, or that "*deductio ad domunum*."

Games appear elsewhere in this question as well, returning to emphasize the hazards of chance that define the interactions of an emergent system. Thus sports like rugby give way to gambling as HCE "laid out lashings of laveries [a £1 note] to hunt down his family ancestors and then pled double trouble or quick quits to hush the buckers up" (134.02–04). There is neither certainty nor stability in this gamble on double or quits, only a shifting set of odds on a particular outcome. HCE doesn't resolve into a single figure; instead, we have to weigh his various elements one against another, betting critically on a particular outcome, knowing all the time that the text's constraints afford other portraits, other configurations of this dynamic, interactive figure. The pun on *played* and *pled* in this passage deftly emphasizes the complexity of the situation. Caught in an emergent game, the reader plays while pleading for relief from the interaction of the clauses and their multivariant meanings that afford far too many HCEs to make the idea of character practical. In response, this passage offers nothing like resolution, but only a set of odds—"tre to uno tips the scale"—based on the next turn of the card: "ace of arts, deuce of damimonds, trouble of clubs, fear of spates" (134.09, .07–08). The punning exchange of *pled* and *played* thus suggests that Joyce himself has doubled down on the *Wake* by transforming what began as an attempt at summation into an emergent, interactive game.

Boss Fight

Throughout the three levels of this essay, I have examined the ways in which aspects of the critical and theoretical work developed around ludic theory provide a new framework for thinking about I.6 as an experiment in emergent gaming. This pivotal chapter of the *Wake* is organized around chunks of data that work like objects in a programming table, and the reader then uses them to construct an unfolding array of interactive combinations. These pieces are, in turn, governed by the constraints of the text itself, by procedures for generating meaning that sometimes even appear in the diegetic world itself, as in the word ladders and chains in question 8. Constraints, however, create affordances—new possibilities for amalgamation shaped by rule and procedure. The textual objects of I.6 thus do not resolve into a fixed pattern of either plot or symbol, but instead open up the possibility of emergent meaning. Interactions between individual pieces on the pages produce levels of meaning that have to be played rather than read. Few games, however, are purely emergent, and despite the possibilities for the radical dissolution of plot and character exemplified in the catalogue that explodes across question 1, other kinds of structures assert themselves—as the often brilliant work of critics like Epstein and Gordon make clear. Despite its playful structure, in other words, the *Wake* is finally caught between the ludology and narratology, between narrative and game. Like so many other oppositions that appear in the book, this one too can be mapped onto the agonistic battle between Shem and Shaun. Seen this way, the eleventh question—in length and complexity a companion to the first—becomes at once the chapter's climax and a kind of boss fight. It ends Joyce's initial attempt at summarizing the *Wake*'s key features by inviting us to consider the book as a contest between reading and play, between fiction and rule.

Possible worlds theory, which has itself been profitably examined as a tool for exploring the *Wake*, contends that there is a basic distinction between the way a fictional world is described and the actual world we imagine.[32] No matter how lengthy or how detailed Flaubert's narrative account of a shop window might be, for example, it nevertheless remains incomplete, opening up a space that we as readers rush to fill in with details. *Ulysses*, at times, is particularly eager to close this gap between real and possible worlds, as when Joyce labored over "Wandering Rocks" with stopwatch, map, and *Thom's Directory* to lay out the movement of his characters across 1904 Dublin. Even here, however, the world fashioned in the text is incomplete, and so we complete it ourselves, filling in the blanks imaginatively. (And on Bloomsday we do this work literally, laying the book back across the modern city.) The imaginative work involved in completing a fictional world depends upon the principle of coherence or what Marie-Laure Ryan calls "the principle of minimal departure."[33] Thus we might well imagine in the Dublin of *Ulysses* some dusty velvet curtains hung in the window above Sweney's, but we don't imagine Bloom startled by a backfiring car or dodging laser beams fired by aliens. Such events depart too sharply from the world evoked in Joyce's text, though they might well be perfectly coherent within some other fictional world. In the *Wake*, however, this principle of coherence or minimal departure breaks down since—as we saw in the first question—anything might seemingly appear.

Although fictional worlds generally depend upon coherence, games do not, since the rules governing them always impose artificial constraints that typically cannot be explained within the fiction itself.[34] As Juul argues, incoherence arises because games depend upon rules and thus are never quite alternative possible worlds in themselves. This is particularly true of video games, where the unique constraints of the system—be it a joystick, keyboard, or graphical engine—insist on the tension between rules and fiction: "This means that when we find it too hard to imagine a video game fiction, we can resort to explaining the events in the game by appealing to the rules.... If the effort required to fill in a blank in the game world becomes too big, we have to resort to a rule-oriented explanation." The fiction can only unfold within a particular set of rules, and thus the game's emergent, unpredictable possibilities are constricted, its world always balanced between coherence and constraint. Juul thus argues that rather than thinking of the game as a coherent world, "we could call this type of fictional world an *incoherent world*, meaning that there are many events in the fictional world that we cannot explain without discussing the game rules"[35] I.6, I now want to conclude, can best be understood precisely as an incoherent world in which the climactic struggle between the two brothers in the eleventh question models the larger tension in the text between fiction and rule.

Understood simply, Shem functions in this section of the book as a figure for writing, fiction, and creativity, a role that the next chapter explores at length in its famous description of the "Haunted Inkbottle" with its "imeffible tries at speech unasyllabled" (182.31, 183.14–15). Shaun, on the other hand, defends the importance of logic, constraint, rule, and orthodoxy, becoming the young Stephen of *A Portrait* who detests the soccer pitch. In the Mookse and Gripes parable, for example, the Shaun-like Mookse gathers together the rules of language, law, and logic to offer a "widerproof" of his superiority: "I have now successfully explained to you my own naturalborn rations," he concludes, the final word here punning on *ratio*, the Greek term for reason, which has been rationed out generously to Shaun (155.29, 159.24–25). This attempt to measure the Mookse against the Gripes forms part of a larger motif in the chapter that links Shem to chaotic creativity and Shaun to religious orthodoxy. Thus Shaun briefly becomes the "dogmad Accanite," a phrase that evokes a dogmatic understanding of the universe, in which all questions can be answered by reference to rules (158.03). Shem, on the other hand, is a "dubliboused Catalick," a drunk (boozed) or dubious Catholic who throughout this section is associated with a whole range of heretics (158.04). And as Shaun's increasingly hostile response to a request for help reaches its end, he grows pathologically insistent on the stability and fixity of rule-governed space. "My unchanging Word is sacred," he exclaims, as he tries to stabilize words and worlds simultaneously, insisting on preserving "the rite words by the rote order" (167.28, .33).

When measured against the playfulness of language in the *Wake* as a whole, of course, it is easy to dismiss Shaun in this question as a mere caricature, particularly since his furious tantrum in the eleventh question is immediately followed by the extraordinary portrait of Shem's creativity in I.7. When we see I.6 as a game rather than a text, however, Shaun becomes not just an agent of oppression or another of Joyce's pilloried critics[36] but instead the necessary constraint that makes play possible. From "the bowels of his misery," Shem unfolds "the continuous present tense integument" of a coherent possible world, his writing "slowly unfold[ing] all marryvoising moodmoulded cyclewheeling history" (185.33–186.02). This extraordinary image of fictional totality from I.7 might well describe *Ulysses*, which that same chapter calls the "usylessly unreadable Blue Book of Eccles," its fictional world so coherent, so extensive that we can still walk Dublin's streets imagining ourselves in the very shoes and footsteps of Bloom or Stephen

(179.26–27). To my knowledge, however, there is no day dedicated to HCE and certainly no attempt to reenact the events of the *Wake* in a Chapelizod pub. This is because *Finnegans Wake* is less a book that points to the world than a game we readers play. The counterpart to the Bloomsday reenactment of *Ulysses*, after all, is the *Wake* reading group in which we gather to play the text with one another. Between the two of them, the brothers Shem and Shaun create the magic circle in which play occurs: the former creating a fictional world, the latter insisting endlessly on the rules that constrain it. Thus they fashion here at the climax of I.6 not the coherent totality of *Ulysses* but the incoherent fictional world of a game.

Save or Quit?

When Joyce pauses in I.6 to provide an overview of *Finnegans Wake*, he steps back from the novel as coherent possible world in order to focus instead on the affordances of a writing that operates between Shem and Shaun, between rule and world, between the logocentric and the ludocentric. The *Wake*, in this sense, does not contain all of "cyclewheeling history" as Shem might imagine, nor can it be reduced to a fixed set of characters and events as Shaun might wish. As Nuvoletta realizes at the moment the Mookse and the Gripes descend into pointless argument in I.6, "The Mookse had a sound eyes right but he could not all hear. The Gripes had light ears left yet he could but ill see" (158.12–13). Each is incomplete without the other, but they do not simply resolve into some more complete whole. Instead, between them they create any number of emergent possibilities in what Nuvoletta calls "the waste of all peaceable worlds" (158.09–10). Rather than Candide's best of all possible worlds, I.6 offers instead a vision of game worlds created and destroyed, their pieces reshuffled and rearranged in the "collideorscape"—here literally in an act of play that Issy observes while looking down on her feuding brothers. Video games, Juul argues, can only ever be "half real"; caught as they are between rule and fiction, their uniquely emergent potential is always dependent upon the narrow constraints of the magic circle in which they are played. In these games "the incoherence of the fictional world is less likely to be experienced as a problem" because "breaking the coherence of the fictional world does not so much foreground the way a game projects a fictional world as it foregrounds the rules, the game as an activity."[37] This is simply another way of reiterating Beckett's claim that *Finnegans Wake* "is not about something. It is that something itself." And that something, it turns out, is a game that we play collectively and in groups.

The playthrough I've offered in this one chapter, of course, is simply that—one emergent possibility selected from the others and developed within the affordances and constraints of the game called *Finnegans Wake* I.6. Media critics from Marshall McLuhan through Donald Theall and Lydia Liu have argued that the *Wake* is a kind of machine, what Derrida famously called a "1000th generation computer."[38] I have tried to argue, however, that Joyce was less the engineer he once claimed to be and more of a game designer, one uncannily aware of the balance between ludology and narratology, between constraint and creation. From his earliest writings through his mature works, he explores thematically and even stylistically the importance of games as a creative medium, but only in his final work does he actually design a game of his own. In their first draft, the questions and answers of I.6 may have started as an attempt at summation that might satisfy readers looking to find the elements of a novel-like character and plot. In crafting this section of the book, however, Joyce transformed the *Wake* from a novel into a game, from a coherent fictional world into an incoherent one that churns between Shem and Shaun. The game can be played again and again, the kaleidoscope turned so its pieces are rearranged. And with each playthrough—a term I hope you now find more feasible than "interpretation" or "reading"—you must simply decide if you wish to save or quit: to preserve a particularly rich or skillful result, or to test again the affordances and emergent potential of *Finnegans Wake*.

Notes

1. For a concise description of the *Wake*'s development, see the introduction to *How Joyce Wrote "Finnegans Wake": A Chapter-by-Chapter Genetic Guide*, ed. Luca Crispi and Sam Slote (Madison: University of Wisconsin Press, 2007), 3–48.

2. In his letters and drafts, Joyce used the siglum of a square to represent the book's title.

3. This answer encodes not only Weaver's incorrect guess about the book's title but also one of Joyce's Parisian addresses: 2 Sq. Robbiac.

4. The catalogue became an important stylistic element of the latter stages of *Ulysses*, evident in the interpolations of "Cyclops" and the lengthy lists (of objects, money, and places) that appear in "Ithaca."

5. In July 1927, Joyce wrote to Weaver, "I am working day and night at a piece I have to insert between the last and [the siglum for Shem]. It must be ready by Friday evening. I have never worked against time before. It is very racking" (*LettersIII* 163). For a more detailed genetic account of this chapter's evolution, see R. J. Schork, "Genetic Primer: Chapter I.6," in *How Joyce Wrote "Finnegans Wake."*

6. Danis Rose, *The Textual Diaries of James Joyce* (Dublin: Lilliput Press, 1995), takes similar note of the chapter's summative quality, contending that despite its fascination, it "does not add anything to the narrative," 104.

7. Joyce provides a full list of the sigla in a letter to Harriet Shaw Weaver written on March 24, 1924, revealing that these figures were present at the book's earliest compositional stages (*LettersI* 213). For further evidence of how important the sigla are, see also a letter written in 1926 (*LettersI* 242). For a now central critical discussion of these marks, see Roland McHugh, *The Sigla of "Finnegans Wake"* (Austin: University of Texas Press, 1976), a study which actually coined the term *sigla* to describe these marks.

8. Many critics have seen I.6 as an essential structural pivot in the *Wake*, since the list of sigla appended to each question offer something like the schemas now regularly used to interpret *Ulysses*. See, for example, Robert-Jan Henkes and Erik Bindervoet, "Oversystematizing the *Wake*: The Quiz Chapter as the Key to a Potential Schema for *Finnegans Wake*," *Genetic Joyce Studies* 4 (2004). Online.

9. Edmund Epstein, *A Guide through "Finnegans Wake"* (Gainesville: University Press of Florida, 2010), 81–82.

10. I borrow this last term from McKenzie Wark, *Gamer Theory* (Cambridge: Harvard University Press, 2007), 1–25. This book offers a provocative theory of modernity as a kind of game: "Games are not representations of their world. They are more like allegories of a world made over as gamespace. They encode the abstract principles upon which decisions about the realness of this or that world are now decided" (21). As violence, governance, economics, and even narrative become mapped onto games, "play becomes everything to which it was once opposed. It is work, it is serious; it is morality, it is necessity" (12).

11. Frank Budgen writes that Joyce purchased a game called Labyrinth in Zurich, which "he played every evening for a time with his daughter Lucia," then used as a kind of model for the "Wandering Rocks" episode of *Ulysses*. See *James Joyce and the Making of "Ulysses"* (Bloomington: Indiana University Press, 1960), 123.

12. For a discussion of queered masculinity in *A Portrait*, see Joseph Valente, "Thrilled by His Touch: The Aestheticizing of Homosexual Panic in *A Portrait of the Artist as a Young Man*," in *Quare Joyce*, ed. Joseph Valente (Ann Arbor: University of Michigan Press, 1998), 47–76.

13. Jesper Juul, *Half-Real: Video Games between Real Rules and Fictional Worlds* (Cambridge: MIT Press, 2005), 69.

14. Finn Fordham has created a useful taxonomy of the different levels or types of interpretive approaches to the *Wake*. These include "structural, narrational, theoretical, inspirational, philological, genetic, and exegetical." See Finn Fordham, *Lots of Fun at Finnegans Wake: Unraveling Universals* (Oxford: Oxford University Press, 2007), 7. The totalizing critiques I describe here tend to emerge primarily as narrational or exegetical approaches.

15. See Joseph Campbell and Henry Morton Robinson, *A Skeleton Key to "Finnegans Wake"* (Novato, Calif.: New World Library, 2005), and John Gordon, *"Finnegans Wake": A Plot Summary* (Syracuse: Syracuse University Press, 1986).

16. Samuel Beckett, "Dante . . . Bruno. Vico . . . Joyce," in *Our Exagmination Round His Factification for Incamination of "Work in Progress,"* ed. Samuel Beckett et al. (London: Faber & Faber, 1972), 14.

17. Lydia Liu develops a fascinating reading of the *Wake* as a key text in the rise of information culture, arguing that its discrete chunks of data provided a testing ground for Claude Shannon's theory of information coding. See Lydia Liu, *The Freudian Robot: Digital Media and the Future of the Unconscious* (Chicago: University of Chicago Press, 2011). For Liu, the *Wake* becomes not only an exemplary avant-garde text but an exemplary digital text as well.

18. Lev Manovich, *The Language of New Media* (Cambridge: MIT Press, 2002), 124.

19. Clive Hart, *Structure and Motif in "Finnegans Wake"* (Evanston: Northwestern University Press, 1962), 77.

20. Allen Newell and Paul S. Rosenbloom, "Mechanisms of Skill Acquisition and the Law of Practice," in *Cognitive Skills and the Acquisition*, ed. John R. Anderson (Hillsdale: Erlbaum, 1981), 75.

21. Modern game programmers almost never begin from scratch, but instead work with languages, engines, and design environments in which significant operational chunks (like the rendering of a door or the physics of jumping) already exist and are simply called upon from a preconstructed library in order to assemble some larger world.

22. Epstein, *Guide*, 70.

23. Katie Salen and Eric Zimmerman, *Rules of Play: Game Design Fundamentals* (Cambridge: MIT Press, 2004), 95. Here is how they describe this concept: "the term is used . . . as short-hand for the idea of a special place in time and space created by a game. . . . As a closed circle, the space it circumscribes is enclosed and separate from the real world. As a marker of time, the magic circle is like a clock: it simultaneously represents a path with a beginning and end, but without beginning and end." This model of the game as circle clearly invokes both the Viconian cycles of the *Wake* and the book's cyclic structure in which the last sentence flows syntactically into the first.

24. James J. Gibson, *The Ecological Approach to Visual Perception* (Boston: Houghton Mifflin, 1979), 127–43. An affordance is a quality of an object, person, animal, or environment that allows an agent to perform an action. In one of Gibson's examples, "a graspable rigid object of moderate size and weight affords throwing. It may be a *missile* or only an object of play, a *ball*" (133). A QWERTY keyboard affords the entry of twenty-six letters, ten numerals, and a fixed number of symbols. In this example, the constraints are fixed and relatively limited, but they nevertheless afford a number of actions including the composition of this essay.

25. European modernism has often been treated as a rejection of constraint and thus of a piece with the Romantic tradition that stretches back at least to Blake. Woolf's critique of Edwardian realism, Joyce's willful embrace of obscenity in "Circe," and Picasso's tribal masks fastened onto naked bodies signal, in their various ways, an understanding of creativity as a rejection of form, tradition, rule, and constraint. Alongside this branch of modernism, however, there is another one that embraces the importance of constraints as themselves a mechanism for generating creative response. This is evident, for example, in H.D.'s strict metrics as well as Yeats's mystic symbols, and it reaches a kind of climax in the midcentury Oulipo movement, an avant-garde group that created procedures for making poems and novels. These include writing a novel without the letter *e*, for example, or creating an S+7 poem, in which a familiar work of art is changed by replacing each noun with the one seven places away from it in a dictionary. Digital texts and digital games, in particular, draw heavily on this branch of modernist innovation, since they begin not with a blank canvas or empty page but with the highly constrained rules of a programming language and the hardware on which it runs.

26. After seeing the early drafts of the *Wake* in 1926, Pound wrote to Joyce that "nothing short of divine vision or a new cure for the clapp [sic] can possibly be worth all that circumambient peripherisation"—*Pound/Joyce*, ed. Forrest Read (New York: New Directions, 1970), 228.

27. N. Katherine Hayles, *My Mother Was a Computer: Digital Subjects and Literary Texts* (Chicago: University of Chicago Press, 2005), 198.

28. Bruce Clarke and Mark B. N. Hansen, "Introduction: Neocybernetic Emergence," in *Emergence and Embodiment: New Essays on Second-Order Systems Theory*, ed. Clarke and Hansen (Durham: Duke University Press, 2009), 9.

29. The earliest draft version of the question in Joyce's notebooks, for example, runs to only four handwritten pages (at most two hundred words), while the version that first appeared in *transition* was only two and a half pages long (*JJA* 47:5–11, 257–75). In its final form, it runs to fourteen pages.

30. T. S. Eliot, "*Ulysses*, Order, and Myth," *Dial* 75 (November 1923), rpt. *Selected Prose of T. S. Eliot*, ed. Frank Kermode (London: Faber & Faber, 1975), 177.

31. Roland McHugh, *Annotations to "Finnegans Wake,"* 3rd ed. (Baltimore: Johns Hopkins University Press, 2006), identifies *Giroflé, Girofla* as both an opera and "a singing game" (129). The phrase "Africa for the fullblacks" refers to New Zealand's famed Rugby team and the game's fullback position. *Arcs* and *stumps* refer to cricket.

32. See, for example, Margot Norris, "Possible Worlds Theory and the Fantasy Universe of *Finnegans Wake*," *James Joyce Quarterly* 44 (Spring 2007): 455–74.

33. Marie-Laure Ryan, *Possible Worlds, Artificial Intelligence, and Narrative Theory* (Bloomington: Indiana University Press, 1991), 48–60. Ryan refines a list of what she calls "criteria accessibility relations" that bridge real and possible worlds.

These include such things as chronological compatibility, logical compatibility, and linguistic compatibility among many others.

34. In many video games, for example, players are afforded multiple "lives" for the characters they play, typically without any explanation for this strange process of resurrection that shatters any kind of linear timeline. More frustratingly, other games include doors that cannot be opened, objects that cannot be moved, or non-player characters who repeat the same line endlessly.

35. Juul, *Half-Real*, 130.

36. Joyce developed the extended portrait of the time-obsessed Shaun, in part, as a response to Wyndham Lewis's attack on *Work in Progress* and *Ulysses* in *Time and Western Man* (Boston: Beacon Press, 1957).

37. Juul, *Half-Real*, 195.

38. Jacques Derrida, "Two Words of Joyce," in *Post-Structuralist Joyce: Essays from the French*, ed. Derek Attridge and Daniel Ferrer (Cambridge: Cambridge University Press, 1984), 147.

7

Shem's "strabismal apologia"

The Split Vision of the Famine in I.7

CHRISTINE SMEDLEY

The Celt's *Mea Culpa*

In his assault on Shem's literary excesses, Shaun refers to his brother's writing as a "strabismal apologia," a description which captures the split mode of the chapter itself (189.08). The expression encodes both *strabismus*, a doubled or cross-eyed vision, and *abysmal*, here describing a profoundly inadequate confession. *Abysmal* implies that the confession or defense emerges from the abysm of despair, as in Oscar Wilde's *De Profundis*, an important intertext for *Finnegans Wake* in general and this chapter's exculpatory defense of the dissolute, exiled Irish artist. Another possible model for I.7, John Henry Newman's *Apologia Pro Vita Sua*, combines autobiography, rebuttal, and apology, understood traditionally as an expression of contrition or regret.[1] In the same way, the Shem chapter is often read as one of Joyce's most transparently autobiographical works, and it has been criticized for the apparent rawness of its self-disclosure and the pettiness of its invective.[2] Yet as with so much of Joyce's semiautobiographical fiction, he creates only an illusion of self-portraiture, a parody of self-defense. Indeed, through this burlesque of the life of the artist as seen "askance," distrustfully or scornfully through the eyes of another, he mockingly yokes together narratives of personal and national culpability and persecution, ultimately dismantling both by exposing the limitations of any narrative locked into such a one-sided perspective.[3]

Following a tradition of minority nationalist writers such as John Mitchel, Joyce's apologia merges personal history with the history and spirit of the nation. Yet by conflating racial mixing with the history of nations—

"Miscegenations on miscegenations" (18.20)—Joyce parodies the myth of Irish national or racial purity. The Shem chapter begins as an attempt by Shaun to explain his brother's degenerate Celtic temperament by tracing his lowness back to impure genealogical origins, a movement which corresponds to Joyce's earlier effort in "Ireland, Island of Saints and Sages" to account for "the curious character of the modern Irishman" (*CW* 160). Shaun's attack on Shem opens by establishing his inferior roots: "A few toughnecks are still getatable who pretend that aboriginally he was of respectable stemming (he was an outlex between the lines of Ragonar Blaubarb ant Horrild Hairwire and an inlaw to Capt. the Hon. and Rev. Mr Bbyrdwood de Trop Blogg was among his most distant connections)" (169.01–06). As in Joyce's essay, which subversively posits impurity as the distinguishing feature of the Celtic race, Shem's bloodline promiscuously mingles the high and low: he is the illegitimate offspring ("outlex" as outside the law and "between the [authorized genealogical] lines") of Viking chiefs and Norwegian royalty and of the common—Beardwood, an apparent reference to a friend of Joyce's father, and Bloggs as "a mock English working-class name"—mixed with the criminal, through the reference to the wife-killer Bluebeard.[4] In his essay, Joyce similarly asserts a hybrid Irish identity: "Our civilization is a vast fabric, in which the most diverse elements are mingled" (*CW* 165).

Joyce's essay begins with an equation of nation and self. He writes, "Nations have their ego[s], just like individuals" (*CW* 154). Such a transposition would have appealed to Irish cultural nationalists who fundamentally sought to integrate individual subjectivity with the national spirit.[5] Yet the essay proceeds to unravel nationalist constructions of an essential, authentic, or unified racial essence.[6] Indeed, "Ireland, Island of Saints and Sages" dissects the singularity of an Irish national identity in a manner similar to his depiction of the fluidly mutating, endlessly splitting and reconciling ego of the Shem-Shaun amalgam. In I.7 the split ego of the two brothers informs and explains the chapter's narrative mode: an ironic apologia of Shem/Joyce voiced through his rival alter ego, Shaun/Stanislaus. Such a divided self exposes the futility of accusation and undermines any serious imputation of blame when the target is no more than a "dividual chaos" (186.05).

Shem/Joyce's martyrdom at the hands of his critics fuses with a larger narrative of colonial persecution so that Shaun's attack exposes the "empirative of my vendettative," an imperialist's vindictive vendetta or an uncharitable "blood-feud" against his underdog brother (187.31). Finn Fordham points out the paradoxical nature of Shaun's attack: "Shaun has consistently been viewed by critics as more suspect—a braggart, a bully, and a hypocritical sentimentalist—with Shem being the revolutionary artist and anti-hero, the outcast with whom we commiserate."[7] Yet Shem's tales of persecution and exile, facetiously equated with the economic exploitation and lynching of black Americans, also parody narratives of Irish victimization, deployed by writers like Mitchel, whose *Jail Journal* parallels his own political persecution, imprisonment, and exile with the victimization of the nation, thus constructing a role for writers as what David Lloyd calls "self-appointed martyrs of nationalism." Lloyd describes an Irish nationalist ideology that necessarily collapses personal and national identity, subsuming the discrepancies and irreconcilability of the real into a fictive whole: "The whole man, the man of integrity, becomes thus the man who is integrated with and reproduces the spirit of his nation."[8] Though Shem and Shaun have typically been viewed as antithetical, they are also widely recognized as an amalgam. As James Fairhall notes, "They are a recycling of a single person, their fractitious father HCE." Fairhall traces the divisive conflicts that the warring twins embody, including Parnellites and the anti-Parnellites, the Pro-Treaty and Anti-Treaty forces, and concludes, "The fact that all these conflicts reflect cleavages in HCE's psyche subverts essentialism—the notion of a pure, essential, undivided Irishness, at the most basic level, that of the individual subject."[9] Likewise, the identities of the two brothers never fully merge in this chapter, and the conflicting perspectives and shifting poles of guilt and innocence, justice and mercy, truth and untruth, victim and oppressor are never resolved into an anticipated unity. As with the condition of strabismus, the two eyes appear to be looking in different directions at once.

Joyce also follows writers such as John Mitchel, and later Michael Davitt and Jeremiah O'Donovan Rossa, in placing the Famine at the heart of Ireland's foundational narrative.[10] Paul Ricoeur's concept of the "social imaginary," through which "cultures create themselves by telling stories of their own past," underscores the role of narrative in shaping personal and social identity.[11] While the "foundational symbols" constructed by historical victors may glorify past events and actors, victims find their identities through narratives of the collective trauma of conquest and humiliation. As Ricoeur contends, "It is very important to remember that what is considered a founding event in our collective memory may be a wound in the memory of the other."[12] The Famine, or the Hunger as Mitchel, Davitt, and Rossa renamed it, engendered a wounded Irish national identity rooted in shame and the desire for vengeance. As Davitt writes, "The history of the famine years will ever be a record of Celtic humiliation."[13]

Despite some important analysis by Mary Lowe-Evans, Bonnie Roos, and Miriam O'Kane Mara,[14] there has been a lack of any substantial study on the many references to the Famine in *Finnegans Wake* and only cursory recognition of the profuse Famine imagery in I.7, a chapter thematically structured around the alimentary processes of an ailing Irish body—eating, drinking, and defecating. The Shem chapter also alludes directly to the story of Esau and Jacob, wherein the elder brother, at the point of starvation, sells his birthright for a bowl of pottage. The thematic links of the Esau/Jacob story with its parallels to Black '47 and "souperism"[15] resonate with the episode's clusters of allusions to Exodus and the plagues of Egypt—the diseases of livestock, pestilence, famine, and drought—and more generally to the chapter's many references to food, cooking, hunger, thirst, gluttony, and deprivation. There are also allusions to many works related to the Famine, including Yeats's *The Countess Cathleen*, Thackeray's *The Irish Sketch Book*, and John Mitchel's *Jail Journal*, along with numerous poems and ballads. Joyce's conflation of pottage and "messes of mottage" throughout the chapter registers his ambivalent engagement with traumatic collective memory and the need for a language that would adequately represent it (183.22–23).

As part of the *Wake*'s larger motif of brother battles, the fraternal dyad in I.7 signifies the colonial binary of the Irish and English as sibling rivals. As Christopher Morash records, "Writing Ireland as England's horrid twin extends back to the period before the Famine."[16] Much has been written about the construction of Irish identity as the barbarian other to Britain's progressive, civilized self.[17] In I.7, Shaun's hyperbolic explication of Shem's innate "lowness" literalizes an Ireland that Joyce described in his critical essay as "a country destined by God to be an eternal caricature of the serious world" (*CW* 120). Ventriloquizing British middle-class sentiment during the time of the Great Famine, Shaun's attack recycles claims that the Famine was a providential visitation upon a morally inferior nation. In the second section of the chapter which Joyce referred to as the "improperia," the sins for which Shem is condemned are exactly those Irish Catholic excesses to which Protestant England attributed the Famine: verbal and financial prodigality, coarse appetites, drunkenness, and an innate physical and moral dirtiness. As Morash points out, these narratives of "national sin" justified Anglo-centric interpretations of the Famine as righteous and necessary punishment.[18]

The central framing biblical narratives for I.7 figured prominently in the nineteenth century's interpretations of the Famine. One of the most damning charges Shaun levels against Shem-Cain is fratricide. Since Shaun-Abel was brought up "on his keeping and in yours," Shem's violence against his morally superior brother repeats Cain's protestation, "Am I my brother's keeper?" (191.11–12). Shem's apparent "shirking" of his brotherly duty clearly invokes Famine discourse. Shem, who identifies himself as "cannibal Cain," explicitly registers the repressed shame of actual cannibalism that occurred during the Famine as well as encoding a foundational act of violence (Cain as the first murderer) as a cornerstone in the chronology of self and nation (193.32).[19] Historically, the relationship between the two nations had been spoken of by the Anglo-Irish in terms of a brotherly affection, especially since the Act of Union.[20] Yet during the Famine, widespread British opinion opposed providing financial assistance to Ireland. Thus free market economics frequently trumped an ethics of Christian charity. In I.7, Shaun's accusation seems to rebound to himself when, in his childlike pledge of veracity (punning on "Cross my heart, hope to die / Stick a needle in my eye"), he inadvertently echoes a critique of Britain's exploitation of its excessively hospitable Irish brother and its subsequent Malthusian denial of charity during the Famine: "That the host may choke me if I beneighbor you without my charity!" (193.26–27). McHugh points out that the line refers to the belief that the Eucharistic Host will choke the guilty. Read in the context of the Famine, the line exposes Shaun's suppressed guilt, that the gluttony of the British Empire will appropriately choke the oppressor as he swallows ill-gotten bread. Alternatively, "host" may be read as an embodiment of the victimized Celt self-defensively choking his freeloading guest; the line betrays Shaun's recognition that Cain/Shem's violence may be justified as an act of retribution for British parasitism.

The parable of the prodigal son was also superimposed onto contemporary events during the Famine years. Joyce places this narrative at the forefront of his mock apologia for an improvident Irish national temperament. Christine Kinealy writes that Sir Charles Trevelyan, the chief administrator of relief during the Famine, "viewed events in Ireland through a moral and providential prism. Comparing the Irish poor to the 'prodigal son' in the Bible, he said that they could not be turned away. At the same time, they were not to be given a 'fatted calf' but 'the workhouse and one pound of meal per day.'"[21] I.7 repeats this biblical tale of two rival brothers: the "wastefully extravagant" prodigal son, Shem, confronted by the smug righteousness and smoldering resentment of his older brother, Shaun. Shaun as "Justius" is modeled on the slighted older son of the parable, who rigidly adheres to "law, merit, and reward" rather than "love and graciousness."[22] Shem, like the parable's younger son, wastes his inheritance in profligate company: "you squandered among underlings the overload of your extravagance and made a hottentot of dulpeners crawsick with your crumbs" (193.01–03). Significantly, in the biblical prototype, it is a famine that forces the arrogant and debauched youth into the humiliating profession of a swineherd, after which he humbly seeks his father's forgiveness. As in the parable, the prodigal Shem is often associated with pigs. He is described as a "sowman's son," "whimpering to the name of Low Swine," who tells the bourgeois intelligentsia "the whole lifelong swrine story of his entire low cornaille existence" (169.14, 173.05–06, .19–20).[23] The deployment of such moral fables to explain and justify the unprecedentedly catastrophic impact of the Famine also fueled sectarian rhetoric within Ireland when the more profitable North of Ireland was asked to subsidize the increasingly impoverished Catholic South. In describing the use of such biblical parallels, Kinealy notes, "The probity of Ulster versus the sloth of Connaught was an interpretation that was invoked frequently."[24] The Irish themselves internalized such scripts, viewing the disaster as, in part, a consequence of their own squandering of what had been an abundant potato crop in the years preceding the blight.[25]

Appropriately, one of the accusations focuses on Shem's wastefulness, specifically in relation to food:

> Malingerer in luxury, collector general, what has Your Lowness done in the mealtime with all the hamilkcars of cooked vegetables, the hatfuls of stewed fruit, the suitcases of coddled ales, the Parish funds, me schamer, man, that you kittycoaxed so flexibly out of charitable butteries by yowling heavy with a hollow voice drop of your horrible awful poverty of mind. (192.05–10)

The passage compresses multiple, conflicting indictments among the various parties held responsible for the Famine, as well as more contemporary and personal accounts of economic mismanagement and laziness, as in the reference to Shem as "collector general," alluding to Joyce's famously spendthrift father's employment for the Collector-General of Rates. Shem as "malingerer in luxury" embodies the British view of the idleness and extravagance of Irish landlords and peasants whose habits inevitably led to their downfall. The sense of the Irish as sham beggars pervaded the British press at the time of the Famine, influenced in part by Thackeray's *Irish Sketch Book* and its descriptions of the indolent poor: "they come crawling round you with lying prayers and loathsome compliments that make the stomach turn[,] . . . refuse them and the wretches turn off with a laugh and a joke" (38). Shem as a malingerer makes a poor mouth, "yowling" dramatically about his "horrible awful poverty," while failing to do his duty to his nation and exploiting those who would give him aid. At the same time, Shem's furtive removal of food and drink out of Ireland in carts, hats, and suitcases recalls one of the nationalist's central indictments against the British, the forced export of food from the country even during the worst years of the Famine. As Mitchel posited, "All the grain and cattle the people could raise . . . it all went away, of course; it was all consumed in England."[26] A constant refrain in the historical reconstructions of Mitchel, Davitt, and Rossa relays the perversity of "ships laden with Irish produce, sailing from the same shores to England, with the exported fruits of Irish toil and land, to be turned into rent for the Irish landlords in the English market."[27] But in the Wakean passage, blame for British "plunder" slips into a gossipy accusation of Parnell for misappropriating the "Paris Funds," or the Irish Nationalist deposits banked in Paris during the time of the split between Parnellites and anti-Parnellites. Coupled with the reference to Kitty O'Shea ("kittycoaxed"), the charge typifies Parnell's persecution by the press after his adulterous affair was revealed.[28] Like the "drunken old harridan" that Mr. Casey recalls in *Portrait*, "bawling and screaming" the words, "*Priesthunter! The Paris Funds! Mr Fox! Kitty O'Shea!*" Shaun's effort to assign blame devolves into rancorous and petty mudslinging where there is more than enough guilt to go around (*P* 36).

According to Shaun, Shem's obligation to his nation emerges due to his birth one generation after the Famine. Like Joyce, Shem is "butting in rand the coyner of bad times": "the bad times" or "*an Drochshaol*" is the Irish name for the Famine (186.29). Post-Famine Ireland is a "place of burden, your bourne of travail and ville of tares, where after a divine's prodigence you drew the first watergasp in your life" (190.21–23). The phrase "divine's prodigence" merges the rhetoric of providentialism (divine providence) with a direct allusion to the prodigal son and also refers to the gifted prodigal Irish artist's debt to his nation (as a prodigy). This passage further embeds a reference to Jesus's parable of the tares, in which God's elect are likened to wheat while the damned are compared to weeds (tares).[29] Such biblical plots were thus imposed onto contemporary events where the catastrophic effects of the potato blight were read by many as an apocalyptic fulfillment of prophesy. An Irish national sin, variously identified as waste, indolence, or excessive alcohol consumption—as in Shaun's iterations of "Tamstar Ham of Tenman's thirst"—was interpreted as having precipitated a righteous punishment (187.22–23).[30] Joyce's conflation of the sentimentalized line "vale of tears" and "ville of tares" also taps into Famine imagery of the starving poor, "endeavoring to satisfy the cravings of devouring hunger with grass and turf."[31] Shem's refusal to "saffrocake himself with a sod" suggests his rejection of the role of Irish martyr as constituted through such nationalist ideological constructions (172.20).

Historians continue to debate the responsibility for the Irish Famine.[32] But if fault can be assigned, it should be placed upon the excesses and evasions of ideology during and after the event. Ricoeur's final works call attention to the manipulation of memory by ideology. In such cases, he writes, "The resource of narrative becomes a trap when higher powers take over this emplotment and impose a canonical narrative by means of intimidation or seduction, fear or flattery."[33] Morash describes the way ideological constructions shaped the British response to the blight: "As the providential interpretation of the Famine as supernatural punishment for 'national sin' developed into a justification for starvation, disease, emigration, and death, it began to merge with that other great narrative of 'depopulation,' Malthus's 'principle of population.'"[34] In their recourse to the same stock of biblical plots and images, nationalist writers reproduced imperial discourse as an identical, though inverse, image. James S. Donnelly asserts, "As a result of these enduring ideological filters, it was extremely difficult or even impossible for nationalists to find a place in their interpretation or memory of the Famine for facts or circumstances that contradicted or conflicted with reigning nationalist orthodoxies."[35] Moreover, like the ultra-nationalist Citizen—the Cyclops figure in *Ulysses*—Shaun's nationalist account of history "folds back upon itself and encloses itself within its own sufferings to the point of rendering itself blind and deaf to the suffering of other communities."[36] I contend that in I.7's "strabismal apologia," analogies of impeded vision are similarly deployed to critique a blinkered nationalist perspective. When Bloom and the Citizen trade barbs in their dispute over the relevance of Irish history, the Citizen's vituperative and exclusionary discourse on the Famine leads to this exchange:

—Some people, says Bloom, can see the mote in others' eyes but they can't see the beam in their own.
—*Raimeis*, says the citizen. There's no-one as blind as the fellow that won't see, if you know what that means. (*U* 12.1237–40)

Seen through Joycean optics, both the nationalist and imperialist versions of history appear as mutually distorting and oppressive perspectives.

Recipes for Revolution

As critics have long noted, a key theme in the *Wake* is communal feasting.[37] Yet it is collective hunger, inducing shame and deforming bodies, which marks the text as a repressed other of Irish folk history. Throughout the *Wake* Joyce imbricates Famine memory and personal autobiography through the iconography of food. According to Mara, "[Ireland's] understanding of famine as a political symbol for English oppression politicized Irish eating behaviors and intensified food as a way to mark identity."[38] In I.7, Shaun's calibanization of Shem is predicated, in large part, on his appetites: as Shaun alleges, "his lowness creeped out first via foodstuffs" (170.25–26). Allusions to the Famine in I.7 are paralleled by the typically Shaun-like fixation on food. Shem's perverse appetites, indigestion or "painful digests," self-imposed refusal of food, claims that "he kukkakould flowrish for ever by the smell" of a "czitround peel," and subsistence on alcohol rather than food contrast sharply with Shaun's lip-smacking description of the foods Shem avoids: "None of your inchthick blueblooded Balaclava fried-at-belief-stakes or juicejelly legs of the Grex's molten mutton or greasilygristly grunters' goupons or slice upon slab of luscious goosebosom with lump after load of plumpudding stuffing all aswim in a swamp of bogoakgravy for that greekenhearted yude! Rosbif of Old Zealand!" (183.21, 171.10, 170.32–171.02). In the catalogue, Shaun's gastronomic relishing of the sounds of language also highlights the consumption of a martyred Irish body ("fried-at-belief-stakes" smothered in "bogoakgravy"). It also exposes an aristocratic, imperialist gluttony, "blueblooded Balaclava" suggesting both a pastry ensconced piece of meat (baklava) as well as a hooded thug, with the added allusion to the Battle of Balaclava, thus signifying the disastrous appetites that fueled the Crimean War. Shaun's appetite for the "Rosbif of Old Zealand" again registers the nationalist grievance against the British exportation of Irish goods during the Famine. Joyce had previously recorded such a sentiment in "Hades" when Bloom reflects, "Roastbeef for old England. They buy up all the juicy ones" (*U* 6.393–994).

The most direct reference to the politicization of food discourse occurs in the passage where Shaun describes the making of Irish stew in brutally violent language:[39]

> the more carrots you chop, the more turnips you slit, the more murphies you peel, the more onions you cry over, the more bullbeef you butch, the more mutton you crackerhack, the more potherbs you

pound, the fiercer the fire and the longer your spoon and the harder you gruel with more grease to your elbow the merrier fumes your new Irish stew. (190.03–09)

Shaun's recipe for stew encodes multiple references to the Famine. The "slit" turnips were an important food substitute for the potato during the Famine years, and as Roger McHugh records, "the poor would be glad to eat them slice by slice roasted on the tongs."[40] Perhaps the most obvious allusion to the Famine is the "murphies" which, as Roland McHugh points out, is slang for potatoes. "Murphies" are also a metonym for Irish peasants, whom Thackeray's narrator in *The Irish Sketch Book* denigrates as feckless and indigent "potato-people" whose reliance on the single crop apparently precipitated the disaster. These Murphies were indeed "peeled" by Robert Peel, the British prime minister from 1841 to 1846, whose delayed and often punitive response to the blight, in the form of a professional police force in Ireland (known colloquially as "Peelers") and his proposed Coercion Bill, were seen as having exacerbated Irish suffering.[41] In this new Irish stew, onions as a source of tears bring to mind the "poignings" (143.19) of I.6, a portmanteau which punningly conflates the French *oignon* with Poynings' Law, which marked the beginning of Tudor rule in Ireland.[42] Bullbeef or "bullybeef" is "tinned corned beef," whose production "had a devastating impact on the impoverished and disenfranchised people of . . . Ireland. Pushed off the best pasture land and forced to farm smaller plots of marginal land, the Irish turned to the potato. . . . Eventually, cows took over much of Ireland, leaving the native population virtually dependent upon the potato for survival."[43] Evoking emigration, "Crackerhack" becomes a grisly play on the crackerhash, or biscuits and salt meat, served aboard the "coffinships" of the Irish exodus. In his alternate guise as virulent nationalist, Shaun marshals famine rhetoric as a means of fomenting violence in this "new Irish stew"; the recipe's more general pun on the word *stew* as "a state of suppressed agitation, worry, or resentment" is reinforced by the fierce fire and the fuming that follows from the stirring of a Faustian spoon. (Shaun's line follows from the proverb "He who sups with the devil hath need of a long spoon.") In *Ulysses*, Joyce depicts hunger as a potentially explosive ideological tool. Witnessing the violent appetites of the men at the Burton, Bloom thinks, "Hungry man is an angry man," and he is repelled by their apparent rapaciousness: "Every fellow for his own, tooth and nail. Gulp. Grub. Gulp. Gobstuff. . . . Eat or be eaten. Kill! Kill!" Significantly, Bloom views the men drawn together by hunger as "One stew" (*U* 8.662–703). In the same way, Shaun links hunger and violence when he likens the Irish artist's post-Famine progeny to a herdlike mass of "the hungered head and the angered thousand" (188.36). In Shaun's improperia, Shem is accused of shirking his duty; here he avoids participation in a discourse that, to some degree, incited a desired, though belated, Irish revolution. Thus Shem is he "who sleep[s] at our vigil and fast[s] for our feast" (189.29–30). Morash describes the way Famine imagery in late nineteenth- and early twentieth-century Ireland was "constructed as an archive of free-floating signs," "textually generated shards of memory," which may become "part of an individual's sense of identity."[44] Shaun's "Irish stew" is a smorgasbord of such iconic Famine imagery, and Shem's abstinence, fasting in the face of such meaty textual bounty, suggests Joyce's skepticism toward this recipe for national union, concocted from such morsels of memory. Again, Ricoeur describes the paradox of an excess of memory—where actors become locked in a futile compulsion to repeat a nation's perceived humiliations and wounds—and too little memory—in which inconvenient or painful elements of the past are elided or actively suppressed: "What some cultivate with morose delectation, and what others flee with bad conscience, is the same repetition-memory. The former love to lose themselves in it, the latter are afraid of being engulfed by it." They "do not attain what Freud termed the work of remembering."[45] As Morash notes, the desire to create identity through such memory can result in new atrocities when used to construct a cohesive but largely fictive identity for a nation, a tribe, a race united in opposition to another imagined whole.[46]

Abuses of memory must be replaced by what Ricoeur describes as a "just memory," one directed toward the future instead of the past. As Ricoeur asserts, "The victim at issue is the other victim, other than ourselves."[47] Accordingly, Joyce's treatment of the Famine includes several pointed references to contemporary or emerging genocidal events including the persecution of black Americans, Jews, and Armenians. As a "nogger among the blankards" or "nigger" among white men (*blanke* in Dutch: white man), Shem is often the target of slurs related to the racist defamation and violence against blacks in the United States and Africa (188.13). Shem is also depicted as Jewish; his very name identifies him as the biblical son of Noah, progenitor of the Semitic races. Shaun's attack on Shem occasionally slips into the persecutory rhetoric of the Nazis: "heal helper! one gob, one gap, one gulp and gorger of all!" (191.07–08). McHugh glosses the words as a play on the slogan "Heil Hitler! Ein Volk, ein Reich, ein Führer." Similarly, Shaun compares Shem's outsider status to the massacre of Armenians, made "menial" or servile, by nationalist Turks: "you were as popular as an armenial with the faithful"

(190.25–26). He likens his brother's exclusion, based on his abject smell, to the forced deportation of the Armenians along with other non-Muslim minorities such as Greek Christians during the ethnic cleansing campaigns of the early twentieth century: "not even the Turk, ungreekable in purscent of the armenable, dared whiff the polecat at close range" (181.22–24). The phrase associates the forced extermination of Armenians from their historical homeland in Turkey with the cruel practice of the British foxhunt—Wilde famously described the ritual as "the unspeakable in full pursuit of the uneatable."

In a chapter filled with recriminations, ALP identifies Shem's true sin as that of forgetting: "because ye left from me, because ye laughed on me, because, O me lonly son, ye are forgetting me!" (194.20–21). Beneath the ironic excesses of Shaun's attack, Joyce articulates the failure of the artist to give voice to the Famine dead, many of whom were buried anonymously in mass graves. Joyce makes oblique references to such victims throughout the *Wake*, as in the "hungerlean spalpeens" (32.15–16) of I.1.[48] But as Cormac O'Grada points out, the stories of most of those who suffered during the Famine are not recorded in either official or folk archives.[49] At the end of the chapter, Shem identifies himself and Ireland as "one black mass of jigs and jimjams, haunted by a convulsionary sense of not having been or being all that I might have been or you meant to becoming" (193.34–36). Joyce's obligation to write about Ireland's traumatic past and to imaginatively move the nation beyond it—signaled by the phrase's slide from past to present participle—is a compulsion that convulses the body and the writing of the Irish artist: "jimjams" is American slang for *delirium tremens* as well as a reference to Joyce himself. Though I.7 works to undermine ideological constructions of memory imposed by British historians and Irish Nationalists alike, it also encodes the melancholy of the artist/nation which is paralyzed by that memory.

Although Ricoeur emphasizes the need to correct oppressive narratives of history with multiple "kaleidoscopic" versions of history, he also suggests there are events which resist representation.[50] He singles out the unprecedented "great crimes of the twentieth century," centrally the Jewish Holocaust, "situated at the limits of representation, [which] stand in the name of all the events that have left their traumatic imprint on hearts and bodies: they protest that they were and as such they demand being said, recounted, understood."[51] In the same way, Joyce acknowledges his inability to adequately represent the Famine dead and self-referentially mocks his previous attempts as adolescent "whistlewhirling your crazy elegies" or the presumptuous "giving unsolicited testimony on behalf of the absent"

(192.34, 173.29–30). But by the chapter's end, Shem's abasement puts him in contact with a subaltern "downandoutermost where voice only of the dead may come," which is also the point where he reconnects with the betrayed mother, ALP (194.19–20).

A central motif in Famine poetry is the mother's lament, often delivered at the grave of her child. In I.7 ALP, "our turfbrown mummy," intercedes on behalf of her son and functions as a literal embodiment of the land (194.22). She is both Mother Ireland and her mummified remainder, remnants of the historical past. Her tidings are a historical bricolage, "old the news of the great big world," which incorporate only "scraps" of the age-old quarrel: "sonnies had a scrap" (194.23–24). Her tale of Irish "woewoewoe!" and "waywayway!" encodes the Famine's twin traumas of mass death and emigration (194.24). But she is also a maw, a mouth; the "giddy-gaddy, grannyma" harkens back to Shaun's final utterance: "*Awmawm*" (195.03–04, 193.30). As Margaret Kelleher points out, in Famine literature, "female images are chosen to represent the Famine's worst consequences, in characterizations ranging from heroic self-sacrifice to 'monstrous' perversions of 'Nature.'"[52] As maw, ALP recalls the Famine iconography of the mother's devouring mouth: horrific images recorded by Mitchel of "insane mothers [who] began to eat their young children, who died of famine before them."[53] ALP's mouth also runs like sewage, spewing out the language of the common folk, not recorded in official versions of history; she mingles the frivolous gossip and recipes of a lost community and a contemporary popular culture with raunchy evocations of the Irish emigrant's sterile return: "dry yanks will visit old sod" (194.27). At the same time, ALP's narrative weaves in references to the impact of the tragedy on the physical landscape, such as "Tallaght's green hills": the name is derived from the Irish *Taimhleacht* or "plague-grave" (194.35). ALP is described as "babbling, bubbling, chattering to herself, deloothering the fields on their elbows leaning with the sloothering slide of her" (195.01–03): as river touches land, her deluge of language unearths the "traumatic imprint" of Irish history's anonymous dead at the same time as it opens up fertile grounds for the future.

Conclusion: Moving beyond "glass eyes for an eye" (183.36)

The irreconcilability of vision encoded in Shem's "strabismal apologia" functions on multiple levels: personal, national, and textual. References to disabled eyesight obviously have an autobiographical valence in the Joycean oeuvre. Roy Gottfried argues that Joyce's compromised eyesight during the writing of *Ulysses* translated into the production of an "irritated text," whose intentional opacity and indeterminacy destabilize language at its foundation. Gottfried contends that, for the reader, "the limits of Joyce's own vision are replicated, making any and all readers empathetic with and symptomatic of his handicap."[54] Similarly, John Bishop places Joyce's eye difficulties at the center of the *Wake*, proposing that the writer's myopia underscores the text's "meoptics," the text's night vision.[55] Joyce began the "Shem the Penman" chapter in February 1924 and revised it through the late 1920s. In these years, Joyce's eye troubles migrated to what had been his stronger eye, when the iritis that began in 1908 in his right eye spread to his left (*JJII* 535). In 1919, Joyce wrote to Harriet Weaver, "My eyes are so capricious . . . this time the attack was in my 'good?' eye" (*JJII* 454). In 1924, Joyce underwent a second iridectomy on his left eye (*JJII* 566). This traumatic surgery left him dependent on his right eye while he was composing the Shem chapter. With a patch over one eye, he wrote to Weaver, "my one bedazzled eye searched the sea like Cain-Shem-Tristan-Patrick from his lighthouse in Boulougne" (*JJII* 567). Shortly thereafter, conjunctivitis and then episcleritis developed in his right eye. The condition of strabismus causes "the inability of one eye to obtain binocular vision with the other because of an imbalance of the intrinsic muscles." Though Joyce did not suffer from the congenital strabismus that would severely impact his daughter Lucia, these eye troubles forced him to shift back and forth between two defective visual poles. Thus the naturally occurring phenomenon of ocular dominance, or the tendency to prefer visual input from one eye over the other, was exacerbated for Joyce. The Shem-Shaun amalgam can be read as a divisive pair of rivals that cannot ultimately be divided, but whose fight for dominance prevents binocular vision, the fusion of what are in fact two disparate images of Irish identity into a single whole. In his "strabismal apologia," the oscillating, one-sided perspectives of Shaun and Shem convert a physical reality into a textual strategy. The fight for dominance between Joyce's left and right eyes materializes what, in the *Wake*, is allegorized as the struggle between warring twins. For Joyce, symptom becomes cure—or at least a prescription for a more faithful re-visioning of the self and the past.

The "strabismal apologia" therefore corresponds to a split perspective where the artist, as seen through the lens of his competitive and antagonistic other/brother, engenders a schizophrenic *mea culpa* written in both first and third person. They are two pairs of I's/eyes that cannot see eye to eye or merge into a unified whole. Thus when the narrative transfers to Shem's perspective, the apologia is appropriately blurred and doubled. As Rose and

O'Hanlon contend, when Shem tries to speak, he "utters the accusations of Shaun. He thereby accuses himself of betrayal and cowardice."[56] Moreover, the confusion of identity increases with the apology's shifting deployment of pronouns. In the passage, it is unclear whether Shem is talking about himself in the second person or addressing Shaun, who is now the Cain figure: "to you, firstborn and firstfruit of woe, to me, branded sheep, pick of the wasterpaperbaskel" (194.12–13). The apology of Shem the Celt materializes only in a moment of fractured, disunited disclosure, seeing both sides at once and suggesting a mutual disinheritance: "My fault, his fault, a kingship through a fault!" (193.31–32). The textual strategy of the Shem chapter thereby effects what Ricoeur describes as a transformational model of memory exchange, "taking responsibility, in imagination and in sympathy, for the story of the other," which is "a matter not only of subjecting the founding events of both cultures to a crossed reading," but also a setting free of "that part of life and of renewal which is found captive in rigid, embalmed and dead traditions."[57] In his cross-eyed re-visioning of the Irish Famine, Joyce suggests that to split the Eye/I is to acknowledge the other in a profound way.

Notes

1. "Apologetics," http://en.wikipedia.org/wiki/apologetics.

2. See, for example, William York Tindall, *A Reader's Guide to "Finnegans Wake"* (New York: Farrar, Straus and Giroux, 1969), 131, and Adaline Glasheen, *A Census of "Finnegans Wake": An Index of the Characters and Their Roles* (Evanston: Northwestern University Press, 1956), xx.

3. *Strabismus* is from the Greek "to squint." An additional meaning of *squint* is to look askew or askance, with disapproval or distrust. See Walter William Skeat, *An Etymological Dictionary of the English Language,* 3rd ed. (Oxford: Clarendon Press, 1882), 588.

4. Roland McHugh, *Annotations to "Finnegans Wake,"* (Baltimore: Johns Hopkins University Press, 1991). I am indebted to McHugh for many of my glosses, too many to acknowledge individually.

5. David Lloyd, *Nationalism and Minor Literature* (Berkeley: University of California Press, 1987), 4.

6. "Nationality (if it really is not a convenient fiction like so many others to which the scalpels of present-day scientists have given the coup de grâce) must find its reason for being rooted in something that surpasses and transcends and informs changing things like blood and the human word" (*CW* 166).

7. Finn Fordham, *Lots of Fun at "Finnegans Wake"* (New York: Oxford University Press, 2007), 39.

8. Lloyd, *Nationalism and Minor Literature* 71, 70.

9. James Fairhall, *James Joyce and the Question of History* (New York: Cambridge University Press, 1993), 224.

10. In literary representations of the early twentieth century, the Famine became "a central and increasingly controversial event in the national chronology." See Margaret Kelleher, "Irish Famine in Literature," in *The Great Irish Famine*, ed. Cathal Póirtéir (Dublin: Mercier Press, 1995), 240–41. Major nationalist reconstructions of the Famine include John Mitchel, *The Last Conquest of Ireland (Perhaps)* (Glasgow: Cameron and Ferguson, 1869); Michael Davitt, *The Fall of Feudalism in Ireland* (Shannon: Irish University Press, 1970); Jeremiah O'Donovan Rossa, *Rossa's Recollections, 1838–1898* (Mariner's Harbor, N.Y.: privately published, 1898).

11. Paul Ricoeur, "The Creativity of Language," interview with Richard Kearney, in *A Ricoeur Reader: Reflection and Imagination*, ed. Mario J. Valdes (Toronto: University of Toronto Press, 1991), 475.

12. Paul Ricoeur, "Memory and Forgetting," in *Questioning Ethics: Contemporary Debates in Continental Philosophy*, ed. Mark Dooley and Richard Kearney (New York: Routledge, 1999), 9.

13. Davitt, *Fall of Feudalism*, 55.

14. Mary Lowe-Evans, *Crimes against Fecundity: James Joyce and Population Control* (Syracuse: Syracuse University Press, 1989); Bonnie Roos, "The Joyce of Eating: Feast, Famine, and the Humble Potato in *Ulysses*," in *Hungry Words: Images of Famine in the Irish Canon*, ed. George Cusack and Sarah Gross (Dublin: Irish Academic Press, 2006), 159–95; Miriam O'Kane Mara, "James Joyce and the Politics of Food," *New Hibernia Review* 13 (Winter 2009): 94–111.

15. On "souperism," or "the alleged attempts of evangelical missionaries to use hunger as an instrument to win converts to the Protestant faith" during the catastrophic years of the Famine, see Irene Whelen, "The Stigma of Souperism," in *The Great Irish Famine*, ed. Cathal Póirtéir (Dublin: Mercier Press, 1995), 135–54.

16. Christopher Morash, *Writing the Irish Famine* (Oxford: Clarendon Press, 1995), 48.

17. See especially Seamus Deane, *Civilians and Barbarians* (Derry: Field Day Theater, 1983).

18. Morash, *Writing the Irish Famine*, 92–93.

19. At this point, Shaun's identity has shifted from a caustic imperialist to "Shaun the Patriot," an aggressively nationalist type. On this slippage elsewhere in the *Wake*, see Emer Nolan, *James Joyce and Nationalism* (London: Routledge, 1995), 151–58.

20. Terry Eagleton, *Heathcliff and the Great Hunger* (New York: Verso 1995), 127.

21. Christine Kinealy, *A Death Dealing Famine: The Great Hunger in Ireland* (London: Pluto Press, 1997), 138.

22. Arland J. Hultgren, *The Parables of Jesus: A Commentary* (Grand Rapids: Wm. B. Eerdman's, 2000), 70–82.

23. The aptness of this biblical model for poor Irish was magnified by their stereotypical association with pigs. Thus writes Friedrich Engels, echoing the earlier characterization of Carlyle: "The Irishman loves his pig as the Arab his horse. . . . he eats and sleeps with it, his children play with it, ride upon it, roll in the dirt with it." See Engels, *The Condition of the Working Class in England in 1844* (Dortmund, Germany: Tredition, 2012), 92.

24. Kinealy, *A Death Dealing Famine*, 143.

25. See Cormac O'Grada, "Black '47 and Beyond," *The Great Irish Famine in History, Economy, and Memory* (Princeton: Princeton University Press, 1999), 208.

26. Mitchel, *Last Conquest*, 116–17.

27. Davitt, *Fall of Feudalism*, 66.

28. Davitt calls the Paris Funds quarrel "an absurd press controversy" that "arose from a willful misunderstanding of what was a manifest act of carelessness on the part of an old veteran in the Irish fight" (*Fall of Feudalism*, 672).

29. At the time of harvest, the reapers separate the tares from the wheat and burn them. Jesus explains the parable as a justification of God's final judgment: "The Son of man shall send forth his angels, and they shall gather out of his kingdom all things that offend, and them which do iniquity; And shall cast them into a furnace of fire: there shall be wailing and gnashing of teeth. Then shall the righteous shine forth as the sun in the kingdom of heaven" (Matthew 13:41–43). As Morash points out, Protestant evangelicals and Catholic prophesiers alike frequently made use of such apocalyptic themes in their interpretations of the Famine. Morash, *Writing the Irish Famine*, 128–34.

30. See, for example, the Reverend Hugh M'Neile, "The Famine, a Rod of God; Its Provoking Cause—Its Merciful Design," in *Sermons by Eminent Living Divines of the Church of England* (London: Richard Griffin, 1856), 67–100.

31. Christopher Morash, "Literature, Memory, Atrocity," in *"Fearful Realities": New Perspectives on the Famine*, ed. Christopher Morash and Richard Hayes (Dublin: Irish Academic Press, 1996), 112. Morash contends of such iconic images, "They have an ideological function—indeed they are almost pure ideology, insofar as they create an illusion of complete identity between the individual and society" (114).

32. For an excellent overview of conflicting historical interpretations of the Famine, see especially Christine Kinealy, who writes, "The question of culpability remains the most controversial aspect of the Irish Famine" (*A Death Dealing Famine*, 10).

33. Paul Ricoeur, *Memory, History, Forgetting* (Chicago: University of Chicago Press, 2004), 448.

34. Morash, *Writing*, 93.

35. James S. Donnelly Jr., *The Great Irish Potato Famine* (Thrupp, Stroud, Gloucestershire: Sutton, 2001), 244.

36. Ricoeur, *Memory, History, Forgetting*, 500. For an excellent analysis of the Citizen's Famine rhetoric in the "Cyclops" episode, see Julieann Ulin, "'Famished Ghosts': Famine Memory in James Joyce's *Ulysses*," *Joyce Studies Annual 2011*: 20–63.

37. See especially Joseph Campbell and Henry Morton Robinson, *A Skeleton Key to "Finnegans Wake"* (Novato, Calif.: New World Library, 2005), 38–39.

38. Mara, "Politics of Food," 95.

39. While Shem is a passive piscivore or chickenhearted "virgitarian," Shaun is the belligerent butcher who later announces, "I'll brune this bird or Brown Bess's bung's gone bandy. I'm the boy to bruise and braise. Baus!" (171.03, 187.26–27). In a welter of disturbingly aggressive references, the line combines "Brown Bess," the name given in the British army to the flintlock musket, as well as slang for a harlot, with allusions to forced sex with a prostitute and buggery ("brown" "bung"). *Brune* also suggests browning meat and the slang expression for firing indiscriminately, as well as to "brain," to kill by smashing the skull. *Braise* is a synonym for *stew*, and *Baus* is both the Irish *bas* or death and the German *bauz!* an interjection that translates as "Smash!" (McHugh). Thus Shaun's alliterative German-studded declaration encodes the same violent rhetoric that associates aggressive appetites ("One gob") with the genocidal rise of Hitler. For more on Joyce's prescient suspicions about Hitler and the writer's use of what he called "bully German" in the *Wake*, see John Gordon, "Joyce's Hitler," in *Joyce through the Ages*, ed. Michael Patrick Gillespie (Gainesville: University Press of Florida, 1999), 179–89.

40. Roger McHugh, "The Famine in Irish Oral Tradition," in *The Great Famine*, ed. R. W. Dudley Edwards and Thomas Desmond Williams (Dublin: Lilliput Press, 1994), 399.

41. Kinealy, *Death Dealing Famine*, 142. Elsewhere Joyce contends, "The spirit of the country has been weakened by centuries of useless struggle and broken treaties... while the body has been shackled by *peelers*, duty officers and soldiers" (*CW* 123, my italics). Mitchel writes of Robert Peel's Coercion Bill, "It meant more police, more police-taxes, police surveillance, and a law that everyone should be kept at home after dark" (*Last Conquest*, 98).

42. The gloss for "poignings" is from Fritz Senn, "Explications for the Greater Glossary of Code Addenda to No. 1," *A Wake Newslitter* 2 (1962): 130.

43. Jeremy Rifkin, *Beyond Beef: The Rise and Fall of the Cattle Culture* (New York: Plume, 1993), 56–57.

44. Morash, "Literature," 117–18.

45. Ricoeur, *Memory, History, Forgetting*, 79.

46. Morash, "Literature," 118.

47. Ricoeur, *Memory, History, Forgetting*, 89.

48. *Spalpeen* is "a [derogatory] Anglo-Irish term for itinerant farm labourers."

See Richard Wall, *An Anglo-Irish Dialect Glossary for Joyce's Works* (Syracuse: Syracuse University Press, 1987), 59. According to O'Grada, these poor migrant farmers and their dependents "accounted for most of the Famine's dead" (123), in "Famine, Trauma, and Memory," *Bealoideas* 69 (2001): 121–43.

49. O'Grada, "Famine," 132. As Ulin contends, this "trauma of being unable to mourn properly or to bury the dead surfaces repeatedly" in Joyce's earlier work ("Famine Memory," 30).

50. In his critique of the notion of an inclusive Irish collective memory of the Famine, O'Grada prescribes an approach in which the historian seeks out "the range or kaleidoscope of memories or evidence on particular topics" ("Famine," 132). He asks, "How could the memory of such an uneven and divisive disaster as the Irish Famine be truly collective?" (140). Joyce's fragmentary, conflicting, and endlessly shifting narrative on the Famine seems to conform to just such a mode.

51. Ricoeur, *Memory, History, Forgetting*, 498.

52. Kelleher, "Irish Famine," 239.

53. Mitchel, *Last Conquest*, 121.

54. Roy K. Gottfried, *Joyce's Iritis and the Irritated Text: The Dis-lexic "Ulysses"* (Gainesville: University Press of Florida, 1995), 9.

55. John Bishop, *Joyce's Book of the Dark: "Finnegans Wake"* (Madison: University of Wisconsin Press, 1986), 226. Recent scholarship has reevaluated Joyce's impaired vision, establishing that Joyce was not, in fact, myopic but farsighted (hyperopic). This finding reinforces my emphasis on strabismus, as hyperopia is associated more closely with binocular disfunction, amblyopia (lazy eye), and strabismus. I am indebted to Jan van Velze, "'Noticeably Longsighted from Green Youth': Ocular Proof of James Joyce's True Refractive Error," presented at the XXIII International James Joyce Symposium at Trinity College, Dublin, on June 13, 2012.

56. Danis Rose and John O'Hanlon, *Understanding "Finnegans Wake"* (New York: Garland, 1982), 111.

57. "Reflections on a New Ethos for Europe," in *Paul Ricoeur: The Hermeneutics of Action*, ed. Richard Kearney (London: Sage, 1996), 6–9.

8

Fluid Figures in "Anna Livia Plurabelle"

An Ecocritical Exploration of I.8

MARGOT NORRIS

"Finnegans Wake tells the story of the planet—of mountains, rivers, and the sky, and of the rubbish, the rivers and mountains of it," Finn Fordham writes in *Lots of Fun at "Finnegans Wake."* This leads him to suggest "ecocriticism" as a worthy critical approach to a work in which Anna Livia Plurabelle's blending with the river Liffey makes her a "mythical and environmental figure."[1] Fordham's early suggestion is slowly taking hold, and I will try to amplify the ecological significance of the fluid figures in I.8 while also showing how they complicate current debates within the field of ecocriticism itself. The heart of the problem lies in the theoretical challenge Timothy Morton aims at what he calls "the ecological imaginary," that is, at the way fantasies of nature are created by art, only to inevitably dissolve, thereby having nature, as a concept, give writers "the slip," as he puts it.[2] What does he mean by this? Is there no such thing as "nature," no material or vital substance uncreated by human beings that has existence on our earth? Or does he mean that while the substances we think of as "nature" have existence on earth, they exist in human perception or awareness only as a mental construct, as concept, idea, or language? What happens if we test this problem against a text like Anna Livia Plurabelle? Does Joyce evoke "nature" again and again in the chapter only to have it give the text, and the reader, the slip? The chapter's fluidity has long been recognized as more than just a thematic issue, an allusion to rivers, streams, and natural change in persons or landscapes. The very shift of river into woman, or geography into man, is produced by stylistic and verbal fluidity, by meanings flowing from one concept into another as a letter or a sound shifts within a word or a string of words. My tracking of nature in "Anna Livia Plurabelle" will therefore inevitably display a similar fluidity, as I will try to make the very concept of the "figure" multiple, mobile, and elusive.

Tim Wenzell's *Emerald Green: An Ecocritical Study of Irish Literature* offers a further impetus for giving attention to the role of nature and environment in the work of Joyce. He writes, "Despite the large body of writing in Irish studies, particularly in the last fifteen years, very little of this writing has focused on Irish authors and their observations of the natural world." But although Wenzell remedies this dearth by devoting an important chapter to such Joycean contemporaries as Yeats, Lady Gregory, George Moore, and AE, he effectively overlooks Joyce as a contributor to this conversation. This may be largely because the urban settings of *Dubliners*, *Portrait*, and *Ulysses* function poorly as a response to the "wasteland of the post-Famine landscape," which is an important focus of attention for Wenzell.[3] But Cheryll Glotfelty offers a broader answer to the question "What then is ecocriticism?" that makes far more room for Joyce's own accommodation to the topic.[4] Her answer encompasses general representations of nature, the connection of human culture to the physical world, and negotiations between the human and the nonhuman—all issues foregrounded in the language and preoccupations of "Anna Livia Plurabelle." The *Wake* may not address the problem arguably at the heart of ecocriticism, namely, what Lawrence Buell calls the "human accountability to the environment," which endows literary texts with an ethical responsibility.[5] But I will argue that by deliberately not making the natural environment subservient to human interests, the *Wake* manages to produce an ecologically sensitive orientation for the reader. And it goes even further by constantly underlining the natural and material underpinning of human products, human bodies, and even human identities.

ALP is, of course, not the first Joycean woman to be identified with nature. Molly Bloom's fondest memory of her husband recalls, "yes he said I was a flower of the mountain yes so we are flowers all a womans body yes" (*U* 18.1576–77)—a romantic trope she assimilates to her identity, remembering "Gibraltar as a girl where I was a Flower of the mountain" (*U* 18.1602). Molly is a Bloom, to be sure, but she is also a flow-er, a stream of words, a metaphorical and stylistic river like her successor, Anna Livia Plurabelle, who too will be a stream of words that is the medium of two fictional washerwomen. Joyce in a 7 March 1924 letter to Harriet Shaw Weaver calls their speech "a chattering dialogue across the river by two washerwomen who as night falls become a tree and a stone. The river is named Anna Liffey" (*SL* 301).[6] And so it begins:

> O
> tell me all about
> Anna Livia! I want to hear all
> about Anna Livia." (196.01–04)

Danis Rose and John O'Hanlon transform that very first letter, that opening "O" into "eau," "a typographical representation of the cyclic nature of water" whose triangular form then widens to normal paragraph width "to symbolise the spreading of the river flowing from its source."[7] Does the fluidity of the language here give the river as a natural phenomenon the slip? Or is the figure of the river—which oozes out of sounds, words, shapes, and images to virtually inundate us with its conceptual ubiquity—here giving language the slip?

The washerwomen should anchor the chapter in a more or less conventional fictional world, we would think—a world focused on "the place and the people involved in the action" that makes a "plot summary" of the *Wake*, like John Gordon's, possible.[8] Joyce himself grounded the washerwomen in a real-life experience according to Richard Ellmann, who remembers him telling Arthur Power that the idea for the ALP chapter "came to him on a trip to Chartres, where he saw women washing clothes on both banks of the Eure" (*JJII* 563n46). Yet there appears to be more to the *Wake*'s transformation of the workers known as washerwomen, who in "Clay" ply their trade with "red steaming arms" in the hot, wet spaces of the Dublin by Lamplight laundry (*D* 101). By taking them out of an indoor place in an urban setting and putting them to work outdoors on the riverbanks, Joyce is able more readily to remind us that washerwomen are not only social constructs but also constructs of natural entities—living bodies, creatures, matter. Their later transformation to the tree and stone that Joyce adumbrates in his letter to Weaver suggests this fluidity of their being. And so the washerwomen begin their tale. It is told, not written, or at any rate imagined as told before being transformed into writing, and therefore itself consists of sound, an emanation or production of natural phenomena, as sound is produced by animals, streams, and wind.[9] Joyce, worried about the success of the ALP chapter, went walking along the Seine the night he finished it, "to listen by one of the bridges to the waters," according to Ellmann, who reports that "He came back content" (*JJII* 564n50). His writing signified sound to him, not only the sound of human speech but its similarity or kinship to the sound made by the flow of a river. It is not surprising, therefore, that the washerwomen's opening complaints about an "awful old reppe" (196.11) will echo or resound with the names of hundreds of rivers.[10]

The sounds are those of their names rather than their motion, to be sure, but the rivers are thereby conjured up as sounding all the same. But are these river names merely an "eccentricity" geared to please with their "'flowing' sonority and 'sound sense'" as John Bishop suggests? If so, what is the point, since few readers "are likely to struggle through very many pages of prose so tortuous as the *Wake*'s simply because, though they may not mean anything, they sound nice."[11] James Atherton raises the same issue—"nobody has ever been able to suggest what purpose is served by this inclusion of names"—but he offers the curious possibility "that perhaps the reader will unconsciously absorb the effect of rivers from reading river names."[12] What would be this "effect," unconsciously absorbed? I will propose that this effect is an ecological sensibility, the construction of an "ecological imaginary" that turns the reader's attention back not only to the words or names of rivers but to their referents, not merely as concepts but as moving, rushing, winding, coursing, ubiquitous, global phenomena in the real world that speak themselves in the form of sound. Not only do the river names themselves produce lovely sounds, as Bishop notes, but they oblige us to picture them, or try to picture them visually, to place them on our mental map of the world, and to remember their function and role in human lives all over the planet. Bloom fills his iron kettle in "Ithaca" by turning on the faucet to let the water flow, we remember. "Did it flow? / Yes. From Roundtown reservoir in county Wicklow of a cubic capacity of 2400 million gallons" (*U* 17.163–65). That tap water in a kitchen begins as river water, we are reminded. And rivers will not be the only natural phenomena conjured up in the ALP chapter. There will be mountains and plains, with all their vegetation, and animals and the foods made out of them, and the bodies of creatures and of humans, all transformed into one another—conjured up for us insistently by the prose, which seems incapable of overwhelming this ecosystem with its simultaneous cultural narrative.

Returning to the washerwomen, we first see them urge one another to tell all about Anna Livia. Yet they instead begin by talking about an indistinct male figure, a "he," an "old cheb" (196.06), a "roughty old rappe" (196.24), "duddurty devil" (196.15), derided for a variety of sins and flaws that render him not only morally but also physically dirty: "Look at the shirt of him! Look at the dirt of it! He has all my water black on me" (196.11–12). The text here layers levels of activity and levels of representation. Gossip about the dirty devil becomes what we now slangily call "dishing dirt"—not only metaphorically but also literally, as the women perform the literal as well as the figurative act of washing dirty linen in public: "He has all my water black on me." The story is already winding and winding. Instead of telling us about Anna Livia, it has veered off to tell us about her man, whose name itself takes strange turns when it is mentioned at all. One moment he is "King fierceas Humphrey" (196.21), but when the question of his name is raised—"How elster is he a called at all? Qu'appelle?"—he becomes "Huges Caput Earlyfouler" (197.07–08), a huge screw-up, as it were, kaputt, fouling up early on like Adam and Eve in the Garden of Eden. Rose and O'Hanlon ask the same question: "But what was he called, then, Henry the Fowler or Hugh Capot, or what?"[13] The only thing that is quite certain at this point in the chapter is that he is described negatively, that he is derided, and that what is disliked about him translates both figuratively and materially into dirtiness. The washerwomen engage in a double activity of the mind and the body; they tell and they wash, and the washing of stained linen requires physical effort and produces physical results in polluting the water. Ecological effects have slipped back out of the gossip, and the metaphors of manual labor and effort have produced sore wrists—"My wrists are wrusty rubbing the mouldaw stains" (196.17–18)—as well as material and organic decay: rust and mildew, polluting the Moldau River.[14] "As you spring so shall you neap" (196.23) is the fluid adage describing the nadir of the figure we will identify as HCE.

Soon we get a description of this man, this HCE, as a self-confident and arguably dashing fellow who is quickly satirized with similes from different angles of nature: "And the cut of him! And the strut of him! How he used to hold his head as high as howeth, the famous eld duke alien, with a hump of grandeur on him like a walking wiesel rat" (197.01–04). His proud posture elevates him to the height of Howth hill, but his humpback—a feature of his body as well as his name (Humphrey)—makes him look like a weasel or a rat. He is also quickly linked to ALP, although whether she is his wife remains a question ("were him and her but captain spliced?" [197.12–13]). Their putative wedding vows are both marine and avian, evoking water fowl, eider ducks and drakes, wild geese and ganders: "For mine ether duck I thee drake. And by my wildgaze I thee gander" (197.13–14). And their union is turbulent, conjuring sailors on troubled waters, the mythical flood of Deucalion ("duke alien"), the biblical deluge of Noah, the journey of a proto-Odyssean "Phenician rover" (197.31), navigating "dredgerous lands and devious delts" (197.22). We are reminded here of Leopold Bloom, unable to manage a rowboat with Molly when the waters became rough, "the tide all swamping in floods," Molly remembers (*U* 18.958–59). The *Wake*'s male is an aggressive sailor, however, as "he raped her home, Sabrine asthore" (197.21) until with his "runagate bowmpriss he roade and borst her bar" (197.35). Although the washerwomen include several cultural references in their description of HCE—health insurance, work as a miner, a journey past madhouses and hospices—their language insistently erupts in references to land, water, animals, and weather, all of it wild, animate, in motion. The moments of peace are relatively rare and evoke the married couple, if that is what they are, in their guises as river and mountain: "Flowey and Mount on the brink of time make wishes and fears for a happy isthmass" (197.14–15). Christmas, a time of truce in warfare, becomes an isthmus, a strip of land uniting larger masses of land separated by bodies of water.

The washerwomen do produce a cultural narrative, of course: the story of a man suspected of doing something very wrong, whose misdeeds have been in the news, a man who is an aggressive partner to his woman, yet still a worker and wage earner—"He erned his lille Bunbath hard, our staly bred, the trader. He did. Look at here. In this wet of his prow" (198.05–07). And when their story turns to his wife, she too displays a troublesome cultural dimension as a downtrodden woman of the sort we find in many of the stories of *Dubliners*. When her husband is depressed, "hungerstriking all alone and holding doomsdag over hunselv" (199.04–05), she cooks for him, tries to cheer him up, works until her "pyrraknees shrunk to nutmeg graters while her togglejoints shuck with goyt" (199.21–22), only to be lucky to escape his abuse—"if he didn't peg the platteau on her tawe, believe you me, she was safe enough" (199.25–27). These descriptions remind us of the underside of poor and troubled lives, like that of Mrs. Fleming, "the stupid old bundle" who cleans the Bloom home incompetently and needs to leave "on account of her paralysed husband getting worse theres always something wrong with them disease or they have to go under an operation or if its not that its drink and he beats her" (*U* 18.1097–1102). Even so, Anna Livia does her best, even playing the fiddle on a wobbling chair in her window, perhaps for donations like Molly after Bloom lost his job at Hely's and left her "strumming in the coffee palace" (*U* 18.562). But the human social drama here depicted cannot suppress the ecological narrative. For one thing, ALP's efforts to feed her husband conjure up the animal and plant life that keeps people alive—fish ("fisk"), eggs ("eygs"), bacon on toast ("beacons on toasc"), green tea ("Greenland's tay"), and coffee mocha ("Kaffue mokau") (199.16–18). And her prayer—uttered after even her most desperate ploy to solicit "all the neiss little whores in the world" (200.29–30) for her husband seems to have failed—is again submerged in her identity as the river.

"By earth and the cloudy but I badly want a brandnew bankside, bedamp and I do, and a plumper at that," she begins,[15] invoking earth and clouds, and requesting a new bankside, a river version of a corset or girdle to make herself once again attractive to the love of her life, her "*life in death companion*," her "*maymoon's honey*." Her man is old and infirm, we gather, "*my old Dane hodder dodderer*," "*my much-altered camel's hump*," "*my fool to the last Decemberer*," still trapped in a "*winter's doze*" from which she prays he will awake so that he may once more "*bore me down like he used to*" (201.05–12). The seasons, conventionally troped as times of life and as images of moods, are here also grounded as responses to nature and weather, to winter and December as times of coldness and passivity. With the husband as the "*frugal key of our larder*," the couple appears now to have "*run out of horsebrose and milk*" (201.09–16)—leaving ALP to figure out how they can survive while her husband remains in his somnolent state. She grasps at the straw left to down-and-out women, like the syphilitic whore in the black straw hat in *Ulysses* who had "begged the chance of his washing," as Bloom remembers (*U* 16.714–15). ALP asks if some lord of the manor or some knight might not "*dip me a dace or two in cash for washing and darning his worshipful socks for him*" (201.14–15). The river here transforms into a proleptic washerwoman, like the one telling her story, a figure that conjoins the river and labor. But first she rests and dreams of the freer life of a Continental vacation: "*I'd lep and off with me to the slobs della Tolka or the plage au Clontarf*," she sings, eager to feel "*the gay aire of my salt troublin bay*" (201.18–19). The Liffey here would love to leap over her banks and veer off into distant bays and streams where she might experience greater sensations of open air and wind, a desire that to Kimberly Devlin signals "her need for release" from the burdens and restrictions placed on the lives of women in difficult situations.[16] The evocation of "the young May moon" in "*maymoon's honey*," coupled with the reference to Dublin's Tolka River, draws a sharp contrast between the stifled ALP and the happy Molly Bloom singing and flirting with Boylan on the banks of the Tolka while her husband trails after them.

But the old, depressed, and idle husband is not ALP's only problem, as we learn when the washerwomen now look more closely at the wife. Like May Dedalus and several of the women in *Dubliners*, she has many children, although the number is here both uncertain and impossibly exaggerated: "How many aleveens had she in tool? I can't rightly rede you that. Close only knows" (201.27–28). If she "confined herself to a hundred eleven" (201.29)— enduring pregnancy or confinement with twins and triplets ("twills and trills") and groups of "sparefours and spoilfives"—then in all likelihood she belongs to a species other than human, perhaps a fish or a mammal producing a "litter" (202.01–02). However, the great number may also invoke ALP as a primal mother, as an Eve who brings forth not only Cain and Abel ("Kund and abbles" [201.33]) but thereby all succeeding generations. We are reminded here of the implicit association of *mer* and *mère*, of Mulligan citing Algy in calling the sea "our great sweet mother" (*U* 1.80), a reference that prompts Stephen Dedalus on Sandymount strand to think of midwives and childbirth and "naked Eve" (*U* 3.41). And like Stephen thinking backward in time, the washerwomen now go back to ALP's beginning, her early courtships and her "girly days" (203.08). This foray into her past will once again foreground Anna Livia as the river, but her fluidity throughout these passages is also expressed stylistically and epistemologically in the form of the washerwomen's uncertainty about all the aspects of her being. ALP can't be pinned down, as it were, can't be reduced to a set of facts or characteristics, or to a single clear identity. The conversation here is full of questions that require going back to get uncertain answers. "For the dove of the dunas! Wasut? Izod? Are you sarthin suir?" (203.08–09), one of them asks the other, and the reply is full of negatives, making it clear that nothing is certain with the river and its female counterpart. The questions pressing the need to move backwards to answer them mimic the movements of waves in the water.

The journey back in time to ALP's youth and her early courtships produces some of the most lyrical passages evoking not only the human figures but also the nature they embody. We may wish to recall here Molly Bloom's early romantic encounters with Mulvey, back in Gibraltar, and with Bloom on Howth Head—set outdoors amid ferns and flowering shrubs, with goats and earwigs, overlooking the sea, and sprinkled with tropes of nature. ALP is the fluid stream—"She was just a young thin pale soft shy slim slip of a thing, then, sauntering, by silvamoon lake"—while HCE belongs to the land "making his hay for whose sun to shine on, as tough as the oaktrees" (202.26–30). When one washerwoman corrects the other, "You're wrong there, corribly wrong" (202.34–35), an earlier scenario is evoked that goes back to the river Liffey's source in Edenic Wicklow: "It was ages behind that when nullahs were nowhere, in county Wickenlow, garden of Erin" (202.35–203.01).[17] Time and space function analogously here, with the action of going back in time recalling the tracing to the source, and with the ecological images becoming so strong that they overpower the social courtship narrative of the female and male figures as ALP goes "foaming under Horsepass bridge with the great southerwestern windstorming her traces" (203.02–03). Her movement is fluid as she spins and grinds, swabs and thrashes her way through the countryside, "for all her golden lifey in the barleyfields and pennylotts of Humphrey's fordofhurdlestown" (203.05–07). But the questions pushing the story further and further back continue: "Dell me where, the fairy ferse time! I will if you listen" (203.16–17). And so begins one of the most engaging, and arguably controversial, moments in "Anna Livia Plurabelle." "Well, there once dwelt a local heremite, Michael Arklow was his riverend name": here the washerwoman begins her story about a priest whose laundry she has done ("with many a sigh I aspersed his lavabibs" [203.17–19]) and his erotic encounter with a very young girl.

"On the one hand here is a priest slaking his thirst in a stream, naturally enough; on the other here is a priest unable to restrain kissing a girl, partly because she is 'so young'—reason enough for a social outcry," Finn Fordham writes in his trenchant, detailed examination of this scenario.[18] Molestation by priests exploded into the news in Ireland in the 1990s, Fordham notes, but Joyce's seemingly uncensorious treatment of the issue in the *Wake* remains problematic. The moral knottiness of the representation is compounded by the sensuousness of the prose. On a weekday in June or July, presumably a hot time of year, the priest plunges "both of his newly anointed hands" into the stream, "oso sweet and so cool and so limber she looked" (203.20–21) or into the young girl's hair, "parting them and soothing her and mingling it, that was deepdark and ample like this red bog at sundown" (203.24–26). The girl, in turn, colludes with his overture, "her enamelled eyes indergoading him on to the vierge violetian" (203.28–29). On the social level of the narration, we appear to get here the beginning of the story of ALP's troublesome catering to abusive men, a pattern that we have already seen perdure into old age. But the more stunning implication that becomes so dramatically visible in these passages is the contrast between human exploitation and its abuse and sin and nature's inherent moral innocence, even in the midst of its turbulence and predation. If the priest is merely washing his hands in the water that glints back to him with the indigo and violet colors of the rainbow, then the moment is lovely and his gestures are natural and soothing. If the stream is a girl, then the gesture is without excuse in spite of the prose: "He cuddle not help himself, thurso that hot on him, he had to forget the monk in the man so, rubbing her up and smoothing her down" (203.32–34). We get this contrast throughout a chapter that begins with HCE's misdeeds and repeatedly speaks of faults and sins: humans are capable of sin, but even destructive storms and animal sexual activities are not. The mythic moment that this points to is, of course, the great Fall in the garden of Eden, when the world was transformed from an inherently innocent nature into a cultural exile of sin and sexual shame.

Ostensibly, on the social level, the encounter between the "bold priest" and the "naughty Livvy" did the girl no harm, but raised her self-esteem and made her feel grown up: "she ruz two feet hire in her aisne aestumation. And steppes on stilts ever since" (204.02–05). Or, perhaps, we merely hear of a rise in the water level or an elevation of steppes, as a result of the priest's intervention. We now learn that ALP had even earlier sexual or pseudo-sexual encounters when two "lads in scoutsch breeches" waded through her waters with bare feet before she became powerful enough to support canoes or barges (204.05–09).[19] But when she is young, she is as innocent and vulnerable as Leda, "leada, laida, all unraidy . . . too frail to flirt with a cygnet's plume" (204.10–11). And as she becomes even more youthful, she "laughed innocefree with her limbs aloft and a whole drove of maiden hawthorns blushing and looking askance upon her" (204.18–20). Figurative language turns inside out here as tropes transform the natural traits of hawthorn, a shrub of the rose family, into "blushing" embarrassment and disapproval while the toddler laughing on the ground with her limbs aloft becomes as "innocefree" as Yeats's famous isle—as innocent and free as "The Lake Isle at Innisfree." As the washerwomen turn back to their laundry, even the clothes, which began with HCE's dirty shirt turning their water black, now take on the innocence of nuns' "coifs and guimpes," priests' surplices, and a baby's "pinny" (204.29–31). There are still "old Veronica's wipers" to be washed (204.30), but they merely conjure up the veil with which Veronica wiped the face of Jesus on his way to Calvary, and too are steeped in innocence. "Baptiste me, father, for she has sinned!" (204.36) evokes the whole problematic concept of original sin, which transforms even human infants into moral penitents requiring spiritual cleansing with the waters of baptism. The story of nature's transformation into the realm of the cultural and the moral is played out by laying onto the story of the river and the human infant the oppressive weight of biblical mythology and Catholic doctrine and ritual.

The washerwomen's narration now returns to HCE's scandal, first as it exploded in the weekend newspaper, the aptly named "Sitterdag-Zindeh-Munaday Wakeschrift" (205.16–17), and then by mocking balladeers in the pubs and hotels ("the Rose and Bottle or Phoenix Tavern or Power's Inn or Jude's Hotel") everywhere "in cit or suburb or in addled areas" (205.24–25). The social and cultural story here pretty much squelches nature until ALP emerges to deal with the crisis: "So she said to herself she'd frame a plan to fake a shine, the mischiefmaker, the like of it you niever heard" (206.06–08).

Her plan is cultural, at first, as she borrows a mailbag as well as a lantern from one of her sons, then makes herself tidy to join in the "mascarete" (206.14). The masquerade, however, returns to the river, according to McHugh's gloss of the French *mascarete* as a tidal wave in an estuary.[20] And so the narration has returned to the water, as the washerwomen are now clearly in a boat, with one of them rowing at the other's command: "Here, sit down and do as you're bid. Take my stroke and bend to your bow. Forward in and pull your overthepoise" (206.22–24). The vessel sounds more like a galley than a rowboat, perhaps in keeping with the classical resonances Rose and O'Hanlon find in the description of ALP's preparations for her mission, which they believe echoes Juno making herself beautiful to beguile Zeus in the *Iliad* (119).[21] We now receive an image of the human ALP bathing in the stream, a poetic juxtaposition of river-woman and river, in which the natural rises to the surface once more. Washing in mud, she applies not turpentine but "turfentide and serpenthyme," mixing soil and water, animal and herb (206.34). The products we apply to our bodies or cense them with are derived from nature, we are reminded, including wax and grains of incense. And so are our adornments of hair and dress, like the garland ALP weaves for her hair, of "meadowgrass and riverflags, the bulrush and waterweed, and of fallen griefs of weeping willow" (207.02–04). Jewelry too is derived from nature, with bracelets and anklets and amulets for a necklace made of pebbles and rubble, and "rhunerhinerstones," stones from rivers, and "shellmarble bangles" like pearls derived from oysters (207.07).

Over and over this chapter reminds us that human bodies are products of nature, and so is the food that is used to sustain them, the soap and shampoo that washes them, the clothing that covers them, the cosmetics that beautify them, the ornaments that adorn them. Figures of these entities have become so thoroughly subsumed into culture, transformed into commercial products, and even become synthetic in recent history that their origins in nature have been effectively suppressed and forgotten. ALP revives and restores them, and even if not all of her outfit escapes manufacture, there is still that "band of gorse" that adorns her hat, the "potatorings" that serve as earrings, the "fishnetzveil" that keeps the sun from wrinkling her "hydeaspects," and the "nude cuba stockings" that are "salmospotspeckled" (208.08–12). As a cultural figure she is certainly ridiculous, what with that clothespin on her nose, perhaps to keep herself from smelling the "rrreke of the fluve of the tail" (208.24–25) produced by the pollution and debris that swamp her waters and constitute her get-up: "Everyone that saw her said the dowce little delia looked a bit queer" (208.29–30). As the washerwomen's questions return to her mission, to "what was the game in her mixed baggyrhatty" (209.10), attention returns to the cultural, to the gifts that she disburses like Santa Claus handing out Christmas boxes and birthday gifts to her many children. The gifts are as multitudinous as their recipients, and their list goes on for several pages. ALP's role as the river remains foregrounded chiefly in her rapid, unstoppable motion as "arundgirond in a waveney lyne aringarouma she pattered and swung and sidled" (209.18–19), while the youths that run after her are both the river's offspring, "rivulets ran aflod to see," and human children, "juveline leads and ingenuinas" emerging "from the slime of their slums and artesaned wellings" (209.30–33). The gifts likewise are both natural and cultural, although we are once again reminded that such venerable commercial products as Altoids mints ("deltoid drops, curiously strong") are made of natural substances (210.09). Even such manufactured objects as a "bucket, a packet, a book and a pillow" (211.09) have a natural basis, although "an old age pension" (211.13) does not, and the material basis of the "stonecold shoulder" she gives "Donn Joe Vance" (211.32) has become purely metaphorical.

ALP's response to sin and scandal has been revealed as generosity and giving, a version of the caritas that we have seen in Leopold Bloom and even in Molly, throwing a coin at a wounded veteran, in *Ulysses*. Its analogue is the endlessly life-sustaining gift of water, on the one hand, and the endlessly culture-sustaining gift of words, on the other. We are back to Timothy Morton's reminder that for human perception, nature is merely language, and to my counterpoint, that the referent of far more words than we may have appreciated is nature. A "stonecold shoulder" may be a trope, but it is one that conjures up a material stone and a living shoulder, nonetheless. The generous and even wild flood of words that has showered us in "Anna Livia Plurabelle" is capable of endowing us with the gift of an ecological sensibility if we are willing to listen, to hear it rise through and over the cultural narrative with which it is interwoven. And so we return in the end of the chapter to the washerwomen who have now nearly finished their labor. In the dusk they anticipate a poignant ending to their workday. "My branches lofty are taking root. And my cold cher's gone ashley," they say, as they ask about the time and about the disassembled and reassembled Waterhouse's Clock (213.13–17). Roland McHugh adds a note here, perhaps derived from C. K. Ogden, that "[a]t this point the woman who is to be turned into a tree sees herself pictured upside down in the water, in the form that she later takes"— an image that suggests that she pictures herself drowned. Or, perhaps, she is turned into a German stream (*Bach*) as she laments her sore back ("O, my back, my back, my bach!" [213.17]). The other woman presumably alludes to her cold flesh (*chair* in French) as having turned to ashes, like an ending in cremation. Genesis 3:19 tells us that "Dust thou art and unto dust shalt thou return," a reminder that the phenomenon of death dramatizes the materiality of the human body as it is subsumed, in one form or another, back into nature. The famous transformation of the washerwomen into tree and stone turns its own tropology upside down as the figurative image conjures up the more literal transformation of the dead human body into ground and the vegetation and materials it produces.

Yet the washerwomen still have work to do on this night, and the laundry they now lay out to dry is indeed cultural: the hostel sheets slept on by a man and his bride, a butcher's apron, "[s]ix shifts, ten kerchiefs" (213.27), convent napkins, and a baby's shawl. These are all items close to the human body, touching the body, to be sure, even if their material origin is subordinate to their cultural use. But even as they work, the women begin to deteriorate physically, their hearing and their vision becoming weaker, their gait becoming creaky and limping, suffering from "hobbledyhips" (214.21). McHugh mentions that according to C. K. Ogden, Joyce may have collaborated on such notes, as "Their words are no longer clear to one another," and "As the story goes on the river becomes wider and the 2 women become parted." They still reprove each other, and in a last outburst one of them complains of her widow's life of poverty and trials: "Amn't I up since the damp tawn, marthared mary allacook, with Corrigan's pulse and varicoarse veins, my pramaxle smashed, Alice Jane in decline and my oneeyed mongrel twice run over" (214.22–25). Poverty and age take their toll on the body, the human body with its diseases (as McHugh glosses Corrigan's pulse) and varicose veins, the dog's body with its lost eye and traffic perils, and family members also "in decline." "My sights are swimming thicker on me by the shadows to this place" (215.09–10): hearing and vision are not only media of natural and environmental perception but are themselves aspects of the body's living materiality. But before shutting down completely, "[c]an't hear with the waters of. The chittering waters of" (215.31), they call up Anna Livia and her family one last time. ALP has been in physical motion throughout their conversation, but now, like the declining washerwomen, she too is in temporal motion, in transition: "Anna was, Livia is, Plurabelle's to be" (215.24).

And so the chapter ends, with the washerwomen still talking but failing. They have difficulty hearing—"[c]an't hear with the waters of"—and moving. Throughout the chapter it is the river that has been in motion, winding and veering uncontrollably, while the washerwomen have been moving in place, either washing on the banks of the river or rowing in a boat. Now they become more and more stationary. "My foos won't moos. I feel as old as yonder elm" (215.34–35), one of them complains, while the other says, "I feel as heavy as yonder stone" (215.36–216.01). They invoke the stationary similes of tree and stone here, still natural phenomena, to be sure, but without the magical vitality of the river. Yet even as the world becomes invisible, the washerwomen remain surrounded by nature. There are flittering bats in their night, and field mice making noises, and "[d]ark hawks" listening (215.36). In the end, the quest for storytelling remains, now turned to ALP's children. "Tell me of John or Shaun. Who were Shem and Shaun the living sons or daughters of?" (216.01–02). But even when the boys are transformed into tree and stone, the emphasis is on their living existence, on the vitality they share with their still moving river-mother. "Telmetale of stem or stone. Beside the rivering waters of, hitherandthithering waters of. Night! (216.03–05). The relationship between the washerwomen and the river has been not only one between teller and tale but also one between the production of words and the power of their referents to invoke the material, the vital, the living and sustaining power of nature. There may be no nature in human perception without words or language, but there would be no words without the material bodies, the vital organs, the living substances that are necessary to produce them. The human dead produce no language, and without the living human body there would be no words on this planet.

How do we summarize what the "Anna Livia Plurabelle" chapter offers to an ecocritical look at a literary text? The answer, if we review the evidence, is surprisingly complex—particularly if we are willing to reflect on the challenges that its narrative everywhere poses to a romanticized view of nature, to "European romanticism's canonization of nature," as Lawrence Buell calls it.[22] The washerwomen's story begins with nature's pollution, with dirty water, and with the social degradation of its citizens. ALP and HCE are not pastoral figures but cultural examples of the urban poor. Yet the representation of their plight constantly reminds us that the interconnection between nature and culture does not end on the borders of the city but flows through the undercurrents of Dublin life just as the Liffey flows through its geography. Food, clothing, hygiene, health, and labor are all interconnected with the material and natural world, and to the extent that these aspects of social life become problematized, their grounding in nature complicates the evocation of nature's purity, simplicity, and beauty. We may not expect the chapter to offer a political edge to its ecological evocations, but in its juxtaposition of the lyrical and vulnerable aspects of nature, it does. The aesthetic and healthy features of the natural world may be more easily discernible in rural and pastoral settings, but their urban transformations also give warning of their erosion and degradation. This is the dual and competing message of the washerwomen's simultaneous natural and cultural narrative, told in an equally conflicted and complicated style. In the midst of a story about the fall and sin, the washerwomen's words, sentences, and rhetoric still move with the energy that is implicit in the concept of fluidity, of the river, and the river-woman, and of their own identities. Romanticized nature may be difficult to retrieve, but even in the midst of urban life, it remains available to the imagination. Molly Bloom certainly taught us that:

> God of heaven theres nothing like nature the wild mountains then the sea and the waves rushing then the beautiful country with the fields of oats and wheat and all kinds of things and all the fine cattle going about that would do your heart good to see rivers and lakes and flowers all sorts of shapes and smells and colours springing up even out of the ditches primroses and violets nature it is. (*U* 18.1558–63)

Here in *Ulysses*, and throughout I.8 of *Finnegans Wake*, we are given ample evidence that Joyce was much more than a homocentric writer.

Notes

1. Finn Fordham, *Lots of Fun at "Finnegans Wake"* (Oxford: Oxford University Press, 2007), 20, 66.

2. Timothy Morton, *Ecology without Nature: Rethinking Environmental Aesthetics* (Cambridge: Harvard University Press, 2007), 1–2.

3. Tim Wenzell, *Emerald Green: An Ecocritical Study of Irish Literature* (Newcastle upon Tyne: Cambridge Scholars, 2009), 3, 51.

4. Cheryll Glotfelty, "Introduction," *The Ecocriticism Reader: Landmarks in Literary Ecology*, ed. Cheryll Glotfelty and Harold Fromm (Athens: University of Georgia Press, 1996), xviii–xix.

5. Lawrence Buell, *The Environmental Imagination: Thoreau, Nature Writing, and the Formation of American Culture* (Cambridge: Belknap Press of Harvard University Press, 1995), 7.

6. The Wikipedia entry on the river Liffey tells us that it "was also known as the Anna Liffey, possibly from an *anglicization* of Abhainn na Life, the Irish phrase that translates into English as River Liffey" (http://en.wikipedia.org/wiki/River_Liffey).

7. Danis Rose and John O'Hanlon, *Understanding "Finnegans Wake"* (New York: Garland, 1982), 115.

8. John Gordon, *"Finnegans Wake": A Plot Summary* (Dublin: Gill and Macmillan, 1986), 1.

9. Bernard Benstock writes in *Joyce-Again's Wake: An Analysis of "Finnegans Wake"* (Seattle: University of Washington Press, 1965), "The *Wake* is, after all, as critics have frequently asserted, an aural book, and re-echoes often the facets of an oral recitation," 167.

10. See John Bishop, *Joyce's Book of the Dark: "Finnegans Wake"* (Madison: University of Wisconsin Press, 1986), 336. Bishop here reminds us that by October 1927 "Joyce estimated that he had worked 350 river-names into 'Anna Livia,' and within a month wrote of having 'woven into the printed text another 152.'" He adds, "Readers given to calculating these things estimate that the final version of the chapter contains anywhere from eight hundred to a thousand rivernames."

11. Ibid., 337.

12. James S. Atherton, *The Books at the Wake* (Carbondale: Southern Illinois University Press, 1959), 45.

13. Rose and O'Hanlon, *Understanding*, 115.

14. The Vitava River (German: Moldau) courses under a number of bridges through the city of Prague in a way similar to the course of the Liffey in Dublin.

15. See David Hayman, *The "Wake" in Transit* (Ithaca: Cornell University Press, 1990), where he discounts "the voices of I.8 as mere echoes of an absent ALP" and argues that "there are only two clear instances of ALP's utterance in 'Finnegans Wake'—both found in Book IV," 193. But the italicized representation of ALP's "prayer," if that's what it is, suggests at the very least a verbatim representation, even if it is produced by the narrative of the washerwomen.

16. Kimberly J. Devlin, *Wandering and Return in "Finnegans Wake"* (Princeton: Princeton University Press, 1991), 155.

17. The Wikipedia entry for the river Liffey tells us that "The Liffey rises in the Liffey Head Bog between Kippure and Tonduff in the Wicklow mountains, forming from many streamlets. It flows for around 125 km (78 mi) through counties Wicklow, Kildare, and Dublin before entering the Irish Sea at its mouth at the midpoint of Dublin Bay" (http://en.wikipedia.org/wiki/River_Liffey).

18. Fordham, *Lots of Fun*, 67–68.

19. See Suzette A. Henke, *James Joyce and the Politics of Desire* (London: Routledge, 1990), 179. Henke, like Finn Fordham (68), attributes the preoccupation with infantile sexuality in these passages to the influence of then current Freudian theory: "Joyce acknowledges, like Freud before him, the erotic delights of polymorphous perversity that characterize infantile sexual experiments."

20. Roland McHugh, *Annotations to "Finnegans Wake"* (Baltimore: Johns Hopkins University Press, 1991), 206.

21. Rose and O'Hanlon, *Understanding*, 119.

22. Buell, *Environmental Imagination*, 56.

9

Moveable Types

The Character System in "The Mime of Mick, Nick and the Maggies" in II.1

CAROL LOEB SHLOSS

Book II, chapter 1 is the most overtly performative chapter of *Finnegans Wake*. It both reiterates the performance techniques of the entire book, where letterforms enact their own fate in a "cellelleneteutoslavzendlatinsoundscript" (219.17), and leads us to a new space of play. Every evening, the text announces, there is activity in the "Feenichts Playhouse" (219.02)—no fees charged in this Phoenix Park theater—where interested persons can watch a "wordloosed" drama enacted. It is a twilight activity, located between night and day, light and darkness, and "the whole thugogmagog" recurs, with different omissions, because of the various principals, the "respective titulars neglecting to produce themselves" on cue (222.14–16). Though the play is supposed to end with the enactment of a "Magnificent Transformation Scene showing the Radium Wedding of Neid and Moorning and the Dawn of Peace, Pure, Perfect and Perpetual" (222.17–19), the transformation fails to take place.

Instead, the children who enact their assigned roles return home "unlitten" (unenlightened, in darkness), with "miseries" entwined with "laughters low" (259.03–08). Clearly this is play of a distinctive and disturbing cast, and if it takes the form of a formal dramatic production, it also serves the characteristic purposes of children, who "trailing their teenes behind them" (227.12–13) are playing at "the shifting about of the lassies" and the "tug of love of their lads" (253.25–26). That is, they are competing and trying out erotic roles before those roles assume the obligatory shape of their adult lives. Thus they pose questions presented by any courtship narrative: What kinds of "children" participate in this performance? How are they sorted out—winning and losing, and assuming prominence or neglect? The questions are both substantive and narratological.

Stories, like social groups, are constructed through, by, and in competition. Narratives both delimit characters and thrust them into a distributional system, which demands the allocation of fictional space. Thus questions of ordination and subordination are at the heart of any fictional enterprise, even one as unique as *Finnegans Wake*. To describe the method by which such sorting is achieved, the way that symmetry or asymmetry is constituted, is to describe the narrative's pull toward democracy or inequality and to comprehend the forms of social relations, which encompass the diverse populations that people these novels. How are specific human figures inflected into narrative? How are they brought to the fore or conversely made to recede or disappear?

In this chapter, Joyce gives us a world with many actors but few success stories. The narrative seems preoccupied by the issue of "minority," creating a fictional world where the issue of subordination—and hence of insubordination—is always a powerful subtext. The "shifting about of the lassies" and the "tug of love of their lads" take a precarious turn whose trajectory this essay will follow.

To discuss a character system in the *Wake* is, of course, fraught with the expansions and multiplicities of Joyce's generic and constantly mutating conception of fictional identity. Although he begins this chapter with a list of actors, suggesting a series of fixed and consistent persons who will later interact, the list is deceiving, written as if it were an occasion for its own deconstruction or a pose that will later be dismantled. "Did it ever occur to you *prior to this* by a stretch of imagination that you might be very largely substituted by a complementary character?" the narrator asks,[1] suggesting that we look for constantly modulating traits and names and associations rather than stable narrative boundaries.

Glugg, Izod, the Floras, Chuff, Ann, Hump, Saunderson, Kate, and the Customers all enter the text with this seeming contradiction implicit in their presence. To name is to imply a singular identity; to narrate is to imply a course of action, and yet we are hard pressed to find individual sensibilities or simple behaviors. Gradually we learn that Wakean "characters" are more aptly described as "character spaces," or locations, as it were, where types of performances occur. Glugg, for example, is not just a particular sensibility, not just a young male with an identifiable interiority, but a type of boy, "the bold bad bleak boy of the storybooks" (219.24) who is associated with "Nick" or Beelzebub ("Bill C. Babby" [230.04]) and who will repeatedly occupy a place of exile. Chuff, similarly, is "the fine frank fairhaired fellow of the fairytales" (220.12–13), who is associated with "Mick" or "Michelangelo" (230.03). He is on the side of the angels. "Izod," for a third example, is always changing into another version of herself, another manifestation of young womanhood, while always remaining "placed" as that manifestation of girlhood, adolescence, and gradually awakening sexuality. Joyce indicates her "placement" by giving her various names with a family resemblance—Issy, Izzy, Isolde, Isabeau, Isabey, and in this chapter Izod—while he suggests her generalizability by the shifting letterforms themselves. She is a position in life, just as the other "characters" in the *Wake*, amid all of their various manifestations, mark other positions: mother, father, brother, old man, young man, knight, king, bishop, rival, friend, and so forth.

Joyce identifies his own compositional strategies in this chapter with the word *circumpictified* (230.32): encompassing, circumscribing, and surrounding inscriptions that enclose rather than distinguish the specificity that we usually try to recognize in the construction of narrative fiction. He creates *poetographies* (242.19): writing through poetic image, writing whose opacity remains on the level of signification, rather than moving transparently to allude to or imply referential personalities. If character in the Mime cannot be construed simply, then neither can action. "Psing a psalm of psexpeans, apocryphul of rhyme!" (242.30–31) is a phrase built on a children's rhyme: "Sing a song of sixpence, a pocket full of rye." In Joyce's hands, it is also as close as we will get to the description of a plot: "Sing a song of invented sex experience in poetic figures." Cumulatively the character glyphs add up to a narrative, but the unprecedented nature of their construction leaves many questions to be confronted.

The problem that this essay will address is the nature of the structural positions these "characters" hold within the literary totality that they inhabit. How, and to what extent, can we create a "character system" or a descriptive configuration from these gestures toward personalities that are always moving, always substitutable, and always exceeding the boundaries of conventionally rendered individuality? How are they inflected into the total work of art? Who emerges into prominence? Who is assigned minor roles? What is the socioformal organization of this chapter?

The conceptual framework behind this analysis was created by Alex Woloch in his book *The One vs. the Many: Minor Characters and the Space of the Protagonist in the Novel*. "How," Woloch asks, "can we redefine literary characterization in terms of a distributional matrix: how [is] the discrete representation of any specific individual . . . intertwined with the narrative's continual apportioning of attention to different characters who jostle for limited space within the same fiction universe?"[2]

Woloch's contribution to narrative theory is the creation of a model that avoids the tension between structure and reference—the opposition between the character as an individual and the character as part of a construction. As he explains, "In this framework, distribution relies on reference and takes place through structure" (17). This strategy serves also to bring out the socioformal dimension of narrative—quite apart from the dynamics that we might infer or extrapolate from social interactions outside the form. The character system, Woloch continues, offers "not simply many *interacting* individuals but many *intersecting* character-spaces, each of which encompasses an *embedded* interaction between the discretely implied person and the dynamically elaborated narrative form" (18). The space of a particular character emerges only vis-à-vis the other characters, which crowd him out or potentially revolve around him. "It is precisely here that the social dimension of form emerges, revolving around the inflection rather than the simple reflection of characters."[3]

Woloch is concerned, as his title implies, with the one and the many, with the tension between depth psychology and social expansiveness. The protagonist, according to him, is not a narrative given but rather emerges out of a complex narrative universe as other characters, all with their own potentials, are cast aside, disappearing from discourse as more and more space is allotted to the character who becomes the protagonist by virtue of his or her expropriation of fictional space.

In this schema, minor characters all have the potential to be the generative, central force of the narrative; they all have interiorities that could be pursued but which are not. And in their marginalization, in the elimination of their functions, we find the implicit political dimension of narrative as a form. Woloch calls minor characters the proletariat of the novel, for like their counterparts in real social space, their worth is reduced to function and their primary task is to disappear, either by exploding or by becoming engulfed in someone else's story. They are the socially subordinate actors in an imaginary drama, precluded from the actualization of full human consciousness, reduced to exterior form—suffocated or convulsed—"wounded, exiled, expelled, ejected, imprisoned or killed (within the discourse)."[4] The full extent of their interiority is denied, their perspective never pursued; they are configured only as subordinates.

To use this framework allows us to ask how Joyce creates protagonists and minor characters in "The Mime of Mick, Nick and the Maggies." How does the text allot attention among the actors in the drama? Who comes forward as the narrative progresses? Who is exiled or wounded or assigned a subordinate role? What is the function of inferiority? *Finnegans Wake*'s method of characterization suggests other questions as well. If characters in the *Wake* are not singular but represent a type, if they retain a family resemblance amid constantly shifting rearticulation, then is the whole (movable) type endorsed or left in obscurity? Can we infer a politics of attention from examining Joyce's character system?

Initially we notice that Joyce opens the chapter with a cast of characters, most of whom will be discarded without playing any narrative roles whatsoever. Who is "Ann" or "Kate" or "Saunderson"? Joyce names them only to forsake them. Their minorness serves primarily to create a sense of plenitude, as if a full-blown drama were about to take place. It is the same drama that is promised by naming a time ("the pressant" [221.17]) and identifying the workers behind the scenes. "Messrs Thud and Blunder" are responsible for the "futurist onehorse balletbattle pictures" (221.18); shadows are provided by "the film folk," who also supposedly offer "[l]ongshots, upcloses, outblacks and stagetolets" (221.22–22, the rented stage, the stage toilets) as if the performance were a polyglot assemblage of dance, theater, and film. "Harley Quinn" and "Coollimbeina" arrange dances, and the entertainment proposes "[j]ests, jokes, jigs and jorums" (221.25–26), costumes and wigs, music, and a community prayer. That is, Joyce sets the stage for something that never happens; he assembles a great performance apparatus for a drama that fails to enact itself. Just like "Ann" and "Kate" and "Saunderson," the other supporting staff members immediately disappear from the narrative. Their function, for want of a better way to describe it, seems to be to call attention to theatricality in and of itself. The text recedes from the "theater" it sets up—the inferior actors and the artistic directors disappear—at the same time that its language continues to dramatize itself. Joyce silences another set of sustaining characters while he maintains the "play" of language supposedly created to call them into being.

Instead of presenting a performance piece, the text proceeds to describe "play" of an entirely different sort—that of children experimenting with intimacy through the opportunities provided by slightly lewd guessing games. As mentioned above, Joyce calls this "the shifting about of the lassies" and "the tug of love of their lads" (253.25–26). In a much-quoted letter to Harriet Weaver, Joyce described the basic idea as

> Angels and Devils or colours. The Angels, girls, are grouped behind the Angel, Shawn, and the Devil has to come over three times and ask for a colour, if the colour he asks for has been chosen by any girl she has to run and he tries to catch her. As far as I have written he has come twice and been twice baffled. (*SL* 355)

He did not tell Miss Weaver that the colors were those of girls' drawers, but his note to her did privilege "the Devil" as the primary player in the narrative. His coming, guessing, failing, coming again, and being thwarted another time provides the focus of the clue.

Given this emphasis, it is interesting to note that the final text makes no distinction among the remaining actors. Three remain in equal tension: Chuffy, Glugg, and Izod, who is described initially among her peers. She is one of many:

> Aminxt that nombre of evelings, but how pierceful in their sojestiveness were those first girly stirs, with zitterings of flight released and twinglings of twitchbells in rondel after, with waverings that made shimmershake rather naightily all the duskcended airs and shylit beaconings from shehind hims back. (222.32–36)

This experimentation with "first girly stirs" will be Joyce's subject for the remainder of the chapter—only those characters, which participate in this shrouded dalliance, will remain in the narrative. Like the neighborhood children in Joyce's short story "Eveline," these Wakean children flit about at twilight. But unlike their earlier counterparts, they exhibit the first awakenings of sexual awareness in adolescence, the fluttering urges of the body, the sense of another, undiscovered and yet anticipated dimension to human being and embodiment. These "zitterings" and "twinglings" are experienced as something "naughty" and not quite known, seen at dusk, dimly, shyly—and as necessarily involving a partner.

The sexual tension experienced by Izod is, then, the founding condition of the "game" that will unfold. At this point in the narrative, it is her story, and Glugg and Chuffy (or "Shem" and "Shaun") will ascend into the foreground only to the extent that they will answer this initial need. Chuffy is a figure of safety. He is angelic and good ("Chuffy was a nangel" [222.22]). Glugg is the figure of adolescent daring, sexual knowledge, a "person" of taunting behaviors, invitation, hence "the devil" or the dark side of experience ("But the duvlin sulph was in Glugger.... He was sbuffing and sputing, tussing like anisine, whipping his eyesoult and gnatsching his teats over the brividies" [222.25–27]).

If he guesses right, if he answers the riddle posed by Izod, the two will be partnered, and the text indicates that this is a partnership desired by both. She is a tease. She wants the "duvlin sulph" to guess her colors and give chase. The text gives to her all the colors of the rainbow: "Not Rose, Sevilla nor Citronelle; not Esmeralde, Pervinca nor Indra; not Viola even" (223.06–07)—"I am ... all thees thing" (223.09). Were the text to end here, the subjectivities of Chuff, Glugg, and Izod could all lay claim to priority in the narrative's distribution of attention. Two adolescent boys of opposing natures vie for the "hand" of a girl ready for partnered play: "And they are met, face a facing. They are set, force to force" (223.15).

Given this formal, spatial parity, it is interesting that excellent and influential readings of this chapter then undercut the distribution of the character system by focusing solely on the interiority of Glugg, as if he were already identified as the protagonist. This is a privilege that is awarded at the expense of the character space of Chuff, but especially of the character space of Izod, who, at this point in the tale's unfolding, is still very much present, still very much occupying a space that is active, ready to choose, ready to play, and filled with desire: "she pranked alone so johntily. The skand for schooling" (223.33). She is about to be naughty (joining the school for scandal), but in the hands of critics, she has been demoted, as if the drama of the chapter lies in guessing the riddles rather than posing them.

One example of this privileged attention can be found in Margot Norris's essay "The Politics of Childhood in 'The Mime of Mick, Nick and the Maggies.'"[5] Norris reads the chapter in the light of Joyce's previous work, but especially as a countertext to *A Portrait of the Artist as a Young Man*. Whereas *Portrait* places the artist as a hero who tries to free himself from the myths of religion, state, and home in the tradition of the European *Bildungsroman*, the "Mime," Norris argues, undercuts or critiques this idea of development and self-liberation. It does this through reevaluating the nature of childhood, the meaning of exile, and the role of class in the education of the artist. It is the failure of knowledge, the insufficiency of education, that is the central drama of the "Mime," she asserts. Glugg does not succeed in solving the riddle of colors; he recedes from competition and stalks around in futile and sputtering disregard. His experience demonstrates the limits that class can place on the Enlightenment's idealization of pedagogy and the successful socialization of the child.

At first, Norris continues, the piece seems jocular, as if it were a childish version of a story about the artist's growing autonomy. She quotes another of Joyce's letters to Harriet Weaver on 22 November 1930 in which he judges the chapter to be "the gayest and lightest thing I have done in spite of the circumstances" (*SL* 355). It is filled with nursery rhymes and images of flower girls and children's laughter. But the gaiety, according to her, is specious, bought at the price of ignoring the actual social circumstances of children's experience, as if "real" childhood were replaced by a symbolically expurgated version of itself, as if adults were lying about social conditions, idealizing childhood as a utopian location. Using Max Horkheimer as her guide,[6] she writes, "Children symbolized the Golden Age as well as the promising future. The rationalistic society gave children legends and fairy tales so that they might mirror hope back to their disillusioned elders."[7]

Norris's essay addresses children's culture as a whole; it identifies children as a class, whose fate is often far different from the gloss adults put on it. She further generalizes by using children to emblemize the subordinate position of the Irish people under a colonial regime. But then, despite this attention to all children in the *Wake*, she focuses on one child:

> In the "Mime" plot of a little devil unable to guess the little girls' riddle, rebuffed and ostracized from the game, going off to write literature and returning to a miserable home, Stephen's Icarean odyssey and vocation are rescribed. Reread through this infantile narrative, *Portrait* becomes the tale of a sensitive boy whose poverty eventually made him an unfit suitor for a bourgeois girl.[8]

Without casting doubt on the resonance of such intertextual reading, without challenging Norris's thesis—that class has a powerful effect on children's assumption of identity and power—we can still notice that the only child whose disenfranchisement she illustrates is Stephen Dedalus's counterpart, the "little devil," Glugg.

The "Mime" offers much more complexity, much more divided and dispersed attention to the interactive lives of children. Competition, even among children, requires instigation, and it requires competitors. Joyce's text offers all. Intimate relationship or special notice, the desired outcome of this sport, similarly entails multiplicity: the girl and boy must meet, they must emerge out of the many possibilities of the courtship ritual, and they must do this together. Norris's method accounts for the "one" but not the "many" in the field of possible choices. That this game fails to bring Izod and Glugg together does not diminish the space of either character in the narrative structure. As we will see, Joyce continues to give consideration to all the contestants, making the issue of emerging from the troupe a subject of narration as well as the precondition of the text's creation.

Izod, or Issy, is initially presented in the midst of "the Floras." They are described as "Girl Scouts from St. Bride's Finishing Establishment" and as a bunch of "pretty maidens," who stand in an ambiguous relationship to her. The narrator says that they "pick on her," regard her as their "pet peeve," and also stand guard over her (220.03–06). She is presented in the midst of squabbling adolescent intrigue. How Izod, or someone like Izod, will emerge out of this group is the question that is posed by any courtship narrative. One thinks, for example, of Elizabeth Bennet in Jane Austen's *Pride and Prejudice*, with her four sisters and bevy of young female neighbors. Austen's text does not assume that Elizabeth will prevail in winning the hand of Darcy, but instead creates a narrative jostling out of which Elizabeth emerges. Her sensibility grows as other potentially "triumphant" sweethearts vanish from the story. They vanish not only in the sense that they do not win the hand of a potential husband but also in the sense that they complete their function. Their narrative work is done.

Izod begins the "Mime" among many young women, but she is given choices that are not identified for the other girls. She has "jilted" Glugg and is "being fatally fascinated by" Chuff (220.10–11). But the narrative next presents a contradictory trajectory. Instead of entertaining Chuff's courtship, Izod remains focused on Glugg, questioning him many times before the formal colors game begins: "And bids him tend her, lute and airly. Sing, sweetharp, thing to me anone!" (224.15–16). This is a "come on" that shortly will be reversed seemingly by all the flower girls, who by this time are collectively lined up in provocative positions: "The youngly delightsome frilles-inpleyurs are now showen drawen, if bud one, or, if in florileague, drawens up consociately at the hinder sight of their commoner guardian" (224.22–24). They are showing their bottoms at the same time that they rebuff Glugg: "Warewolff! Olff! Toboo!" (225.08).

Has Izod emerged from the pack of possible girls to be chased or not? The game veers from Joyce's initial description of the children's game to a new version where only one girl, Izod, is involved. Instead of all the girls being "at the ready" to be chased if one of their colors is chosen, only one poses riddles and receives (only to reject) answers. The formal structural pattern of the narrative has begun to shift. It will retain this ambiguity of "the one vs. the many" for a considerable narrative space, but gradually Izod will come forward with a sensibility, an interior emotional life that distinguishes itself (by taking up more and more narrative space) from that provided to the other Rainbow Girls.

Her suitor, Glugg, fails to answer the riddle of "colors." He tries to guess three times: "Have you monbreamstone? . . . Or Hellfeuersteyn? . . . Or Van Diemen's coral pearl?" (moonbeam stone, hellfire stone, or pearl from Australia's Van Diemen's Land). No. No. No. "He has lost" (225.25–28).

Norris takes this loss to be one of class standing, or rather the revelation of a class standing that the artist (Glugg) never had despite aspirations to win the hand of a bourgeois woman. The mystery he cannot penetrate, according to her, is one of a chivalric code or an aristocratic figure, or a form of behavior beyond the ken of the lower classes. The game thus mirrors a real rejection or humiliation in the referential world, which bars crossing class boundaries in marriage or courtship. Glugg is rebuffed just as Stephen Dedalus was rebuffed by Emma Clery, and their loss is the sign of the artist's *Deklassierung*, a lack of social standing which no amount of "cultural capital"—talent or education—can bridge.[9]

John Bishop understands Glugg's failure from an entirely different perspective. He points out that all of Glugg's answers refer to light that is only visible at night—and, as Bishop reads all of the *Wake* as occurring within the "troped head" of a sleeping giant, that vision is of a particular interior "ocular" type: the reflection of desire rather than actual sight. All of the characters, in this mode of reading, are refractions of the self as that self plays out interior conflicts that remain obscured or pushed into the subconscious during daylight hours. Bishop writes, "That the occulted color HCE tries to discover by 'gazework' within his 'glystering juwells' should be 'heliotrope' would account for the positioning of the 'Colours' chapter at the center of *Finnegans Wake*."[10]

Bishop looks at the entire trajectory of the book, finds that this is its midpoint, and that Finnegan is beginning to "turn toward the sun" or to ascend from the depth of his nighttime adventures. He starts "inexorably to float up toward sunrise, resurrection and the wakened rediscovery of sunlit vision."[11] In this system of thinking, all the character spaces are subsumed under the "troped head" of HCE, the sleeping giant. HCE has various manifestations (sometimes darkness incarnate, sometimes light), but all are aspects of one psyche. All the conflicts are internal; all serve ultimately to reveal the disturbances of life that fail to rise to the surface of consciousness but that play out in anxiety-ridden sleep. Resurrection, in this schema, is a unification of consciousness, the end of conflict, an awakening to the solace of a harmonious self, a self in which whatever is "ambothed upon by the very spit of himself" (230.02) becomes both/and, no longer the conflict of either/or.

This reading views Glugg as an aspect of HCE, the sleeping male protagonist, as if sleep did not have its own priorities. But one can argue that dreams, too, allot attention to various representations of the self, and that sleep, imagined as a grounding condition of Joyce's representative strategy, need not invalidate the character system of *Finnegans Wake*. It requires only the readjustment of the symbolic realm, which continues to bring forth and to exile aspects of desire, or shame, or burial, or resurrection with distinctions analogous to wakefulness. The subconscious, too, allots attention and finds representations of its own complexity.

Bishop can thus be seen, like Norris, to privilege Glugg, to see his action as formative—not of social reality but of interior experience—but formative nonetheless. Though he is represented as socially outcast and rejected "Shames" (93.21) or "Pain the Shamman" (192.23) or "The Memory of Disgrace" (413.03), though he is "acheseyeld" (148.33)—exiled, hurting, with painful eyes—his character space is given most exegetical attention, as if, in sleep, dark thoughts inexorably hold sway over other manifestations of the psyche.[12]

The irony of the Mime's allocation of attention can be viewed from both Norris and Bishop's reading of the meaning of Glugg's loss. For although this "character" fails to guess the answer to Izod's riddle, although he is exiled from the girls as a consequence, he is *not* exiled from the text. Failure does not lead to disappearance. He continues to take up (disgraced) narrative space. Indeed, he is followed through his departure, wrathful responses to failure ("he swure. . . . He would split. He do big squeal" [228.04–06]), and banishment: "From the safe side of distance! Libera, nostalgia! . . . He would . . . trashold on the raging canal, for othersites of Jorden" (228.24–31).

Clearly Glugg's narrative function has not been completed. The text reveals that suffering or loss is, despite the surface gaiety of the narration, of real concern. It takes up space. Glugg is represented as someone who "made melodi of malodi" (229.10)—created poetry out of pain—and as someone who went "in for scribenery with the satiety of arthurs" (229.07, Society of Authors). Writing is thus associated with revenge or with a reversal of fortune: "He would jused sit it all write down just as he would jused set it up all writhefully rate in blotch and void" (229.26–27).

In the text, the narrator then makes excuses for Glugg's "chromitis" (232.02). It offers reasons for his being "off colour" and for his having "recourse of course to poetry" (230.01, .24), but all of this self-justification is interrupted by a simple call to return. He does not go back to the sequence of the narrative—he has never entirely left it—but to the central drama of the game. He is now Mr "Moramor" (231.28, more love), for Issy has summoned him: "Isle wail for yews. O doherlynt!" (232.13). That is, to have followed Glugg's narrative position in this manner is to have partially digressed. It is to have ignored one of the founding conditions of the play.

Following the logic of space or "weight" or attention in the narrative, what remain are "girly stirs": the issue of female desire, especially as it is embodied in Izod. She is equally affected by Glugg's failure to guess: "It's driving her dafft like he's so dumnb. If he'd lonely talk instead of only gawk. . . . Speak, sweety bird!" (225.17–20). Long before Glugg's tantrum, indeed at the moment of his failure—"Shape your reres, Glugg! Foreweal!" (225.29–30)—the text dwells on her interiority. She is sad and dysphoric. "Yet, ah tears, who can her mater be?": Who is her mother? What is the matter? Who is her mate? "She's promised he'd eye her. To try up her pretti. But now it's so longed and so fared and so forth. . . . Alabye! Fled" (225.32–34). "Alabye!" (all goodbye) is a response to "farewell," but it is also an "alibi," a slight of hand, an invitation to look in the wrong direction at a critical moment. Was the guessing game a sham, a set piece with a foregone conclusion that has nonetheless gone awry? What is implied by "She's promised he'd eye her"?

As a result of this misguided guessing, Izod retreats into "the many." That is, she fails to come forward as a single and singular actor in "the shifting about of the lassies" and "the tug of love of their lads." The failure at "colours" has consequences beyond Glugg's banishment. All the girls wilt, but Izod is particularly affected: "The flossies all and mossies all they drooped upon her draped brimfall. The bowknots, the showlots, they wilted into woeblots" (225.35–36). There are tears; there is woe. For want of Glugg, the girls gather around Chuff ("Ring we round, Chuff! . . . All's rice with their whorl!" [225.30–31]) turning, at the hands of the narrator, into an "angel's garland" (226.22–23).

What follows is one of the most rending passages of subjectivity in the *Wake*. Like Glugg's angry leave-taking, Issy's unhappiness claims a significant place in the structure of narration as it draws to a close. Then she rejoins the group of girls. That is, the circle dance is not simply a lovely sight of innocence (the outsider's perspective) but an unwelcome retreat from not being chosen as a principal actor (the insider's sense of things). To come into prominence is the driving force of narrative distribution as well as the driving force of mating games. Issy doesn't make it. Her feelings are described, and then she is once again engulfed by the collective Floras.

> Poor Isa sits a glooming so gleaming in the gloaming; the tincelles a touch tarnished wind no lovelinoise awound her swan's. Hey, lass! Woefear gleam she so glooming, this pooripathete I solde? Her beauman's gone of a cool. Be good enough to symperise. (226.04–08)

Amid ugly feelings, she remains alone. Glugg is not, according to the text, just any young man, but her "swan" (swain), her "beauman" (beau), and he has cooled off. The voice that narrates does not regard this narrative development neutrally (it's only a game; they're only children), but names her as poor and pathetic and in need of sympathy. The voice swerves in an uncharacteristic way; it holds empathy, and it tries to mitigate individual wounding by placing the gloom in perspective first of wordplay and then of history. "Bring tansy, throw myrtle, strew rue, rue, rue" (226.10–11): Think of spices, it suggests. Rue is one of them. Think of this experience in the ages and ages of passing time. "And among the shades that Eve's now wearing she'll meet anew fiancy, tryst and trow. Mammy was, Mimmy is, Minuscoline's to be" (226.13–15). Remember that courtships have gone amiss since Eve and the beginning of human records; this is a book about repetition and renewal: she will meet a new fiancé who is trustworthy. Think of past, present, and future (what was / is / is to be) to hold this failure in its proper perspective. Then the narrative returns to the present and to the specific: "Lord Chuffy's sky sheraph and Glugg's got to swing" (226.19–20). The girls return to the protection of the angelic (Chuff is both "sheriff" and "seraphim"), and their collective dance begins.

Once again the narrative voice resorts to lyricism and to the observation of girlish vanities. Cashmere stocking, garters, shoes, caps, and pinafores are part of the performance repertoire, soon to be put in motion during this twilight show. "And they leap so looply, looply as they link to light. And they look so loovely, loovelit, noosed in a nuptious night" (226.27–28). Izod is subsumed in the group. Once the bearer of all the colors ("I am all . . . these things"), now she is indistinguishable from her troupe of "[q]uanty purty bellas" (224.28).

"Say them all but tell them apart" (226.30). The narration then starts its own kind of pantomime. Not content with describing a dance of colors, not satisfied with observing corporeal relationships or naming the dynamic of young bodies in motion, it emphasizes its own linguistic choreography. Presumably the subject of narration, its *histoire*, is the Floras—or the Rainbow Girls, as they have often been called. But the narration begins its own kind of ferocious play.

This play is no different from the selection and combination and recombination that characterize all Wakean language, but it is brought into relation with the subject of dancing. The dance of words calls particular attention to itself, to its own dexterity, to its assumption of tension and kinetic force. That is, this is mimesis acknowledging its origin in the body. If dance is writing with the body, this passage of the *Wake* subsumes that writing into another choreography that eats its subject in the process of identifying it.

> R is Rubretta and A is Arancia, Y is for Yilla and N for greeneriN. B is Boyblue with odalisque O while W waters the fleurettes of novembrance. Though they're all but merely a schoolgirl yet these way went they . . . dancing goes entrancing roundly. (226.30–35)

The capital letters identify a rainbow—not a reference to a rainbow—but the word itself: RAYNBOW. And while the circling continues—"And these ways wend they. And those ways went they" (227.13)—the letterforms reverse themselves, calling attention away from the teenage girls who presumably invoke the reference to the dexterity of language itself. "Winnie, Olive and Beatrice, Nelly and Ida, Amy and Rue [WOBNIAR]. Here they come back" (227.14–15).

Whatever energy, verve, finesse, or creative expressiveness might in some circumstances be allotted to the girls' dance remains located in the narrating voice. The Floras simply circle and circle again, repeating a movement without expressive gesture, moving, symbolically, around Chuff as his "angels garland." Their actions are centered not in their own youthful exuberance but on him as their guardian. They are oddly eccentric to the action they create, a pattern but no more than a pattern.

That Issy has been absorbed into this group is of the utmost importance. She is granted neither of the two conventional novelistic possibilities for her: that she emerge with a developing interiority, in and of herself across time; or that she develop in relation to many other persons, across social space. Instead she recedes into the herd of young girls, or as Joyce puts it, "all the gay pack . . . all the flowers of the ancelles' garden" (227.15–18). That is, having emerged into psychological fullness, albeit a dysphoric one, she recedes into an asymmetric structure, no longer unfurling and interjecting with a full place in the semantic structure of the text.

Thus when Glugg comes to guess again, he is guessing, this time, with a kind of ambiguity. Is he vying for Izod or simply trying to succeed in identifying one of the girls' colors? The return to play is initiated by her call: a "claribel cumbeck to errind" (232.16)—a clear call back to his errand. The call indicates both a lack and a desire: she wants him.

For a moment, Izod is described as having some kind of prior claim on him: "And around its scorched cap she has twilled a twine of flame to let the laitiest know she's marrid" (232.14–15). She's "married"; she's merry; she asks if her brother is jealous or intensely interested: "Is you zealous of mes, brother? . . . You suppoted to be the on conditiously rejected?" (232.21–23). But it is a short-lived prominence.

In response to the summons, the "devlin sulph" stands before the entire group: "he [was] again agog, before the trembly ones" (232.32–33). He is described in opposition to the girls, "vicereversing" their "perfection," "virid with woad" (vivid with rage), full of "complementary rages . . . from his punchpoll to his tummy's shentre" (227.19–22). "He threwed his fit up to his aers, rolled his poligone eyes, snivelled from his snose" (231.29–31). His motives are alluded to as suspect: "Now a run for his money! Now a dash to her dot" (*dot:* dowry in French). In short, the narrative develops his interior life, demonstrates fury, frustration, and economic aspiration, and then, with an abrupt shift, warns the girls against the very sensibility it has just annunciated: "Angelinas, hide from light those hues that your sin beau may bring to light!" (233.05–06).

Again Glugg fails. But whom does he fail? One or many? "He is guessing at *hers* for all he is worse." Or "how he hates to trouble *them*" (233.11, 15, my italics). And what is this game of "[f]ind the frenge for frocks and translace it into shocks of such as touch with show and show" (233.09–10)?

This seems to be edgy sexuality, temptation fleetingly dangled, invitation offered in the guise of innocence—and thus failure that is also half invited and half thwarted. What would success at this game be? The text never tells us. Instead Glugg is once more banished: "Get! . . . [a]nd he did a get . . . and slink his hook away" (233.7–29)—only to be replaced in the narrative by Chuff, who takes the story in the direction of pure fantasy, which plays on the girls' desires for home, status, a hearth with a cat, a car, and the prospect of bourgeois prosperity.

Instead of one girl being chosen, the girls remain together in an adoring flock, referred to as "Mayaqueenies" (234.13). "[T]hey went peahenning a ripidarapidarpad around him . . . in neuchoristic congressulations, quite purringly excited. . . . sending him perfume . . . to setisfire more then to teasim" (234.19–25). The teasing is intended to lure him: "that he, the fine-hued, the fairhailed, the farahead, might bouchesave unto each but everyone . . . his kissier licence. Meanings: Andure the enjurious till imbetther rer" (234.26–29)—endure the injurious until you bed her. Like the dance scenes of Jane Austen's novels, where sexual selection occurs under the guise of genteel gesture and conversation, these girls, albeit in a more provocative way, are vying for Chuff's attention. They are in a state of disequilibrium, for the competition implied by their faceless numbers has already insinuated itself into the formal structure of the narrative.

Thus when the narrative returns to Glugg ("But low, boys, low, he rises" [240.05]), its asymmetry is established—not as an imbalance between Chuff and Glugg, the ostensible competitors—but as an inequality between the many girls ("young shy gay youngs" [242.16]) and the rare commodity of male partners. "And, to make a long stoney badder and a whorly show a parfect sight, his Thing went the wholyway retup" (242.22–24). This attention to Glugg seems to emphasize one person's unsatisfied lust, but the narrative distribution of attention has already created a much broader field of disappointed and misaligned eros.

Toward the end of the chapter, Joyce returns to the ostensible form of a dramatic play. He reintroduces a setting. The moon rises and the dramatic action is called to a close. "Chickchilds, comeho to roo. Comehome to roo, wee chickchilds doo, when the wild-worewolf's abroad" (244.9–11). Children return to their homes (chickens come home to roost), but they come also with rue—the same rue that has been a subtext for the duration of this strange erotic play. The danger seems to be Glugg's mere presence in the vicinity (he has consistently played the role of werewolf), but nothing is clear. "It darkles (tinct, tint) all this our funnaminal world. . . . We are circumveiloped by obscuritads" (244.13–15).

The narrative creates a moment of silence—"Quiet . . . Tranquille" (244.28) —and an image of that tranquility: "The time of lying together will come and the wildering of the nicht till cockeedoodle aubens Aurore" (244.32–33). People will sleep through the wild night until the dawn. It takes an inventory of sleeping animals—elephants, rhinoceroses, hippopotamuses, pigs, beagles, peacocks, and camels rest—and it alludes to the night as a time for strolling lovers: "Darkpark's acoo with sucking loves. . . . Soon tempt-in-twos will stroll at venture and hunt-by-threes strut musketeering. Brace of girdles, brasse of beauys" (245.17–20).

But the dysphoria that has dogged all the contestants in the guessing game continues despite the theatrical gesture toward peace. The narration alludes to their state of being as "troublebedded" (245.30) and says, "But meetings mate not as forsehn" (245.22–23). Mating did not go as foreseen.

Only at this point does Izod, now in her guise as Icy-la-Belle, reemerge. She speaks in her own voice, and she speaks as a seductress: "My top it was brought Achill's low, my middle I ope before you, my bottom's a vulser" (248.11–12). "This kissing wold's," she says, "full of killing fellows" (248.24). The choice of partners can go terribly wrong, despite one's most colorful self-presentation. The narrative then describes her "lair": it is a "house of breathings . . . the breathings of her fairness, the fairness of fondance and the fairness of milk and rhubarb and the fairness of roasted meats and uniomargrits and the fairness of promise" (249.06–13).

For a moment, the seduction seems to work: "And Sunny, my gander, he's coming to land her. The boy which she now adores" (249.18–19). The narrative takes the stance that it is the group itself, all the girls, who defeat Glugg. "All point in the shem direction as if to shun" (249.28). "All laugh" (249.33). "Twentynines of bloomers gegging een man arose" (249.36–250.01). Twentynine to one. But Izod makes a move to become the protagonist of her own story, to leave the group and to assert a place for herself aside from "the floral's school" (250.33). "Twice is he gone to quest of her, thrice is she now to him. . . . And their prunkqueen kilt her kirtles up and set out. And her troup came heeling" (250.27–30). She is a maid with "the wont to be wanton" (251.06). She is a "young sourceress," he is "a fammished devil" in search of "eternal conjunction" (251.12–13).

The narrative itself lends encouragement to this venture: "Come, thrust! Go, parry!" (252.04), but it doesn't work. "[E]xceedingly nice girls can strike exceedingly bad times unless so richtly chosen's by" (252.22–23). This is the tale of a "naturel rejection" (252.28). It is dysphoric; it records not union but people who are "splitten up or recompounded" (253.34–35). The narrator exclaims, "what doom is here!" (255.12). "So angelland all weeping bin that Izzy most unhappy is" (257.01–02): the heavens (angel land) and even England are crying because Issy is miserable. Her failed move toward narrative centrality is marked by an ugly residue of feelings.

The dancing also stops: "They go round if they go roundagain before breakparts and all dismissed. They keep. Step keep. Step. Stop" (252.29–31). Somehow the disappointed sexual venture has affected the dancing. Briefly the narrative returns to the form of a performance that can have an arbitrary and definite end: "The curtain drops by deep request" (257.31–32). But the joyful circling had ceased long before: "For a burning would is come to dance inane. Glamours hath moidered's lieb and herefore Coldours must leap no more. Lack breath must leap no more" (250.16–18).[13] Aside from the allusion to Macbeth's sleeplessness, this is a dirge, a song to lost vitality, to the confusions (moider: confuse, bewilder) of courtship, to the failure of embodiment itself.

What has happened in this play where Glugg fails "tiercely" and where Izod repeatedly sits weeping (253.19)? Were this a Jane Austen novel, one could claim that a courtship ritual had failed and a daughter had returned home to her parents in defeat. One could notice the economics of partnership: that the competition for money, stability, position, and sexual attraction had been thwarted. This does happen. "For she must walk out. And it must be with who. Teaseforhim. Toesforhim. Tossforhim. Two. Else there is danger of. Solitude" (246.33–35). But it is not all that happens.

Uniquely in *Finnegans Wake*, character is not singular. Izod is Icy-la-Belle who is Izzy, who is Issy, who is a type or example of herself. That is, Izod marks a structural position in life, just as Glugg and Chuff, in their specific competition of "colors," also signify a more general male tendency toward strife. This is a world family and not just one family; it is a story of regeneration itself and not just the fading away of one set of parents and the upsurge of their boisterous offspring. Thus we cannot locate this courtship ritual in a specific time, as, for example, we locate Austen's characters at a juncture between the fall of the landed classes of England and the ascendancy of the monied professional classes. What implications does Joyce's singular fictional strategy have for evaluating the distribution of novelistic resources we have followed throughout this essay?

We might see in this unchanging changeability, the constant shifting of identities, a critique of the ritual itself, for none of the participants escape without "a hidden wound" (247.23). Izod enacts the drama of young girls who must wait to be chosen and who, in this narrative, have power only insofar as they are objects to be viewed with desire. That is, she embodies her own fated place in the mime itself. It is not an accident that she and her cohorts in the "floral school" are dancers. They circle and circle, named as visual perfection and viewed according to the colors of their drawers or "understamens." But their dancing, we can also notice, is not the dance of exuberance or self-expression or even of mastery. It is, in this mime, a consistent space for self-display.

While neither contestant, Chuff or Glugg, "wins" in the sense of being successfully mated, Chuff does claim the company of the girls. It is unwanted in Issy's case, but he has the cultural resources and the "purity" to accompany them and to command their attention. In the cosmic drama that is implied by their names, the Archangel Michael vs. Nicolas or Lucifer or Beelzebub, and by the allusion to the Christian book of Revelation, they are supposedly enacting a "Magnificent Transformation Scene showing the Radium Wedding of Neid and Moorning and the Dawn of Peace, Pure, Perfect and Perpetual" (222.17–19). That is, their identification with good and evil is supposed to lead to a place beyond conflict and to the defeat of evil itself. The "duvlin sulph" should, according to this schema, be overcome.

It is here that we can see the ironic reversal worked by the text insofar as it allows Issy to emerge with an active character space. For she desires "the duvlin sulph"; it is precisely his darkness or sexual experience that she finds lacking, and in this lack we find the source of dysphoria, the unstated but driving force of the narrative distribution of space. "Childs will be wilds" (246.21–22). Those "first girly stirs" are not simply circumstances to be viewed lasciviously, but occasions, were the world different, for the expression of female desire.

But the referential world, the novel's *histoire*, is not different. In this text, attention tends to be given to male choosing and to male telling. To some extent, Norris and Bishop are right. Glugg may fail, but he is given multiple chances to act. Chuff succeeds, insofar as he succeeds, simply by being a heavenly prince. He is innately a principal, and the text treats him as such. Issy is the *aporia*, the trouble point of narrative attention, who emerges, only to withdraw, who speaks, only to be occluded. Her narrative space both exists and is usurped by others, with resulting gloom.

The principal usurper is, of course, not identified in the *histoire*, for it is the speaking voice which composes and transforms all of these implicit tensions into signs. The primary actor has also been the primary voyeur, "the cause of all our grievances, the whirl, the flash and the trouble" (220.27–28). It is "the chroncher of chivalries" (254.07), the whirling dervish of vocables, the creator of the "soundscript," the arranger of letterforms, which mix and match, perform, bamboozle, and dazzle. If there is a politics of attention in "The Mime of Mick, Nick and the Maggies," it is centered on this puppeteer, this linguistic dervish, who, invisibly behind the scenes, turns the Rainbow Girls into their observed embodiment, robbing them of their own *jouissance*.

This voice flirts and flaunts, turning "[p]rettimaid tints" into their own alphabetic representation: "apple, bacchante, custard, dove, eskimo, feldgrau, hematite, isingglass, jet, kipper, lucile, mimosa, nut, oysterette, prune, quasimodo, royal, sago, tango, umber, vanilla, wisteria, xray, yesplease, zaza" (247.34–248.02). By the end of the "Mime," the narrator asks, "Who is Fleur? Where is Ange? Or Gardoun?" (252.31–32). And well it might ask, for the girls, as acting subjectivities, have been engulfed by their own assembly into a show-off language. The weight, movement, style, breath, and flow of tension through space that normally characterize dance have been transformed into the poetic body of the text, into a "wordloosed" drama. "Alabye! Fled!" Budding adolescence has been only a narrative pretext whose primary focus, we now see, remains on staging its own corporeality, its own voice, its own terrible, consuming voice.

Notes

1. David Hayman, ed., *A First-Draft Version of "Finnegans Wake"* (Austin: University of Texas Press, 1963), 237.

2. Alex Woloch, *The One vs. the Many: Minor Characters and the Space of the Protagonist in the Novel* (Princeton: Princeton University Press, 2003), 13.

3. Ibid., 17–18.

4. Ibid., 25.

5. Margot Norris, "The Politics of Childhood in 'The Mime of Mick, Nick, and the Maggies,'" *Joyce Studies Annual* 1990, 61–95.

6. Max Horkheimer, "The End of Reason," in *The Essential Frankfurt Reader*, ed. Andrew Arato and Eike Gebhardt (New York: Continuum, 1987), 41.

7. Norris, "Politics of Childhood," 64.

8. Ibid., 70–71.

9. Ibid., 78.

10. John Bishop, *Joyce's Book of the Dark: "Finnegans Wake"* (Madison: University of Wisconsin Press, 1986), 238.

11. Ibid., 239.

12. Ibid., 240.

13. The allusion is to *Macbeth* II.2.39–40: "Glamis hath murther'd sleep, and therefore Cawdor / Shall sleep no more—Macbeth shall sleepe no more."

10

"MUTUOMORPHOMUTATION"

Horus and Set as Principles of the Digital and Analog in II.2

JEFFREY DROUIN

II.2 is perhaps the most polyvocal chapter of *Finnegans Wake*. The format is unique: it separates the voices of the Earwicker family into spatial regions of the page, resulting in a simultaneous discourse embodying what the television show in the next chapter describes as "*verbivocovisual presentment*" (341.18–19). The spatial separation is an interesting reflection of Shaun's geometry lesson as the children do their homework upstairs in the Earwicker pub. The format mimics a children's copybook with annotations in the margins, where Shaun and Shem comment on the narrowed central body of text, which flows like a river (perhaps visually representing ALP), and in footnotes, where Issy voices her responses. However, the simultaneous juxtaposition also resembles a periodical layout or cinematic split screen, a synaesthetic medium of words, sounds, and moving images that impinge upon the combined faculties of the eye and ear. Thus the *Wake* positions itself within the media ecology of the 1920s and 1930s, experimenting with the instantaneity afforded by the associative nature of language to make vastly disparate times and places simultaneous to one another.[1] In that way, Shaun and Shem, as the representatives of the eye and ear, respectively, take center stage in this chapter along with their archetypes Cain and Abel of the Old Testament and Horus and Set of Egyptian mythology.

In fact, an underexplored area of II.2 is the conflict of Horus and Set, who illuminate the broader stakes in the merging of Shaun and Shem into a complete adult male. Like the brothers in the *Wake*, Horus and Set represent the unification of contraries such as eye/ear, upper/lower, good/evil, and Apol-

Ionian intellect/Dionysian creativity that are required for attaining the status of the new father. However, there is more afoot than the abstract resolution of cosmic essences, since the unification occurs as a geometry lesson amid multiple references to modern scientific and media revolutions. The connection linking all of the concepts in II.2 resides in the dichotomy of eye and ear, which were understood in Joyce's day to be founded upon fundamentally different physiological processes involving digital and analog sensory streams.[2] A large part of the *Wake*'s modernism consists in its synthesis of principles that are ineluctably opposed but mutually dependent.

During the geometry lesson, Shaun makes the two-part "grand discobely" (294.12–13) of sexual knowledge and rational analysis that unites him and Shem to become the adult male who in II.3 will lead Issy in an attack against their father. Shem helps Shaun to learn the Cartesian method of measuring space—he "must, how, in undivided reawlity draw the line somewhawre" (292.31–32)—simultaneously tricking him into acquiring sexual knowledge by drawing their mother's genitalia. As usual in the *Wake*, this Oedipal process entails much more than the development of the complete human male and the overturning of the generational cycle.

The transformation is driven by the boys' association with contrary parts of the body, though a rigid dichotomy does not always hold. In general, Shaun represents the upper half of the body and Shem the lower half. At first, Shaun comments from the right margin upon the center river-text, while Shem comments from the left. About midway through the chapter, the stream of language overflows its banks and then recedes, causing the boys to merge and switch sides, both left/right and upper/lower. Shaun, as the upper half of the body and the eyes, is associated with vision; Shem, as the lower half and the ears, is associated with hearing. Edmund Epstein notes that the cells of the retina receive visual impulses in discrete "packets" that enter the optic nerve and the brain in a discontinuous stream, while the ear perceives sound through the continuous wave motion produced over the cilia in the organ of Corti.[3] Thus Shaun represents a digitalized sense modality while Shem represents an analog one. In that way, seeing is an analytic process associated with Cartesian rationalism and the intellect, while hearing is a synthetic process for the re-creation of the world.

In Joyce's schema, the analog triumphs because its homologous relation to continuous reality allows the ear to synthesize the disparate materials it encounters. Modernist scholars have pointed out that the advent of electric media in the late nineteenth century precipitated a shift away from the Enlightenment emphasis on vision, with its linearity and atomism. Hearing became the new metaphor to describe a networked field model of knowledge production characterized by simultaneity, syncretism, and inclusiveness.[4] In this context, the mythic method that Joyce developed in *Ulysses* and greatly expanded in the *Wake* reflects the acoustic model of instantaneous polyvocality enabled by electric media.

A number of Shaun and Shem's characteristics outlined in earlier parts of the *Wake* foreshadow their amalgamation in II.2 and the blending of the digital and analog that it entails. Epstein notes that for much of I.7, Shaun's metamorphosis into Justius accompanies a self-righteous verbal attack on his lower brother, asserting the supremacy of visual digitalization.[5] When Shem, as Mercius, defends himself, he "does not champion the audible over the visible; he includes both senses in a complete presentation of the world."[6] It is for that reason that Shem, as the more complete analog principle, creates the film reel that announces the beginning of the forward flow of time in the *Wake*. The long word "Quoiquoiquoiquoiquoiquoiquoiq!" (195.06) represents the sound of a movie projector starting up, when the Movietone soundtrack is audible before the film is visible.[7] In early sound film, the sound was produced through an analog magnetic or optical band embedded in the filmstrip alongside the discrete photographs that create the illusion of continuous motion. Thus the mixed medium of sound film serves as an example of the combination of digital-Shaun and analog-Shem information streams, alongside each other within the figurative filmstrip of the text, but with the emphasis on Shem-analog as the creative principle that holds it together. For that reason, Shem as the analog principle becomes the primary mover of events in this chapter and of their repercussions in the ones that follow.

While the visual and audial syncretism might seem a straightforward way of reading the *Wake*, what is less intuitive is that the principles of the digital and analog also recall the battle between Horus and Set. Epstein notes that the black eye which Shaun delivers to Shem after they have switched sides (304.01R) seems to originate from the battle in which Set destroys Horus's eye and Horus destroys Set's genitalia.[8] In that arrangement, Shaun takes on the characteristics of Horus while Shem takes on those of Set. However, because of their reversal and merging after the river-text recedes, each brother takes on some of the contrary qualities of the other and his associated god, meaning that Shem-Set becomes Shem-Horus and obtains the injured eye.

There is much more to the Horus and Set connection than in the segment mentioned by Epstein. The plot elements of II.2 perform a thorough retelling of their conflict as Joyce found it in a handful of Egyptology sources primarily by E. A. Wallis Budge.[9] Budge indicates the name Horus means "he who is above" and Set "he who is below," forming a model for Shaun and Shem as the upper and lower halves of the body, as well as what many Egyptologists consider to be a geographical conflict between the two halves of the kingdom.[10] Horus is a god of light who possesses the power of the rising Sun. He is affiliated with the protection of the solar disc, which is often referred to as his "eye," and he was predominantly worshipped in Lower Egypt, which is the northern half of the kingdom. His archenemy is Set, god of disorder and darkness marked by effusive sexuality, who was predominantly worshipped in Upper Egypt, which is the southern half of the kingdom. As the god of upper limits and light, Horus is associated with Shaun as the upper half of the body and digitalized vision, along with its faculties for intellectual analysis and moral oversight. As the god of the desert, or unlimited analog space, Set is associated with Shem, who provides the transgressive, dark, creative magic associated with the nether regions of the body. Just as Shaun and Shem are connected through the body of their mother, ALP or the river Liffey, so are Horus and Set connected through the body of the river Nile, which is often associated with Isis, mother of Horus and sister of Set. Thus the mix of upper and lower has an ironic resonance in this chapter, where Shaun-Horus comes out on the bottom and Shem-Set on the top after the textual stream of ALP-Isis retracts into her riverbed. The post-flood topsy-turvy suggests a temporary ascendance of disorder and antiestablishment animus, which has deep implications for the multifaceted revolution that is about to occur.

The Horus-Set conflict is part of the Osiris resurrection cycle, which forms one of the models for the Earwicker family in II.2. The correspondences are HCE-Osiris, ALP-Isis, Shaun-Horus, and Shem-Set, while Issy represents a young version of Isis. The great god Osiris once walked the earth in the form of a man and ruled with Isis, his wife and sister. Set (also called Seth), the brother of Osiris and Isis who wanted the throne for himself, tricked Osiris into entering an ornate box, which he sealed with lead and sent down the Nile and out to sea, turning it into his coffin. Isis, in her grief, brought the coffin back to Egypt and buried it. One night Set was hunting by moonlight and detected the buried body of Osiris. He tore the body into fourteen pieces and scattered them around the kingdom. Isis relentlessly searched for the members of Osiris and brought them back together but was never able to locate the phallus. So she fashioned one, placed it on the body, and then, with power words provided by Thoth, brought Osiris briefly back to life to unite with her. As a result, she became impregnated with Horus, subsequently giving birth and raising him in a secret place. Osiris died again shortly after being resurrected by Isis. The gods were so moved by Isis's devoted pleas to bring back Osiris that they resurrected him in the afterworld with a new body, making him ruler of the dead. Osiris, as a king-god, is associated with royalty, so that in funerary texts "the living king was identified as an earthly Horus and the dead king (his father/predecessor) as Osiris."[11] As one of Joyce's sources put it, "Osiris represented the past, and Horus the present, or, as we have it expressed in *The Book of the Dead*, 'Osiris is Yesterday, and Rā (i.e., Horus grown up) is to-day.'"[12] Thus the Osiris myth has as much to do with resurrection as with legitimate succession to the throne, and in that way it serves as an ironic model for the revolutionary "succession" of the children over HCE-Osiris led by Shaun-Horus, who is on the journey to becoming the new HCE.

Joyce's sources in Egyptology provide much material for Shaun and Shem, as the maturing Horus avenges his father's murder by attacking his usurping uncle Set. Horus's battle with Set is a story of the triumph of good over evil, light over dark, and in some periods it even carried a political allegory legitimizing the dominion of Lower Egypt over Upper Egypt. During the fight, Horus crushes Set's genitals, sending his yells of pain throughout Egypt.[13] In one version, Set takes the form of a black pig when striking fire into the eye of Horus, while in other versions Set casts filth into the eye and makes it sick (Budge *Ani*, 384–85).[14] Eventually Horus triumphs over Set to attain the rightful succession to Osiris. Thoth, the divine scribe and god of knowledge, arbitrates the fight and declares Horus the victor—but not absolutely: "his duty was to prevent either god from gaining a decisive victory, and from destroying the other; in fact, he had to keep these hostile forces in exact equilibrium."[15] In some versions of the myth, Horus and Set were separated, reunited, and reconciled, symbolizing the peaceful unification of the lands of Egypt. The most striking embodiment of the combined gods' contrary attributes and the two halves of the kingdom is in figures of the dual god Horus-Set, in which their heads, as the typical falcon and Set-animal (a fantastic creature resembling an aardvark), appear together on the body of a man. Such an embodiment perfectly exemplifies the uneasy unification of Shaun and Shem into a complete human being, which may well have been inspired from such a figure that appears in Budge's *Gods of the Egyptians*.[16] Still, Shaun and Shem retain many of the propensities that initially put them in conflict, even though they take on each other's properties like Horus and Set. Hence Shaun becomes outraged at having lost his purity to Shem's influence and abuses him with a stream of invective. Budge, quoting Plutarch, informs us that Egyptians who tend to worship Horus "'hold [Set] in the greatest contempt, and do all they can to vilify and affront him.'"[17]

Many of the key moments in II.2 are inflected with elements of the Osiris complex and the Horus-Set conflict. The second page features an arrangement of the main deities, where the narrative describes HCE as being buried within his body as a Euclidean line, "Length Withought Breath," like Osiris, "who, entiringly as he continues highlyfictional, tumulous under his chthonic exterior but plain Mr Tumulty in muftilife . . . a manyfeast munificent more mob than man" (261.13–22).[18] Bishop explains that after Set hacked Osiris's body into fourteen pieces and buried them around the lands of Egypt, "Egyptians came to understand that the body of Osiris encompassed the entire material universe" in a way similar to HCE at the beginning of the *Wake*, where he "dreams of a landscape stretching from Phoenix Park to Howth Head without perceiving himself as the scattered central subject who contains it."[19] Thus, in the beginning of II.2, HCE is "tumulous," tomb-like or entombed "under his chthonic exterior," buried within his body as a chthonic deity, one who dwells like Osiris under the ground of the native land. "Tumulty" signals tomb (or tumulus) as well as tumult, while "multilife" suggests simultaneous contrary states such as life/death, wake/sleep, present/past, and god/human that characterize Osiris. Also, HCE is "more mob than man" in a reflection of Osiris's collective identity as the god of the dead. On the same page, the text asks a series of questions imploring the world to give HCE a fair "trial" and to find out who he really is (261.23–262.19), which echoes Isis entreating the gods to resurrect Osiris. Shem-Set's left-margin comment "*Dig him in the rubsh!*" (261.03–04L) is simultaneously a war cry to "kick him in the ribs" and a reminder of his burying Osiris's body parts in the brush, as well as ALP-Isis's digging them up (in the rubbish that is one of HCE-Osiris's signifiers). The whole ordeal is summarized as a "horrorscup" (261.25), a cup of horrors having the predictive properties of the horoscope, foreseeing Horus's *coup* against the usurping Set and the conflict that is about to erupt between Shaun and Shem. Shem-Set is determined to give HCE-Osiris the resurrection he deserves, for which he must first be killed in a horrifyingly violent fashion and then succeeded by Shaun-Horus. In order to pull off this Oedipal plot, Shem must help Shaun to learn Euclidean geometry and the facts of life so that together they can take over HCE's kingdom.

The writing of the Nightletter and its violent threats catalyzes a number of key transformations that are, appropriately, associated with Thoth and the role of literature in revolutions. ALP and the children focus on writing but disagree on the medium in which ALP's letter shall be disseminated. Following ALP's suggestion that the children write a letter about HCE (278.13–20), Issy's lengthy footnote expresses sexual and murderous thoughts in an inspired outburst that overflows the margins of the river-text's banks and far exceeds the amount of page space she is normally given. Throughout the screed, Issy threatens their parents with her sexuality, which is one of the characteristics she obtained through Shem's agency in II.1: "This isabella I'm on knows the ruelles of the rut and she don't fear andy mandy." Her final gesture boasts that "tough troth is stronger than fortuitous fiction" (279. n1), punning on the name of Thoth and his power over writing and truth. Thus the creative impulse for her sexual rebellion also drives her desire to write, which aligns her with Shem-Set. Similarly, when a version of the letter appears in II.2 (280.04–27), it is followed by a number of references to the centrality of literature and letter-writing in revolutions. Shem comments, "*Le hélos tombaut soul sur la jambe de marche*" (280.09–11L), translating as "Les héros tombant seul sur la Champs de Mars," or "The heroes falling alone on the Champs de Mars (battlefield)." There is also a pun in French that translates as a threat that the sun (*hélos*, or Horus) will fall into his tomb (*tombeau*) on the walking legs (*jambe de marche*) of Shem-Set as lower half of the body. Shortly afterward, the text switches to clear French to say that despite the upheavals of modernity, the generations of various flowers sprout up fresh and laughing as on the days of battles (281.04–13).[20] Shaun's comment upon this state of affairs identifies "THE PART PLAYED BY BELLETRISTICKS IN THE BELLUM-PAX-BELLUM. MUTUOMORPHOMUTATION" (281.01–10R). In other words, the purely aesthetic writing of *belles lettres* facilitates the entire process of war and peace, causing their metamorphosis into one another, or their "MUTUOMORPHOMUTUATION." Thoth, as the god of writing and referee of the warring Horus and Set, lurks here as the arbiter between Shaun and Shem and is implied to be the power that holds them together in equilibrium.

The conflict of Horus and Set colors the river-text's overflowing and the joining of Shaun and Shem. The process begins with Shaun's attempt to tackle his first geometry homework problem, to "[c]oncoct an equoangular trillitter" (286.21–22), an equilateral triangle that is also a three-sided or three-dimensional letter. At this point, Shem, now identified as "Dolph" (286.25), begins to raise a storm by teasing Shaun about his difficulty in solving the problem: "Can you nei do her, numb?" (286.25). Shaun, now identified as "Kev" (286.27), confirms that he is stuck, "Oikkont" (286.26), while his simultaneous marginal comment sees the impending coalescence of their contrary energies: "PROPE AND PROCUL IN THE CONVERGENCE OF THEIR CONTRAPULSIVENESS" (286.16–22R). Issy makes two comments to confirm this notion. The first labels Shaun-Kev as "the disordered visage" (286.n3), meaning that his face is getting "bent out of shape" and also taking on the properties of Set (Shem), the god of disorder. Her second comment refers to both of them as "[s]inglebarrelled names for doubleparalleled twixtytwins" (286.n4): each in his menacing manner, single-barreled like opposing (parallel) guns, is actually entwined and mixed ("twixty") and identified with the other ("twins"). The boys echo archetypal brotherly battles as Shem offers more help and they continue to bicker. Shem asks, "I cain but are you able?" (287.11–12), followed by "So let's seth off betwain us" (287.12–13), emphasizing their twinlike nature as he begins to give Shaun the coordinates for drawing ALP's genitalia (287.08–17). In these two phrases, Shem identifies himself with Cain, the murderous brother in Genesis, as well as Seth, simultaneously the third son of Adam and Eve and the Egyptian god Set.

As soon as Shaun and Shem "seth off," the river-text begins to overflow with a Latin discourse providing a key to understanding the structures of identified contraries and resurrection that drive the *Wake* (287.20–28). According to McHugh's translation of "the Roman tongue of the dead," the passage announces the exhibition of "a small piece of second-grade imperial papyrus" concerning Paris as the location "whence such great human progeny is to arise," as if prophesying that city's artistic fervor in the 1920s and 1930s when Joyce lived there. This Egyptian document invites us to be "seated joyfully on fleshpots" and to "turn over in our minds" the ancient wisdom of "both the priests," Giordano Bruno and Giambattista Vico, namely, "that everything recognises itself through something opposite & that the stream is embraced by rival banks." This clear signal that Shaun and Shem are experiencing "MUTUOMORPHOMUTATION" and switching sides across the textual riverbanks is amplified by the description of Dolph (Shem) as the "dean of idlers" (287.18) who is tutoring Kev (Shaun) for a nefarious purpose. Dolph is "rebelliumtending mikes of his same" (287.29–30), ensuring that Kev, who will later be labeled as the archangel Michael, will rebel against their parents and take on some of Shem's disorderly qualities. Again, the Thoth-like power of writing and truth that upholds Shem-Set's contrarian creativity is powering the revolution through *belles lettres*: "chanching letters for them vice o'verse . . . and blending tschemes for em in tropadores and doublecressing twofold thruths" (288.01–03).

After the river-text recedes, the references to literature emphasize the burgeoning revolution as a resurrection. The top of the page borrows vortex imagery from Vico and W. B. Yeats's *A Vision*, as McHugh notes, to echo Thoth's role in the resurrection cycle: "in truth, as a poor soul is between shift and shift ere the teath he has lived through becomes the life he is to die into" (293.02–05). Shaun's first left-margin comment indicates that he now has knowledge of the "*Interplay of Bones in the Womb*" (293.02–04L), referring to sex but also to the gestation of the resulting fetus. The comment emphasizes the process of resurrection as a rebirth, which is confirmed by his second left-margin comment referring to revolutionary literature of Joyce's day, the vorticisms of Yeats and Wyndham Lewis (293.05–08L).

The rest of the story hinges on the part of the Horus-Set conflict establishing legitimate succession. Shaun's reaction to viewing ALP's genitalia completes the Oedipal process of coming to terms with the incestuous nature of sexuality, thereby making him an adult. He expresses the facts of life as a demonstrated geometrical proof, *quod erat demonstrandum* (Q.E.D.): "Qued? Mother of us all! O, dear me, look at that now!" (299.03–04). His mixed reaction is at once horrified and filled with wonder, with a sudden urge to return to orthodoxy in his desire to join the police (300.01). Issy correctly senses that Shaun, becoming excessively moral like the archangel Michael, is about to attack Shem, the deceitful devil or St. Nick, for compromising his purity: "Picking on Nickagain, Pikey Mikey?" (300n1). The details have changed, but the conflict between good and evil in the Horus-Set story still applies here. Shem-Set provokes Shaun-Horus by saying that "you were always one of the bright ones, since a foot made you an unmentionable" (300.01–03), meaning he was bright (like Horus) and pure until he became infected with his lower (foot) instincts. As the brothers trade insults, more vortex imagery appears as the "Wherapool" (300.09), the mixing cycle that draws them together—and down. At the same time, Shaun's comments in the left margin emphasize the "pure" part of sex, "*primanouriture*," and its institutional privileges, "*ultimogeniture*" (300.01–03L). That is, he attempts to redeem his newfound sexuality through its procreative purpose, embodied in his birthright that has unfortunately become a reversed form of primogeniture. Simultaneously, Shem's right-margin comment delights in the "dirty" part of sex: "SICK US A SOCK WITH SOME SEDIMENT IN IT FOR THE SAKE OF OUR DARNING WIVES" (300.01–08R). The sock continues the "low" foot imagery to represent a turgid phallus stuffed with dirt that is apparently enjoyed by wives, and which contains decayed matter that nourishes plants and other life. Shaun-Horus's claims appear to be narrow: he has a "creactive mind" (300.20–21), or a creative and reactive mind only, while Shem's "sock" represents the complete cycle of death and life, the "corructive mund" (300.24) or continuously revolving world (*mundus* in Latin) with its mud that works as both putrefaction and fertilizer.

Thoth plays a central role in the plot dealing with birthright and succession to the throne of HCE-Osiris. Budge's translation of the Papyrus of Ani, which was one of Joyce's sources, describes Thoth as an agent of truth in the succession of Horus: "Hail, Thoth, who didst make the word of Osiris to be true against his enemies . . . on the night of setting up the 'Senti' of Horus, and of establishing him in the inheritance of the possessions of his father Osiris."[21] After the unification of opposites, Shaun is urged to "[p]ose the pen, man" (303.02), like Thoth the scribe, after which the text indicates that "Kev was wreathed with his pother" (303.15), or entwined (like a wreath or woven text) with his brother Dolph, who provides the creative impulse. The line clearly echoes the biblical story of Cain, who was wroth with his brother Abel, but also invokes the Egyptian story of Horus and Set. Shaun-Horus is still trying to assert his supremacy with reference to his *"intertemporal eye"* (303.06–07L). However, Shem-Set comments on their being wreathed, in the right margin, by calling himself and Shaun "TROTHBLOWERS. FIG AND THISTLE PLOT A PIG AND WHISTLE" (303.03–08R), echoing Issy's pun on Thoth and truth from the Papyrus of Ani and invoking the version of Set as a pig. The connection with Thoth as the god of writers and publishing is further reinforced by puns on Irish authors' names, including Steele, Burke, Sterne, Swift, Wilde, Shaw, and Yeats, whose activities are further linked to Irish revolutionary leaders such as Daniel O'Connell, James Connolly, and Charles Stewart Parnell (303.05–12). In other words, the revolutionaries, exemplifying the combined creative and rational faculties like writers of truth, undertook to rid Ireland of the usurping foreigners (Set).

The moment in which Shaun seals his "MUTUOMORPHOMUTATION" with Shem is cast entirely in terms of the Horus-Set conflict. Shaun, no longer able to withstand his brother's taunting, punches Shem in the eye. As discussed above, the punch represents the instant in which Shaun and Shem attain each other's significant qualities. Shaun is able to act violently because he is no longer in possession of his virginal purity, owing to Shem's nefarious influence. Shem, happy that his plan has therefore succeeded, makes two simultaneous statements in the body and right margin of the page. He gleefully accepts the blow—"Thanks eversore much, Pointcarried!" (304.05)—claiming "point carried" (won) and also invoking the name of Henri Poincaré, the French mathematician who defended non-Euclidean geometry and the principles of relativity on which Einstein's theories were later based. Shem has therefore adopted something of the rational analysis and its visual basis that reside in Shaun's territory, meaning that he now possesses the injured eye: "I'm seeing rayingbogeys rings round me" (304.08–09). In another polyvocal moment of the *Wake*, Shem simultaneously acknowledges his black eye in the right margin, "WITH EBONISER" (304.01R), hailing it as the moment of mutual transubstantiation in which the "EUCHRE RISK" (Eucharist, 304.03–04R) attains the substance of the body of Christ during the sacrament of Holy Communion. In the margin, Shem repeats his thanks in French, "MERCI BUCKUP" (*merci beaucoup*, 304.04–05R), but retains his disorderly nature in threating Shaun to "MIND WHO YOU'RE PUCK-ING, FLEBBY" (304.06–09R). The threat comes specifically from a satirical version of the Horus-Set conflict known as *The Contendings of Horus and Set*, in which Horus is cast as a weak puckish figure, Set as a buffoonish strong man, and Osiris as a sharp-tongued curmudgeon.[22] Shaun responds to Shem's threat by saying, "Honours to you" (304.09–10), meaning, on one level, "that's Horus, to you," to which Shem retorts as Set, "I'd love to take you for a bugaboo ride and play funfer all if you'd only sit and be the ballasted bottle in the porker barrel" (304.11–14). This reference to the game in which Set tricks Osiris into entering his own floating coffin and turns it into a funeral constitutes the same threat to Shaun-Horus.

The final moment in the plot occurs when Shaun and Shem join forces and the children collaborate on the "NIGHTLETTER" (308.16) threatening to murder their parents. The two boys reconcile and decide to make HCE give them "his Noblett's surprize" (presumably in the category of literature), proclaiming together: "With this laudable purpose in loud ability let us be singulfied. Betwixt me and thee hung cong" (306.04–07). In other words, they are raising the battle cry to be "singlefied" (united) in purpose and engulfed in sin, predicting their rebirth as the new father with the rising Sun in the East (Hong Kong). Following this agreement, all three children collaborate on a series of titles inspired by their learning in various subjects, showing their new ability to write and disseminate as provided by the power of Thoth. Shaun's marginal comments just before the Nightletter, as the children are counting to ten, summarize powers like "*Bimutualism*" and "*Interpenetrativeness*" that have guided their mutual metamorphosis (308.02–16L).

Finally, in their newly banded creative power, the children collaborate on writing the Nightletter which threatens a generational takeover. The letter conveys their best "youlldied greedings" to ALP, HCE, and the "old folkers" below and beyond (308.17–19)—a blasphemous inversion of the yuletide rituals in which the departed elders are honored. Instead, the children threaten their ancestors by wishing them "all very merry Incarnations . . .

through their coming new yonks" (308.19–22): that is, resurrection in the afterworld, which in Egyptian religion was called Amenti and was located far to the West (New York). Shem's final gloss in the right margin makes a bold proclamation of his character and its embodiment of attributes like those of Set: "KAKAOPOETIC LIPPUDENIES OF THE UNGUMPTIOUS" (308.05–10R), which according to McHugh translates as prone to do evil (*kakopoiêtikos*), libido, and unconscious. Issy gets the last say, in which she draws some hieroglyphs that look like crossbones and a hand thumbing a nose, expressing her hope that HCE will "enjoyimsolff over our drawings on the line" (308.n2). Thus the final words of the chapter conflate geometry with the declaration of a battle line or, more specifically, the threat to draw a line around their father's neck.

The geometry lesson of II.2 actuates a conflict that conflates Egyptology and literary material with the early twentieth-century scientific revolution. When ALP's diagram is revealed and the text refers to "old Sare Isaac's universal of specious aristmystic" (293.17–18), Issy's footnote confirms the overthrow of Newton by contemporary physics with a reference to Edwin Arthur Burtt: "are we going to be toadhaunted by that old Pantifox Sir Somebody Something, Burtt, for the rest of our secret stripture?" (293.n2). Burtt was an American philosopher who published *The Metaphysical Foundations of Modern Physical Science* (1924), *The Metaphysics of Sir Isaac Newton* (1925), and *Religion in an Age of Science* (1930) while Joyce was working on the *Wake*.[23] Burtt believed that the philosophy resulting from the science of Einstein (or "Eyeinstye," 305.06), which Issy seems to invoke as a new authority, would replace the absolute time and space of the Newtonian worldview. The notion is confirmed by a reference to "the Great Ulm" (293.14), a great Elm blended with the German city of Ulm, which McHugh informs us is Einstein's birthplace.

Einstein's relativity theories depend on non-Euclidean geometry and the four-dimensional space-time continuum, which establishes a conflict with the Euclidean geometry lesson in II.2. Shem-Set and Issy advocate an analog model of the universe. Joyce was thinking about the folds and warping that characterize non-Euclidean geometry as early as spring 1921, when in a letter to Claude Sykes he referred to "Penelope" as the most "amplitudinously curvilinear" episode of *Ulysses* (*LettersI* 164). Thus there is a direct connection between geometry and the Oedipal processes of II.2, since the boys associate the continuous curvature of the universe with a woman's body. Shaun continues to resist his troubling new knowledge of sexuality right up to the moment of epiphany, when he still asserts the Euclidean three-dimensional model on which Newtonian mechanics is based: "Scholium, there are trist sigheds to everysing" (299.01–02). When Shaun finally strikes Shem, tacitly admitting defeat in the argument over which geometry is best, Shem's cry of "Pointcarried" (as discussed above) also bears with it Poincaré's defense of non-Euclidean geometry and four-dimensional space-time. Shem's reference to his own "present momentum, potential as I am" (304.08) indicates his self-identification with quantum mechanics, which is largely based in potential states.

The Nightletter is revolutionary not just for its content but because it is delivered as a U.S. telegram sent overnight. Its eastward travel to Ireland through the instantaneous electric medium follows the bark of Rā as it carries the solar disk through the afterworld toward dawn. The printed letter moving through electricity is what causes II.2 and the *Wake* in general to question the status of print in the media ecology of the 1920s and 1930s. References to electric media abound and are also associated with the multiple simultaneous revolutions coming to fruition in II.2. For instance, early in the chapter the text associates the cycle of rebirth with electric media. Various birds and features of the landscape are "televisible" while HCE is asked to "cometh up as a selfreizing flower," accompanied by "the phoenix, his pyre . . . still flaming away with trueprattight spirit" (265.07–11).[24] The phoenix, a Greek mythological bird associated with fire and the sun, regenerates from its own ashes. It most likely originated from the Egyptian Bennu bird, which was similarly a self-created solar deity involved with the resurrection of Osiris. In this context, the "selfreizing" HCE who simultaneously razes and raises himself enacts both the phoenix and Bennu myths. The "trueprattight" or tripartite spirit that fuels his flame is the combination of Shaun-Horus, Shem-Set, and a third unnamed medium bearing the powers of Thoth. In the context of II.2, where all developments result in the writing *and* dissemination of the letter, Thoth seems to be a model for this mysterious "third person," somewhat like the Holy Spirit in the Christian trinity, which fuels the dynamism between God the Father and God the Son, or in this case between HCE-Osiris and the soon-to-be-combined Shaun-Horus/Shem-Set. However, Thoth's powers seem to be evolving into the new arena of electric communication because the effects of these phenomena are now "televisible," visible from afar by means of an extrasensory medium. The electricity of the Nightletter is exactly the invisible medium on which the resurrection cycle turns.

The instantaneous and synaesthetic possibilities of electric media and the "new post" are broadcast by the "two millium two humbered and eighty thausig nine humbered and sixty radiolumin lines to the wustworts of a Finntown's generous poet's office" (265.25–28): that is, the 2,280,960 inches in the three miles between Chapelizod and the General Post Office, Dublin, multiplied by twelve. The word *radiolumin* signifies a ray of light and also suggests the poetic revolutionary potential of radio, which usually carries sound signals but is actually a light medium. The synaesthetic transformation of light to sound is described again where a traffic beacon appears as the "grene ray of earong" (267.13): simultaneously the "green ray of hearing" and the "green ray of orange" combine the colors of the Irish republican flag to become "the green ray of Erin." As the paragraph cycles through the colors of the rainbow, the sound/vision matrix becomes the place "[w]here flash becomes word and silents selfloud" (267.16–17), or flesh becomes Word in an inversion of the Creation in Genesis; it also appears as a flash of light in which silence becomes sonorous as in a talking movie. Radio and television are mentioned in various ways throughout II.2, yet the more consistently invoked electric medium is cinema.

Early in II.2, ALP refers to the hollywood bush (265.17), which also establishes the Hollywood movie industry as a recurrent theme throughout the chapter. During the textual flood, ALP's story about "the Ides of Valentino's, at Idleness" (289.27–28) unmistakably refers to romantic 1920s movie star and sex symbol Rudolph Valentino—idle, a "lover" like Set, and embedded in the idolatry of celebrity worship. The shortening of Rudolph into Dolph plus the fact that he is idle links him back to Shem as "Dolph, dean of idlers" (287.18) and his dangerous sexual magic that infects both Issy and Shaun with revolutionary thoughts. Set is as much a bad boy idol as any movie star.

However, the moniker "Dolph" refers to Set's dangerousness in another way. Just before the reference to Rudolph Valentino, the mention of the Earwicker family business prompts Issy to ask, "Had our retrospectable fearfurther gatch mutchtatches?" followed swiftly by a mention of "the prence di Propagandi" (288n7, 289.02). Issy's question about the mustachioed "führer" simultaneously evokes the images of a mustachioed movie villain and Adolf Hitler. Thus the contraction of Rudolph and Adolf into the single coin "Dolph" signals the duality and confusion of Set as a simultaneously creative/destructive force. Hitler was very much a phenomenon of the silver screen in newsreels and propaganda films like those of Leni Riefenstahl. Hence "beam slewed cable" (289.09): the media revolution takes on the characteristics of Cain and Abel and their forebears Horus and Set as the movie projector beam and wireless transmission have superseded cabled telegraphy. Cinema and interwar politics replay a contemporary version of the Egyptian archetypes enabled by post-electric technology.

Perhaps the most prophetic moment of II.2 occurs when the text refers to Shaun-Horus and Shem-Set's duality as "Doll the laziest" (Dolph the "idler") and "Doll the fiercst" in "unitate" with "the vectorious readyeyes of evertwo circumflicksrent searclhers never film in the elipsities of their gyribouts those fickers which are returnally reprodictive of themselves" (298.09–18). In other words Horus, "the victorious eye," and Set are two "circlers" ever/never looking around (or circumflecting) in the elliptical space-times of their Vichian gyres, eternally reproducing and predicting themselves in new media of the future that resemble the rotating reels of a movie camera/projector. The connection to geometry emphasizes the cosmic nature of the resurrection. The "vectorious" gods move about in curvilinear space-time as championed by Poincaré and Einstein, "in all directions on the bend of the unbridalled, the infinisissimalls of her facets becoming manier and manier as the calicolum of her umdescribables" (298.29–32). Finally unbridled, Shaun-Horus and Shem-Set are free to travel in all directions on the bends and folds of their mother ALP-Isis as her facets multiply and infinitesimal calculus brings them into her unmentionables—the mystical secrets of the universe that are more profane than holy. In their completeness, they follow a continuous analog trajectory as they create the conditions for the new kingdom to come.

The "MUTUOMORPHOMUTATION" of the digital and analog through Shaun-Horus and Shem-Set drives the Oedipal parricide/regicide cast as media revolution in II.3. Troy hears in the "pipping" static emanating from the radio in the bar room the appearance of Apep (314.24–26), the giant snake who personified evil in Egyptian mythology and became synonymous with Set.[25] The deceiver enters the stronghold by way of the radio receiver: the acoustic model has succeeded; the revolution will be televised. Shem-Set is now ready to spread disorder through the united children of HCE while the patrons enjoy the television drama of Butt and Taff. Though the children perform a variety of extremely violent acts on HCE, he never really dies. Instead, the children have nullified his sexual authority, leaving him to enjoy a kind of impotent retirement. Thus HCE-Osiris exits as King Roderick O'Conor, the "last pre-electric king of Ireland" (380.11–13).

Notes

1. For recent studies on the *Wake* and electric media, see Elena Lamberti, "From Linear Space to Acoustic Space: New Media Environments and New Modernist

Forms," in *Modernism*, vol. 1, ed. Astradur Eysteinsson and Vivian Liska (Amsterdam: John Benjamins, 2007), 431–48; Laurent Milesi, "H Y P E R W A K E 3D," in *joyceMedia: James Joyce, Hypermedia & Textual Genetics*, ed. Louis Armand (Prague: Litteraria Pragensia, 2004), 66–72; and in the same volume Donald Theall, "Transformations of the Book in Joyce's Dream Vision of Digiculture," 28–43.

2. Joyce would not have understood the digital to mean the computational information storage or binary computer code with which we are familiar today, though certainly the general concept of binaries applies to the *Wake*. Rather, the digital was understood as a series of discrete, quantitative values, regardless of medium. The Cartesian three-dimensional coordinate grid is just such a device because it divides and quantifies continuous reality into discrete units for measurement and description. The analog, on the other hand, would have been understood as continuously variable values that reflect the actual contours without artificial segmentation.

3. Edmund Epstein, *A Guide through "Finnegans Wake"* (Gainesville: University Press of Florida, 2009), 90. For an excellent general treatment of the physiology of the eye and the ear in the *Wake*, see chapters 8 and 9 in John Bishop, *Joyce's Book of the Dark: "Finnegans Wake"* (Madison: University of Wisconsin Press, 1986). Technically, all sensory data are "digital," traveling through the nervous system in discrete packets once they are past the sensory organs. However, as documented in both Lamberti and Theall, Joyce's artistic contemporaries believed the ear to transmit analog signals to the brain, even if the scientific community might have understood otherwise. For that reason, the eye and the ear in Joyce can be taken to represent the digital and analog, respectively.

4. Lamberti, "Linear Space," 434.

5. Epstein, *Guide*, 90. A comprehensive table of Shaun and Shem's opposing qualities appears on 83.

6. Ibid., 90.

7. Ibid., 91.

8. Ibid., 137.

9. The most comprehensive sources for Egyptology in the *Wake* are Bishop; James S. Atherton, *The Books at the Wake: A Study of Literary Allusions in James Joyce's "Finnegans Wake"* (Carbondale: Southern Illinois University Press, 1959; reprint, New York: Arcturus Books, 1974); and Mark L. Troy, "Mummeries of Resurrection: The Cycle of Osiris in *Finnegans Wake*" (PhD diss., University of Uppsala, 1976). According to Atherton, Joyce's main sources for Egyptian mythology were one of E. A. Wallis Budge's translations, *The Book of the Dead: Facsimile of the Papyrus of Ani in the British Museum* (London: British Museum, 1890) and one of his scholarly monographs, *Osiris and the Egyptian Resurrection*, 2 vols. (London: Medici Society, 1891) (192n3–4). Troy indicates Budge's *The Gods of the Egyptians; or, Studies in Egyptian Mythology*, 2 vols. (London: Methuen, 1904; New York: Do-

ver, 1969) as another major source (21). Bishop claims that Budge's translation of the Papyrus of Nu was also such a source (91). This essay uses the following editions of Budge to quote from Joyce's primary sources: for the Papyrus of Nu, *The Book of the Dead: An English Translation of the Chapters, Hymns, Etc., of the Theban Recension, with Introduction, Notes, Etc.* (New York: Barnes & Noble, 1969); for the Papyrus of Ani, *The Book of the Dead: The Hieroglyphic Transcript and Translation into English of the Ancient Egyptian Papyrus of Ani* (New York: Gramercy Books, 1995); for other references, see Budge's *Gods of the Egyptians.*

10. Budge, *Gods* 2:243.

11. Edmund S. Meltzer, "Horus," in *The Oxford Encyclopedia of Ancient Egypt*, vol. 2 (Oxford: Oxford Univ. Press, 2001), 119.

12. Budge, *Gods* 1:487.

13. Ibid., 475, 497.

14. Budge, *Ani*, 384–85.

15. Budge, *Gods* 1:405. Thoth was very important to Joyce, as indicated by the characterization of newspaper editor Myles Crawford in *Ulysses*, whose "scarlet beaked face, crested by a comb of feathery hair" (*U* 7.31–32) clearly evokes the ibis bird in Egyptian depictions of the god.

16. Budge, *Gods* 2:242.

17. Budge, *Gods* 2:252.

18. In another segment of II.2, HCE is compared with dead King Tut (and therefore Osiris): "flat as Tut's fut" (291.04), to which Issy replies, "O hce! O hce!" (291n1).

19. Bishop, *Book of the Dark*, 98.

20. Roland McHugh, *Annotations to "Finnegans Wake"* (Baltimore: Johns Hopkins University Press, 1980), 281. I am indebted to McHugh for providing many other glosses throughout my essay.

21. Budge, *Ani*, 427. According to Budge's note on this episode, a senti is a two-pillared canopy under which a king was crowned (427n1).

22. Donald B. Redford, "Contendings of Horus and Seth," in *The Oxford Encyclopedia of Ancient Egypt*, vol. 1 (Oxford: Oxford University Press, 2001), 294. The story deftly parodies the contradictory versions of the myth that sometimes cast Horus and Set as brothers instead of nephew and uncle.

23. McHugh sees on 263 a reference to a popular science book, Sir Arthur Eddington's *The Expanding Universe* (1930), which explains recent developments in physics stemming from Einstein's relativity theories. Eddington was the scientist who first confirmed aspects of Einstein's general theory of relativity by experiment and helped to make him a public figure.

24. Milesi indicates that the holograph notebook, VI.B.46.204ff., mentions John Logie Baird, inventor of the first television technology in 1925, and indexes television terms that were used primarily on 349 in II.3 ("H Y P E R W A K E 3D," 67).

25. Troy, "Mummeries of Resurrection," 52.

11

Irish History and Modern Media

Generating Courage in II.3

ENDA DUFFY

"The Irish proletariat has yet to be created," wrote Joyce to his brother Stanislaus after leaving Ireland,[1] hinting at what he may have had in mind when in *A Portrait* he speaks of "the uncreated conscience of my race" (*P* 253). Can we take this declaration as Joyce's challenge to himself, which he finally faces in *Finnegans Wake*? His letter explains that while the coming Sinn Fein anticolonial revolution in Ireland will mark a progress, it will be merely a stage on the path to the real revolution, that of the Irish workers. Joyce's politics have long been obscured, while he is valorized for potentially radical linguistic excess. Recall, nevertheless, that the post–Cold War phase of Joyce criticism was kickstarted when Dominic Manganiello showed that Joyce, at the very moment when he was defining the scope of his aesthetic vocation, first re-created himself as a socialist radical.[2] If the *Wake*, as the most radical novel of the twentieth century, is to be given its due, we can claim that in it Joyce accepts the challenge he implicitly poses in 1905. In it Joyce, the greatest Irish creator, creates the Irish proletariat. This claim does not mean merely that he at last represented the workers, the class that *Ulysses* largely ignored. Rather, as a Marxist, Freudian, Nietzschean, and Darwinian (even if he kept these evangelists of modernity at arm's length), who also invoked Vico and Bruno, Joyce knew the dream of historical progress enough to be a revolutionary: to want, first for Ireland but then for the world, a new civilization in which the people would share in the fortune their work generated. Only such a tremendous ambition justifies, and matches, the *Wake*'s overwhelming complexity. The keywords of the book's working title, *Work in Progress*, herald the potential for change: they focus on work, on progress, and their interrelation. Maria Jolas, publisher of *Work in Progress* in *transition*, noted that the missing apostrophe in the *Finnegans Wake* made that title a cautionary admonition to the powers that be.[3] The Finnegans are the workers of the world, and Joyce foretells their rebellion. To face the full force of the twentieth century's most revolutionary book, we must hear "Finnegans Wake" as a war cry.

Chapter II.3 of *Finnegans Wake* is its longest, possibly its wildest. It includes both the last portion of the novel Joyce wrote, in 1938, next to the very first—the pages on Roderick O'Conor, last high king of Ireland, with which this chapter ends, a section composed during a holiday at Bognor Regis in 1923.[4] It is set in the public bar of the Mullingar House, where HCE presides before a rabble of drinkers in a room beneath that in which his three children do their homework. This chapter caps the genre of tavern texts for which Joyce is famous: the morose *Dubliners* story "Counterparts" and the pub scenes in "Lestrygonians," "Sirens," "Cyclops," and "Oxen of the Sun" in *Ulysses*. The episode of *Ulysses* that II.3 most resembles, however, is "Circe," in its indoor setting, drunken male carousing, and narrative transitions from quasi-realistic description to tall tales with a phantasmagoric edge. Both "Circe" and II.3 are about being drunk in a public room in the wild night city, and in both this drunkenness is relayed as a multisensory bombardment of voices, images, lights, tale-telling and cajolement, whiskey and beer. II.3 opens with scenes of wild drinking in the pub and closes with the scene of HCE, when the drinkers have at last dispersed after Sackerson has called closing time, lapping up the dregs before he lapses into a dream of his own high kingship. The chapter features entertainment, conviviality, hospitality, pub gossip, controversy, tipsiness, and dreams of glory. It floats forward on a Guinness- and Jameson-fueled orgy of stories to top stories, shouts from the doorway, people rushing to the backyard to relieve themselves, snatches of old songs, and repeatedly ignored orders to clear the premises.

II.3 describes possibly the greatest night out ever in a Dublin pub. Can this drunken madness have the germ of revolution in it? Is Joyce here giving us more than a satire on what has come in Ireland to be known derisively as "closing-time republicanism"—the tendency of people after a night in the pub to loudly champion an Irish republic, independent of Britain? Can a pub revolution have any purchase on a real one? Can a wild night in a pub, presented in an enigmatic work of fiction, really shatter a given consensus and substitute "idology" for the dominant "ideology"? In the course of II.3, Joyce mentions "decumans numbered too" or Document Number Two

(369.24–25). This was an alternative to the treaty with the British following the 1919–21 War of Independence that founded the Irish Free State, offered by the 1916 leader Eamon de Valera. The *Wake*, in turn, may be a "Document Number Three," offering an even more radical version of an Irish society beyond the treaty compromise. How, in the sound and fury of a drunken night, could such a vision be made explicit?

Currents and Clashings

In fact, little out of the ordinary happens in II.3. In the public bar, a radio comes to life, and "the pip of the lin . . . pinnatrate[s] inthro an auricular forfickle" (310.09–10). HCE uncorks bottles of beer, all raise their glasses, and soon they are listening to the story of how Kersse, the Dublin tailor, is asked by the Norwegian sea captain to make him a suit. The tailor and captain quarrel; the pub drinkers quarrel. The sailor goes off to sea and returns; Kersse offers him his daughter in marriage. The radio interrupts the story with the weather forecast and advertisements for porter and tea. Kersse offers his daughter—and imagines her embraces. Celebrants of the marriage sing and shout in a luminous aura: "And Dub did glow that night. In Fingal of victories" (329.14). There follows bliss, sex, and then children, and the radio story ends. Kate, the servant, enters to tell HCE that his wife ALP demands his presence upstairs. With HCE gone up, there is cheering and what Joyce's notes called a Maori war cry: "Ko Niutirenis hauru leish! A lala!" (335.16).[5]

A new story begins, apparently told via television (a very new invention in the 1930s) by the comic duo Butt and Taff. It details how the Irish soldier Buckley, a private in the British army during the 1853–56 Crimean War, shot the Russian general. Buckley got the general in his sights but, impressed by his grand uniform, hesitated to shoot. Next, he realizes that the general has lowered his trousers to defecate and, from a sense of human empathy, hesitates to shoot again. But then he sees that the general has taken up a sod of turf to clean himself and, outraged "At that instullt to Igorladns!" (353.18–19), he admits, "I shuttm, missus, like a wide sleever! . . . Shurenoff!" (352.14–15, 354.05). All this is told in a comic dialogue between the lively Butt, who did the shooting, and the more timid Taff, who eggs him on. They are interrupted five times by grandiloquent stage directions about "*the heliotropical noughttime . . . the bairdboard bombardment screen*" (i.e., the television, invented by Logie Baird) (349.07–09), and, at the moment when the general is finally shot, by the famous account of "*The abnihilisation of the etym*"

(353.23), which seems in 1938 to speak of nuclear fission and to foretell the atomic bomb.

As the story ends, nothing less than a new cycle in the Viconian cycles of history is announced, and HCE tries to explain himself and his role in the new era. He launches into a confession. The radio interrupts with a musical program; the pub drinkers accuse HCE again. Challenged, he cries, "Guilty, but fellows culpows!" (363.20). The four old men in the snug will have none of his excuses, and with song, legalese, and news reports they taunt him. Soon "The Sockerson boy" (370.30), who may be HCE's curate (the assistant at the bar), calls time. The drinkers grow more raucous, singing "Like wather parted from the say" (371.07–08), as their departure is described in terms that anticipate the book's ending: "they were all trying to and baffling with the walters of, hoompsydoompsy walters of" (373.05–07). At last they are gone, and there unfolds a fantastic seven-page rumination, the first thing Joyce ever wrote for the *Wake*, a full-scale "Epistlemadethemology for deep, dorfy doubtlings" (374.17–18, epistemology-theology for dear, dirty Dubliners). In it, HCE "bares sobsconscious inklings shadowed on soulskin" (377.28) when he signs himself "King Roderick O'Conor, the paramount chief polemarch and last preelectric king of Ireland" (380.11–13). He drinks the leftover dregs and, slumped in a chair alone, sings the rebel song "Follow Me Up to Carlow." Thus ends the section.

II.3 is a stream of broadcast voices that come in over each other on different wavelengths as on a radio receiver; they must be listened to together. The world of II.3 is that of the urban milieu as envisaged in Georg Simmel's essay "Metropolis and Mental Life" (1903) or Walter Ruttmann's film *Berlin: Symphony of a Great City* (1927): a panoply of images, lights, smells, and sounds compete for our attention, with jarring, jolting interruptions ("Punk" [367.07]), frequency changes, language switchings from Gaelic to Russian to Chinese, ghostly apparitions, and the voices of many half-drunken men talking at once. Nevertheless, the differences between these wavelengths are relatively discernible. The text alternates between the relatively realistic setting of the bar and the stories of Kersse the tailor and how Buckley shot the Russian general, with the Roderick O'Conor passage surfacing as a fantasy of the possibly near-comatose HCE at the end. After the opening exhortation, the accounts of serving drinks and downing them, of Kate's arrival to summon HCE upstairs, even of HCE's public confession and the brouhaha of the customers are as near as *Finnegans Wake* gets to direct narration. The two stories, the confession and the O'Conor sequence are interleaved with the quasi-realist moments, so that II.3 is a series of panels, each relaying a tale, while the hinges between them are provided by realistic passages on the activities in the pub. David Hayman suggests that Joyce's challenge as he composed this section was not the structures of the tales themselves but the transitions between them.⁶ By zoning in on these transitions, Hayman hopes to break out of one possible dilemma in reading II.3: the reader tends to search for meanings in possible relations between the different panels, while knowing that unified meaning is the very phenomenon foiled by this tissue of soundings. Could we rethink the hinges between the four principal panels—the Kersse story, the Russian general story, HCE's confession, and the O'Conor sequence—not as transitions but as staged clashes, to make audible the cultural clashing of these divergent sequences?

Confrontation is the chapter's topic and trope. What are the principal clashes or confrontations staged here? There are the obvious clashes of human beings: Buckley shooting the general, Kersse arguing with the captain, HCE being shouted down by the four old men, Butt and Taff, the doubletellers of the Russian tale, far from full agreement, even the peremptoriness of offstage ALP in calling HCE upstairs. II.3 is the very bellicose heart of the book. The Easter Rebellion in Dublin, the Russian Revolution, and the Crimean War in which the general was shot, along with various other wars and battles, especially the Battle of Clontarf, fought north of Dublin in 1014, and the Battle of Waterloo, which feature throughout the *Wake*, are constantly invoked. The section ends with a song about Fiach McHugh O'Byrne's defeat of Queen Elizabeth's army at Glenmalure, south of Dublin, in 1580. Shot through the linguistic remix we have endless references to historic and recent battles, wars, and revolutions, as well as to the competitive games of chess, horse racing, and soccer ("Shimmyrag's" [366.21] refers to Shamrock Rovers). The switch point for these currents is the climactic story that contains both personal struggle and actual battle: the account of Buckley shooting the Russian general. "I shuttm" (352.14), says Butt, who is Buckley, who may be *Ulysses*'s Buck Mulligan and, some claim, Shem, HCE's own wayward son. Butt's shocked, prideful phrase is the switch where the personal and the political converge.

If we can hear the sound currents that encounter each other at the switch point of "I shuttm," then we can discern the larger forces that clash in this section. These currents occur at different levels of audibility; they are increasingly submerged depth charges that radiate outward from this central flash point of conflict. The first of these emphasizes the matter of Ireland, whether as a place, a history, or a source of identity for the characters and of enrichment for the hoard of allusions. Next up in this aural tissue of references is the focus on the new technologies of radio and television. The second paragraph offers detailed technical terminology on the radio set; later, as Butt and Taff begin telling their tale, they seem to be a pair of comics heard and seen on the pub television screen. In II.3, history telling is technologized. Irish history, whether mythic or recent, most often told as the story of the struggle for national independence, is here confronted with the scientific-inflected modernity represented by the new media technologies of radio and television. Ireland's medieval struggles with the Danes, in the Kersse story, and the Irish struggle since 1169 with the British, suggested in the second story, are now only to be made audible, and latterly visible, through the new technical media of radio and television. National history telling contrasts with the means of telling it: the past is told through the media of the future. The convivial face-to-face world of the pub talkers, the print transmission involved in books and letters, and the more anonymous world of new media broadcasts confront each other here. Technology intervenes in an older order of family, gossipy community, and the identity granted by national allegiance. Limning these new media ecologies, II.3 explores what happens when new media communicate old messages. As Donald Theall notes, Marshall McLuhan was inspired by these Joycean soundings.[7]

The *Wake*, written between the wars, gives us the noises generated by the confrontation of technologically powered new media and older myths of belonging. As these cross-currents meet, each word, in its reservoir of sound associations, dredges up a string of associated meanings: while the word heard on the radio or television is made possible by the new technology, the past is contained in the word's sound. Thus Joyce's method of punning is accentuated by the mediation of technologies of sound (and image) transmission. Sounds mediated by technology beg to have their immediate impact on the human's physiology more clearly noted; the reader-hearer registers the sound's physiological effect, which is, however, impacted by what she remembers of its imbedded history. The text machine, acting on the mind's ear (and the mind's eye) generates clashing feelings in us.

Such feelings in II.3, I suggest, cover four major thematic terrains. The first is the issue of hearing itself, which is presented in contradistinction to seeing. The effect of the heard is confronted with the effect of the seen. II.3 begins with a radio report and the pleasures of the technologically enabled audible; at the same time, the great personal sin of HCE involves looking. The stakes of reading-as-seeing the silent text (as when the letter is reread) are not forgotten either. The respective powers of the seen and the heard in the persuasive transmittal of information face off here.

This clash of cacophony and visuality then sets the conditions for a further register of contrasts, between the raucous all-pervading comedy and a potential seriousness surrounding the fights, violence, shooting, and shame. The bellicosity of II.3 might be expected to give it a somber quality, but the textual machine, like a hurdy-gurdy, propels the reader to comedy and merriment. Does this mean that Joyce, like Swift, is satirizing the action he displays? This clash of laughter and the bellicose generates the chapter's energy. II.3 is a raucously comic soundscape instead of a visualized, seemly commemorative history of war.

A further incongruity that confronts the reader is how drunkenness and alcohol consumption set the scene for accounts of revolutionary intent and struggle. John Bishop has taught us to think of the *Wake* as a book of the dark.[8] More obviously, in II.3, it is a book of the drunk. Given Joyce's drinking,[9] and the drunkenness of his father, who as a onetime investor in a Chapelizod distillery is a model for HCE, we may ask how far we might take here the idea of a drunken text. What is heard and seen changes under the influence of drink; what is comical changes, too. Is the ideal reader of this section a drunken reader? Is a sensory bedevilment, even an addictive reading of the soundscape and visual scene, the book's demand? Is the laughter necessarily drunken also?

These conflicts lead us to the fourth issue, that of courage versus cowardice. The sound effects, the comedy, the drunkenness, facing their opposites—the silent seen, the sober truth—all generate a species of courage that reaches its high point in the section and in the book, when Butt does seize the moment and acts: when he shoots the general in the backside. Shooting someone in the back may be the definition of cowardice, but it at least implies that the shooter takes action. Can sounds, comedy, and even alcohol make one brave? (Conversely, does the deliberative quality of the seen, of seriousness and sobriety, render one cowardly?) Is courage, as a particular amalgam of human mood, energy, and resolve, an affect that can be generated by a fantastic text-machine, which it takes courage to read and which also generates courage in the reader? II.3 demonstrates the enormous cultural forces that must be generated in order to imagine and instill courage in characters and, more so, in readers. Can this book give us courage? Butt gets courage, but he is only a cinematic comedian, a "Chorney Choplain" (351.13), and after hearing of his exploit, HCE seems scared once more. By the end, was Roderick O'Conor, who was last high king of Ireland before the British took over, and who tried to fight them, a coward or the last courageous man in Ireland before now? The chapter's text-machine generates a panoply of affects; the reader can gauge if she has been given by the text the gift of courage herself.

Irish Histories of Rebellion

To grasp how in II.3 courage is generated out of clashing sound streams, consider the episode's central confrontation: between the Irish setting, history, and politics on the one hand and new media radio and televisual modernity on the other. First, it is made clear that the story of how "Bullyclubber burgherly shut the rush in general" (335.13–14) is an "eeridreme" (a dream of Eire, Ireland) offered by "The Irish Race and World" (342.30–32, "The Irish Racing World" or the Irish race, the Irish world). "Da Valorem" (de Valera, Irish prime minister) has been invoked, as has "the lost Gabbarnaur-Jaggarnath" (342.11–14, the last governor general of the Irish Free State, who was replaced by the first president of Ireland when de Valera's new constitution was adopted in 1937). Moreover, the realistic setting, a public house on the outskirts of Dublin, is emphasized, and Dublin place-names proliferate in this "tale of a tublin." Endless references to Irish historical struggles and strugglers ensue, from "Faun MacGhoul" (354.06, Finn McCool) to "the lomondations of Oghrem" (340.08–09), which refers to the Battle of Aughrim of 1691 and the air lamenting that Irish defeat. (Remember also "The Lass of Aughrim" in "The Dead.")

This arrangement goes well beyond references to historical contexts expected of any Irish novel; a design emerges, culminating in the Roderick O'Conor passage. This passage is the most sustained and explicit attention to Irish history and to an Irish political figure in the book—and the first part of the *Wake* that Joyce wrote. O'Conor, as the "last preelectric king of Ireland" (380.12–13), marks the end of Irish self-rule and the ascendancy of the British in Ireland. O'Conor's complicated career as Irish medieval warlord and chieftain of Connaught does not constitute a clear-cut narrative of defeat. He offered fealty to King Edward II, but also defeated the British forces, even to the gates of the Pale. He was deserted by neighboring chiefs, yet reentered alliances with them afterwards. His eventual defeat was aided by his traitorous sons; he had the eyes of one of them put out as a punishment, abdicated in favor of his eldest, and retired to the Abbey at Cong. Thus his story is one of victories as well as setbacks, of a king who held his own in the face of a British-Norman takeover of Ireland and who reacted to changing power structures across Europe with a fighting spirit and a determined realpolitik on all fronts. The father of potentially traitorous sons, he is a model for HCE.

In terms of the Viconian cycles, his fall ushered in a new era of Irish history in which the island was ruled by Britain. This era had just ended when Joyce wrote his book of HCE, who in the *Wake* reprises O'Conor as in *Ulysses* Bloom reprises Odysseus.

II.3 ends by drawing attention to the fall of a figure that led to seven hundred years of British rule in Ireland; it begins, however, with many references to the new, present epoch, the years just before the *Wake* was begun, when the Irish at last threw off British rule. The *Wake*, by implication, wants to record how Ireland, as in the time of Roderick O'Conor, is once again on the cusp of epochal historical change. References abound here to the recent revolution in Ireland, from the 1916 Rising to the War of Independence of 1919–21, the Anglo-Irish treaty that led to the founding of the Free State, the Civil War that followed, and the political maneuverings that continued up to the new constitution of 1937. The drinkers' first toast is "Our svalves are svalves aroon!" (311.17), which as "Ourselves, ourselves alone" is the English translation of the Gaelic "Sinn Fein, Sinn Fein amhain!"[10] The 1916 Rising was often called the "Sinn Fein Rebellion," and the members of the Sinn Fein party, who won the majority of parliamentary seats in Ireland in the 1918 election, went on to unilaterally form their own Dublin government, precipitating the War of Independence. Sinn Fein members have already been cited in the chapter's second sentence as "Finnfannfawners" (309.09–10), that is, "Sinn Fein Amhain-ers." This version unites Finn, that is, Finn McCool, and Tim Finnegan, too, with Sinn Fein, the political force ushering in the new Ireland and also, in the rhyming substitution, implicates Shem and Shaun in the "Finnfann," that is, in the Sinn Fein nexus (Sinn Fein: Shem-Shaun). Shem and Shaun—"Sinn Fein amhain!": the sons *are* the new Ireland.

Yet these allusions are only the beginning. As Kersse and the Norwegian captain negotiate, and the captain goes to sea again, we hear that he will be gone "from our lund's rund turs bag til threathy hoeres a wuke" (320.21–22), that is, "from Ireland's round towers back until treaty whores or heroes awake." The epochal treaty of 1921 was signed by the British government and Irish representatives. These Irish were either heroes or whores, and this difference of opinion led to the Civil War of 1921–22. The Kersse story continues to connect Irish independence to waking up and to "Finn again" with the following: "And old lotts have funn at Flammagen's ball. Till Irinwakes from Slumber Deep" (321.17–18). Here "Finnegans Wake" is connected to the line "When Erin wakes from slumber deep" from the song by the "new Irelander" Thomas Davis, "The West's Awake." This ballad, with its focus on sleeping and waking offering obvious Wakean parallels, calls on the Irish to awaken and rise against the British by reminding them of those who fought in "O'Conor's van"—that is, under Roderick O'Conor. It rises to "But hark! A voice like thunder spake, 'The West's Awake, the West's Awake!'" very much in the *Wake* spirit; the song is threaded through the chapter.

Moments later, when HCE returns from the outhouse, the Sinn Fein fight for Irish independence is connected to the radio broadcast in the phrase "Our set, our set's allohn" ("Ourselves, Ourselves alone," the Sinn Fein cry, is related to a radio set, to ohms of electricity, and to the Irish victory over the Danes at Clontarf in 1014, which is comically relayed as a tennis score—"Clontarf, one love, one fear" [324.15–23]). Other Irish battles against the enemy are also cited. The chapter cannot drop the Sinn Fein slogan, which it next delivers in mock-Chinese: "tsay-fong tsei-foun a laun" (325.14); soon Kate brings the message to HCE from ALP, "his fain a wan" (333.27).

The Kersse story resounds with the sounds of the Sinn Fein rebellion of 1916–21; the story of Buckley's shooting of the Russian general, which on the surface seems more keyed to matters of revolutionary struggle, has its political allusions resonate more with the politics of the post–Civil War Free State. The pub drinkers toast their eagerness to hear it with the cry, "So the truce, the old truce, and nattonbuff the truce, boys. . . . Slant. Shinshin" (336.19–20). "The truce" ended the Civil War, and so it was the "truth" of the new state. "Slant" suggests "Slainte," the toast "Health" in Gaelic, while "Shinshin" ("chinchin," a toast in Italian) as the first half of "Sinn Fein" is literally "Us, Us." Here Taff, he "*of the peat freers . . . looking through the roof towards a relevution of the karmalife*" (338.05–06), responding to the audience's call "For Ehren, boys, gobrawl," may be de Valera/Shaun to Butt's Shem. He stands for the rustic Ireland of the peat fires and its freedom. He is soon named as "Da Valorem" (342.11), which combines de Valera's actual mix of fearful caution and courageous resoluteness in these years, as he eggs Butt on with the taunt "Gambanman! Take the cawraidd's blow!" (344.06–07, "Gombeenman! Take the coward's blow!"). Butt responds with some Synge-song "cultic twalette" (344.12), "Celtic twilight" as "twaddle," explaining he hadn't the heart to shoot the general when "the weight of his arge" (344.34, his aged arse) was displayed. He admits that this hesitancy is close to "the cowruads in their airish pleasantry" (344.18, the cowardice of the Irish peasantry), but Taff will entertain no insult to that Irish class, so he orders Butt, "And don't live out the sad of tearfs, piddyawhick" (346.22–23), that is, "Don't leave the sod of turf out of the story."

In the tale, Butt shoots the general when he sees that he has taken up a sod of turf to clean his backside. This clump is no mere handful of earth. It is a sod of peat, the very symbol of the Irish peasant, fruit of the bogs since made a literary subject by Seamus Heaney. This is the same peasant who, as the comic-gnomic Mulrennan in *A Portrait*, Stephen had professed to truly fear. Butt shouting, "my oreland for a rolvever" (352.09, "My Ireland for a revolver"), cries "We insurrectioned" and "I shuttm, missus" (352.14). Taff sums the situation up: "Aha race of fiercemarchands counterination oho of shorpshoopers"—that is, "a race of fierce merchants counter a nation of shopkeepers": the insurrectionary Irish against the British (352.25–26). This conflict led to "dawnybreak in Aira" (353.32–33), "Daybreak in Eire," through a "donnybrook in Eire," and eventually, "Withal aboarder, padar and madar, hal and sal, the sens of Ere with the duchtars of Iran. Amick amack amock in a mucktub" (358.20–22). These words offer a flow of Gaelic to say, "All aboard, father and mother, the sons of Eire and the daughters of Eireann, *avic* [my son], *amach* [out] *amock* [amok, or my pig]." The end of this sentence is a premonition of the novel's final line ("A way a lone a last a loved a long the" [628.15–16]), echoed in Gaelic. It brings in the image of setting out to sea in a ship that ends this section and prefigures the image of the Liffey flowing out to sea in the conclusion of book IV. It also reminds us of the parent-child relation in "Avick" ("my son;" earlier Taff had asked Butt, "Shattamovick?" [354.01–02]). All that remains is for HCE, in his defense, to claim that "Jambuwel's defecalties is Terry Shimmyrag's upperturnity" (366.20–21, "England's difficulty is Ireland's opportunity")—"Terra Shamrock" being Ireland. Finally, HCE dreams that he is Roderick O'Conor, the last high king, and, at the very end, "Faugh McHugh O'Bawlar," that is, Fiach McHugh O'Byrne, a Wicklow chieftain who in 1580 defeated the British in the Battle of Glenmalure.

II.3 reverberates with echoes of Irish history and contemporary Ireland's situation. Cries of rebellion, centered on the Kersse story, give way to a sense of independence achieved and a retrospective look at the decisive revolutionary action in the Russian general story. This progression leads, by the end of II.3, to a millennial perspective, in which Ireland's recent and bloodily achieved independence, involving war cries, courage, and actual shooting of the powerful, is compared to the struggles that led, eight centuries earlier, to the British conquest, vanquishing the last high king. Also reverberating throughout II.3 and confronting this tale of history and politics is the progression in media technologies from radio to television, which was occurring as Joyce wrote.

Media Conflicts

The use, early in II.3, of extensive technical language regarding radio ("the magnetic links of a Bellini-Tosti coupling system with a vitaltone speaker" [309.18–19]) following an account of the "birth of an otion" [309.12]) might seem mere technobabble. Yet the radio as the medium for communicating the Kersse story is unequivocally announced, just as the Buckley story, told by Butt and Taff, is clearly "teilweisioned" (345.36). Further, soon every medium of communication is referred to: the story is told by correspondents of "The Irish Race and World" (342.32), a newspaper; the stage direction calls, "Phone for Phineal" (346.12); Taff asks, "Can you come it, Budd?" (346.31), a radio receiver's call; and there is a pervasive sense of wonder at how "the fictionable world" (345.36) will be made more fictionable still when "*Amid a fluorescence of spectracular mephiticism there caoculates through the inconoscope . . . the figure of a fellowchap*" (349.18–20). Moreover, this television is seen as a medium whose technological prowess matches the warfare being described. "The bairdboard bombardment screen" (349.09), the television invented by Logie Baird, which bombards light on its "photoslope in syncopanc pulses" (349.11–12), both reports on, and is, "the charge of a light barricade" (349.11). Yet "Say mangraphique, may say nay por daguerre" (339.23): the French sentence "*C'est magnifique, mais c'est ne pas Daguerre*" can be translated as "It's magnificent, but it's not as true to life as photography" (invented by Daguerre), or as "It's magnificent, but it is not true to the war [*guerre*] itself." By adding radio and television to an environment already saturated by communications media, Joyce ups the ante in his exploration of the possibilities of mimetic representation.

In general, the new media are associated with light: television is "the light barricade," and once Buckley's shot is fired, it is "dawnybreak in Aira" (353.31–32), while the second sentence of the chapter had announced that its topic is "the fright of his light" (309.02). Television punctures the "heliotropical noughttime" (349.07), and written communications—such as the letter, Document Number 2, the treaty, and possibly this book itself—are associated with this night of nothingness: "Leave the letter . . . written in smoke and blurred by mist and signed of solitude, sealed at night" (337.11–14). The new technology, then, gets associated with light, futurity, decisiveness, and victory; the old with night, nothingness, and (in relation to the letter) guilt.

Yet this chapter offers no mere endorsement of new media. Rather, it implies a radically re-envisioned sense of space, place, and the *scene* of history. As many have pointed out, the *Wake*, to be felt, must be read aloud: that is, the sound is what matters. To say this is to claim that Joyce is obliterating the visual, denying us a story based on helping us to create in "the mind's eye" a scenario in which we situate a simulacrum of the "[i]neluctable modality of the visible" (*U* 3:1). He obliterates visuality, the critical wisdom goes, and demands a more sensual reception of the noise of the text through "the mind's ear." Donald Theall, championing the Joyce who presages the logics of new media, suggests that Joyce is creating a text machine that interpellates us neurobiologically through all our senses, thus anticipating the virtual reality aspirations of digital media.[11] Yet one can, imagining "this swishingsight teilweisioned" (345.36), go even further: in demanding that the moment of Butt's great courage be televised, Joyce appears to be trying to rethink seeing, to rethink its place in communication for the era of modernism's new art form, cinema. Can the text, in its soundful word manipulation, ever better the visuality of cinema—which had, with the late 1920s talkies, not only images but sound? The *Wake* is a nightbook; that is, it is a book without light, as it is set in the night. Out of that dark comes the light of technological visual communication, this televisualization of stories. II.3 records movement-image tales so that they can move the reader in a new way, even to courage. After realism, the novel is no longer a matter of static image after image—no longer Daguerre, not photographic. And perhaps it is no longer war.

By the end of II.3, HCE is ruminating upon whatever he has learned from the televised story, as he half-drunkenly compares himself to "Roderick O'Conor, . . . last preelectric king of Ireland" (380.12–13). It is still nighttime, and it is as if he is sleeping, so that only in plumbing a remembered store of (dream) images, the chapter can show us how, first, images and the visual are inescapable in stories and, also, how visuality is interwoven with sound memories such as the song "Follow Me Up to Carlow," which are not visual at all. As it is still night, it is appropriate that HCE should be associated, through O'Conor, with the end of an epoch, so that "he bares sobsconcious inklings shadowed on soulskin" (377.28) only to himself, without the benefit of a new light. Renewed courage is implied, but the "Carlow" of the song only becomes "Starloe!" (382.30) in the chapter's final word: there is only meager starlight at the end.

Where, then, might a new literary visuality, a new daylight for the era of the techno-visual, be found in the *Wake*? To generate new courage, especially when it retells stories rich in Irish revolutionary references, the *Wake* works up a new grammar of what the mind's eye can envision. As a book of the dark until the very end, the *Wake* does not really supply such a newly lighted (surreal) scenography. Yet it does offer repeated rehearsals for it.

These are the moments, some of the most suspenseful in the text and yet rare when compared with Joyce's earlier works, where we are granted access to the oldest communication form of all, human dialogue. How, the text at these moments prods us to ask, does the new radio and televisual telling stack up against direct spoken communication? Amid the scenes of shouting, laughter, and song there are three key scenes of dialogue in the chapter: the extensive one after the two stories, in which HCE tries to defend himself against the four old men; the subsequent one in which Sackerson clears the bar; and the other, placed strategically between the radio story of Kersse and the television story of Buckley, where the maid comes in to inform HCE that ALP wants him upstairs. The scene in which HCE defends himself is notable for his admission that he is "Guilty . . . !" (363.20); appropriately for this argument, he cries (echoing the Bible and Mr. Deasy's anti-Semitic invocation in *Ulysses*), "I appeal against the light" (366.02). Without the light, modernity lacks the scenography of modern perspective and thus of the modern organization of space and (in Foucault's terms) the carceral gaze that relates the two. Without it, HCE's sense of his own guilt is always unanswerable but also never erasable. It persists, "blurred by mist and signed of solitude" (337.13–14) in the old order of light and vision, which Joyce had tried to erase by setting his book in the lightless nighttime.

There remains only the spoken words between servants and served. Sackerson and Kate the maid are the two real workers in the chapter—the only two who communicate clearly, whose communication is in each case effective. Kate enters "in her serf's alown" (333.13–14) and speaks "in her amnest plein language, from his fain a wan, his hot and tot lass, to pierce his ropeloop ear" (333.26–28). This invokes again, in both English and Irish, "Ourselves Alone" and "Sinn Fein Amhain," the Irish rebel slogans. It compares Kate and ALP to a hottentot.[12] It also offers her the best Wakean tribute: that she speaks the damnedest plain language. Next, at this moment ALP—or by association Kate, the servant—has her woman's language associated with life with its rights and with the splitting of the atom: "and her birthright pang that would split an atam" (333.24–25). Atom splitting is a topic of this chapter: it crops up again most famously when Buckley finally shoots the general, and this move is compared to "The abnihilisation of the etym" (353.22). Here, pages earlier, Einsteinian atom splitting is related to the largely unseen women, to their life making and its sound, an implied cry of pain, and to the fact that they work and communicate. Kate, however, has her communication here reported only in the third person. It is only later that the washerwomen—women, workers, life makers, talkers, and atom smashers—who are present at the arrival of the new light, will be allowed to speak to one another and to us directly. Joyce has not yet, in II.3, given voice to the Irish proletariat. But inspired by technology, spurred on by history, he has begun the task of imagining a new light, and thus a new conception of space itself and its reorganization, that will allow a radical version of that Irish worker to at last come into being in the narratives of Ireland.

Notes

1. Quoted in Bernard Benstock, *Joyce-Again's Wake: An Analysis of "Finnegans Wake"* (Seattle: University of Washington Press, 1965), 247, footnoted as having been taken from Vivien Mercier, "Dublin under the Joyces," in *James Joyce: Two Decades of Criticism*, 288.

2. Dominic Manganiello, *Joyce's Politics* (London: Routledge and Kegan Paul, 1980).

3. Quoted in Martin Malinger and Richard Kain, *Joyce: The Man, the Work, the Reputation* (New York: New York University Press, 1956), 275. See also Benstock, *Joyce-Again's Wake*, 249.

4. There are a number of excellent readings of this chapter. See Finn Fordham's "Part II, BUTT: 'I Shuttm!'" in *Lots of Fun at "Finnegans Wake": Unravelling Universals* (Oxford: Oxford University Press, 2007), 89–174.

5. Roland McHugh, *Annotations to "Finnegans Wake,"* 3rd ed. (Baltimore: Johns Hopkins University Press, 2006), 335.

6. See David Hayman, "Male Maturity or the *Pu*blic Rise & Private Decline of HC Earwicker: *Chapter II.3*," in *How Joyce Wrote "Finnegans Wake,"* ed. Luca Crispi and Sam Slote (Madison: University of Wisconsin Press, 2007), 250–303.

7. See Donald F. Theall, "Beyond the Orality/Literacy Dichotomy: James Joyce and the Pre-history of Cyberspace," *Postmodern Culture* 2:3 (1992): 1–24.

8. John Bishop, *Joyce's Book of the Dark: "Finnegans Wake"* (Madison: University of Wisconsin Press, 1986).

9. Austin Briggs, "Joyce's Drinking," *James Joyce Quarterly* 48 (Summer 2011): 637–66.

10. The Gaelic word *amhain* is pronounced "ah-waun."

11. Donald F. Theall, *Beyond the Word: Reconstructing Sense in the Joyce Era of Technology, Culture, and Communication* (Toronto: University of Toronto Press, 1995), and *James Joyce's Techno-Poetics* (Toronto: University of Toronto Press, 1997).

12. On Africa in the *Wake*, see Sheldon Brivic, *Joyce through Lacan and Zizek: Explorations* (London: Palgrave Macmillan, 2008), 181–94.

12

Joyce's Countergospel in II.4

DAVID SPURR

Some will say, Is not God alone the Prolific?
I answer, God only Acts & Is, in existing beings or Men.

William Blake, *The Marriage of Heaven and Hell*

The material of the final chapter of book II belongs to both the first and last stages of the *Wake*'s composition. This fact in itself suggests that it represents an abiding preoccupation for Joyce, a matter from which he might wander freely throughout the years of *Work in Progress*, but to which he had ultimately to return. I wish to show that this brief chapter has an essential function in defining the very nature of Joyce's art in *Finnegans Wake*. My argument will be that Joyce's manner of recasting the Tristan and Isolde myth in the framework of the New Testament Gospel has the effect of a countergospel in which the doctrine of the "word made flesh" is both literally applied and completed by an operation in which the flesh is made word. In linguistic terms, the production of the word by the human body is given new value, making it equal to if not greater in importance than the word's signifying function. Language is rediscovered as bodily utterance. The decisive moment of this new dispensation occurs in what Joyce calls a "joysis crisis" (395.32) marked by the figure of the thrusting tongue, the fleshly organ of the word. In the process of evoking this moment, the chapter brings into play a set of reflections on the nature of language and its relation to desire. This way of reading takes the *Wake* to be more than a series of language games and more than a compendium of mythic and historical allusions. Instead, I choose to read this chapter as in some ways rewriting the Gospel, because like the Gospel, this work has the epiphanic character of what Leopold Bloom calls, in another context, a "wondrous revealment" (*U* 13.731); the *Wake* as a whole, I would argue, is a prolonged unveiling of language as the site of convergence between body and spirit and as the event in which they are joyfully bound together.

This manner of reading II.4 is derived from both the history of how the chapter came into being and from an analysis of the form and content of the final text. In the case of II.4, however, the story of how in several stages Joyce divided and then reunited his material helps us not only to appreciate the synthetic power of the chapter but also to see that synthesis as representative of Joyce's larger project in writing the *Wake*. Chapter II.4 has its origins in a four-page manuscript written in April 1923, now in the National Library of Ireland, in which four old men, doubling as the four waves of Ireland, witness the forbidden kiss of Tristan and Isolde, then break into a plaintive chorus of remembered love.[1] Joyce initially thought of the two sets of persons—the four old men and the lovers—as belonging to the same scene. By September 1923, however, Joyce had separated the material into two distinct sketches, "Tristan and Isolde" and "Mamalujo." The latter, with revisions, was published in the April 1924 issue of Ford Madox Ford's *Transatlantic Review*, and both sketches were later included in David Hayman's *First-Draft Version of "Finnegans Wake."*[2] Stylistically, the first of these derives from the "Nausicaa" episode of *Ulysses*, with its parody of the sentimental girl's romance story: "It was a just too gorgeous sensation . . . he being exactly the right man in the right place."[3] In contrast to this style, "Mamalujo" reproduces the fatigue and repetition of the "Eumaeus" episode in the earlier work:

> here now we are the four of us old Matt Gregory and old Marcus Lyons and old Luke Tarpey the four of us and sure thank God there are no more of us and sure now you won't go & leave out old Johnny Mac-Dougall the four of us and no more of us and so now pass the fish for Christ' sake amen.[4]

In the first-draft version Joyce seems to have already had a sense of the exhaustion of the New Testament Gospel, of its belatedness and estrangement from the events to which it bears testimony. A new kind of book was needed to remake the word as flesh.

In 1938, after fifteen years devoted to other parts of his book, Joyce turned again to the "Tristan" and "Mamalujo" sketches in order to recombine them. This new fusion of the two motifs follows the same basic order as the original manuscript of 1923, while significantly expanding the material devoted to the four old men. As Sam Slote summarizes the genetic sequence, "The character of Mamalujo was born through 'Tristan and Isolde,' only to be spun out separately and then, ultimately, reintegrated back into the textual matrix some fifteen years later."[5] This means that the figure of Mamalujo, as history and as gospel, was conceived out of the transgressive if romanticized erotic encounter of Tristan and Isolde. The tension, in the first as well as the final version of 1938, arises out of the difference between the erotic encounter itself and its interpretation, as it acquires meaning by being recalled and formulated in language. Joyce's ultimate return to the material of the original sketch was in keeping with the evolution of his work toward this fundamental question of language and its relation to desire, a project he shares in a larger sense with the four old men, be they the four masters of the Annals of Ireland or the four evangelists of the New Testament. We may thus consider the final chapter of Book II, placed strategically at the center of the book's formal order, as reenacting a primal scene of the *Wake* in its manifestation of an original and abiding dialectic between bodily desire and symbolic value, that is, between body and spirit, flesh and word.

Given the complexity of its genesis and its linguistic texture, the structural scaffolding of chapter II.4 is relatively straightforward. As the previous chapter has ended with the image of a ship setting out from the Irish capital, this chapter begins with the song of the seabirds that follow Tristan's ship on its way to Cornwall. The scene corresponds to the first act of Wagner's opera, which takes place on board the ship: Tristan has been sent by his uncle, King Mark, to bring from Ireland the king's intended wife, the princess Isolde. The birds' song, "shrillgleescreaming" (383.26), mocks the old king mercilessly while celebrating the "big kuss of Tristan with Usolde" (383.29)—the big kiss that also seals their destiny as *Liebestod*: death by love. A narrative voice then calls attention to the "big four"—Matt Gregory, Marcus Lyons, Luke Tarpey, and Johnny MacDougall—referred to as the "four maaster waves of Ireland"[6] (384.06) and as the four winds playing about the ship. The talk among the four alternates between envious remarks concerning the lovers on whom they are spying and nostalgic reminiscences of their own youthful days. At the end of the chapter the four join in song, and a narrative voice concludes on a wistful note. Scattered throughout the chapter are fragments of Robert Burns's "Auld Lang Syne," a song of remembrance and forgetting, and references to Dion Boucicault's melodrama *Arrah-na-Pogue* (1864), in which a kiss figures literally as an act of liberation.

A brief digression might be permitted here in order to remind ourselves that in writing the *Wake* Joyce was far from working in isolation and that both his themes and his techniques are a direct reflection of the larger literary field of the 1920s and 1930s. For example, if we go back to 1922, we note that, apart from the publication of *Ulysses*, the other major literary event of that year was T. S. Eliot's *The Waste Land*. Joyce's sketches for the *Wake* in 1923 rework several motifs in Eliot's poem: the indissoluble mixture of memory and desire, Wagner's Tristan, a dispossessed king, an old man witnessing a youthful sexual encounter, death by water, the cry of gulls—as well as Eliot's method of juxtaposing fragments from various myths, songs, and other discourses. In Eliot these serve as the shattered remnants of a tragic spirit—"These fragments I have shored against my ruins,"[7] whereas in Joyce the parodic mode turns them to a comedic purpose which is no less prophetic. Where Eliot's poem resonates with the Old Testament voices of Ezekiel and Ecclesiastes, Joyce is more concerned, in what was to become this chapter of the *Wake*, with the function of the New Testament Gospel as the attempt to render an exceptional and transformative event in written form.

A striking feature of this chapter is that each of the four evangelists' names occurs respectively at the beginning of a paragraph, in the order "Johnny" (386.12), "Marcus" (388.10), "Lucas" (390.34), and "Matt" (393.04). Before the first of these occurrences we read that "they all four remembored who made the world and how they used to be at that time" (384.35–36). Thus we witness several nostalgic versions of a common memory that includes scenes of Dublin, of college days, of clergymen, and of women, among a myriad of historical and geographical allusions obscurely related to these subjects. Given the formal position of each of the four names at the beginning of a paragraph, the temptation is to read each name as introducing the material that follows it, and as corresponding in some meaningful way to that material, as if the middle pages of the chapter (386–93) were divided into four parts in the manner of the Gospel. The problem is that there is no necessary connection, beyond mere contiguity, between each name and the text that immediately follows it. In addition, the respective identities of the four old men tend to merge in and out of one another and to shift in gender, while the pronominal mode of the nostalgic discourse alternates between the first person plural and the third person—"we," "they," or "he," but not "I." The four old men are collective, not independently subjective witnesses to the past and to one another. An exception to this rule occurs when one of the four makes an interjection in his own name: in the paragraph beginning "Marcus," for example, a reminiscence of college days and young romance is interrupted by a series of telephone calls to Ireland "(hello, Hibernia!)" from each of the four old men "(Matt speaking!)" (388.30). But the discourse interrupted in this manner cannot be assigned with confidence to any one person.[8] The four old men, moreover, are not just men but also "heladies" (386.15) and "shehusbands" (390.20), further adding to the promiscuity of their respective identities.

Joyce's customary method is to use canonical texts such as the *Odyssey* or Vico's *Nuova Scienza* as loosely fitted frameworks for his own material, which bears at best an indirect relation to the traditional work toward which it gestures. Such is the case with his use of the four Gospels here. The names may be seen as punctuating the text, like the four parenthetical interjections of "up" that occur respectively on pages 386, 393, and 397, and which Roland McHugh takes to be the hiccups of the four old men as they reminisce over their drink.[9] I suggest that the importance of the four names as used in this way lies not so much in the respective contents of what follows their appellation as in the order in which they appear.

Several documents attest to the fact that Joyce attached a certain importance to the order of the four Gospels in the New Testament[10] and that he liked to establish correspondence between the four evangelists and other fourfold phenomena. His letter to Harriet Weaver of October 12, 1923, includes a plan of the verses eventually placed at the end of chapter II.4 (398–99), where the names of the four evangelists correspond respectively to the four masters of the Annals; the four liturgical colors of blue-black, "moonblue," red, and black; the four days in the Church calendar, respectively and in chronological order, of Palm Sunday, Holy Tuesday, Spy Wednesday, and Good Friday; the four provinces of Ulster, Munster, Leinster, and Connacht; and the four Irish accents of Belfast, Cork, Dublin, and Galway (*SL* 296–97). The canonical order of the Gospels is particularly important when applied to the geography of Ireland. If we imagine the breast of a Roman Catholic as a map of Ireland with North at the top, the act of making the sign of the cross follows the order which Joyce designates: Ulster, Leinster, Munster, Connacht, or North, South, East, West. Joyce also employs this device in the quiz chapter of the *Wake*, where the multiple choices given as possible answers to a question about an "Irish capitol city" are "a) Delfas," "b) Dorhqk," "c) Nublid," and "d) Dalway" (140.08–36): as if Catholic Ireland were crossing itself at the respective points of Belfast (N), Cork (S), Dublin (E), and Galway

(W). The sign of the cross is a bodily performance of the doctrine of the Holy Trinity. In Catholic ritual, the gesture is often accompanied by the names of the Trinity uttered as the forehead is touched (*in nomine Patris*), followed by the lower breast (*et Fili*) and ending with the horizontal movement from shoulder to shoulder (*et Spiritus Sancti*).

Given this apparent attachment to the traditional order, what is striking about chapter II.4 is that the names of the four evangelists appear most prominently in an order that reverses the positions of the first and last gospels: Johnny, Marcus, Lukas, Matt (386–93). Joyce seems to have had some reason for reversing the canonical order. In fact, he began to play with the order of the Gospels as early as 1924, in a notebook he began while on summer holiday in Saint-Malo and finished in Paris later that year. Page 76 of this notebook (*JJA* 32) lists the evangelists in two different orders, one under the heading of "waves" and the other under "winds." The four coordinates of the compass are also listed in a way that establishes a correspondence between compass points and Gospels, depending on whether the latter are the names of waves or winds:

	Waves	*Winds*
N	Matt	Mark
S	Mark	John
E	Luke	Luke
W	John	Matt

In their character as waves, the evangelists appear in canonical order according to the order North, South, East, West. But in this notebook the old men are not just waves; they are also winds circling about the lovers' ship (as at 394.13–17), where they are reported as "flapping and cycling ... around the waists of the ships, in the wake of their good old Foehn again, as tyred as they were, at their windswidths in the waveslength": the *Foehn* is the south wind that sweeps through the valleys of Switzerland. As winds, the "quad gospellers" (112.06–07) occupy positions which according to their canonical order places them respectively at the compass positions WNES, a clockwise movement as one travels from point to point of the compass. We begin to witness a geometrical pattern expressive of religious doctrine: when connected to the waves and wind of God's original creative act (Genesis I:2),[11] the traditional order of the Gospels corresponds both to the sign of the cross on which each of them hangs the subject of its tale and the movement of time in which they collectively look forward to the moment of fulfilment.

In light of this almost medieval system of signs, the order in which Joyce's evangelists are named in II.4 (as John, Mark, Luke, Matthew) takes on an oddly perverse character. Referring once again to the two charts in the Buffalo Notebook, the four in this new order now occur in the sequence WSEN: a counterclockwise movement, in keeping with the *Wake*'s movement from the present through the past in its resistance to history as progress in time, a resistance reproduced in the narrative structure of the *Wake*. As winds, again according to the new sequence (John, Mark, Luke, Matthew), Joyce's gospellers follow the order SNEW: the sign of the cross made upside down, from bottom to top, beginning with the Son rather than the Father. A thematic explanation is possible for each of these "reverse" patterns: in the counterclockwise movement, time reflects the nostalgic, backward-looking character of the old men, obsessed by the memories of days they cannot relive. The sign of the cross in reverse reflects more generally what I shall call the heretical nature of Joyce's countergospel, in which the Son as word made flesh takes precedence over the law of the Father. Joyce's counter-cross thus recalls the history of the Christian heresies of Arianism, Pelagianism, and Nestorianism, all of which dispute orthodox doctrine concerning the nature of Christ and his relation to God the Father.

The unorthodox order of Joyce's evangelists has its counterpart in his wholly original interpretation of the union of word and flesh, which centers on the figure of the tongue. The key passage here is the paragraph beginning at 395.26. Let us recall the narrative context as rendered in one of Joyce's principal sources, Joseph Bédier's 1900 version of *Le roman de Tristan et Iseut*. On their voyage to Cornwall where Iseut is to marry King Mark, Tristan and Iseut find themselves hopelessly in love after having innocently drunk the secret potion that had been intended for Iseut's meeting with King Mark. Seeing tears in Iseut's eyes, Tristan asks her what it is that torments her. She replies, "L'amour de vous" (The love of you). Bédier then writes, "Alors il posa ses lèvres sur les siennes," and so he put his lips to hers (38).[12] In Joyce's version the incident is introduced with the words "For it was then a pretty thing happened of pure diversion mayhap" (395.26–27). What then transpires in Joyce's text can be paraphrased in the following way: Tristan makes a gesture with his hand "at the justright moment" (395.27). Isolde gives a little cry of "Jesus Christ!" ("joysis crisis" [395.32]) and puts her lips to his, having thereby "renulited their disunited" (395.33), reuniting the two lovers by relighting the fire between them. At this point Tristan, whose performance is compared to that of a champion football player, seizes the opportunity of a lover's lifetime by thrusting his tongue between her teeth, which are compared to both lines of forwards: "rightjingbangshot into the goal of her gullet" (396.01–02). This handsome feat is followed by what sounds like a cheer, "Alris!" (396.03), presumably as the members of the football crowd all rise spontaneously to their feet.

To understand this passage as anything more than a farce, we need to know the history of the principal motifs that it brings into play: the kiss, the tongue, and the shout. Let us take each of these in turn. Apart from the Tristan myth, one of the recurring motifs of this chapter is Dion Boucicault's play *Arrah-na-Pogue*, which tells the story of another kiss. The title character is a young Wicklow woman called Arrah-na-Pogue or "Arrah of the kiss" for a famous incident that, according to the play, took place during the Rebellion of 1798. When the rebel Beamish McCoul was imprisoned in Wicklow jail, a plan for his escape was devised by his fellow insurgents. The plan was written on a piece of paper and communicated to the prisoner under the jailor's nose through a ruse devised by Arrah. As Shaun the Post tells it, "She had rowled it up and put it in her mouth; and when she saw [Beamish], she gave it to him in a kiss."[13] In its character as an act of transmission, Arrah's kiss resembles the one remembered by Leopold Bloom in the "Lestrygonians" episode of *Ulysses*, when he and Molly lay together on Howth Hill: "Softly she gave me in my mouth the seedcake warm and chewed" (U 8.907), and a few lines later, "Hot I tongued her. She kissed me. I was kissed" (U 8.915). Molly herself recalls this moment on Howth Hill in 1888 when she "gave him the bit of seedcake out of [her] mouth" and "got him to propose" to her (U 18.1573–74).

What all of these kisses have in common is the use of the tongue or its surrogate. They are versions of what in English is called the French kiss and in colloquial French is called, more colorfully, "*une pelle*," a shovel. The importance of this kind of kiss in Joyce is that it makes the tongue into a sexual organ as well as an organ of speech. This double function of the tongue is present in the history of kisses on which Joyce draws and which he extends in his own work. In Boucicault, the escape plan passed from Arrah's mouth to Beamish's provides a substitute for the tongue in the French kiss, while serving the other function of the tongue as a means of communication. The rolled-up escape plan is the tongue thrust into Beamish's mouth in the form of writing; it is literally the message of freedom for him. Joyce underscores the double function of the tongue—as the organ of both desire and signification—as being ancient and universal, when in reference to this scene in Boucicault's play he writes of "the passing of the key of Twotongue Common" and "the carrier of the word" (385.04–05). The seedcake passed from Molly's mouth to Bloom's is another surrogate for the tongue, inviting both his real tongue to her mouth in exchange for the seedcake ("Hot I tongued her") and his speech in the form of the marriage proposal. There is finally, in Joyce as in scripture, a connection between the tongue and the divine, as suggested allegorically, if ironically, in the story "Grace," where Tom Kernan's fall from grace is marked by the severing of his tongue. In *Portrait* we are reminded more than once that the tongue figures in the sacrament of Holy Communion: at Stephen's first communion, "he had shut his eyes and opened his mouth and stuck out his tongue a little" (*P* 47) to receive the host. At the end of chapter 3, we read, "He would hold upon his tongue the host and God would enter his purified body" (*P* 158). Taking all these examples together, we note that in Joyce the tongue serves the ends of both desire and signification, of both flesh and the word.

Joyce's preoccupation with the tongue has precedent in the New Testament, most notably in the Acts of the Apostles. In the scene of the Pentecostal gathering of Acts 2, the apostles are visited by "tongues [*glossai*] as of fire" from above and begin to speak in "other tongues" (*eterais glossais*), which are miraculously heard as if everyone spoke in the same tongue. Joyce follows the biblical source in playing on the double sense of tongue as bodily form and language, but also in imagining a wondrous reversal of the dispersion of languages that took place in the episode of the tower of Babel. With this in mind, Joyce's own text can be read as a double reconciliation: that of the coming together of tongues no longer foreign to one another and as the healing of the historical rupture between tongue as body and tongue as language.

Let us now consider the cry or shout, the spontaneous utterance that signifies independently of differentiated linguistic codes. The cry of "Alris!" as Tristan scores the kiss with Iseut, or Isolde, recalls the shout in the street heard by Stephen Dedalus and Mr. Deasy in the "Nestor" episode of *Ulysses*. In that episode the schoolboys have gone outdoors to play field hockey as Stephen visits Deasy's study in order to receive his wages. The conversation between these two turns to theology, with Deasy claiming that "all human history moves towards one great goal, the manifestation of God" (*U* 2.381). Another kind of goal has just been scored outdoors, and the boys raise a shout. "That is God," says Stephen. "A shout in the street" (*U* 2.383–86). Stephen's position is thus clearly distinct from Deasy's. The manifestation of God is not to be delayed, deferred to the end of history. It is here and now, in the spontaneous joy of childhood play and in every lived moment, for those with eyes to see or ears to hear it. With this in mind, we can return to the episode of the kiss of Tristan and Isolde in the *Wake*, concentrating this time on its potentially spiritual sense.

Joyce's narrative parodies both Bédier's romanticizing of the medieval legend and the popular sentimental romance as published in the magazines read by Gerty MacDowell ("our angel being, one of romance's fadeless wonderwomen" [395.30–31]). However, if we consider that the story here is told from the point of view of the four old men, it follows the rhetorical mode of the Gospel as witness to a transformative event. This is the "joysis crisis" (395.32), where Joyce transforms the advent of Ιησοῦ χρίστοῦ (Jesus Christ) into his own version of the *krisis*, the Greek word for the decisive moment, a word most commonly translated in English versions of the New Testament as the moment of judgment (as in Matthew 5:21, Mark 6:11, Luke 10:14, John 5:27) but also as condemnation (John 5:24) and sentence (Luke 23:24). As distinguished from the Greek *dike*, which refers to justice in terms of custom or right, the *krisis* is the crucial act of deciding between two mutually opposing alternatives, such as life or death. Thus Christ announces the Last Judgment, which shall deliver its sentence of life or death, whereas in the Tristan myth the lovers seal their own death sentence by means of their forbidden kiss.

The *Liebestod* theme, which gives its title to the final aria of Wagner's opera, is already at work in Joyce's story of the fateful kiss: "you dote on her even unto date" (395.31–21), even unto this day, even unto death. But the paragraphs that follow plead for a more merciful judgment, in keeping with the "cup of kindness" drunk by the four old men as they sing "Auld Lang Syne." Just after the cheer that greets the kiss, the question is asked, "Could you blame her, we're saying, for one psocoldlogical moment? What would Ewe do?" (396.13–14). Here the attention is shifted from the girl to the one passing judgment, who can assign blame only in a coldly logical, so-called logical moment devoid of kindness, and who is directly interrogated as to his or her response to the same circumstances. The question "What would Ewe do?" suggests the heretical identification of Eve, the mother of man, with Mary, mother of the Lamb of God, while implying both that the sexual act is the natural response to an animal impulse and that the lamb of innocence is the direct offspring of sexual instinct. In other words, the "joysis crisis" redeems the transgressive act of the body by introducing a new logic of *krisis*. Joyce's *krisis* is no longer constrained to choose between contraries: his language brings about the joyful fusion of body and spirit where Christian doctrine sought to render them asunder.[14] What Joyce has preserved from the original sense of *krisis* is that of an event or a decisive moment. In this sense, Joyce's crisis is the event of the word itself: the word as event in its material and bodily form and in the potentially transformative power of this event for our experience of language.

We now have in place the essential elements of Joyce's heretical countergospel, which preaches the liberation from original sin through the jouissance not merely of the flesh but of the manifestation of spirit in the flesh, in the here and now. It is important to distinguish what Joyce is doing in *Finnegans Wake* from what Stephen Dedalus thinks he is doing in *Portrait* when, in writing the villanelle, he conceives that "In the virgin womb of the imagination the word was made flesh" (*P* 182–83). Whereas Stephen merely sublimates the poetic process into a form of religious inspiration, the *Wake* performs a much more radical and original transformation that privileges the nature of language as event. It is through the event of language that jouissance occurs, as bodily utterance or inscription gives expression to desire.

Let us explore this notion of jouissance as the event of language that joins body and spirit. In the first chapter of *Portrait* little Stephen asks, "kiss. Why did people do that with their two faces?" (*P* 11). Stephen poses the question of the relation between desire and meaning, a question carried forward all the way into the *Wake*. In the history of kisses just reviewed, each is both an act of pleasure and an effective sign: if in Wagner's opera the kiss seals the fatal destiny of the lovers, Arrah's kiss communicates the way to freedom for Beamish, whereas Molly's kiss plants the seed of desire and of speech in the fertile ground of Bloom's mind. In this binding of the signifier to the gestures of bodily desire, the use of the tongue is essential in its nature as both the instrument of speech and the fleshly organ of jouissance. Molly Bloom says of being kissed by Lieutenant Mulvey, her first lover, that "it never entered my head what kissing meant till he put his tongue in my mouth" (*U* 18.770–71). It is a brilliant play on words: Mulvey's tongue literally enters her head and, through this movement, conveys the real meaning of the kiss to her mind. Molly thus testifies to the role of the tongue in giving meaning to pleasure and pleasure to meaning, as body and spirit are joined. The shout for joy made when a goal is scored and the crowd leaps to its feet is another moment of perfect concord, taking place on the threshold, as it were, between the body as instinctive utterance and language as signification. Joyce thus works against the Pauline doctrine of the Gospel, which systematically insists on the opposition of flesh and spirit in such passages as Romans 8:3 and Galatians 5, where Paul calls for the "crucifixion" of the flesh in the name of the spirit. In the theological framework which Joyce both gestures toward and refuses, spirit as meaning is made flesh, not in an act of transubstantiation but rather as an affirmation of the essential nondifference between spirit and flesh in the substance of being. If the "joysis crisis" occurs in the form of a sporting conquest over a sentimental girl, that is, if the parodic mode favors the banal and profane, it is because to destroy the opposition between spirit and flesh is also to destroy that between the sacred and the profane. Rather, in the *Wake*, the sacred is collapsed onto the profane, as it was in the original Gospel in the scene of Christ's birth, for example, or of his triumphant entry into Jerusalem on the back of an ass.

In Catholic liturgy, the ritual most directly concerned with the matter of flesh and spirit is the sacrament of the Eucharist. Given Joyce's preoccupation with the Eucharist in every one of his works of prose fiction, a brief exposition of the nature of this sacrament may perhaps be permitted here. In the Eucharist, as formulated by Thomas Aquinas, the consecrated bread and wine are transformed into the substance of the body of Christ, leaving only the accidents of the bread and wine themselves. This substance is the eternal and underlying reality of being, as opposed to the accidents of the material world perceived through the senses. The sacrament thus serves as a sacrifice of the worldly, sensual substance to the sacred and divine substance of Christ, so that the complete substance of the bread and wine are converted into the complete substance of Christ's body and blood.[15] For our purposes, what matters is that for Aquinas as for orthodox Catholic faith, something material is entirely transformed into something divine; there is a one-way passage from one thing to another. From an orthodox point of view, the heresy of Joyce's implied position lies in its refusal to give priority, in this union of contraries, to substance over accident, to the divine over the human, to the spirit over the flesh. This refusal to choose is also a refusal to exclude or suppress; it thus refuses the economy of sacrifice, in which something of worldly value must be given up for something transcendent. Both refusals convey the good news that body and spirit have always been one and that the substantial jouissance of this union is at hand, without the cost of sacrifice and free of the sentence of the law.

The scripture of this countergospel is the language of *Finnegans Wake* itself, with its consistent refusal to choose between one word and another, always preferring to unite rather than divide. As we know, this is done by splicing and joining the morphemes within language and thus, in Saussurean terms, collapsing the vertical axis of selection onto the horizontal axis of combination. To this fusion of the elements within a given language, such as English, is added the grafting of elements from other languages onto the stem of the initial language, a process made visible in the draft versions of the *Wake*. The process of fusion is therefore both intra- and inter-linguistic, but it does not stop there. Our excursion into the doctrine of the Eucharist finally brings us back to a further union within the nature of language in the

Wake: the fusion of language as a system of meaning with language as sound. In Joyce's book the signifying function of language, normally dominant, is undermined by and even made subordinate to its phenomenal character as the bodily production of the word. This phenomenon is related to Lacan's notion of *la langue* as the concept according to which language is haunted by an internal split between two incommensurate elements, sound and sense, which neither coincide nor exist wholly outside of one another. In this internal split, as Lacan is interpreted by Mladen Dolar, the bodily production of speech produces jouissance: "enjoyment becomes the inner element of speech itself—it inundates speech, yet without engulfing it."[16] Joyce's language captures this enjoyment, for example, in the word *flshpst*, as when Tristan, kissing Isolde, "druve the massive of virilvigtoury flshpst the both lines of forwards" (395.36–396.01). Here *flshpst* is more a sound than a word, the sound of the wet, fleshy tongue slipping between Isolde's teeth and into her throat. The tongue is body rather than signifier, even if its motion, as gesture, also signifies. In this case, however, the bodily production of sound is that of jouissance. The jouissance of language is beyond meaning; it is what is left over after language has discharged its signifying function.

Does the language that puts into play this jouissance make sense? Yes and no, in the indeterminate, borderline manner of *Finnegans Wake*. In the *Wake*, the binding of the spirit onto the flesh is the condition of jouissance, because the site of this binding represents the encounter of sense with that which escapes sense: the non-sense of the body in its irrepressible, unpredictable, and indeterminate desire. In the French kiss, the tongue searches in the dark of the other's body; the thrust of erotic impulse exceeds meaning, even the meaning grasped by Molly when, French-kissed by Mulvey, she knew for the first time "what kissing meant" (*U* 18.771). The Wakean tongue is the idiom that evokes this excess of the real which other languages suppress. The *Wake* perhaps comes closest to an embodiment of this excess in its systematic cultivation of the site at which, in language, sense is exceeded by the non-sense of the body.

It is only with the song at the end of the chapter (398.32–399.34) that we can, with Joyce's authorization,[17] assign verses to each of the four old men, both as the Four Masters of Ireland and as the four evangelists of the New Testament. These verses were conceived in 1923, before Joyce began to play with the canonical order of the Gospels. Now placed at the end of the chapter, they return the evangelists to their traditional places, as if these men were done wandering, at least for the time being. The four verses are thus assigned respectively to Matthew, Mark, Luke, and John and to the provinces of Ulster,

Munster, Leinster, and Connacht, with the corresponding "accents" of Belfast, Cork-Kerry, Dublin, and Galway-Mayo. The importance Joyce assigns to accent is in keeping with his insistence on speech as bodily production, for accent is the ineradicable mark of geographical or social origin on the speech-making organs of the body. The four successive stanzas of the final song, moreover, are saturated with the language of desire, as if the promise of bodily jouissance had become the latest good news of the Gospel. The song is introduced by an English version of the Hebrew *Shema* or the invocation to Israel, "Hear, O hear, O Israel," but here the name of Israel is replaced by that of "Iseult la belle," while Tristan, "sad hero," is also made the object of address (398.29). The first verse moves forward into the Christian era by setting the song in an *Anno Domini nostri sancti Jesu Christi* (398.32), a year never precisely identified, but nonetheless putting the subject of the song under the sign of Christ, as befits the evangelist singers. From this point the song's four stanzas follow a distinct progression: in Matthew's stanza, a "girleen" (let us call her Isolde) is forbidden by a menacing Shaun-like figure from being courted; in Mark's verses she figures as a Dingle version of Venus Anadyomene, riding in on the surf "in her curragh of shells of daughter of pearl" (399.05), whereas in Luke she is the object of a tender marriage proposal.

In the final stanza, the voice of John brings this sequence to its consummation, as Isolde is bedded in a frankly erotic encounter: "Grand goosegreasing we had entirely with an allnight eiderdown bed picnic to follow" (399.23–24). Whereas each of the evangelists has spoken in a different grammatical person (thou, she, you), John has the privilege of speaking in the first person: "I tossed that one long before anyone" (399.20). The song concludes with Isolde's testimony to her own pleasure, sworn by a traditional symbol of Irish Christian faith: "By the cross of Cong, . . . you're the mose likable lad that's come my ways yet from the barony of Bohermore" (399.25–28)— from the Bothar Mor or Great Road. While throughout the song Christian symbols are freely mixed with Isolde's sexual career, the correspondence between the two semantic fields intensifies in the fourth stanza, where the erotic encounter begins on a "wet good Friday" (399.21) and lasts all night before Isolde is described "rising up Saturday in the twilight from under me" (399.25–26) and praising her lover by invoking the cross. Whereas in the song as a whole, the life of Christ has been transformed into the adventures of a girl, in the last stanza the signs of Christ's crucifixion, death, and rising from the dead are converted to the scenes of a sexual romp. Isolde rises up from under her lover on Saturday, the Sabbath, whereas Jesus is discovered risen only on Sunday, "the first day of the week" (John 21: 1). In this manner she can be said to upstage Him by anticipating his act of rising. The song of the four old men is in certain ways an elaboration on the "joysis crisis" of the big kiss occurring four pages earlier, as in both cases the amorous encounter is given the magnitude of a religious epiphany. Again, the effect is not that of the profanation of the sacred but rather the sacralization of the profane, both in flesh and in language: the consummation of fleshly desire, as told in the homely Hiberno-English of the song's lyrics, acquires a depth and universality of resonance within the ghostly framework of the Gospel story. For the four old men, the song is a kind of redemption from the sadness, envy, and nostalgia of the earlier prose passages; it not only celebrates the body as its subject matter but as song it also returns to the joy of the body in the vocal production of music.

To have given the last stanza to the voice of John is a happy choice, for John literally has a different vision from that of the synoptic gospels. There are several reasons why Joyce is likely to have favored John's version. John begins, for example, by declaring that the Word [*logos*] was with God in the beginning and that all things were made through the Word, and that in the Word was life and the light of men (1:1–4). The logos is not just an allegory for the figure of Christ; it is the original form of creative utterance. John's formula can thus be understood both in linguistic terms as referring to the constitutive function of language and in artistic terms as affirming the creative power of language. John, moreover, writes differently from the other evangelists, using the objects of daily experience—bread, water, and light—in his exposition of Christ's meaning. He is the only one of the four who, in chapter 21, tells the story of Christ's resurrection in novelistic detail and suspense: Jesus reveals himself indirectly to his disciples "when the morning was now come" (21:4), and obtains assurances of love from Simon Peter while entrusting him with the pastoral care of Jesus's followers. This is the only Gospel in which the resurrected Christ does something so familiar as to cook breakfast for his companions (21:9–12). John is also the only one of the four evangelists who insists that the *krisis* or judgment is not to be deferred to Christ's second coming but is already constituted by the event of Christ's presence: "And this is the [*krisis*], that light is come into the world" (3:19); "Now is the [*krisis*] of this world" (12:31). Joyce shares with John this insistence on the word as a decisive event in the here and now.

In the celebratory address to the evangelists which follows their song on the final page of this chapter in the *Wake*, to each name is added the suffix *hew*, as if acknowledging each as a hewer, a maker; but to John's name is given the most extravagant ornament: "Johnheehewwheehew!" The sign of making is combined with spontaneous shouts of joy, and these are topped with the single syllable of the succeeding line: "Haw!" (399.29). Is this the braying of the ass which Jesus rides into Jerusalem in John 12:14–15? In any case, it has no proper semantic value: it is the spontaneous bodily utterance that both precedes and exceeds meaning, like the "shout in the street" (*U* 2.383–86), which Stephen identifies with God.

Joyce again pays homage to John two lines later with the words, "And still a light moves long the river" (399.31), echoing John 1:5: "And the light shineth in darkness." The final two lines of the chapter, which also close book II of the *Wake*, are as follows: "Its pith is full. The way is free. Their lot is cast. / So, to john for a john, johnajeams, led it be!" (399.35–36). The first of these lines contains three sentences, each composed of monosyllables arranged in two iambic feet. The sequence is musical more than it is narrative or logical, and yet the respective evocations of fullness, freedom, and fate are like the simple wonder of John's words when he recognizes the risen Christ: "It is the Lord" (21:7). It is finally with John that Joyce seems to identify in the final line. The address "to john for a john" recalls both the evangelist and the name given to the commonest of men. According to the *OED*, John is "the representative proper name for a footman, butler, waiter, messenger, or the like." In this double function of the proper name, the sacred is again joined to the profane, while the name itself is joined to Joyce's "Christian" name in "johnajeams." On one hand, "johnajeams" is Hamlet's John-a-dreams in the soliloquy of act 2, scene 2, line 565, a "dull and muddy-mettled rascal" unpregnant of his cause. But "johnajeams" is also the fusion of the most spiritual of the evangelists with the textual body of Joyce's own dream Gospel: John of James, or James's John.

At the end of John's book the evangelist says that if all the things that Jesus did were to be recorded, "I suppose that even the world itself could not contain the books that should be written" (21: 25). Joyce seems to have written the *Wake* with a similar view in mind. His intention is not to write an infinite number of books but to write one book which through its profusion of signs, freed from their ordinary forms, charges them with such multiplicity of meaning as to signify everything that might be written. Beyond this, John's idea of putting into books the things that Jesus did constitutes a kind of reversal of the doctrine expressed at the opening of his Gospel: "the Word was made flesh" (1. 14); to put the acts of the incarnate Christ into a book is to render the flesh back into words. Here is where Joyce both joins with the Gospel and writes it anew, in a form where the body continues to shine through the word. Such a conclusion is not intended as a fetishization of either the body or language, for each is nothing without the other, and for Joyce there is, as in Stephen Dedalus's view of the world, a nothingness at the heart of both.[18] No doubt this nothingness lies at the heart of *Finnegans Wake* as well, but it is precisely this hole at the center that not only makes possible the language of Joyce's book but also opens it up to the advent of a radical alterity.

Here is where we might draw tentative lines of affinity between the spirit of the *Wake* and the idea of faith as put forth in Derrida's *Foi et savoir* (Faith and knowledge). Derrida claims that religious faith has historically been associated with three kinds of places: the island, such as the island of Patmos where John experiences Revelation; the promised land; and the desert, or, more radically, a desert in the desert: the absolute nothingness which "makes possible, opens, splits, or renders infinite the other" precisely because it lies outside the general structure of experience.[19] The radical confrontation of nothingness is the event at the origin of religion, understood in its etymological sense (Latin *relegere*: to gather, assemble, and *religere*: to tie, bind) as the gathering together of pure singularities before the formation of social and political structures, before the opposition of the sacred and the profane: the "not yet" of the first page of the *Wake* (03.11), where Joyce evokes the void of Genesis 1:2. There is thus at the heart of faith itself a faith without dogma which risks absolute darkness, but which also opens the way to a relation with the singularity of the other and to the unforeseen. It is the belief that the world could be created again from the beginning, getting it right this time. In literary terms, this faith corresponds to a linguistic performativity free of any given language, a new way of speaking which loses itself in itself while also announcing at least the possibility of its translation of a radical otherness.[20] It is in this sense that the *Wake* can be read as written in a visionary mode. What Derrida calls the "pure singularities" of being thus become the singular linguistic forms, which Joyce uproots and recombines in an act of faith that both precedes and goes beyond any existing anthropological or theological horizon. This faith in the redemptive promise of a language, of a world free of dogma yet always open to possibility and renewal, is the unstated, everywhere implied faith of *Finnegans Wake*.

Notes

1. The 1923 *Finnegans Wake* manuscripts at the National Library of Ireland are online at the following address: http://catalogue.nli.ie/pdflookup.php?pdfid=vtls000252560.

2. The two sketches, which figure as distinct from one another in British Library MS 47481, are reprinted in David Hayman's *First-Draft Version of "Finnegans Wake"* (Austin: University of Texas Press, 1963), 208–19.

3. Ibid., 208.

4. Ibid., 213

5. Sam Slote, "Prolegomenon to the Development of Wakean Styles: New Acquisitions at the National Library of Ireland," *James Joyce Quarterly* 42 (Fall 2004): 26.

6. Hermann Maas was a theologian and contemporary of Joyce active in the *Pfaffernotbund*, the group of German Protestant pastors opposed to National Socialism.

7. T. S. Eliot, *The Waste Land*, in *Collected Poems, 1909–1962* (New York: Harcourt, Brace, 1970), 69.

8. In one of his commentaries on references to the New Testament Gospel in *Finnegans Wake*, Roy Benjamin claims that it is Matthew, not Mark or some other person, who is delivering the "howldmoutherhibbert" ("Old Mother Hubbard") lectures (388.29), that the phrase "from sea to sea" (388.30) is Joyce's elaboration on "the first gospel's theme of inclusion," and that these two elements together envision "both a new role for women and a new trend toward the universal," especially characteristic of Matthew. Roy Benjamin, "Intermisunderstanding Minds: The First Gospel in *Finnegans Wake*," *Joyce Studies Annual* 2010, 222. But it seems arbitrary to attribute the "sea to sea" theme particularly to Matthew when this theme belongs to the lecture which his telephone call interrupts. The movement toward universality is, of course, common to each of the four Gospels. In Mark 11:17, for example, Jesus quotes Isaiah: "Is it not written, 'My house shall be called a house of prayer for all the nations'?"

9. Roland McHugh, *Annotations to "Finnegans Wake*," 3rd ed. (Baltimore: Johns Hopkins University Press, 2006).

10. The canonical order Matthew, Mark, Luke, and John dates from the Synod of Laodicea, 363 AD.

11. The word *spirit* in the King James Version ("the spirit of God moved upon the face of the waters") translates the Hebrew *ruah*, which in its primary sense means breath, air, wind.

12. Joseph Bédier, *Le roman de Tristan et Iseut* (Paris: Gallimard Folio, 2009), 38.

13. Dion Boucicault, *Arrah-Na-Pogue*, in *The Dolmen Boucicault*, ed. David Krause (Dublin: Dolmen Press, 1972), 127.

14. "That which is born of the flesh is flesh; and that which is born of the Spirit is spirit" (John 3:6).

15. Saint Thomas Aquinas, *Summa III, Article 75, Question 4, Summa totius theologiae*, 6 vols. (Zurich: Olms, 2000–2003).

16. Mladen Dolar, *A Voice and Nothing More* (Cambridge: MIT Press, 2006), 144.

17. Letters to Harriet Shaw Weaver of October 12, 1923 (in *SL* 296–97), and of November 2, 1923 (in *LettersIII* 82).

18. "On that mystery and not on the madonna which the cunning Italian intellect flung to the mob of Europe the church is founded and founded irremovably because founded, like the world, macro and microcosm, upon the void" (*U* 9.840–42).

19. Jacques Derrida, *Foi and savior* (Paris: Seuil, 1996), 29.

20. Ibid., 31.

13

Salvation, Salves, Saving, and Salvage

The Linguistic Underpinnings of III.1

KIMBERLY J. DEVLIN

One theme of *Finnegans Wake*, particularly prevalent in book III chapter 1, is organized around the four words listed in my title, which are interrelated through sounds and/or meanings. *Salvage* is the "act of saving imperiled property from loss"—the property at stake is the elusive letter that resurfaces and disappears throughout the text. One meaning of *salve* is "flattery or commendation," both of which we hear in the chapter's interrogatory discourse. A salve is also a balm, often aromatic. *Salvation* evokes the "deliverance from the power or penalty of sin: redemption" or "the agent or means that brings about such deliverance"—the attempted agent is the figure known as Shaun. *Saving* can mean "rescue," "economy," or, in extreme cases, accrual to the point of hoarding—a theme of the chapter's central fable, the Ondt and the Gracehoper. *Deliverance* in its more secular contexts is associated with "delivery" as "utterance or enunciation," "the act of conveying," and "the act or manner of speaking or singing": these meanings are related to Shaun's vocations and voices. *Delivery* is also related to transit and transmission, Shaun's role as the carrier of the letter.[1] In III.1, Shaun is identified as a "salve a tour" (409.31): the phrase contains all but one of the letters of *saviour* (implying perhaps that he lacks, specifically, an *i*). This incomplete saviour is simultaneously on "tour," in peripatetic motion, and hence identified—with partial irony—as "the walking saint" (427.28): he emerges as a "salve" who is pedestrian in both senses of the word. He is also identified as "the salus of the wake" (427.29)—the health (*salus* in Latin) of what remains of the paternal legacy (HCE's wake) and the solace of the weak. These titles in themselves are "salves," the flattering connotations of which are questioned, however, both through Shaun's obesity and sluggishness ("hastehater of the first degree" [408.11]), and the dishonest assurance of his fable. This essay will attempt to illustrate the ways this string of roughly homophonic words helps to illuminate III.1 (in conjunction with many other literary devices) and in closing will examine one of Shaun's limited assumptions about linguistic salvage.[2]

From Transition to Transmission

Before the central figure of Shaun comes into view, we receive a brief transition from book II to book III, which may be explained in the latter's opening lines. III.1 opens with a foreboding reference to the possible time, which thematically connects it to II.4: if read through a pessimistic lens, this prior chapter dramatizes that the passage of time brings senescence along with purely voyeuristic and vicarious sexual pleasure. The "joysis crisis" (395.32) celebrated by Tristan and Isolde may be accessed by the Four only through listening and watching—as opposed to feeling and experiencing. The ominous sound of the imagined chiming clock is followed by an indication of the somatic state of the dreamer, alive but simultaneously inert: "And low stole o'er the stillness the heartbeats of sleep" (403.05). Under a "white fogbow," paired images of the parents, HCE and ALP, then shimmer into view, in forms that remind us of the dream's recurrent artifactuality. The imago of the father, for instance, is described as a "remembrants," a remembering of a pictorial representation—such as one painted by Rembrandt—that is "mobiling so wobiling": it is blurred through its unsteady outlines, both mobile and wobbly. But some of its "fixtures"—features in a picture—are fixed enough to delineate (403.06–11). "His kep [that] is a gorsecone" (403.08) connects him to HCE in the park, who wears a "caoutchouc kepi" (35.08), a rubber military hat. The cap resembling "gorsecone" links him also to Finn MacCool, the mythic giant embedded in the landscape of Dublin and its environs, who "shows one white drift of snow among the gorsegrowth of his crown" (128.20–21): on one level, this figures either the furze or snow on top of Howth, the head of the giant; on another, it intimates a man whose crown of hair has turned white with age; on yet another, it obliquely refers to Christ's crown of thorns, here made from another form of vegetation. Tinged with fears and wishes, the paternal imago may sport a *becco*, a beak signifying a cuckold (in Italian),[3] and a *hornhide* (403.13–14), rough skin or perhaps a virile erect phallus.[4] But horns, such as antlers (as we know from "Circe"), are of course another feature of the betrayed husband. Other fantasmic features of the father—the red or "ruddled" nose of a possible drunkard, the blue teeth, and the threatening stare—explain why this image is "befear[ed]." The envisioned mother, "exhibit next," by way of contrast, is an object of desire: "The most beautiful of woman of the veilch veilchen veilde"—veiled and associated with violets (*Veilchen* in German), the signifier of modesty.[5] As "Anastashie," she is associated with the princess Anastasia, rumored to have survived the slaughter of the tsar and his family during the Russian Revolution, and here (and elsewhere) symbolic of desires for resurrection (*anastasis* in Greek), for the deliverance from death, desires which are the logical opposite of the fears of permanent mortality (403.10–15).

The parental representational exhibits appear only to be commanded to immediately disappear: "Come not nere! Black! Switch out!" (403.17). This visual vanishing is appropriate because Book III as a whole focuses on the replacement of the father by the son. The star of III.2 is Jaun, a lascivious priest, whose name echoes "Don Juan." In III.3, Jaun turns into Yawn, who resembles the recumbent HCE as a "mountainy molehill" (474.22): the paradoxical phrase may suggest that the son's form is similar to the father's, but in diminished proportions. In a central scenario in III.4, a son diverts maternal affection and attention away from HCE when he cries and awakens ALP after a nightmare about "phanthares"—panthers, phantasms, and a phantar (a "clumsy thing, thick-set person" in Irish): in this referenced dream within the dream, the disturbing ghost turns out to be the father (or the "fawthrig") himself (565.17–19). In III.1 we witness the emergence of the son, Shaun, whose name contains the word "sun," traditionally, in the biblical lore of Noah, one sign of salvation. But the human son of III.1 will emerge as a potential usurper, and the material sun as an artificial and limited source of illumination: the light shines from a mere "belted lamp" (404.13) and by the chapter's conclusion it has burned out, with two letters extinguishing themselves in the process ("yep, the lmp wnt out for it couldn't stay alight" [427.15–16]). The initial mission of the fraudulent son/sun is to "amove allmurk" (404.10): that is, to remove and replace the father as old King Mark and to move from above (hence "amove") the murk that temporarily darkens the dreamtext. He is then questioned by unnamed interlocutors, who offer "salve" in unctuously flattering remarks and queries, and who help establish his overdetermined identities. Though it is uncertain as to who is speaking,[6] this linguistic "salve" is a form of what Margot Norris calls "the language of desire,"[7] an attempt to inflate the image of Shaun, who may be an avatar of HCE.

Multiple Mes

At one point in the interchanges of III.1, Shaun's interlocutors praise him by claiming, "How good you are in explosion!" (419.12). Explosion is an apt term for one of Joyce's own writing techniques in *Finnegans Wake*: exploding, shattering, and increasing the means of exposition, decomposing the composure of normative prose. As a result, potential meanings are scattered all over the space of the text, particularly through the use of figurative language: simile, metaphor, metonymy, synecdoche, allusion, resonance, portmanteau, and pun. Identities and antitheses are both destabilized and dispersed, leaving Shaun to attempt—with little success—"to isolate i from my multiple Mes" (410.12). His meanings are constructed in response to the questioning of others—as all attempted self-identifications are—and proliferate as the chapter progresses.

Shaun's "Mes" wander through the chapter as he assumes through the logic of metonymy a series of ambulatory guises. With his "Hobos hornknees" (409.16–17), he is a descendant of the errant and peripatetic Leopold Bloom, who travels mainly by foot, and eventually of Odysseus, when Shaun makes his sea-born exit in his barrel, "Beyond cods' cradle and purpoise plain" (427.20–21). Through the synecdochic reference in "my heaviest crux and dairy lot" (409.17–18), one of Shaun's roving occupations emerges as a milkman, whose figurative cross is presumably his pail. A romanticized vision of this potential vocation forms a fantasy of the young Stephen Dedalus: "He thought it should be a pleasant life enough, driving along the roads every evening to deliver milk, if he had warm gloves and a fat bag of gingernuts in his pocket to eat from" (*P* 64). In the dream of the *Wake*, the "warm gloves" expand into an epic of protective clothing and the "fat bag of gingernuts" into an epic of fattening food (see 404.16–33 and 405.21–407.21).

As many scholars have noted, Shaun emerges most centrally as a parodic Christ, who in the course of the gospels does a lot of walking: as Shaun explains, "There's no sabbath for nomads" (410.32). This pseudo-saviour is simultaneously a postman, due to Joyce's animation of the pun on "deliverance," which suggests both salvation and running an errand, here carrying the mail.[8] He is also a lamplighter, a "linkman laizurely, lampman loungey" (427.01): a "link" is a torch formerly used to light the ways through the streets. The two modifiers of the nouns emphasize once again his laziness. Because his sources of information are "Rooters and Havers" (421.32), on one level the news agencies of Reuters and Havas, the text may imply that Shaun is a newspaper carrier as well, who aspires to learn and receive his messages through aerial transmission, from wireless "maypoles" that pick up the echoing motions of telegraphic traveling sound waves (421.32). The waking source of these peripatetic roles may be a vision from "Nausicaa" focalized through the imagined perspective of Bloom. After he sees a final firework illuminate the twilight, the text follows a series of other apparitions of light:

> From house to house, giving his everwelcome double knock, went the nine o'clock *postman, the glowworm's lamp at his belt gleaming* here and there through the laurel hedges. And among the five young trees a hoisted *linstock lit the lamp* at Leahy's terrace. By screens of *lighted* windows, by equal gardens a shrill *voice [of a newsboy]* went crying, wailing: **Evening Telegraph, stop press edition!** . . . And far on Kish bank the anchored lightship twinkled, winked at Mr Bloom. (*U* 13.1169–81, my italics, with the exceptions noted in boldface)

A lightship, or course, is a transmitter of pulsating illumination for wandering sailors (one of the vocations of HCE), and also a post, like Shaun, a "beamish" boy in both senses of the adjective (405.16), whose light is initially described as a "flasher" (404.11): in one of his inanimate forms the son of III.1 may well be, like his father, a "Rockabill Booby in the Wave Trough" (104.06–07)—the Rockabill Lighthouse near Dublin County. In another figure of illumination, the simile used in the description of Shaun's fall—"like a flask of lightning over he careened" (426.29–30)—connects him to Satan, who Jesus beholds "as lightning fall from heaven" (Luke 10: 18). A "flask of lighting" is also slang for a glass of gin, according to McHugh: the container serves as a metonym for Shaun's traveling barrel. As a "Lettrechaun" (419.18), the Wakean son is not only a letter carrier, but also through resonance a "leprechaun," the folkloric elf who when caught leads one to hidden treasure; given Shaun's peripatetic guises, it is pertinent that the creature is also traditionally a shoemaker and sometimes called "the Irish footman."[9]

Through ongoing allusions, Shaun is identified with a series of tenors, such as John McCormack (who was made a "count" by the pope [418.17])[10] and Mario "the principot of Candia" (408.11), in reality entitled the Count of Candia: we know from the "Aeolus" chapter of *Ulysses* that the latter resembles Christ. The Italian tenor Tamango is respelled as "Tamagnum" (404.26) to suggest the Latin phrase *tam magnum*, meaning "so great": the Wakean portmanteau is used as an adjective to describe the size of Shaun's "choker" or cravat. The tenor named de Reszke slips into III.1 as an infinitive verb when Shaun decides "to resk at once" in a state of exhaustion from carrying his weighty mailbag (408.04). "I'll reeve tomorry" (408.22) alludes to the tenor John Sims Reeve, while describing simultaneously Shaun's dream (*rêve* in French) of marrying tomorrow. Shaun sports a fake ruby ring, called "the paste of his rubiny winklering" (413.34), evoking the tenors Rubini and Winckelman.[11] Because of Shaun's ability to attract multiple young women through heliotropic forces, as a "meednight sunflower... the solase in dorckaness" (470.07), the overdetermined references to his praised vocal powers may be rooted in the pun Bloom remembers in "Sirens": "Tenors get women by the score" (*U* 11.686).

Shaun's oratorical skills stem from another double-entendre related to the concept of "deliverance": "delivery" can suggest conveyance (of mail, milk, or news) or the act of speaking or singing: "Song! Shaun, song!" his audience cries (414.14). The dubious healing powers of his voice as a figurative salve are implied in the double-entendres in their praise: "How mielodorous is thy bel chant, O songbird, and how exqueezit thine after draught!" (412.07–08). Is Shaun's beautiful chant melodious, exquisite, and sweet as honey (*miel* in French)? Or does it resemble a belch with a malodorous aroma, squeezed out as the "after draft"—or olfactory current—that follows excessive consumption, in an implication of halitosis, a distinctly unpleasant salve? Likewise skeptical of Shaun's delivery, Mary Lowe-Evans characterizes him as a "Father Vaughnish [*sic*] sermonizer,"[12]—Father Vaughan serving as the historical prototype for the hefty and all-too-worldly Father Purdon from Joyce's short story "Grace." Shaun's biased and secular oratory insinuates that he may simultaneously be a politician—"the vote of the Irish" (407.13–14)—who would travel in the course of campaigning and/or converting: he implicitly mixes religion and politics—the conflation of discourses that Simon Dedalus and Mr. Casey rail against in *Portrait of the Artist*'s opening chapter.

Visual representations of Christ throughout art history often represent him as thin, sometimes even bony. Shaun in contrast, as the "immense" (405.21), is an avatar of many previous corpulent clerics in Joyce's earlier works: the "burly black-vested priest" taking "inspection" of "cringing believers" in *Stephen Hero* (*SH* 146): the "fat priest" who "had just dined so he was really good-natured" (*SH* 177); the "Tub of guts.... lapping up his bacon and cabbage," mocked by Simon Dedalus at Stephen's first Christmas dinner (*P* 32); the Jesuits who are "[f]ed up, by God, like gamecocks" (*P* 71); "Aquinas tunbelly" from "Proteus" (*U* 3.385); Father Coffey in "Hades" with "a belly on him like a poisoned pup" (*U* 6.598–99); the priests "living on the fat of the land" in "Lestrygonians" (*U* 8.34–35); or Father Corrigan with a "nice fat hand," remembered by Molly as "the bullneck in his horse collar" (*U* 18.114–15). Not surprisingly, the priestly Shaun's "spadefuls of mounded food . . . constituting his threepartite pranzipal meals plus a collation" (405.30–32) take on gargantuan proportions. In the context of the Bible, Shaun's association with massive "ingestion" (406.32) may parody Christ's ability to transform five loaves and two fish into a meal for thousands; but being "guilbey of gulpable gluttony" (406.33), despite the narrative disclaimer, Shaun consumes the feast for the populace on his own. In sharp contrast to Christ's ability to fast for forty days, the son figure indulges in what Margot Norris identifies as an obscenely enormous Last Supper-like meal.[13] What is amazing about Shaun's repast is not only its volume, but also what he is willing to eat: table napkins, an accoutrement of dining, on account of their feast-worthy taste ("the faste of tablenapkins" [405.31]), and an enema, whose liquid substance may consist of not only petit pois but also urine/pee—"a clister of peas, suppositorily petty" (406.19). Shaun's "mounded food" (405.30) and "avalunch" (406.09) hint that his meal might mirror one of HCE's recurrent recumbent forms as a "mounding's mass" (8.01), a dormant or active volcanic mountain.

The repeated motif of the well-fed priest is an ongoing reminder of the wealth and power of the Catholic Church. Shaun's meal is replete with what I believe are upscale or pricey items. "[F]ourale to the lees of Traroe" on one level means "farewell to Red Bank oysters" (see McHugh), presumably because Shaun will find and consume them, in even the months without an "r" in them ("without a sign of an err in him"), the annual period when the shellfish were usually unavailable (405.18–20). Oysters are often considered aphrodisiacs, and in *Ulysses* are associated with the randy and relatively wealthy Blazes Boylan. Other items on his epic menu (see again 405.21–407.21) include blood and Jaffa oranges (foreign imports), mock turtle soup, Yorkshire pudding (both with British origins), bacon, steak, "gaulush gravy and pumpernickel to wolp up," loin of veal, and "the best of wine." "[A]ll free of charge, aman" sounds like the closing of a pre-meal blessing, expressing thanks that the feast technically costs nothing, as it is the byproduct of donated offerings to the church.

Shaun's ingestion of food imported from Great Britain may have a subtle additional political significance. One of the causes of the Irish Potato Famine was the export of food out of Ireland, which enabled the British to (almost) starve the Irish out of existence, in what David Lloyd calls the most devastating demographic catastrophe in European history.[14] Shaun's access to British imports may imply a priestly exemption to this lethal economic policy, traces of which are still evident in Joyce's depiction of Dublin in 1904.[15] His consumption of "praties sweet and Irish" (406.11) may be yet another telling detail on his menu. Sweet potatoes, tropical in origin, were almost impossible to cultivate in Ireland on account of the climate. They thus were and remain a gourmand's taste treat.[16]

Shaun is usually associated with the biblical Esau on account of his gluttony and his self-description as a "hairyman" (425.34). He is also called "the fiery boy" (412.13–14)—on one level, the fire boy (as a source of light), on another, the fairy boy. The designation marks him as the pseudo-son, the child left by fairies, gypsies, or other agents of mischief in the changeling myth: Jaun is called "our rommanychiel" (472.22) in III.2, and HCE is later called a "Changechild" (481.02) in the interrogations of III.3. The biblical and folkloric myths both center on fears of illegitimacy and usurpation: the obligation world of the dream would demand proper and lawful father-son succession.[17] In related allusions to Shakespeare's *Henry IV*, part 1, Shem is identified as "bruddy Hal" (234.04) and "merry Hal" (440.36), the legitimate heir apparent, who recognizes the onerous duties of the king as symbolic father and who would rather sow his wild oats, at least for the time being. Despite the ongoing struggles for preference and ascendancy in the dream, both sons through allusive figuration realize that the paternal position constitutes a psychological knot: the role and mandates of "the Father" become an interpellation to be at least partially resisted. The emergent son of III.1 at points openly resents the duties of deliverance imposed on him by the paternal Other: "How all too unwordy am I, a mere mailman of peace . . . as to be the bearer extraordinary of these postoomany missive on his majesty's service" (408.10–14). Danis Rose and John O'Hanlon in their abbreviated translation of this passage substitute "unworthy" for "unwordy":[18] the change suggests Shaun's sense of entrapment in a role he cannot live up to. As he concedes shortly afterwards, "It should of been my other" (408.17), implicitly his rival Shem. "Unwordy" further resonates of "wordless" and "unworldly," both adjectives being patently dishonest as descriptors of Shaun. In speaking, Shaun's *modus operandi* is excess—an ironic illustration, perhaps, of Joyce's "'verbal diarrhoea,'" [*sic*] the phrase Wyndham Lewis used to characterize *Ulysses*.[19] As will be seen in Shaun's identification with the Ondt, he is also thoroughly indulgent in worldly pursuits.

Shaun is much like Stephen Dedalus, who will come to resent the "worldly voice [that] bid him raise up his father's fallen state by his labours" (*P* 84). In contrast to the dutiful and compliant son of the gospels, Shaun often dislikes his peripatetic job of delivering milk and/or letters ("his heaviest crux and dairy lot"), as carrying this cross is menial work (*courvée*: drudgery in French) that is hard on his knee joints and backbone: "Fatiguing, very fatiguing. Hobos hornknees and the corveeture of my spine" (409.16–18). The implied hump here links Shaun to Shakespeare's Richard III, in yet another allusion to usurpation. His wishful confession, "I the mightif beam mairc-anny" (408.16), suggests the limitations of his illumination (he is a beam that is a "might-have-been") as well as his desires to be Marchese Guglielmo Marconi: having invented a system of wireless telegraph,[20] Marconi would not have to undergo tedious travel ("Weak stop work stop walk stop whoak" [411.06]) in order to transmit his messages. Shaun's preference for the pleasures of childhood over the onerous responsibilities of adulthood is heard in his regressive lament for his lost youth: "Those sembal simon pumpkel pieman yers" he longs for fittingly allude through metonymy to a nursery rhyme about food (408.20) as well as to Simon Daedulus, who is explicitly described as childish in *Stephen Hero* (*SH* 87). Shaun's wandering vocation is the will of a fallen and corrupt father, who perhaps "cooks his books" in an attempt at financial solvency: "not what I wants to do a strike of work," Shaun complains, "but it was condemned on me premitially by Hireark Books and Chiefoverseer Cooks in their Eusubian Concordant Homilies" (409.33–36). The father is revealingly plural, as is the multi-tasking Shaun with his "multiple Mes." "Eusebian" is a reference, according to McHugh, to Eusebius's Canons, which harmonized the gospels, a major source—in parodic form—of the portrait of the son in III.1 and III.2.[21] He later claims that his inherited role is a matter "of coerce" (410.02), with its further suggestion of paternal coercion. The irony of Shaun's complaints lies in the hints that he is heir to the father's will because he has killed him, reduced him to the mound of debris that is often one of HCE's signifiers: "Down among the dustbins let him lie! Ear! Ear! Not ay! Eye! Eye! For I'm at the heart of it. Yet I cannot on my solemn merits as a recitativer recollect ever having done of anything of the kind to deserve of such. Not the phost of a nation" (409.02–06). Shaun, aligned with the eye, initially attributes responsibility for the deed to Shem, aligned with the ear. In the recurrent double-speak of his delivery, he then briefly confesses his central complicity ("I am at the heart of it"), only to finally suggest that he has repressed or forgotten the act, and is thus not deserving of implied punishment—as if faulty memory exonerates patricide. The phrase "Not the phost of a nation" condenses "not the ghost of a notion"—no trace of the message is retained in his recital—with "not the post of a nation": the phrase hints at his mnemonic failure in his delivery of a full, clear, or coherent letter to his audience.

The Fable

As a parodic Christ figure, Shaun delivers the word, but in place of parable he opts for the more secular genre of fable. His self-entitlement as "His Gross the Ondt" connotes not only the position of "His Grace," the aggrandizing honorific for an archbishop, but also an ethos of profit, carnality and corpulence (417.11). The Ondt is "that true and perfect host" in only the social sense of the word, and a snobbish one at that: speaking of his rival, the Gracehoper, he decides, "We shall not come to party at that lopp's . . . for he is not on our social list" (415.30–31). These words may be a poke at what Norris identifies as the mean-spirited snobbism of Wyndham Lewis, who is one of the Ondt's allusive identifications.[22] Because Shaun is aligned with space, one irony in his choice of a revised version of the Ant and the Grasshopper is that the original allegory focuses on a moral about time: according to a Google search, the fable illustrates that "It is wise to worry about tomorrow today" or "there is a time to work and a time to play!"[23] In Shaun's version of it, moreover, the story contains no evidence of the industry or work ethic that supports the moral. In the fullest picture of the Ondt, he is thoroughly at leisure, wearing his slippers and pyjamas ("unshrinkables," according to one of Joyce's letters to Harriet Shaw Weaver, as noted in McHugh), smoking an expensive Cuban cigar, prostrate upon his throne, warming himself in his sunroom:

> Behailed His Gross the Ondt, prostrandvorous upon his dhrone, in his Papylonian babooshkees, smolking a spatial brunt of Hosana cigals, with unshrinkables farfalling from his unthinkables, swarming of himself in his sunnyroom, sated before his comfortumble phullupsuppy of a plate o'monkynous and a confucion of minthe. (417.10–16)

If this is Shaun's indirect self-portrait, it is not an illogical one to be produced by a son looking for "my vacation in life" (411.01–02). "Dhrone" condenses "throne" with "drone," the male insect who usually performs no work. Because of the double meaning of "throne," moreover, this could also be a vision of Shaun as the Ondt ensconced in his watercloset: it is reminiscent of the one of Uncle Charles in *Portrait*, who smokes such strong tobacco that he is asked "to enjoy his morning smoke in a little outhouse at the end of the garden" (*P* 60). The "throne" may also connote through metonymy British royalty and empire as well as the seat of elevated church officials, in a historical evocation (in Joyce's mind) of the two most oppressive of Ireland's masters.

In his rendition of the Ondt and Gracehoper, Shaun as "Eatsup" (563.24) —a portmanteau suggesting Esau and appetite—makes sure to emphasize that his rival's punishment is hunger, his own deepest dread: in his comeuppance the Gracehoper doesn't know where to "sirch for grub for his corapusse" and cries, "Not one pickopeck of muscowmoney to bag a tittlebits of beebread! . . . I am heartily hungry!" (416.14–20). The original fable of the Ant and the Grasshopper has often been recognized as one with a morally questionable conclusion—like the parable related by Father Purdon in "Grace." The fable can be interpreted as an illustration of a failed deliverance of Christian charity. At one point in III.1, Joyce explicitly alludes to "Grace," when Shaun cries out "Greedo!" (411.12), an echo of Mr. Cunningham's bungled account of the cardinal who cried out "Credo!" (D 169). "Greedo" is an apt statement of Shaun's worldview, with its creed of worldly accumulation: the word could be roughly translated as "I believe in excess, possession, and gluttony." As Patrick A. McCarthy points out, the Ondt "preaches a gospel of money like that of Father Purdon . . . : *Ad majorum l.s.d.!* (418.4) means 'for the greater glory of pounds, shillings, and pence.'"[24] In its hypocritical conclusion, the Ondt's ultimate reward is his rival's "goods," the harem (Floh, Luse, Bieni, and Vespatilla) who as "houris" (417.28) may be Mohammedan nymphs of paradise or more earthly whores. His "savings" here are a hoard of women and food, earned like a drone with no visible effort.

The fable of the Ondt and the Gracehoper is often read as a struggle between space and time, but the victor is unclear and its interpretations vary. McCarthy argues that "Shem, as the Gracehoper, taunts the Ondt (Shaun) for his inability to 'beat time' (419.08), and this equivocal phrase sums up Earwicker's dilemma: having aged, he feels himself losing his sexual powers and, in order to prove his manhood to himself, either commits or imagines he has committed some sexual act."[25] Tindall interprets the last line of the fable's poem as a critique of the Ondt's artistic skills, as an underlining of his imaginative banality: "how much nicer if having 'song sense' or literary sensibility, he could 'beat time.'"[26] Philip Kitcher explains that the phrase to "beat time" has two resonances: "One is to suggest that the Ondt, unlike the Gracehoper, is clumsy and ill-attuned to the songs and dances of pleasure. The other, which recalls the Gracehoper's earlier 'kick time' (415.24), takes both of them to fail to overcome time, both to be doomed to insignificance because of the finitude of their lives and achievements."[27] Another ambiguity is introduced in the reference to "their dance McCaper" (415.10). One hears Danse Macabre, with its overtones of inevitable and indiscriminate mortality; but in the context of the Gracehoper's raucous party, it is a dance celebrating life, an attempted defiance of death by joyous capering. The party rolls along "zeemliangly to kick time" (415.24), creating further complexities. "Zeemliangly" resonates of "seemingly" and thus implies a mere illusion of kicking time—in the sense of conquering or getting rid of it. And the further resonance of to "kill time" can suggest the wishful defeat of time or, on the other hand, extreme boredom, idling away at meaningless activities when time seems to move too slowly. But the Gracehoper never seems bored, in his characteristic "joyicity" that includes the production of art, initially in the form of music, played on a "pair of findlestilts" (414.23), and in closing in the form of a poem that invokes his *"in risible universe"* (419.03)—one full of laughter. Shaun's fable as a whole, nonetheless, fails in its supposed attempt to deliver a clear moral or philosophical lesson: he appropriately introduces it as "fable one, feeble too" (414.17–18). It merely supports a common notion of the wish worlds of many mortal beings—the ancient Egyptians perhaps most prominently—namely, "You CAN take it with you." This sham illumination may be the implication of Shaun's vision of himself (as the Ondt) in paradise with his saved markedly earthly salves: women, his "houris"; a pricey liqueur, crème de menthe, "confucion of minthe" (a confusing fusion of the after dinner drink with Confucian philosophy); warmth, "his sunnyroom"; food, "a plate o'monkynous"—perhaps another imported gourmet treat, as monkey nuts are cultivated in tropical and warm climates.[28] In the end he closes with an invocation of the Holy Ghost, which instead is respelled as the "holocaust" (419.10–11): in context, it suggests destruction—not through fire (its original biblical definition)—but rather through hoarding and the attendant starvation of another, in a further allusion to the nightmare of the Famine. Michael Davitt explicitly described the Great Hunger as a "holocaust of humanity," in an essay in which he blames equally the British Empire and the Catholic Church ("the political and spiritual governors of the Irish people") for the national tragedy.[29]

The Letter

Over the course of book III chapter 1, Shaun emerges as a man of letters, but only in the most secular sense of the phrase: rather than being devoted to scholarly or literary pursuits, he simply carries the mail. In terms of metaphor, he is the vehicle rather than the tenor; in terms of linguistics, he is aligned with the signifier rather than the signified. His barrel-as-mailbag is analogous to an envelope, the palpable and superficial casing that surrounds the sense of the text, the material of letters—in both their epistolary and alphabetic definitions—although one passage in III.1 undermines the signifier/signified distinction (as I will discuss shortly). As the representative of materiality, Shaun embodies a technique of the dreamtext itself: in its relentless linguistic play, *Finnegans Wake* exploits the materiality of language. As Norris notes, "because the unconscious treats words like objects, it is alive to their sounds, their literal and archaic meanings, and their uses in every known context."[30] Because the chapter focuses on a failed belletrist but avid gourmand, many of the discursive lapses involve distortions that center on food and appetite. Rosary beads surface as "grocery beans" (411.16–17); the imprecation "Please God" becomes "pease Pod" (412.31); the Egyptian Elysian Fields called "Sekhet Hetup" turn into a different kind of paradise in "Suckit Hotup!" (415.35); the location of Moor Park becomes a cry for "morepork" served with "mauveport" (407.19, .21); and the blessing, "Lord have mercy on them," is secularized as "Lard have mustard on them" (409.15–16).

But if Joyce revels in the materiality of language, he is simultaneously sensitive to the language of materiality. Hence Stephen's proleptic reflection in "Proteus," "These heavy sands are language tide and wind have silted here" (*U* 3.288–89). In III.1 the language of materiality is emphasized when verbal fragments on the surface of the letter's envelope make them sound as if they refer to a residence, a building, a solid structure: "Shutter up" (420.29), "House Condamned by Ediles" (421.02–03), "Roofloss" (420.27), "Cohabited by Unfortunates" (421.08–09)—this last phrase suggests this material locale is possibly a brothel, a site of illicit sexuality. Supporting this sense of the letter as a physical space are phrases that sound like signs or messages posted on walls or doors: "Back in a Few Minutes" (421.03), "Key at Kate's" (421.04), "Lost all Licence" (421.09). One phrase describes the letter as "Salved" (421.06), suggesting that it has been saved, if only in fragments, that it possibly contains a salve as a consolation of sorts, or that it expresses the simple message of "Be well!" (*Salve* in Latin).

The penultimate phrase of the letter has a base structure in the song "Come Back to Erin," evoking a plea for the letter to return to the homeland of Ireland: this motif is anticipated in the encased list of eleven addresses of Joyce's residences in Dublin, also known as "Baile-Atha Cliath" (421.20). Julieann Ulin suggests that the song may be a plea to Irish exiles in England, who emigrated in flight of the lethal Great Hunger.[31] The distortion of the song title into "Came Baked to Auld Aireen" (421.14), with its reference to food, connects it to one of the fragments of the presumed contents of the letter—namely, "a lugly parson of cates" (11.23–24), a "gentleman with a beautiful present of wedding cakes" (111.13–14), and a "lovely . . . pershan of cates" (280.15–16). One of Issy's sly footnotes in II.2 hints that the ongoing references to baked goods in conjunction with a man of the cloth refers to a fallen father who bribes children with sweets: "The good fother with the twingling in his eye will always have cakes in his pocket to bethroat us with for our allmichael good. Amum. Amum. And Amum again." "Amum" irreverently condenses "Amen" and "yum" (279.F1). If we want to interpret the motif more innocently, the parson's cakes/cates may represent communion wafers, although untainted clerics in Joyce's fictions are a very rare sight, as I have suggested earlier. Given the Catholic clergy's emphasized voracity and elitism, it is important that "cates" have connotations of delicacies.

Interestingly, the description of the letter blurs its envelope and its contents, its metaphorical vehicle and tenor. On one level, it contains transformative puns on phrases that could be stamped on the outer enclosing writing surface, such as "Kainly forewarned" (421.05, Kindly Forward), "None so Strait" (420.28, No Such Street), or "Overwayed. Understrumped" (421.07, Overweight. Understamped). The return address is the same one we have already seen: "Sender. Boston (Mass)" (420.10–11) reminds us of "transhipt from Boston (Mass.)" (111.09–10). Other elements, however, connect to what we assume to be written in the letter itself: its date "31 Jan" (420.20) translates "the last of the first" (111.10)—the last day of the first month; the "noon sick parson" (420.24) anticipates the "lovelade parson" (617.24–25); "The Reverest Adam Foundlitter" (420.35) foreshadows the "Dirtdump. Reverend" (615.12) that ALP addresses in book IV; "His Bouf Toe" (421.09)—or on one level, his beef tea—echoes "the teastain" (111.20) that marks the version in I.5; the earlier mention of "Mr van Howten" (414.04) repeats almost to the letter "the van Houtens" (111.12) referred to by the hen, Belinda of the Dorans; and as mentioned above, the "Came Baked" entity (421.14) describes the cakes or cates seen elsewhere. Joyce's mixing of the physical encasement of the letter with its supposed content or meaning supports his semiotic demonstration that objects always have a signifying dimension, a linguistic trace, and that signifiers can never be stripped of or separated from their materiality.

Discussing the odd conclusion of III.1, Tindall suggests that Shaun exits in a kind of paradoxical "ascension [that is] more or less horizontal."[32] But the final simile implies descent as opposed to ascent, likening Shaun's enveloping barrel to a visually similar turd, flushed down a toilet or commode, in yet one more circulatory round—or another "commodious vicus of recirculation" (3.02): "he spoorlessly disappaled and vanesshed, like a popo down a papa, from circular circulatio" (427.06–08). The "aromatose" he leaves behind is appropriately fraudulent in its claim to be a trace of "Taboccoo" (427.13) and in its resemblance to perfume: "A reek was waft on the luftstream. He was ours, all fragrance" (427.11–12). The "salve" he leaves in his wake is a balm that is suspect in its aromatic pleasures. In the end Shaun is disposed of but not for long: he wanders into the next chapter on "bruised brogues" as the lusty and hypocritical priest called "Jaunty Jaun" (429.01), whose name connects him through allusion to "Don John Conmee" (*U* 10.174) and jaunty Blazes Boylan.

Before his final excretory departure, Shaun in his savaging of Shem briefly puts in his opinion on language, focusing on his rival's "shemletters" (419.20) in particular. Shaun's denunciations of his brother's discourse in I.7 have been convincingly interpreted as parodic imitations of the class-biased critiques that greeted Joyce's own publications, from writers such as H. G. Wells, Ezra Pound, Wyndham Lewis, Rebecca West, and Virginia Woolf.[33] In III.1 Shaun accuses Shem of "lowquacity" (424.34)—that is, an excessive discussing of low matters: the portmanteau may be a code for Joyce's supposed "cloacal obsession." Shem is also denounced for plagiarism ("The last word in stolentelling!" [424.35]) and for his "strangewrote anaglyptics" (419.19–20): Shaun claims he can read Shem's accretive, polyvocal layers of meaning, but ultimately, as the materialist, he complains about their physical pain: "hellas, it is harrobrew bad on the corns and callouses" (419.28–29). In a related accusation to the audience who brings up Shaun's own "slanguage" and "sinscript" (421.17–18), he replies, "Your words grates on my ares" (421.23)—not only on his ears, but also on his arse (presumably when writing paper or newsprint is deployed as toilet paper, as we see at the end of "Calypso" or in the representation of the Russian General in II.3). Most centrally, Shaun disapproves of the artistic media of his brother's work, its construction from debris or garbage—its "[p]uffedly offal tosh" (419.33): the phrase may loosely echo "this great bulk of filth," the condemnation of *Ulysses* heard from the supposed "spirit" of Oscar Wilde.[34] Before briefly summarizing two versions of the sin in the park, Shaun refers to "them bagses of trash which the mother and Mr Unmentionable . . . has *reduced* to writing" (420.03–04, my italics). Shaun cannot see litter as potentially creative textuality, as Joyce did throughout his career. While writing *Dubliners* in November 1906, he reports to his brother Stanislaus that he has sent a letter to his Aunt Josephine, requesting from her "a Xmas present made up of tram-tickets, advts, handbills, posters, papers, programmes, &c" (*LettersII* 186). Sixteen years later, shortly before embarking on *Finnegans Wake*, he asks his aunt directly to "[s]end me any news you like, programmes, pawntickets, press cuttings, [and] handbills. I like reading them" (*LettersI* 194). Shaun as the limited man of letters does not realize that writing involves a recycling and reformation of the old, the banal, the used, the linguistic disposables—those "stale shestnuts" (183.24–25, chestnuts that may be shit-like?)—that form the basis for the new. Salvage is finally "something saved from destruction or waste *and put to further use*" (my italics): this sort of ecological art, practiced by ALP and Shem (in his role as Joyce's double), is dismissed by Shaun as a reduction rather than viewed as the rich "idioglossary" (423.09) composted and composed in *Finnegans Wake*. Normally marginalized discourses described as "tittletattle" (*LettersI* 136) provide the media for the possible savaging of both HCE and Shem—or for the "litterery bed" (422.35) of their salvation.[35]

Notes

1. All definitions in quotation marks are from the *American Heritage Dictionary* (Boston: Houghton Mifflin, 1992).

2. Two other homophones that may be implicit in III.1 are *savaging* and *savage*. Savaging suggests "attack[ing] without restraint or pity" and is the frequent rhetorical mode when Shaun talks about Shem. Savage, in the sense of uncultivated, unruly, or even primitive, is one of the most stereotypical labels for the Irish and is often implied by Shaun as a crucial characteristic of Shem. As Sheldon Brivic points out, the stereotype extends to the representation of Shem as black or African in origins ("negertop, negertoe, negertoby, negrunter!" [423.33–34]). Shem is also often depicted as his mother's child—and ALP is also associated with being at least part African. See *Joyce's Waking Women: An Introduction to "Finnegans Wake"* (Madison: University of Wisconsin Press, 1995), 59, 63. For further reading on the Irish as a whole being related to Africans (and both being stereotypically marked as racially inferior), see Vincent J. Cheng, *Joyce, Race, and Empire* (Cambridge: Cambridge University Press, 1995), 19–41.

3. I am indebted to Roland McHugh's *Annotations to "Finnegans Wake,"* 3rd ed. (Baltimore: Johns Hopkins University Press, 2006) for the majority of translations throughout this essay. I have also used his text for other sources of information.

4. James S. Atherton, "Shaun A: Book III chapter i," in *A Conceptual Guide to "Finnegans Wake,"* ed. Michael H. Begnal and Fritz Senn (University Park: Pennsylvania State University Press, 1974), 150.

5. Don Gifford, with Robert J. Seidman, *"Ulysses" Annotated* (Berkeley: University of California Press, 1988), 30.

6. The issue of who is speaking remains uncertain and open to critical debate. Atherton claims that the Donkey is the primary cross-questioner in "Shaun A," 156. Anne L. Cavender agrees that "the interrogator is 'the ass'" who "exhibits genuine sympathy for Shaun," in "The Ass and the Four: Oppositional Figures for the Reader in *Finnegans Wake*," *James Joyce Quarterly* 41 (Summer 2004): 678. William York Tindall speculates that "the 'we' may be the twelve men or the four elders," in *A Reader's Guide to "Finnegans Wake"* (New York: Farrar, Straus and Giroux), 234. According to Danis Rose and John O'Hanlon, "*the four interrogate Shaun through the dragoman donkey in the voice of Issy*," in *Understanding "Finnegans Wake"* (New York: Garland, 1982), 210. Joseph Campbell and Henry Morton Robinson simply identify the voice as that of "the people," in *A Skeleton Key to "Finnegans Wake"* (New York: Penguin, 1980), 258.

7. Margot Norris, *Joyce's Web: The Social Unraveling of Modernism* (Austin: University of Texas Press, 1992), 169.

8. Margot Norris, *The Decentered Universe of "Finnegans Wake"* (Baltimore: Johns Hopkins University Press, 1976), 17.

9. *Brewer's Dictionary of Phrase and Fable*, ed. Ivor H. Evans (New York: Harper & Row, 1981), 661.

10. For an excellent study of McCormack and Shaun and the tenor's relationship to Joyce, see Patrick Reilly, "Seansong, or whatyoumacormack," *James Joyce Quarterly* 44 (Summer 2007): 719–36.

11. Four other tenors alluded to are Enrico Caruso (406.15), Michael Kelly (407.16), John Braham (422.26), and Karl Jörn (428.03).

12. Mary Lowe-Evans, *Catholic Nostalgia in Joyce and Company* (Gainesville: University Press of Florida, 2008), 47.

13. Norris, *Decentered Universe*, 17.

14. For an astute analysis of the complex convergence of causes of the Irish Potato Famine, see Lloyd's *Irish Culture and Colonial Modernity, 1800–2000* (Cambridge: Cambridge University Press, 2011), 19–48.

15. Julieann Ulin, "'Famished Ghosts': Famine Memory in James Joyce's *Ulysses*," *Joyce Studies Annual* 2011, 37.

16. I am indebted to my friend and colleague Carole-Anne Tyler for this information on the sweet potato, from a conversation and subsequent email on June 14–15, 2013.

17. According to Possible Worlds Theory, the obligation world in a text is constituted by "a system of commitments and prohibitions defined by social rules and moral principles"—see Marie-Laure Ryan, *Possible Worlds, Artificial Intelligence, and Narrative Theory* (Bloomington: Indiana University Press, 1991), 116. Two of the strongest attempts to defy the obligation world in *Finnegans Wake* are fantasies of patricide and incest. She defines a "wish world" (a term I will use below) as con-

taining desired actions or states that are intrinsically rewarding, "such as making love, eating, or playing games," 117. Eating is obviously a predominant part of the wish world of Shaun.

18. Rose and O'Hanlon, *Understanding*, 210.

19. William F. Dohmen, "'Chilly Spaces': Wyndham Lewis as Ondt," *James Joyce Quarterly* 11 (Summer 1974): 372.

20. Adaline Glasheen, *Third Census of "Finnegans Wake"* (Berkeley: University of California Press, 1977), 186.

21. For an excellent discussion of Joyce's parodies of elements of the Gospels and the Stations of the Cross, see Norris, *Decentered Universe*, 16–22.

22. Norris, *Joyce's Web*, 74. For more on Joyce's dislike of Lewis because of his class condescension, see Dohmen, "'Chilly Spaces,'" 372.

23. See http://www.longlongtimeago.com/llta_fables_antgrasshopper.html and also http://www.dltk-teach.com/fables/grasshopper/mstory.htm. Accessed August 30, 2012.

24. Patrick A. McCarthy, "The Structures and Meanings of *Finnegans Wake*," in *A Companion to Joyce Studies*, ed. Zack Bowen and James F. Carens (Westwood, Conn.: Greenwood, 1984), 614.

25. Patrick A. McCarthy, *The Riddles of "Finnegans Wake"* (Cranbury, N.J.: Associated University Presses, 1980), 87.

26. Tindall, *Reader's Guide*, 231.

27. Philip Kitcher, *Joyce's Kaleidoscope* (Oxford: Oxford University Press, 2007), 286–87n12.

28. http://www.the free dictionary.com/Monkey+nuts. Accessed September 9, 2013.

29. Michael Davitt, *The Fall of Feudalism in Ireland* (London: Harper & Brothers, 1904), 50. The English government and Catholic Church are further denounced by Davitt for promoting the myth that the Famine was an act of divine will, as opposed to the outcome of exploitative economic policies combined with the timidity of the priesthood: "Both, too, agreed in fathering upon the Almighty the cause of the famine. It was the visitation of God!" (50). This clerical passivity in the face of a holocaust could be one source of Shaun's (and the Ondt's) characteristic laziness and complacency. Writing more recently, Mary E. Daly avoids impassioned finger-pointing, but nevertheless concedes that the "Catholic clergy could have been more proactive"—"The Operations of Famine Relief, 1845–47," in *The Great Irish Famine*, ed. Cathal Póirtéir (Dublin: Mercier Press, 1995), 133.

30. Norris, *Decentered Universe* 104.

31. Ulin, "'Famished Ghosts,'" 52.

32. Tindall, *Reader's Guide*, 234.

33. Norris, *Joyce's Web*, 69–70, 85.

34. See James S. Atherton's discussion of Joyce's use of H. T. Smith's *Psychic Messages from Oscar Wilde* in *The Books at the Wake* (Carbondale: Southern Illinois University Press, [1959] rpt. 1974), 49.

35. I am indebted to Christine Smedley and Patrick A. McCarthy for their invaluable insights and suggestions for elaborations of this essay.

14

Jaunty Jaun's Brokerly Advice in III.2

PATRICK A. MCCARTHY

Preamblings

In 1924, as he drafted book III of *Finnegans Wake*, Joyce told Harriet Shaw Weaver how hard it was to describe what he was doing:

> If ever I try to explain to people now what I am supposed to be writing I see stupefaction freezing them into silence. For instance Shaun, after a long absurd and rather incestuous Lenten lecture to Izzy, his sister, takes leave of her "with a half a glance of Irish frisky from under the shag of his parallel brows." These are the words the reader will see but not those he will hear. (*LettersI*, 216)

Over two years later Ezra Pound, unimpressed by Joyce's efforts, declared, "Nothing so far as I can make out, nothing short of divine vision or a new cure for the clapp [sic] can possibly be worth all the circumambient peripherization" (*JJII* 584).[1] Pound's complaints are understandable, but there are also compensations in Joyce's careful dissection of Shaun's "Lenten lecture," in thematic clusters that amplify meaning, and in such memorable puns as Shaun's admission that he often has to eat his own words: "Oop, I never open momouth but I pack mefood in it" (437.19–20). In its presentation of Shaun as a pious lecher, III.2 is both one of the funniest and one of the darkest episodes of the *Wake*.

Wedged between two interrogation chapters, III.2 consists mainly of the monologue that Joyce called a "Lenten lecture," delivered by Shaun under the name Jaun. After encountering Issy and other schoolgirls, Jaun begins a sermon that emphasizes the importance of chastity (431.21–457.24). Issy replies flirtatiously (457.25–61.32), playing the role of Esther Johnson ("Stella") to Jaun's Swift, until he interrupts to say that he is leaving and that she must not cry when he departs: "Esterelles, be not on your weeping what though Shaunathaun is in his fail!" (462.07–08). Jaun proclaims, imagines, or foresees the arrival of his twin brother Dave before taking his leave, after which he is mourned as a god. Originally III.1–2 was a single chapter, but as the later part developed a character of its own, Joyce set it off as a separate chapter focusing on religious rather than secular authority. Still, the continuity between III.1 and III.2 is evident not only in their narrative situation but in their language, which reflects Shaun's appetite, his work as a postman (hence the references to roads, feet, and footwear), his vanity, and his resentment of Shem. At the end of each chapter Shaun bids his audience good-bye, although both times we are assured that the golden boy (the sun) will return.

III.2 begins simply: "Jaunty Jaun, as I was shortly before that made aware, next halted to fetch a breath" (429.01–02). The sentence continues for another seven lines (and the paragraph for an additional fifteen) as Joyce alternately clarifies and complicates what has gone before and connects recurrent themes such as talking and walking. Thus Jaun unties his "bruised brogues" before he speaks, *brogue* meaning both a type of shoe (*bróg* in Irish) and a thick Irish accent; the tongues in his shoes and in his mouth are loosened. Joyce called book III the four watches of Shaun, and Jaun appears to be a watchman who makes his nightly rounds, stopping at times to rest his feet. Yet he spends more time giving speeches than walking, which might be why Joyce calls him a "poor preambler" (429.04), playing on the etymology of "preamble" as a "walking before." Jaun's speech is literally a preamble, here meaning words spoken before he ambles off, as the narrator also implies when he refers to Jaun's "few prelimbs" (431.14).

The opening of III.2 abounds in references to feet, footwear, and walking: besides "preambler" and "brogues" there are "the first cothurminous leg of his nightstride" (the first leg, or part, of his nightly walk, wearing a *cothurnus*, or buskin, like a Greek tragic actor), "hosen" (stockings in German), "halluxes" (hallux: big toe), and "bootblacked" (429.02–03, .05, .17, .21). Jaun, we learn, is "noted for his humane treatment of any kind of abused footgear" (429.07–08), with "kind" playing on the kindness of Jaun's oddly "humane treatment" of footwear. Yet as the chapter proceeds, Jaun's kind manner is revealed as a false front that hides his sadistic character, especially toward Issy. (See, for example, 444.06–445.25.) In the opening, the positive image of Jaun is also undermined in two related passages: "his bruised brogues . . . were plainly made a good bit before his hosen were" and "he had a bullock's hoof in his buskin" (429.04–05, .16–17). Roland McHugh notes that these passages are parodies of Breton proverbs, the first translating as "His boots were made before his socks," referring to an unsuccessful applicant, and the second as "He has a calf's hoof in his shoes," referring to an idiot.[2] The narrator remains unidentified, but the frequently ironic tone of the narration suggests a connection with Shem.

The summer 1928 issue of *transition*, in which Joyce published a version of III.2, also featured an article by Stuart Gilbert on Joyce's new project that attempted to justify its obscurity and difficulty. A year later, *Our Exagmination* included an expanded version of Gilbert's article with a detailed commentary on a passage from the Jaun chapter (the early version of 448.34–452.07).[3] These annotations demonstrated that Joyce's text had a complex logic of its own and was far from surreal or irrational. In this essay I will examine the logic of III.2 in three broad areas: its references to Byron's life and work; Joyce's composition process, as illustrated by revisions in the chapter after its appearance in *transition*; and the role of Dave the Dancekerl in relation to the Shem-Shaun rivalry. Each topic has larger implications for the *Wake* as a whole.

(Don) Jaun and Byron

The narrator says that Jaun "looked a young chapplie of sixtine" (430.31), which, as Petr Skrabanek notes, might identify him as one of the castrati in the Sistine Chapel Choir.[4] Still, Jaun's asexual appearance is misleading, since the girls who feel "his full fat pouch for him so tactily and jingaling his jellybags" (430.30–31) are said to "frole by his manhood that he was just the killingest ladykiller all by kindness" (430.32–33). McHugh's note on "sixtine"—"Byron's Don Juan was 16" (at the beginning of *Don Juan*)—offers a means of explaining this ambiguous portrayal by pointing to Byron's comic hero, with his combination of innocence and sexual appeal, as a model for Jaun. Although Jaun's name is spelled "Juan" only three times in the chapter (461.31, 461.33, 470.33), Adaline Glasheen rightly notes the importance of the Don Juan/Don Giovanni theme in III.2, and among the versions of the story, Byron's is the most likely source for Joyce's emphasis on Jaun's (apparent) innocence.[5]

These references to Byron and his works may serve as examples of Joyce's allusive technique:

435.10: After warning Issy about artists who might ask her to pose in the nude, Jaun adds, "And the volses of lewd Buylan, for innocence!" Byron's "volses" are his verses, especially "The Waltz" (1813), about a dance that was considered so risqué that Byron had to publish the poem anonymously. In "The Waltz," Byron calls Terpsichore, the muse of dance, "The least a Vestal of the Virgin Nine" (line 6), describes the waltz as "Seductive" (line 147) and "Voluptuous" (line 248), and refers to the waltzer's "lewd grasp and lawless contact warm" (line 237).[6] If the waltz is a sexy dance, Byron is a "lewd" lord; "Buylan," punning on (Blazes) Boylan, further associates him with seduction. Perhaps "for innocence" (in place of "for instance") means that "lewd Buylan" wrote "The Waltz" to corrupt the innocent. Here, Jaun condemns Byron by associating him with sexuality: hardly an unexpected association, but one that serves Joyce's purposes. Jaun tries to distance himself from Byron, or at least from his verses, but the way he invests almost every comment with sexual meaning undermines that pretense. Thus a few lines after the reference to "The Waltz," Jaun warns, "There's many's the icepolled globetrotter is haunted by the hottest spot under his equator like Ramrod, the meaty hunter, always jaeger for a thrust" (435.12–14).

436.14–15: "Love through the usual channels, cisternbrothelly, when properly disinfected." The overtones of contamination and immorality in "cistern" and "brothel" cast doubt on how "disinfected" the "channels" might be, but Jaun certainly seems to advocate sister-brother incest, at least as an alternative to homosexuality.[7] Later there is a more specific allusion to Byron's allegedly incestuous relationship with his half-sister, Augusta Leigh (465.17), but the passage already appears to be associated with Byron, since it is soon followed by a distortion of Byron's poem "Maid of Athens" (1810): "Mades of ashens when you flirt spoil the lad but spare his shirt!" (436.32–33). That poem was addressed to Teresa Macri, a twelve-year-old girl Byron met in Greece, which perhaps implies a connection with Jaun's relationship to his sister, a schoolgirl. Although the poem itself is not overtly sexual, it had what Fiona MacCarthy calls "a sordid undercurrent," given the story that Teresa's mother offered her to Byron for 30,000 piastres, a sum that was beyond his means.[8] The allusion to "spare the rod and spoil the child," an adage invoked to justify spanking children, takes a sexual turn when Jaun threatens to spank the girls' bottoms (436.36 ff.), which Edmund Epstein notes is connected a few pages later to "the related area of book burning."[9] As the chapter proceeds, Jaun the moralistic censor has little in common with Byron except, perhaps, a desire for his sister.

444.25–28: In a passage filled with sadistic threats, Jaun warns Issy against sex without birth control, which might result in a "misconception" (444.11), adding that there will be consequences: "I'll have it in for you. I'll teach you bed minners, tip for tap, to be playing your oddaugghter tangotricks with micky dazzlers if I find corsehairs on your river-frock." Robert Gleckner has argued that the corsair reference in this passage is one of several in the *Wake* that associate the outcast Shem with corsairs, and in particular with Conrad, the hero of Byron's "The Corsair."[10] The theme of spanking returns here, but as Jaun tells Issy, it's "For your own good, you understand, for the man who lifts his pud to a woman is saving the way for kindness" (445.11–13).

454.01-02: "So for e'er fare thee welt!" The first sentence alludes to the opening of Byron's "Fare Thee Well": "Fare thee well! And if for ever, / Still for ever, fare *thee well*."[11] The subject is Byron's then-scandalous separation from his wife, Anne Isabella Milbanke, who spread rumors of his immorality, including the relationship with Augusta Leigh. *Welt* is German for "world" (here, perhaps, suggesting "Fare thee well, cruel world"), and English for part of a shoe, as McHugh notes; it might also be a bodily welt caused by a spanking.[12]

464.28-29: "Not forgetting the oils of greas under that turkey in julep." In "The Isles of Greece," a poem within canto 3 of *Don Juan*, a poet laments the domination of Greece by Turkey (the Ottoman Empire); hence, "the oils of greas [are] under that turkey." Joyce sets up the context with puns on patriotic songs—"The Marseillaise," "Yankee Doodle," "The Wearing of the Green"—and references to several European nations (464.21–28). The inevitable food puns in references to Greece and Turkey fit into III.2, where they reflect Jaun's great appetite.

465.17-18: "like boyrun to sibster, me and you, shinners true and pinchme." Jaun simultaneously addresses Issy and Dave (Shem), his twin and other self, whose coming he proclaims. Joyce implies a connection between incestuous relationships, such as that between "boyrun" and his "sibster," and some Irish nationalists who are "Shinners" in several ways: they have shins, they are sinners, and they support Sinn Féin. The connection of Sinn Féin to incest lay in its isolationist policies, as when Jaun tells Issy, "The racist to the racy, rossy. The soil is for the self alone. Be ownkind. Be kithkinish. Be bloodysibby. Be irish. Be inish" (465.30–32). The passage includes a play on the Gaelic League motto, "sinn féin, sinn féin amhain" (ourselves, ourselves alone) as well as other exhortations to stick to one's "ownkind," that is, family (kith and kin, blood siblings), nation, and island (*inis* in Irish). As Len Platt observes, buried beneath the nationalist rhetoric of this passage is an argument for "incest as a way of protecting the purity of the race."[13]

Joyce's reference to Byron and his sister as sinners ("shinners true") would have been clear enough for readers of the 1928 *transition* text, but the basis of the implied comparison between incest and Irish nationalist politics might have been lost on them, since the rest of the passage I have quoted (indeed, all of what is now 465.28–466.03) was added years later. One apparent reason for Joyce's elaboration of the passage was to develop the book's attack on racist ideologies, which became a more prominent theme after Hitler's rise to power. In other respects, too, the Byron references in III.2 evolved over time. For example, an early *Wake* notebook (VI.B.6) contains a crossed-out note, "incest Byron & sister," which the editors of the notebook cite as the source of "Or like boyrun to sibster, me and you, shinners true."[14] The note is prefaced by the symbol for Shem, but in III.2 "boyrun" is identified with both Jaun and Dave, who will take his place. Given Stephen's admiration for Byron in *A Portrait of the Artist as a Young Man*, we might expect the identification of Byron with artists to continue. However, in this chapter, at least, Byronic references also point toward Shaun, especially when they refer to Byron and his sister.

468.27–28, 469.19: Preparing to leave, Jaun drinks a toast to Thomas Moore—"Gulp a bumper at parting and the moore the melodist"—adding, "Farewell but whenever, as Tisdall told Toole." The theme of parting suggested by references to Moore's "One Bumper at Parting" and "Farewell, but Whenever You Welcome the Hour" continues on the next page with Jaun's "Farewell awhile to her and thee!" (469.19), playing on a line from "Childe Harold's Good Night," a poem in *Childe Harold's Pilgrimage* (canto 1). It is an appropriate poem for Jaun to recall just as he prepares to leave Ireland for America:

> Adieu, adieu! my native shore
> Fades o'er the waters blue;
> The night-winds sigh, the breakers roar,
> And shrieks the wild sea-mew.
> Yon sun that sets upon the sea
> We follow in his flight;
> Farewell awhile to him and thee,
> My native Land—Good Night![15]

Since the entire chapter has been a sort of farewell speech, it is fitting that again—as with "Maid of Athens" and "Fare Thee Well"—Jaun's phrasing alludes to one of Byron's many farewell poems. The expatriate theme of "Childe Harold's Good Night" reflects Joyce's own career, and the stanza concludes with a line quoted in the "Nausicaa" episode of *Ulysses*, where, as it grows dark, Bloom thinks, "My native land, goodnight" (*U* 13.1080). It is also a poem that Joyce studied at Clongowes Wood College, where—contrary to what we might expect from *A Portrait of the Artist*—the book used in the English curriculum for Joyce's class included two poems by Byron, "Childe Harold's Good Night" and "The Gladiator," but none by Tennyson.[16] In Joyce's adaptation of Byron, the change from Childe Harold's "Farewell awhile to *him* and thee" to Jaun's "Farewell awhile to *her* and thee!" emphasizes that Jaun is not merely saying farewell to the sun and to his native land ("him and thee") but to Issy and their mother, Anna Livia, to whom he referred a few lines earlier: "Was not my olty mutther, Sereth Maritza, a Runningwater?" (469.13–14). But the mother, as usual, is also Ireland, the country that Jaun must leave. Using the poetic term "Banba" for Ireland, he says, "Somewhere I must get far away from Banbashore, wherever I am" (469.06–07), and later he uses another term for Ireland: "Lood Erynnana, ware thee wail" (469.21). In the last, we hear a final echo of Byron's "Fare Thee Well" and a final reference to Byron's lewdness.

Transition and After

Its publication in *transition*[17] marked an important stage in the chapter's development, but over a decade later, when *Finnegans Wake* was published, III.2 had expanded by about 40 percent. As a result, it is not only longer but richer and even more broad-ranging in its references than the version of 1928. The revisions serve Joyce's artistic ends in various ways. Often they refer to other parts of the book, as when Joyce inserted lines between "I'll sack that sick server the minute I bless him" and "Here she's, is a bell" (*transition* 7–8; 432.33–433.03). The opening of the insert, "That's the mokst I can do for his grapce," evokes the fable of the Mookse and the Gripes in I.6 (152.15–159.18), told by Shaun as Professor Jones, who resembles Jaun and other Shaunian characters in his dogmatic tone and intolerance for other viewpoints. The allusion is a sign that the Shaun-Shem rivalry, while less open in III.2 than in I.6–7, operates here as well and that in some ways Jaun resembles Wyndham Lewis, whose ideas are parodied in the discussion of time-space issues in I.6 and the fable of the Ondt and the Gracehoper in III.1. (Note that "grapce" includes aspects of the Gripes and the Grace[hoper]—both Shemian figures.) As Dirk Van Hulle has observed, Joyce read at least parts of Lewis's *The Art of Being Ruled* in 1926 and wrote the Dave the Dancekerl episode with the book in mind. Joyce alludes to *The Art of Being Ruled* when Jaun calls Shem

"Mr Jinglejoys" (466.18), in response to Lewis's claim that the representation of consciousness in *Ulysses* resembled the bizarre way Mr. Jingle speaks in *The Pickwick Papers*.[18] Below, I will point to another Lewis reference that Joyce added after 1928. In each case the addition implies that Lewis was one of Joyce's targets.

One important feature of the *Wake* is what Joyce calls "The seim anew" (215.23), recurrence with significant difference. An example in III.2 is that Jaun begins by addressing Issy as "Sister dearest" (431.21), and later refers to her as "Dear Sister" (439.26), more simply as "Sis dearest" (448.33), and more extravagantly as "Sissibis dearest" (452.08). Yet while repetition is a principle of the *Wake*, Joyce normally took care not to overdo it. That may explain what otherwise seems an odd decision to change the narrator's comment on the "twentynine hedge daughters": in *transition* (5) the number twenty-nine is said to mean that "it was still a look before you leap year," but in *Finnegans Wake* we are told that "it was still a once-upon-a-four year" (430.03). At first there is no obvious reason for the change, but one appears a few pages later in a sentence that was not in *transition*: "Where you truss be circumspicious and look before you leak, dears" (433.33–34). One play on "look before you leap" sufficed, and the leap/leak pun proved more important for Joyce than the doubled sense of "leap" in the earlier draft.

A comparison of *transition* and *Finnegans Wake* versions of the paragraph that begins "Poof! There's puff for ye" (*transition* 11; 439.15) will provide more examples of how Joyce used the late revision process to broaden, deepen, and enrich his text. One addition to the paragraph was "The valiantine vaux of Venerable Val Vousdem. If my jaws must brass away like the due drops on my lay. And the topnoted delivery you'd expected be me invoice! Theo Dunnohoo's warning from Daddy O'Dowd" (439.17–20). McHugh notes references to *Valentine Vox*, a novel; George Valiantine (American "voice medium"); Val Vousden (Dublin "music hall entertainer"); two plays, *The O'Donoghue's Warning* and *Daddy O'Dowd*; an Irish chieftain, The O'Donoghue; *vaux*: valleys (French for low notes); and several phrases. To this list we might add "topnoted delivery ... invoice," which combines two of Jaun's roles: as a postman delivering an invoice and as a John McCormack-like tenor delivering high notes when he is in voice. Although she cites only one direct reference to McCormack's name in III.2, Adaline Glasheen says that McCormack was "one of the principal models for Shaun-Jaun, who sings McCormack's favorite songs," that McCormack and Shaun are each "strongly identified with Don Giovanni," and that McCormack resembled Shaun in his overeating and consequent obesity.[19] McCormack was a papal count, which connects him to

Jaun's quasi-clerical role, and the fact that he was a tenor means that—whatever the truth of his own life—he was inevitably a Don Giovanni/Don Juan figure for Joyce, since "tenors get women by the score" (*U* 11.686). The erotic associations of high operatic notes are also evident in Joyce's expansion of the *transition* passage "Now something nice" (12) to the *Wake*'s "Now, before my upperotic rogister, something nice" (439.25–26).[20]

Among the most intriguing additions to this paragraph are the references to juvenile fiction by Francis J. Finn, S.J. (1859–1928), an Irish American priest. Joyce refers directly to Father Finn when Jaun lists "that *Percy Wynns* of our S.J. Finn's" (440.09–10) as an example of the "pious fiction" Issy should read. If this allusion to *Percy Wynn* [*sic*] were Joyce's only reference to Finn, it would be of little interest except that Jaun recommends to his sister a book specifically written for boys.[21] But this is just one of eight references in the *Wake* to Father Finn, all in III.2 and all but two in the paragraph I have been discussing. They are found in the following passages:

> 434.19: "Put your swell foot foremost" (*The Best Foot Forward and Other Stories*, 1899; three novellas and two short stories)
> 439.35: "Tome Plyfire" (*Tom Playfair; or, Making a Start*, 1891; novel)
> 439.36–440.01: "ethelred by all pressdom" (*Ethelred Preston; or, The Adventures of a Newcomer*, 1896; novel)
> 440.06: "(mostly boys)" (*Mostly Boys: Short Stories*, 1894; thirteen stories)
> 440.09–10: "that *Percy Wynns* of our S. J. Finns" (*Percy Wynn; or, Making a Boy of Him*, 1891; novel)
> 440.14: "this luckiest year" (*His Luckiest Year*, 1918; novel)
> 440.21: "Chiefly girls" (see *Mostly Boys*, above)
> 457.11: "any lightfoot Clod Dewvale" (*Claude Lightfoot; or, How the Problem Was Solved*, 1893; novel)

Only the first passage appears in *transition* (9) exactly as it does in *Finnegans Wake*. Most of the next six do not appear in any form in *transition*,[22] while the last is a clever revision of a *transition* passage.

Initially, the connection of Joyce's "Put your swell foot foremost" with Finn's *The Best Foot Forward* was surely coincidental, since there are no other references to Finn or his books in Joyce's notes or drafts from the 1920s. Both authors play on the catchphrase "put your best foot forward," but in different ways: it was an appropriate title for Finn's story, in which a class of students and their teacher need to give one another the benefit of the doubt and try to make a good impression,[23] while for Joyce it was an inevitable phrase in a chapter filled with foot references. The parallel with swollen-footed Oedipus might explain why the sentence continues with a suggestion of the disgrace that arises from foolhardy actions: "Put your swell foot foremost on foulardy pneumonia shertwaists, irreconcilible with true fiminin risirvition and ribbons of lace, limenick's disgrace" (434.19–21).

The last of the passages listed above derives from one in *transition* (22), where Jaun says what he would do "If any marauding Clod Dewvale was to hold me up dicksturping me and relieving me of my rights to my onus"—if he were held up by a highwayman like Claude Duval (1643–1670) or Dick Turpin (1705–1739), disturbed and relieved of his rights to his own (or to his burden: his onus). In the *Wake*, Joyce altered the passage to refer as well to Father Finn's Claude Lightfoot: "If any ~~marauding~~ **lightfoot** Clod Dewvale was to hold me up, dicksturping me and ~~relieving~~ **marauding** me of my rights to my onus" (457.11–12). The meaning changes: the highwaymen are still marauders, but one is also lightfooted—surely an asset in that profession. Moreover, "marauding me of my rights to my onus" sounds suspiciously as if someone is giving him an enema, this time more forcibly than when the highwaymen were just "relieving" him. In the end, so to speak, a pious fiction has become entangled with more violent themes.

It is not clear that Joyce ever read a book by Father Finn, since he refers only to titles. Indeed, he might not have heard of Francis J. Finn until at least November 1928, when Finn died. At some point, though, Joyce read about Finn, whose name, with its echoes of Finn MacCool, Huckleberry Finn, Finn's Hotel, Tim Finnegan, and possibly Father Flynn in "The Sisters," would have caught Joyce's attention. It would not have taken him long to recognize that one of the foot references in his chapter could serve as an allusion to *The Best Foot Forward* and another passage could easily be altered to refer to *Claude Lightfoot*.

Although the titles of Finn's other books that Joyce mentions do not include the word *foot*,[24] he inserted more references to Finn's books and author in a single paragraph (439.34–440.21) where they stand as examples of Joyce's reshaping of language toward his own end. The allusion to *Tom Playfair* deprives it of any sense of fair play: "I'd burn the books that grieve you and light an allassundrian bompyre that would suffragate Tome Plyfire or Zolfanerole." Jaun has just warned Issy against certain kinds of books; now, in a passage that was probably inspired by Nazi book burnings of the 1930s, he says he would burn books in a huge bonfire like the burning of the library at Alexandria (48 BCE). (Later, "our nazional labronry" [440.05] is presumably a library with unburned books that Nazis would approve.) The fire would suffocate "Tome Plyfire" (Tom Playfair; playing with tome burning) or Savonarola, who burned what he deemed sinful and was later burned himself. However, "Perousse instate your *Weekly Standerd*, our verile organ that is ethelred by all pressdom" (439.35–460.01), with the reference to *Ethelred Preston*, offers Issy reading of a different sort, along with an allusion to the male sexual organ. Jaun advises Issy to read "*Through Hell with the Papes* (mostly boys) by the divine comic Denti Alligator (exsponging your index)" (440.05–07): *Through Hell with the Papes* alludes to the number of popes in Dante's *Inferno*, "(exsponging your index)" points to the Catholic Church's index of forbidden books, and the allusion to Father Finn's *Mostly Boys* acknowledges that popes tend to be male. The second reference to the same collection, "Chiefly girls," might have been inserted for the sake of balance, unless Joyce knew that Father Finn, after writing books for boys, founded a secondary school for girls.[25] Likewise, the allusion to Finn's *His Luckiest Year* ("this luckiest year") serves mainly to multiply the number of references to his fiction.

The most interesting allusion places Finn's *Percy Wynn* alongside "*Lentil Lore* by Carnival Cullen" and "*Pease in Plenty* by the Curer of Wars" as works approved by the Catholic hierarchy (440.08–15): clearly, even if Joyce never read a word of Finn's writing, he recognized that it would be "pious fiction" in support of Catholic doctrine. As a bonus, the title of *Percy Wynn* echoes the first three syllables of *Percy Wynd*ham Lewis, including the given name, Percy, that Lewis disliked and wished to suppress. Unlike Father Finn, Cardinal Cullen, and St. John Vianney (the Curé d'Ars), Lewis was not Catholic, but he was as dogmatic as any of the others. Placing Lewis in their company may be regarded as an apt response to Lewis's attack on Joyce through his association of Bloom and Mr. Jingle.

Dave the Dancekerl

Throughout his sermon Jaun tries to cover his desires with a mask of piety, but when she finally speaks, Issy is more honest and direct, addressing Jaun as her "pet" and "flusther[ing] sweet nunsongs in his quickturned ear" (457.28–29). She wants him to think of her and not of "sester Maggy," also known as "nurse Madge, my linkingclass girl" (458.10, 459.04), yet her own affections are not limited to Jaun: she had a crush on "young Fr Ml [Father Michael], my pettest parriage priest" (458.03–04), and she mentions a "loveliletter" from her "latest lad," with whom she has been rather intimate: "Why I love taking him out when I unletched his cordon gate.... I felt for his strength, his manhood, his do you mind?" (459.23–29). Her references to "Jer" (458.15) and "Jaime" (461.31) show that she has Shem as well as Shaun in mind.

Jaun's response, leading into his remarks on Dave the Dancekerl, is an extended champagne/eucharistic toast, "with his bubbleblown in his patapet and his chalished drink now well in hand" (461.34–35). Although he says, "Erin go Dry!" (462.04), the paragraph is sodden with references to drink, especially champagne, as Issy is treated as a bride-to-be: "To stir up love's young fizz I tilt with this bridle's cup champagne" (462.08–09).[26] At the same time, in the stirring up of "young fizz," and certainly in another drink—"A stiff one for Staffetta mullified with creams of hourmony" (462.05–06)—not to mention the description of Jaun's "pearlies in their sparkling wisdom . . . nippling her bubblets" (462.11–12)—there are signs of his desire for Issy. Yet it is becoming increasingly evident that although Issy is "a most impatient virgin," as Epstein puts it, Shaun will not act on his desires.[27] Instead, he will leave behind Dave, his proxy (462.16) or alter ego (463.07), to act for him.

Despite his reservations about Dave, who "has novel ideas" and is "a jarry queer fish betimes," even "the poisoner of his word," Jaun embraces Dave as part of himself (463.12–13). This attitude is unlike the one in I.7, where Shaun pillories Shem incessantly. Likewise, earlier in III.2 there are strident attacks on figures identified with Shem, including "Autist Algy," who would take Issy "to the playguehouse" and ask her to pose in the nude (434.35–435.06). However, at one point Jaun inadvertently reveals his connection to Shem, the "black fremdling" and "outsider" (442.01, 442.23; *Fremdling*: stranger or foreigner in German). Jaun says of Shem, "He's a markt man from that hour. And why do we say that, you may query me? Quary?" (442.18–19). "Query" and "Quary" (*quare*: why? in Latin) both refer to questions, but Quary also calls attention to a particular marked man, James Carey, who was killed for informing on the Invincibles after the Phoenix Park murders. Jaun says he would turn his own brother over to the police (443.02–05), thereby acting as an informer, and speaks of "bringing proceedings verses the joyboy," his brother (443.11).[28] Yet he briefly gets his pronouns mixed up: "*We'll* he'll burst *our* his mouth like Leary to the Leinsterface and reduce *he'll* we'll *ournhisn* liniments to a poolp" (442.29–31, my italics). Given Jaun's references first to Shem and then to himself as informers, one reason for his confusion of pronouns may be to reflect the informer's dilemma: how to accuse his accomplices without informing on himself. The vacillation between *we* and *he*, *our* and *his*, might also signal the beginnings of Jaun's partial identification with Shem as part of himself, a moment like the one toward the end of I.7 when Shem proclaims, "My fault, his fault, a kingship through a fault!" (193.31–32). This identification becomes more prominent when Jaun begins talking about Dave.[29]

Jaun says that he and Dave are brothers—"Got by the one goat, suckled by the same nanna, one twitch, one nature makes us oldworld kin" (463.15–17)—and calls him "darling," playing on the meaning of David in Hebrew (462.16, 462.30, 463.34). There are contradictions in his references to Dave, "a squamous runaway and a dear old man pal of mine too" (462.17–18), but eventually the brothers seem almost to fuse into one character. A similar merging may be seen in Joyce's revision of the passage quoted in his June 1924 letter to Miss Weaver: "with a half a glance of Irish frisky from under the shag of his parallel brows." That is substantially how the passage appeared in *transition* (30), but in *Finnegans Wake* there is a significant parenthetical insertion: "with half a glance of Irish frisky (a Juan Jaimesan *hastaluego*) from under the shag of his parallel brows" (470.32–34). In the *Wake*, John Jameson Irish Whiskey signals both Shaun and Shem (John and James), but here we get the name Juan, rather than the usual Jaun. The addition of "*hastaluego*" makes it clear that "Juan" is pronounced "Wan," as in Spanish, rather than in the Byronic fashion, where it has two syllables and rhymes with "new one" and "true one." The insertion also converts the half glass of Irish whiskey to a parting drink like the *deoch an dorais* that Jaun proposed earlier (462.07).[30] Jaun starts to leave but falls, tries again, blesses the girls, and finally disappears, "lost to sight" (471.28). We hear no more of Dave, nor do we see him, because he was Jaun's "innerman," "the shadow of a post" (462.16, 462.21–22), not a person in his own right.[31] Jaun is remembered as a great walker, and his return the next morning is predicted, but for now he and his emanation, Dave, have vanished.

Although it is not easy to say how this might be measured, there is probably more sexual suggestiveness per page in III.2 than in any other chapter of the *Wake*.[32] Early in the episode Jaun proclaims his rise (432.04), and if that has a phallic sound, then we are in for much more very soon. Take, for example, his flat declaration to the girls, "Well, here's looking at ye! If I never leave you biddies till my stave is a bar I'd be tempted rigidly to become a passionate father" (457.05–07). In this passage references to voyeurism, an erection, and father-daughter incest mix with musical terms (stave, bar) and a possible clerical vocation as one of the Passionist Fathers. Yet it is all talk: Jaun boasts, threatens, makes sly (and not so sly) hints, and refers repeatedly to underwear, bottoms, sexuality, and the like, often under the guise of teaching the girls to be chaste. But there is no sexual contact, only what D.

H. Lawrence condemned as "sex in the head." The general effect is to ridicule Jaun's sexual pretensions and innuendos as much as his hypocritical piety.

Jaun is an intermediate stage in Shaun's degeneration, seeming more and more like a bag of wind until he disappears. In III.3 he will enter a new stage, when "His dream monologue [in III.2] was over, of cause, but his drama parapolylogic had yet to be, affact" (474.04–05), monologue once again giving way to interrogation as multiple voices speak to, and maybe through, Yawn.

Notes

1. Joyce adapted Pound's quip in his list of possible titles for Anna Livia's "mamafesta": "*A New Cure for an Old Clap*" (104.22–23).

2. Roland McHugh, *Annotations to "Finnegans Wake,"* 3rd ed. (Baltimore: Johns Hopkins University Press, 2006).

3. Stuart Gilbert, "Prolegomena to *Work in Progress*," in Samuel Beckett et al., *Our Exagmination Round His Factification for Incamination of Work in Progress* (Paris: Shakespeare and Company, 1929), 49–75.

4. Petr Skrabanek, "Epscene License (523.34)," *A Wake Newslitter* 15.5 (October 1978): 74.

5. Adaline Glasheen, *Third Census of "Finnegans Wake"* (Berkeley: University of California Press, 1977), lx, 104–5.

6. *The Poetical Works of Lord Byron*, ed. Ernest Hartley Coleridge (London: John Murray, 1905), 135–41.

7. The phrase "through the usual channels" might have been suggested by a passage in Frank Harris's biography of Oscar Wilde. In the 1916 edition Harris said that Horatio Lloyd, Wilde's father-in-law, had been accused of homosexuality, but in the 1918 edition Harris quoted Robert Ross's correction: "The charge against Horatio Lloyd was of a normal kind. It was for exposing himself to nursemaids in the gardens of the Temple." *Oscar Wilde: His Life and Confessions, Volume 2* (New York: Brentano's, [1918] rpt. 1924), 608. On Joyce's notebook entry derived from this quotation and its evolution into a passage in I.2 (33.21–34.29), see Sam Slote, "Wilde Thing: Concerning the Eccentricities of a Figure of Decadence in *Finnegans Wake*," in *Probes: Genetic Studies in Joyce*, ed. David Hayman and Sam Slote (Amsterdam and Atlanta: Rodopi, 1995), 104–7. Ross sought to distinguish homosexuality from the more "normal" offense of exhibitionism; Jaun distinguishes it from the "usual channels" of heterosexual incest. Jaun's observation that "canalised love . . . does a felon good" (436.18–19) is a veiled reference to the same "channels" (*canali* in Italian).

8. Fiona MacCarthy, *Byron: Life and Legend* (New York: Farrar, Straus and Giroux, 2002), 114.

9. Edmund Epstein, *A Guide through "Finnegans Wake"* (Gainesville: University Press of Florida, 2009), 184.

10. Robert F. Gleckner, "Byron in *Finnegans Wake*," in *Twelve and a Tilly: Essays on the Occasion of the 25th Anniversary of Finnegans Wake*, ed. Jack P. Dalton and Clive Hart (London: Faber and Faber, 1966), 47–49.

11. Byron, *Works*, 377.

12. McHugh points to a reference to "Fare Thee Well" on the next page: "With the Byrns which is far better and eve for ever your idle be" (455.02–03). However, he is mistaken in adding that Byron's poem has a "motto from Burns," since the epigraph to "Fare Thee Well" is from Coleridge's "Christabel." Earlier, Gleckner (45) spotted these allusions and two fainter echoes on 454–55: "Fare thee well, fairy well!" (454.27–28) and "to aye forever" (455.22).

13. Len Platt, "'No Such Race': The *Wake* and Aryanism," in *Joyce, Ireland, Britain*, ed. Andrew Gibson and Len Platt (Gainesville: University Press of Florida, 2006), 169. See also Platt's *Joyce, Race, and "Finnegans Wake"* (Cambridge: Cambridge University Press, 2007) and John Gordon, "Joyce's Hitler," in *Joyce through the Ages: A Nonlinear View*, ed. Michael Patrick Gillespie (Gainesville: University Press of Florida, 1999), 179–98.

14. *The "Finnegans Wake" Notebooks at Buffalo: Notebook VI.B.6*, ed. Vincent Deane, Daniel Ferrer, and Geert Lernout (Turnhout, Belgium: Brepols, 2002), 131 (notebook page 115). The notebook page is also reproduced in *JJA* 30:129.

15. Byron, *Works*, 147.

16. Bruce Bradley, S.J., *James Joyce's Schooldays* (New York: St. Martin's Press, 1982), 106.

17. James Joyce, "Continuation of a Work in Progress," *transition* 13 (Summer 1928): 5–32.

18. Dirk Van Hulle, *Manuscript Genetics, Joyce's Know-How, Beckett's Nohow* (Gainesville: University Press of Florida, 2008), 64, 77–81, 198–99; Wyndham Lewis, *The Art of Being Ruled* (New York: Harper and Brothers, 1926), 414. See also David Hayman, "Enter Wyndham Lewis Leading Dancing Dave: New Light on a Key Relationship," *James Joyce Quarterly* 35/36 (Summer/Fall 1998): 621–31, and David J. Califf, "Clones and Mutations: A Genetic Look at 'Dave the Dancekerl,'" in *Probes: Genetic Studies in Joyce*, ed. David Hayman and Sam Slote (Amsterdam and Atlanta: Rodopi, 1995), 123–47. "Mr Jinglejoys" appeared in *transition* (28).

19. Glasheen, 177.

20. On operatic eroticism see also Matthew J. C. Hodgart and Ruth Bauerle, *Joyce's Grand Operoar: Opera in "Finnegans Wake"* (Urbana: University of Illinois Press, 1997), 86–87.

21. Francis J. Finn, S.J., *Percy Wynn; or, Making a Boy of Him* (New York: Benziger Brothers, 1891). After being raised with ten sisters (no brother), Percy is sent to a Catholic boys' boarding school where the sympathetic Tom Playfair—hero of

another book to which Joyce alludes—protects him against bullies and teaches him to be less "girlish" (18). At the end, Percy earns "the love and respect of his schoolmates" and becomes "a real boy in every sense of the word" (251).

22. The exception is "our verile organ that is red allover" (*transition* 12), altered to "our verile organ that is ethelred by all pressdom" (439.36–440.01).

23. Francis J. Finn, S.J., *The Best Foot Forward and Other Stories* (New York: Benziger Brothers, 1899).

24. Apparently Joyce missed Finn's *That Football Game and What Came of It* (New York: Benziger Brothers, 1897), since he makes no reference to it.

25. "Francis J. Finn," http://en.wikipedia.org/wiki/Francis_J._Finn; accessed March 10, 2013.

26. In "Dante . . . Bruno. Vico. Joyce," his contribution to *Our Exagmination*, Samuel Beckett quotes the remainder of this paragraph and comments, "The language is drunk. The very words are tilted and effervescent" (14).

27. Epstein, *Guide*, 185.

28. Another Wyndham Lewis reference; see Van Hulle, *Manuscript Genetics*, 78–79. In *The Art of Being Ruled*, Lewis uses "joy-boy or joy-man" to refer to a "Nancy" like Oscar Wilde (241).

29. As Wim Van Mierlo notes, "Dave never appears in the flesh; Shaun only invokes his coming" (369). "Shaun the Post: Chapters III.1–2," in *How Joyce Wrote "Finnegans Wake": A Chapter-by-Chapter Genetic Guide*, ed. Luca Crispi and Sam Slote (Madison: University of Wisconsin Press, 2007), 347–83. Nonetheless, at times Jaun seems to speak to Dave, as when he gives him advice on "the wring wrong way to wright woman" (466.15).

30. The emphasis on farewell in Joyce's play on *deoch an dorais* ("dhouche on Doris" [462.07]) is reinforced two lines later by "bridle's cup," which is both a bridal cup and a *bridle* cup, a Joycean version of a stirrup cup.

31. Califf points to a notebook entry in which Joyce wrote, "Shem [is the] inner man of Shaun" ("Clones and Mutations," 123).

32. Platt makes a related claim, that III.2 is "the single most vulgar section in the whole of the *Wake*" (*Joyce, Race, and "Finnegans Wake*," 160).

15

The Daughter in the Father

The Revolutionary Aspect of III.3

SHELDON BRIVIC

God as Multiplicity

The third chapter of the third book of *Finnegans Wake* presents the conformist brother Shaun as Yawn asleep on a hill at the center of Ireland and interrogated by the four evangelists, who draw out a series of voices from within him that include the other members of HCE'S family.[1] The implication is that even the least imaginative member of the family contains all of the others, and indeed all of humanity, and in fact God, as the object sought by Matthew, Mark, Luke, and John.

The God they find, however, is a work in progress, a mathematical structure of human consciousness that pullulates with infinite possibilities of the formations of family, subjectivity, and history to counterpoint oppression with advancement, and a structure that is anchored in gender.

As a sign that what the four senilities are looking for is divine, though what they find is defined by historical categories, the second page of the chapter uses seven words for fear and twenty-eight exclamation marks twice to emphasize their fear of what they seek in him (475.01–16).[2] The passage also refers to parts of him as nebulae and other heavenly bodies (475.12–16). Blake writes, "God only Acts & Is, in existing beings or Men."[3] In his 1912 lecture on Blake, the idealistic half of his two Italian lectures on "Realism and Idealism in English Literature" (the first lecture was on Defoe), Joyce expressed admiration for Blake as a "great genius" and a "fearless and immortal spirit," praising his radicalism.[4]

Yawn's divinity is linked to his being contained by an assemblage led by his father. Matthew asks, "Are you in your fatherick . . . ?" and Yawn answers, "The same. Three persons" (478.28–30). The familial "rick" or pile to which he belongs constitutes both God (the Trinity) and all of humanity as the total potential for human consciousness. III.3 is a major demonstration that the discourse of the *Wake* speaks for multitudes. Through the sequence of its many voices, it develops the great variety of arrangements that these voices can assume.

So the God subject in Joyce does not have the unity of the monotheistic God. It more closely resembles Badiou's idea of the subject as an indeterminate series of encounters whose form cannot be predicted.[5] This model corresponds to Finn Fordham's idea that the figures in the *Wake* are not universals but figures of change on which universals are imposed,[6] what Badiou calls events. One implication here is that a "character" is not a stable form but an interchange with a constellation.

When Shaun is asleep, the voices within him that speak for other people aligned with the forms of the family are free to unfold themselves dialogically. His somnolent state provides a structural bed for the *Wake*, in which the shared identities that make up the collective subject are held down in sleep. In waking, one affirms an individual personality, but dream reveals that one contains a myriad of identities. One of Joyce's main models here is Blake's idea of the sleeping giant Albion, whose body contains all of humanity, which would overcome the separations of culture, gender, and class if it could truly wake, though differences rebound within the sleeping body of III.3.[7] While the image of the gigantic sleeper is established in the first chapter, Yawn attaches himself in III.3 to "your sleeping giant" (540.17). HCE as Finnegan enacts the idea that all humanity is combined in one figure, and Yawn, as the sleeping aspect of HCE, has the ability of dreams to shift roles and contexts rapidly.

If III.3 presents "the map of the souls' groupography" (476.33), this multipersonal assemblage is constantly rearranging itself. The example I will focus on here emphasizes the pattern of nesting, one figure contained in the other, which may correspond to the mathematical idea of belonging to a set. Here the daughter is nested in the father, who is nested in the son Shaun, who is nested in his mother.

It is realistic of the *Wake* to represent the subject as made up of a family of voices. If I say something stern, my father's voice may speak in me. If I say something tender, it may be my mother's voice, and likewise for siblings, friends, teachers, enemies, and so on. These people are inside, and Freud argued that the ego was made up of a series of identifications.[8] But I could say something both stern and tender, paternal and maternal. So the typical phrase of the *Wake* has several meanings that speak for several voices. Here the focus on what disturbs Shaun reveals that even this conservative figure contains the structure of injustice within him in a form that speaks for revolution. This is the "deep" level on which he is subject to unknown possibilities, as opposed to the discourse at the end of III.3, where he asserts the "surface" level of his control over the world.

When—rather than following authority, as Shaun does in his waking role of letter carrier—the subject expresses itself actively, it aims at a truth beyond what it can know, just as Blake's sleeping giant seeks vision. The deeper the old men plumb into Shaun's interior, the further they go from his conscious mind, and the wider they range through the human types that he excludes through his self-possession, they find that these other types express his lacks and dependences. The potential connections that Shaun could realize through his multiplicity must be held down by a world in which the calculations of male rationality control the indiscernible feminine and artistic language of subjectivity.

The Daughter in the Aggressive Father

In the page I focus on (500), the most extreme conflicts in Shaun's mind emerge following the image of his father's wake, as his interrogators press to get at the real nature of the father figure that he takes as the core of his identity. Joseph Campbell and Henry Morton Robinson argue that at this point the inquest reaches "the giant father himself," and "the strangest, wildest cries" are heard.[9] John Gordon claims that they reach down to the dreamer's "most sensitive memories," baring "'all that's buried ofsins'" (499.25), especially HCE'S "longing" for his daughter, Issy.[10] Edmund Epstein, who calls this page "the most powerful passage" in the *Wake*, says that at this point what emerges are the voices of "tormented Irish history."[11]

HCE is usually comatose in the *Wake*, suggesting that the paternal principle is obsolete. When he is seen in action, which is generally in the past, he tends to be aggressive. The most pressing role of the father figure is conquest, usually the ultimate controlling activity of male authority. HCE was described earlier in III.3 as "acting like a bellax" (486.32). Now he is expressed by the opposing battle calls of the Irish rebels and their English conquerors: "Crum abu!" (500.06), which McHugh identifies as a "Fitzgerald war cry,"[12] and "Cromwell to victory!" (500.06), a parallel phrase naming the most terrible devastator of Ireland, Oliver Cromwell. HCE is involved in the passion of battle: "—We'll gore them and gash them and gun them and gloat on them. /—Zinzin. /—O, widows and orphans" (500.07–10). The appearance of "O, widows and orphans" in the midst of the war cries calls forth ambivalence. It is preceded by "Zinzin," which McHugh identifies as a French "onomatopoeia evoking noise." As a sound of interference it indicates the difficulty of holding levels of discourse together. The widows and orphans are both linked as aims to the destructive desire of war, which seeks to create them, and are also seen as painful human images of suffering and loss.

The violence of war destroys families by enforcing oppositions. This antipersonal voice corresponds to propaganda, so the spiritual aspect of life is reduced to the slogans of journalism in a series of newspapers: "Christ in our irish times! Christ on the airs independence! . . . Christ light the dully expressed" (500.14–16). The *Daily Express* becomes the "dully expressed" because the ideology of religion in the newspapers has been put before its beauty.

The "dully expressed" leads directly into the most terrible violence, which is the worst debasement of the feminine side of the subject. This assertion may be motivated by the insecure aspect of the father: "Cloudy father! Unsure! Nongood!" (500.19). In this case, the sacred *Vater unser* is converted into an uneasy one that has to assert himself by raping a daughter: "Slog slagt and sluaghter. Rape the daughter" (500.17). Here the voices from within Shaun imply an indictment of the sovereignty he is attached to and suggest atrocity against the daughter not only of others but of his own family. He cannot destroy the image of the daughter without reflecting on his own.

There is always a great potential for aggression between a father and his daughter. As Jen Shelton observes in *Joyce and the Narrative Structure of Incest*, Joyce pointed out that the relation between father and daughter always involves a margin of uncertainty on which abuse is present as a possibility.[13] The more aggressive the father is, the more any move he makes may tend to overpower the daughter. My book *Joyce's Waking Women* traces a long series of references in the *Wake* to paternal abuse of the daughter and its harmful effects.[14]

From Joyce's point of view, the inclination to rape one's daughter is an extension of the strongest manhood, partially because such manhood is based on doubt. Joyce was the first writer after Freud to reveal the universality of incest as part of his attack on conventional masculinity. The control of history by male violence turns the girl into a commodity, an insight that anticipates Luce Irigaray's essay "Women on the Market": she argues that society has traditionally been organized (by men) around the exchange of women as objects of value.[15] Joyce's lecture on Blake refers to "the two commodities most highly quoted on the stock-exchange today, woman and the people."[16]

But the daughter defiled is also the sensitive side of the man, who voices her protest as it issues from Yawn: "Sold! I am sold!" (500.21). Insofar as this voice is his, he has sold his truest, most sensitive self to partake of power. She is his tenderest feeling, or "meye eyesalt" (484.05), a name which evokes crying and tears. The wail that issues from him expresses not his pleasure but his pain, yet it is a pain he enjoys. On the first page of III.3, Yawn is said to wail "Most distressfully (but, my dear, how successfully!)" (474.05–06). Shaun is the acme of success, just as "my dear" is an upper-class locution here, and Joyce feels that one's success as either a leader or a seducer may be proportional to one's ability to easily sustain distress over the wrongs one has committed.

Just as the name of Cromwell has to evoke horror from any Irishman even while the Irishman may identify with his cause by aligning his values with English status and refinement, so Shaun feels in his mind the anguish of the daughter he brutalizes as he speaks for her predicament. This is indicated by the triple iteration of "me!" (500.23–25). Her name is "I sold" because her being sold constitutes her identity. The glory of the father depends on abusing her, as is indicated in the Greek myth of Agamemnon, who had to sacrifice his daughter Iphigenia before he could win victory in Troy.

Yawn's identification with the defiled daughter is constituted by his containment in the father as the foundation of an authority that isolates its wielder from human feeling: "—Are you in your fatherick, lonely one? /—The same. Three persons. Have you seen my darling only one? I am sohohold!" (478.28–30). The obliteration of the daughter by the coldness of the father extends from the structure of the patriarchal family to business and imperialism. So Yawn as HCE boasts of his reputation on the market "for daughters-in-trade being lightly clad" (532.25–26). His success can be measured by his ability to sell daughters. This passage is followed by a description of his business arrangements, which center on his effort "to illsell my fourth part in" an African woman without a mouth named Blanchette Brewster (537.23–25). As I have argued elsewhere, ALP is often, if not usually, described as African as an expression of the analogy between women and slaves.[17] Shaun/HCE's ownership of Blanchette is presented as "byusucapiture" (537.23); McHugh defines *usucapion* as "acquisition of ownership by long use." The colonized woman for sale is linked to his daughter when he denies that he had her "resolde" (538.08). The whole twenty-six-line transaction is something he denies, yet Edward W. Said, in *Culture and Imperialism*, claims that the wealth and refinement of European culture has depended on colonial acquisitions.[18]

Faulkner suggests in *Absalom, Absalom!* (1935) that the purity of white women depended on the debasement of black ones: the supreme object of desire was an octoroon of the kind cultivated in New Orleans brothels, who had the features of a white woman but could be dominated like a nonwhite one (or like a white woman reduced to a subordinate status by lack of money).[19] Yawn gets nervous and stutters when he thinks of the attraction of Blanchette's "cocoa contours" (538.04). The octoroon represents a gold standard of desire, and Yawn describes the woman he does not trade in as "best Brixton high yellow" (538.09). She is the basis of British class, but "Brixton" also refers to Bristol, the city from which Blanchette hails (537.25), a center for the slave trade that temporarily declined after slavery was abolished.[20]

III.3 emphasizes that in a charter of 1171, Henry II gave Dublin to Bristol. As McHugh indicates, forty-four words of this charter are quoted with little change in the last section of III.3, when Yawn as HCE is boasting of the achievements of his power. The passage appears at the end of sixty-six lines of details of urban hardship (based on B. S. Rowntree's book *Poverty*), such as one foot of dust and a water closet shared by fourteen tenement families.[21]

The quote from Henry begins, "with chartularies I have talledged them" (545.14). "Talledged" is based on "tallage," collection of taxes from feudal dependents, and it suggests—along with "chartularies"—that the inhabitants of a colonized city, or a city ruled by a king, are strictly hemmed in or chartered. The line evokes "London," Blake's song about the "mind-forg'd manacles" of oppression: "I walk thro' each charter'd street / Near where the charter'd Thames does flow / And mark in every face I meet / Marks of weakness, marks of woe" (26–27).

Legitimacy

One of the key verbatim lines from Henry's charter is "they do inhabit it and hold it for me" (545.18). Colonialism brings out a tendency of all government: people live "for" the leader, and he owns them. Dominic Manganiello's book *Joyce's Politics* establishes that his political orientation was toward anarchy, two of his favorite political authors being Mikhail Bakunin and Peter Kropotkin.[22] Joyce repeats the statement from Henry's charter that the Dubliners will have "all the liberties" of the men of Bristol, but he changes Bristol to "Tolbris" (545.20–21) to indicate that the people of Bristol are already taxed and circumscribed (*bris* is a Jewish term for a circumcision). Henry disables his people, so *Henricus rex* becomes "Enwreak us wrecks" (545.23).

Because, as Levi-Strauss pointed out, the central object of exchange in patriarchal societies is always women,[23] capitalism and imperialism are founded on the sale of the daughter. The main purpose of accumulating money is to control the greatest quantity and quality of women. Yawn as HCE says, "my tenenure of office and my toils of domestication first began, with weight of woman my skat and skuld" (539.33–35). McHugh annotates *skat og skuld* as Danish for "taxes, treasure and debt, guilt."

In III.3 woman is transformed by fetishism into a mechanical object: "—Mrs. Tan-Taylour? Just a floating panel, secretairslidingdraws, a *budge* of *klees* on her schalter, a siderbrass sehdass on her anulas findring and forty *croce*lips in her curlingthongues" (511.29–31, my italics). This image is based on a series of works by Dali in which an attractive woman's body is transformed into a vertical stack of furniture drawers:[24] "Was she wearing shubladey's tiroirs [drawers] in humour of her hubbishobbis, Massa's star stellar?" (511.27–28). Drawers, of course, may be parts of furniture or female undergarments.

Woman is seen here as an aesthetic object, as indicated by the references to Dali, Budgen, Klee, and Croce. The image of her as a series of compartments for property organizes the complex operation of her parts. The value of these parts is an exchange value according to a standard of beauty that measures her against an inanimate aesthetic (or pornographic) abstraction by which she can be "resolde or borrough by exchange" (538.08). The actual woman may be valued insofar as she resembles cheesecake or is treated like a resold or borrowed burrough (an area of land): the abstraction of beauty is something one can acquire through possessions, whereas one cannot possess the actual woman.

Insofar as this paternal glory geared to desire is arranged as the fundamental model for all values, the only thing Issy can do to seek justice is to ask for the highest price: "Brinabride, my price! When you sell, get my price!" (500.30). The reference to Parnell's ironic line, "When you sell, get my price," indicates that the potential for love is poisoned by seeking a profit and that both love and politics are ruled by exchange value. Shortly after, the daughter's need for the mother's affection takes over the voice of the brother who contains the father who contains the daughter: "O! Mother of my tears! Believe for me! Fold thy son!" (500.33).

The Daughter in the Father: The Revolutionary Aspect of III.3   261

Badiou argues that the subject contains infinite multiplicity. Joyce here provides a strongly detailed picture of how the subject articulates infinity by recognizing it as a mother who contains a son who contains a father who contains a daughter. The mother has the task of believing in truth, whereas the men believe in theories, and a belief that a theory is true tends to be naïve. The mother is constituted by devotion to the paternal principle, which both Molly and ALP confront at the ends of their novels in the form of Molly's affirmation of God and ALP's vision of Neptune rising. Yet they also claim the power to free humanity by being unfaithful to their husbands. Her belief is the source of the man's confidence as she gives him his phallus, but her infidelity is the source of his intellectually valuable doubt, his Stephen-Shem side. This is the side that seeks her freedom that cannot be sold, a female freedom which is the final goal of Joyce's two major novels.

As Joyce's main deity, ALP is the creator of the *Wake* because the mother represents the source of life: "In the name of Annah the Allmaziful, the Everliving, the Bringer of Plurabilities" (104.01–02). She has the power to awake a world caught in sleep, and Joyce expresses this intensely in words modified from the Egyptian Book of the Dead that identify the mother with a part of the body, just as III.3 tends to identify different persons of the subject with parts of Yawn's body:[25] "My heart, my mother! My heart, my coming forth of darkness! They know not my heart" (493.34–35). Even Shaun can feel the stirring of life if he feels it in his mother as something unknowable.

The ALP chapter of the *Wake* includes the line "she rounded up lost histereve" (214.01), and Joyce, creating Molly and ALP, recovered the lost history of women, so that Anne Enright, an Irish feminist novelist, recently called Joyce one of the great woman writers.[26] The *Wake* moves toward the full realization of ALP's consciousness in her rejection of the delusion of paternal authority at the end to liberate humanity (627–28). That passage and the one I focus on here work against the assertion by the father of all he has accomplished by controlling the mother, the assertion that appears extensively at the end of III.3.

This panorama of the achievements of dominance is often beautiful and has tremendous truth in that civilization has built vast structures of value and security that benefit us prodigiously. It even provides freedom for women, who can now walk in public without veils such as they wore in Homer's time: "In midday's mallsight let Miledd discurverself" (540.33). For her to remove scarves is to discover herself. Yet the engine behind this progress is powered by the abuse of the defenseless, as education has run on flagellation: "enmy pupuls felt my burk was no worse than their brite" (542.18–19). The pupils believe that his paternal birching ("barking" as rubbing the skin off using a rough or sharp object) is proportional to their intelligence (to "burke" is also to suffocate someone). And the teacher believes that the choirboys who are the smartest (*feschest* in colloquial German), the freshest, or the ones with the most prominent fesses are eager to hear the whistling of his cane: "the feshest cheoilboys . . . they are allcalling on me for the song of a birtch" (543.08–10). The inclusion of the phrase "son of a bitch" means that he believes that though they curse him, what they want is his cruelty.

His education of Anna also emphasizes abuse, so the word *learn* means castigate, the alphabet consists of beating, and HCE'S identity is that of a punisher: "her chastener ever I did learn my little ana countrymouse in alphabeater cameltemper, from alderbirk tannenyou with myraw rattan atter dundrum; ooah, oyir, oyir, oyir" (552.36–553.03). As he beats the drum of her skin with his rattan cane, or tans her with his birch, her cries affirming his indoctrination—"o yes, o yours"—are also cries of pain.

In his essay on "The Fourfold Root of Yawn's Unreason," Jean-Michel Rabaté provides a sharp genetically based analysis of Joyce's method of constructing the final section of III.3, known as "Haveth Childers Everywhere," one of the first parts of the *Wake* drafted in 1923. On these twenty-two pages, Yawn as HCE boasts of the cities he has created for ALP. Rabaté emphasizes Joyce's practice of gathering information about cities to accumulate layers of meaning. These levels serve what Rabaté calls the "upward . . . surge" of Yawn's self-assertion,[27] but they also expose contradictions by revealing the falsehood and oppression involved in social creation.

Rabaté's focus on adding and multiplying is a key to the paternal, expansive aspect of the *Wake*, but Badiou presents a number of mathematical functions of logic in his effort to unfold the infinity of the human subject. The aspect of III.3 that I develop here through the pattern of nesting or belonging is aligned with either division or subtraction into the indiscernible, the unconscious, or what is covered up. It moves inward toward the mother rather than outward toward the father. Of the many mathematical structures involved in "the map of the souls' groupography" (476.33), these two seem basic. The outward thrust of the last section of III.3 moves toward waking, which combines the wealth of the existing world with its inevitable crushing and extermination of the world of dream.

If the overall combinatory subject of the novel needs the masculine side to consolidate the physical world of authority and stability, it also needs the feminine interior voice to recognize itself with critical insight by seeing the injustice at the basis of this authority. And the fact that they are parts of the same subject is quite fundamental to III.3 and the *Wake*. This psychoanalytic direction looks inward by interpreting dreams to see the conflict within the subject or the "drama parapolylogic" (474.05), a central activity of III.3, which refers to the four old men as "psychomorers" (476.14–15). Rabaté reports that as Joyce revised III.3, it became saturated with psychoanalytic terminology.[28] Political and sexual injustice depend on the failure to read the opening up of language, and this injustice is based on the isolation of one aspect of the overall human soul from the others, the claim that they are separate when they are all part of each other.

The assemblage of personalities that makes up the subject operates in its changing forms in most significant phrases in the *Wake*. Generally the phrase that marks the appearance of an individual subject speaks for other levels that include the feelings of other figures. For example, the first word of the book, *riverrun*, refers directly to ALP and to the text of the *Wake*, but it also names HCE or Shaun as "reverend" and it speaks for Shem as "reverons" (we dream, muse, rave, or are light-headed). One could go on with the implications here in terms of the continuity of history (four old men), flow that cleans clothes (washerwomen), banks of the river (Shem and Shaun), and so forth. Each meaning of each word is a voice with its own intention. The idea of a single voice becomes an outmoded restriction. The unfolding of these voices accomplishes an enormous step forward for humanity by giving us a bristling, swirling map of the multitudes that each of us contains.

Divinity as Contradiction

In his 1903 review, "The Bruno Philosophy," Joyce quotes with approval Coleridge's version of Bruno of Nola's doctrine: "Every power in nature or in spirit must evolve an opposite as the sole condition and means of its manifestation."[29] One way to relate the coincidence of contraries to the phallic assertive aspect is to consider the implications of the well-known fact that the two sons combine to form the father. Certain mysterious versions of this pattern in III.3 suggest that the father emerges out of the uncertainty generated by the opposition between the two sons: "—Three in one, one in three. / Shem and Shaun and the shame that sunders em" (526.13–14). This opposition may remind one of the "Scylla and Charybdis" episode of *Ulysses*, with its emphasis on Odysseus sailing between the two extremes and the Church being founded on the mystery of paternity that emerges from the void (*U* 9.837–42). The margin of shame on which each brother fails to realize the truth that the other expresses is the area of the unknown and the uneasy, out of which the assertion of authority emerges. HCE is the shame that sunders as the totality that neither can bear to face.

Another version of this pattern speaks of "the point of eschatology our book of kills reaches for now in soandso many counterpoint words" (482.33–34). The goal that emerges from the conflict cannot be clearly expressed, but as John Bishop points out, it can be felt by the heart (*cor, cordis* in Latin):[30] "What can't be coded can be decorded if an ear aye sieze what no eye ere grieved for" (482.34–36). Shem is linked to the ear and time, while Shaun is linked to the eye and space; but they are mixed up in "ear aye" and "eye ere," so it is implied that complete truth could be reached if Shem and Shaun could be combined, an impossibility that would encompass HCE.

The combination is carried further a few lines below with the idea of a text that combines Shem the penman and Shaun the postman: "let me take it upon myself to suggest to twist the penman's tale posterwise. The gist is the gist of Shaum but the hand is the hand of Sameas" (483.02–04). Though this passage is based on Jacob's passing himself off to his father, Isaac, as Esau (Genesis 27: 18–24), it also implies that history can't be carried forward without both brothers. It indicates that the full text combines the meaning of one brother (Shem) with the writing of the other. Yet their names are confused as "Shaum" and "Sameas," neither of which is exactly one or the other.

The conflict between them generates the discourse of God or history: "'Tis the bells of scandal that gave tune to grumble over him and someone between me and thee" (483.06–07). "The Bells of Shandon" is a religious song, and the mysterious someone between the two opponents is God in a line from Genesis where Laban warns Jacob not to do him wrong: "the Lord watch between me and thee" (31: 49). Charged with this schizoid godhead, the combined form is ready to convert pagans around the world. "He would preach to the two turkies and dipdip [baptise] all the dindians" (483.07–08). The twins are described here as a "wombful of mischief" (483.18), and McHugh connects this phrase to the biblical claim that Jacob and Esau fought in the womb (Genesis 25: 22). Each of the opposing views generates the other from its first conception.

The assertion of opposed positions is an active movement that causes conflict, uncertainty, and torment, as well as being the source of creativity and beauty. The unified phallic position of HCE starts from the passive position of being suspended between alternatives. The two versions of this suspension, which are equated with each other in the *Wake*, are the crime in the park in which HCE is constituted by being suspended between a female attraction and a male threat, and the alternate homosexual version of the crime in which HCE encounters the cad and fights (35–37, 516–22). These two versions, the female and the male, correspond to the fall in Eden as either temptation by Eve or disobedience of God (attraction to mother or conflict with father).

The area of experience that is most oppressed—which the *Wake* tends to identify with women—is that in which the greatest possibility for liberation exists. Irigaray, in *Speculum of the Other Woman*, sees the history of philosophy from Plato onward as a masculine construction organized around the power of the father.[31] To free humanity from this edifice, the whole system of logic will have to be reshaped. The recognition of the woman in the man in her afflicted or sold state leads toward the greatest disarrangement of conventional distinctions, as an emblem of the impulsion of the *Wake* to bring everything together.

Central to Joyce's attack on masculine authority is the Lacanian idea that the phallus, as the power to signify, is always based on castration.[32] The pattern appears in the second chapter of *Portrait* when Stephen begins to pursue "E__C__" after he is mistaken for a woman (*P* 68–69). In III.3, God thunders at HCE "to flatch down off that erection and be aslimed of himself for the bellance of hissch leif" (506.07–08). As a result of this loss of manhood, HCE becomes "the fanest of our truefalluses" (506.17–18), which uses the Middle English word *fain* meaning ready or willing. Male assertion is based on a lack.

Many of the grotesque references to HCE's effort to maintain a permanent erection have moral overtones: "I am as cleanliving as could be . . . since I perpetually kept my ouija ouija wicket up" (532.16–18). He is upholding standards (flagpoles), even though he stutters. But HCE as phallus becomes an object of veneration: "Determined Codde or Cucumber Upright. . . . O rhyme us! Haar Faagher, wild heart in Homelan; Harrod's be the naun, Mine kinder come, mine wohl be won. There is nothing like leuther" (536.33–36). The *cod* is both a fish, a symbol of divinity, and a codpiece, while *leuther* refers to both Luther and leather, combining religion with sexual perversion, the hidden side of male authority.

Fifty Shades of Black

Just as authority derives from uneasiness, the final assertion of HCE is preceded by a substantial section wallowing in the homosexual aspect of the crime. This sequence (from 519 to 526) intermittently represents the accusations against HCE in terms of desires that cannot be recognized, having been criminalized and linked to punishment. The prohibitions refer to religious education as a system for defining desires in negative terms. The picture of the Church terrorizing Stephen in *Portrait* through pandying and sermons, which make him throw up, is relatively mild because Clongowes was a genteel upper-class school.

Richard Ellmann reports that in 1893 Joyce was forced for financial reasons to attend a more demotic Christian Brothers school and that he never mentioned it either in his work or to his biographer Herbert Gorman (*JJII* 35). Flann O'Brien presents an account of one of the numerous Christian Brothers schools, and his biographer Anthony Cronin calls it credible: "No matter how assiduous or even intelligent a student was, he was bound to get a hiding every day of his school life."[33] Joyce knew that being whipped continually on the buttocks was a common practice in Irish education (which he saw as influenced by England). It was felt that boys had to sustain such treatment to become men, and this buried world of "perversion" is behind HCE'S final appearance, for his mind would have to be shaped by the actuality of religion and education. Because insecurity leads to assertion in Joyce's work, the homoerotic passages are followed by the image of heterosexual desire, in the form of Issy (526–28).

The extensive and gross series of references to piety as a homosexual system recurs throughout the chapter, being established by a passage in which Yawn tries to differentiate himself from his bad brother by insisting that he has "received the habit." Here the process of joining a monastery is presented as entering a regime of homoerotic sensitivity in lines such as "removed my clothes from patristic motives" and "touching the other catachumens" (483.32–484.12). I have space to mention only a few lines from this sequence when it reaches a sort of climax (at page 520).

It is as if Joyce were reversing Stephen's claim in *Portrait* that all of the priests he has known have been virtuous (*P* 155–56) and suggesting the possibility that Father Dolan might not have been so. As Dolan goes from one classroom to another, beating boys, he repeatedly asks whether any boy "wants flogging" (*P* 48, 51), with the ambiguous "wants" as "deserves" or "desires." It serves the purpose of the Church to convince the boys that if they have sinful thoughts, they must have a desire to be flogged. After some especially vivid "flogging," Dolan might get so excited that he would retire to his room to rest and relieve himself, an abuse that could not be detected.

Such a possibility is raised in a passage on Saint Matthew, who can be aggressive in his questioning of Yawn (522.01–21): "Father MacGregor was desperate to the bad place about thassbawls and ejaculating about all the stairrods and the catspew swashing his earwanker" (520.04–06). Being "desperate to the bad place" may mean that he has reached a dangerous point of sinfulness. Bawling caused by an ass ("thassbawls") in relations to stairrods (balusters) makes MacGregor so desperate that he wanks himself, a British slang term for masturbation that goes back to the nineteenth century,[34] as implied by the phrase "swashing his earwanker."

The system is already understood to operate through sexual dominance in *Portrait*, though it is concealed by censorship. In the first chapter, Simon Moonan is referred to as the prefect's "suck" (*P* 11). In chapter V, the Dean of Studies tells Stephen that if he tries hard, he may be as successful as Simon Moonan. Stephen responds, "I may not have his talent" (*P* 190), which refers to Moonan's talent for sucking. That this sucking may be figurative does not keep such debasement from remaining in force through the pious or Shaun side on which HCE has to depend to build within the system. If the homosexuality represents HCE's sensitive side, that sensitivity is shaped by the educational system.

One Conclusion

How are we to evaluate the HCE that emerges triumphant at the end of III.3? Philip Kitcher celebrates this "sustained upturn" because he feels that the purpose of the *Wake* is to show how to achieve harmonious identity.[35] Kitcher makes perceptive points, and his views may have wide appeal, but I do not think the purpose of the *Wake* is to form an ideal HCE. In *The Sigla of "Finnegans Wake,"* Roland MacHugh, using the siglum for HCE, claims, "If we contrast the . . . [HCE] of book I with that of book III we see in the first case a passive victim of xenophobia and in the second a sadistic instrument of oppression. . . . Comparing III.3 with I.3–4 we may call it . . . [HCE's] comment on the populace as opposed to their comment on him."[36]

The submerged viewpoint of the people, however, gives a subversive charge to every attempt at a higher view. That HCE comes apart in the first book and comes together in the third may be related to the stages of sleep that Bishop traces through the *Wake*.[37] Entering sleep, HCE opens up his personalities, but as he moves toward waking, he grows unified and aggressive. This movement is one of the ways in which III.3 is a microcosm of the novel, leading to the concentration of prolific uplift in "Haveth Childers Everywhere," an uplift that is inconceivable without the disintegration that precedes it to map out its conflicting substance.

Even though it is unrelentingly aggressive and incessantly ironic, the final summation of his achievements is deeply beautiful (547–54). Historically, the domination of the male and the powerful has created the world we know and the spaces where we live, love, and enjoy. There is enough sardonic undertone in the concluding pages to keep us aware that this structure is ridiculous, but it is within this ridiculous structure that beauty, meaning, and feeling have been found throughout human history, and this adds a level of poignancy to "Haveth Childers Everywhere." The alternative possibilities that have been evoked as losses intensify the wonder of a damaged grace.

In the simplest mathematical terms, it is finally the division or the irrational aspect of numbers that gives the multiplication (what can be clearly enumerated) its reality, its ability to encompass the infinity of the situation. This subjectivity cries out behind the objectivity. And Joyce does not end with HCE's bragging, which, as I suggest, is enhanced by having a pitiful undercurrent. As I argue in *Joyce's Waking Women*, the *Wake* ends with ALP's rebellion (627–28).[38] Moreover, the fourth book of the *Wake* also presents the rising of the downtrodden part of the world represented by Asia. This insurrectionary drive is already present as a counterforce in III.3. Without it, the ending would be merely boastful rather than sublime. The daughter in the father makes him human as he dehumanizes her, to prepare for her final insurgent carrying of humanity beyond his wake in book IV.

Notes

1. Good readings of this chapter include those by Joseph Campbell and Henry Morton Robinson, *A Skeleton Key to "Finnegans Wake,"* ed. Edmund Epstein (1944; Novato, Calif.: New World Library, 2005), 287–320; William York Tindall, *A Reader's Guide to "Finnegans Wake"* (New York: Farrar, Straus and Giroux, 1969), 253–83; Danis Rose and John O'Hanlon, *Understanding "Finnegans Wake"* (New York: Garland, 1982), 242–64; John Gordon, *"Finnegans Wake": A Plot Summary* (Syracuse: Syracuse University Press, 1986), 236–53; Edmund L. Epstein, *A Guide through "Finnegans Wake"* (Gainesville: University Press of Florida, 2007), 189–228; and Philip Kitcher, *Joyce's Kaleidoscope* (Oxford: Oxford University Press, 2007), 215–32.

2. These words for fear in various languages are indicated in Roland McHugh's *Annotations for "Finnegans Wake,"* 3rd ed. (Baltimore: Johns Hopkins University Press, 2006). I am indebted to McHugh in many other references in my essay.

3. William Blake, *The Complete Poetry and Prose of William Blake*, newly rev. ed., ed. David V. Erdman (New York: Doubleday, 1988), 40. The quote is from *The Marriage of Heaven and Hell*, which Tindall refers to as "one of Joyce's favorite books" (11).

4. James Joyce, "Realism and Idealism in English Literature," in *Occasional, Critical, and Political Writing*, ed. Kevin Barry (Oxford: Oxford University Press, 2000), 177, 179, 175.

5. Alain Badiou, *Being and Event*, trans. Oliver Feltham (London: Continuum, 2006), 434.

6. Finn Fordham, *Lots of Fun at "Finnegans Wake"* (Oxford: Oxford University Press, 2007), 184. His chapter on "Nirccississes" is one of two recent fine genetic readings that focus on parts of III.3. Another is Jean-Michel Rabaté's essay, "The Fourfold Root of Yawn's Unreason: Chapter III.3," in *How Joyce Wrote "Finnegans Wake,"* ed. Luca Crispi and Sam Slote (Madison: University of Wisconsin Press, 2007), 384–409.

7. The notes for Ellsworth Mason and Richard Ellmann's edition of *The Critical Writings of James Joyce* (New York: Viking, 1959) say, "Blake's Albion, the universal man who symbolizes eternity, is related to that other giant form, Finnegan, in whose life, death, and awakening Joyce finds all human enterprise and aspiration" (*CW* 214).

8. Sigmund Freud, *The Ego and the Id: The Standard Edition of the Complete Psychological Works of Sigmund Freud*, ed. and trans. James Strachey et al., vol. 19: *The Ego and the Id and Other Works (1923–1925)* (London: Hogarth, 1966), 29.

9. Campbell and Robinson, *Skeleton Key*, 309.

10. Gordon, *Plot Summary*, 242.

11. Epstein, *Guide*, 196.

12. In his *Gaelic Lexicon for "Finnegans Wake," and Glossary for Joyce's Other Works* (Berkeley: University of California Press, 1967), Brendan O'Hehir says that *Crom*, pronounced krum, means "crouching" and was an ancient idol overthrown by St. Patrick. *Abu* means "to victory!" (268).

13. Jen Shelton, *Joyce and the Narrative Structure of Incest* (Gainesville: University Press of Florida, 2006), 19–22.

14. Sheldon Brivic, *Joyce's Waking Women: An Introduction to "Finnegans Wake"* (Madison: University of Wisconsin Press, 1995), 102–7.

15. Luce Irigaray, *This Sex Which Is Not One*, trans. Catherine Porter (Ithaca: Cornell University Press, 1985), 170–91.

16. Joyce, *Occasional*, 180.

17. Brivic, *Joyce's Waking Women*, 60–62.

18. Edward W. Said, *Culture and Imperialism* (New York: Vintage, 1994), 80–97.

19. William Faulkner, *Absalom, Absalom!* (New York: Vintage, 1990), 87, 93.

20. "Bristol," *Encyclopedia Britannica*, 1969 ed., 4:220.

21. See the notes for 544.20 and 545.02 in McHugh's *Annotations*.

22. Dominic Manganiello, *Joyce's Politics* (London: Routledge and Kegan Paul, 1980), 67–114.

23. Claude Levi-Strauss, *The Elementary Structures of Kinship* (Boston: Beacon, 1969), 36.

24. Two of these works by Dali are the drawing "City of Drawers" and the statue "Venus de Milo of the Drawers," both done in 1936. See Robert Descharnes, *The World of Salvador Dali* (New York: Harper & Row, 1962), 164, 165, 222. The passage in which Dali seems to be referred to was not present in the 1929 proofs for *transition*, so it does not seem that it could have been added to the chapter until late 1936. See *JJA* 59:25.

25. The most striking example of this pattern appears when one of the evangelists holds three T-shaped objects to Yawn's temple, lips, and breast, and Yawn perceives three different images that represent members of the family, probably Shaun, ALP, and HCE (486.14–31).

26. Anne Enright, remarks after a reading from her novels at the XXXIII International James Joyce Symposium in Trinity College, Dublin, on June 12, 2012.

27. Rabaté, "Fourfold Root," 404.

28. Ibid., 390.

29. Joyce, *Occasional*, 94.

30. John Bishop, *Joyce's Book of the Dark: "Finnegans Wake"* (Madison: University of Wisconsin Press, 1986), 382.

31. Luce Irigaray, *Speculum of the Other Woman*, trans. Gillian C. Gill (Ithaca: Cornell University Press, 1985), 180–90, 243–365.

32. Jacques Lacan, "The Signification of the Phallus," in *Écrits: A Selection*, trans. Bruce Fink (New York: W. W. Norton, 2002), 271, 275.

33. Anthony Cronin, *No Laughing Matter: The Life and Times of Flann O'Brien* (New York: Fromm International, 1998), 25.

34. See Richard A. Spears, *Slang and Euphemism: A Dictionary of Oaths, Curses, Insults, Ethnic Slurs, Sexual Slang and Metaphor, Drug Talk, College Lingo, and Related Matters* (New York: Signet, 2001), 369, 375.

35. Kitcher, *Joyce's Kaleidoscope*, 216.

36. Roland McHugh, *The Sigla of "Finnegans Wake"* (Austin: University of Texas Press, 1976), 22.

37. John Bishop, "Introduction," *Finnegans Wake* (New York: Penguin, 1999), xiv–xxv. Of the various interpretations of the Wake, Bishop's idea that it is about the world of sleep, developed in Joyce's *Book of the Dark*, is one of the most satisfying, and of course the idea of sleep is made obvious in III.3.

38. Brivic, *Joyce's Waking Women*, 94–108.

16

The Porters, Polypragmatic Paradigms, and Pseudoselves in III.4

RICHARD BROWN

What It's All About

In the penultimate chapter of *Finnegans Wake,* Joyce offers a domestic scene of the Porter family which, for all its Wakean strangeness, contains trace elements of the domestic scenery of the "Calypso" and "Ithaca" episodes of *Ulysses* and the final bedroom scene of "The Dead." The chapter is haunted by narrative *mimesis* or holds out the promise of it. Readers from Anthony Burgess, Edmund Wilson, and John Gordon, to the describer writing on the back cover of the 2012 Oxford University Press edition, present the *Wake* as the dream of—or as a story about—the Porter family of Chapelizod. It is to this chapter they most credibly refer.[1] This book is the *Wake,* though, and the kind of mimesis we are given is not contained by the Aristotelian unities. It invokes stranger, more dreamlike, more plural and potentially unrealizable realities, a radically unsettling variety of "unities," subjects, representational paradigms, and points of view.

Finnegans Wake is a polyvocal novel, then, in even more radical ways than are the novels of Dostoyevsky according to the classic account given by Mikhail Bakhtin.[2] It is more multivoiced in more ways and also more determined to explore the multiple potentialities of meaning that can be produced by experimental verbal reformation. These dimensions of the *Wake* make it hard or even impossible to finally settle on what it is about. Its subjects may be almost as many as its readers, and it may in the end be about nothing more than its own polymorphous self.

While we can begin by saying that this chapter is all about the Porter family, we may soon come to think that it is also about what it might mean for a text to be about something or about the various ways by which its reality might be seen to be. For one early reader, Margaret Solomon, this "fourth watch" of Shaun "is about watching" and, of course, in more senses than one.[3] We might reasonably expect a text called *Finnegans Wake* to be about, among other things, waking up or being awake at night, as the parents of small children often are. This chapter takes place just before and up to dawn. We can discern markers of clock time in "half past quick in the morning" and "kicksolock in the morm" (583.30, 584.03), and most readers pick out a core of action in which the parents wake to soothe their restless children back to sleep and then return to their bed. Yet III.4 is also about watching as a spectator does. The children may see their father in an exposed state, and we can approach the chapter through its self-consciousness about watching and about the various kinds of performance—theatrical, cinematic, sporting, and sexual—that may be watched. The narrative moves through a series of "positions." Figuring out whether these are positions adopted by the characters, by different narrators, or by differing positions that might need to be adopted by the reader is only one of the decisions the reader will find it difficult to make, as they attempt to locate their "whenabouts" and to "Expatiate then how much times we live in" (555.03–04).[4]

In III.4 the *Wake* family, who more usually appear in bewildering variations of their Earwicker and Plurabelle names, are introduced as the Porters, and they appear to be located "at home" in their pub in Chapelizod at the western edge of Dublin between the River Liffey and one side of Phoenix Park. The particular location is present in its physical geography and in its historical and cultural resonances, such as the Phoenix Park murders of May 1882, and in more arcane personal echoes of Joyce's father and a job he had in a distillery there from 1873 to 1876 before Joyce was born.[5]

What, a reader might ask, does the use of this version of the family name imply? Perhaps the first resonance of the name is with the definitive Irish-Dublin export "porter" or dark ale, quite likely to be served in a Chapelizod pub, though better known by another family name, Guinness. Joyce explored associations with this, the most famous of Dublin's "porters," in a letter to Harriet Shaw Weaver on January 13, 1925 (*LettersI* 225). He explained to her that Benjamin Lee Guinness (1798–1868), grandson of Arthur (1725–1803), the founder of the brewery, was "Dublin's Noah" and already a key figure in the developing matrix of embedded, interlocking characters, along with his wife, Elizabeth (who Joyce wanted to compare to the fabliau figure of Noah's wife in the English medieval mystery plays), and his two sons, Arthur Edward and Edward Cecil (Lords Ardilaun and Iveagh), who were senior members of the family in Joyce's lifetime. The Irish dark ale, he observes, might be named "*dub lin,*" the black pool from which the whole city takes its Gaelic name. The word *guineeser* (565.10–11), numerous references to the trade of "licensed vintner" (580.24), repeated pseudo-namings (from "noe" [561.05] to "Nuah-Nuah" [590.17]), and connections to the biblical story of Noah's drunkenness and exposure to his sons in Genesis 9:22, the rainbow, and even the other Old Testament warring sons, Esau and Jacob (563.07–09, 563.23), may all count as being associatively connected to the Porter name.

Occurrences of that name in other literary and cultural works are also used by Joyce. Shakespeare's scene of the cursing, word-playing Porter in *Macbeth* is a vital intertextual reference point, and other traces of the play seem significant. The experience of night and the dreams of married couples are essential to both works, although Joyce's story is comic while Shakespeare's is tragic, and Joyce's version of "equivocation" is less a form of political duplicity and more an inevitable feature of the instabilities of the written word that becomes his creative material. Alongside Shakespearean high culture, Joyce invokes the popular music hall song "Oh, Mr Porter, What Shall I Do?" (571.20–21) about an unfortunate young lady who explains to a railway porter that she has boarded a train to Birmingham but mistakenly stayed on board until Crewe, with comic consequences.

Though not named in these direct ways, another significant point of intertextual contact may be with the mysterious "Mrs Porter," who appears as the lover or hostess of T. S. Eliot's cockney sex-criminal Sweeney in the section of "The Fire Sermon" of *The Waste Land* (lines 45–50). Like Joyce's Porters, this contemporary modernist literary cousin is built out of a dense polylingual cluster of intertexts which (in the course of Eliot's six lines) include Marvell's "To His Coy Mistress," a section of John Day's 1641 poem *The Parliament of Bees* about Diana and Actaeon, Ovid's *Metamorphoses*, and the American popular ballad about a native American couple called "Red Wing."[6] Unlike Eliot's dark creations, though, Joyce's Porters are "very nice people" and such a "united family" that they "care for nothing except everything that is allporterous" (560.23, .28, .30–31).

The place, like the names, is defined by means of association with intertextual anchoring points. Sheridan Le Fanu's Victorian gothic novel *The House by the Churchyard,*[7] for instance, fully describes the Chapelizod setting. The novel is invoked at various moments in the *Wake* (most densely in book I, chapter 4, 80.04–12) and here in III.4 Joyce includes the names of three characters: "Gipsy Devereux," "Lylian," and "Black Atkins" (563.20, 588.18). These allusions clinch the correspondence with a novel where strange occurrences abound, even if a more traditional kind of mimesis than Joyce's is needed to allow its gothic and fantastical discourse to operate.[8]

Discovering, recalling, or revisiting any one of these intertexts may satisfy some of the varying desires for meaning on which reading the *Wake* often depends, though none on its own will satisfy them all. A proliferation of mimetic paradigms and discourses are woven into the chapter: narrative prose fiction, the visual arts, theater, cinema, ballet, domestic architecture, the courtroom, the formal toast, advertising, a royal visit, matrimonial case study, crime scene reporting, pornography, the prescribed set moves of such games as chess and cricket, sex manuals, the confessional, and Freud's case study of the "primal scene," experienced, repressed, and displaced in the memory of his "Wolf Man."[9] Such a proliferation of associated scenes redraws the borders of the seen and the obscene and, as conventional mimesis becomes dissipated and dissolved, draws attention to the structures, systems, and discourses of representation itself.

The scene-setting in the opening pages of the chapter is markedly self-conscious. In seven introductory paragraphs, each of which opens with a lowercase letter, members of the extended Porter household are listed as a cast of characters or as actors from a theatrical company. In turn we have such Wakean personae as the four old men or "kinderwardens," who watch the four corners of the beds of the twin sons, Kevin and Jerry, and the daughter, Isobel; "Havelook," the night watchman (556.23) whose job it is to wake and watch; "Kothereen the Slop" (556.32), the bar or kitchen maid; the twelve pub customers or jurors; the "nine with twenty" girls (558.22); and the couple themselves, "Albatrus Nyanzer" and "Victa Nyanza" (558.27–28). Here they assume the names of the great lakes that marked the climax of Richard Burton and John Hanning Speke's voyage of exploration for the conflicted source of the Nile: what Joyce calls elsewhere its paradoxical "soorcelossness" (23.19)—and by implication the ultimate sourcelessness of everything, establishing a suitably problematic prototype for the many roads and journeys that appear.[10]

Unusually perhaps, Joyce himself gave a clue to what he thought the episode of III.4 was "all about." The first section of the chapter that he drafted, as we can see from a letter to Harriet Shaw Weaver on October 10, 1925, is the one which now appears midway through (576.18–577.35) and which draws upon the discursive paradigm of a prayer. It is, as Joyce put it, "a fervent prayer to the divinity which shapes our roads" (*LettersI* 234). The chapter is supposed to be "all about roads" (*LettersI* 229, 232), and while the completeness of that intention seems questionable, the idea of roads reminds us that Chapelizod is an "upturnpikepointandplace" (3.22) on a turnpike to the west of the city; that HCE appears here with a signpost or "stark pointing pole" (566.34–35); and that places can be ones of motion as well as ones of rest.

Mimetic Paradigms

On the most reassuring mimetic level, we are given some conventional grounding in the "interior of dwelling on outskirts of city," an "Ordinary bedroom set" with "Salmonpapered walls," "Bed for two with strawberry bedspread," "Woman's garments on chair," and so on (558.35–559.16). The account of the interior architecture identifies clearly enough the "two rooms on the upstairs" (561.01–02, 562.17) in which "dadad's lottiest daughterpearl" (561.15) and the twins are asleep, and the "chequered staircase" with "one square step" that leads to them (560.09–10). Repeated hints enable us to retain our bearings in this represented domestic space as the couple return, for example, to the "base of the chill stair" (580.23), and then as we (and also "the man in the street") see their love-making, "Casting such shadows to Persia's blind" (583.14–15), from outside the dwelling.

The "Chamber scene" (559.01) recalls other ones in Joyce's works, such as the final scene in "The Dead," where Gretta's clothes are likewise thrown over a chair (*D* 175), or the "Calypso" episode of *Ulysses,* where Bloom has to feel his way around Molly's discarded underwear to get to her library book (*U* 4: 321–23). Like the Blooms' bedroom in 7 Eccles Street, the Porters' bedroom has a picture on the wall: "Over mantelpiece picture of Michael, lance, slaying Satan, dragon with smoke" (559.11–12). Perhaps this picture is one of many popular reproductions of Raphael's *St. Michael Slaying the Dragon,* which once hung in the royal bedchamber at Versailles and is now in the Louvre and reproduced in many places, from Milton's *Paradise Lost* (book 6, lines 316–30) to the fountain on the Boulevard St. Michel in the bohemian quarter of Paris, which was Joyce's "home" in the 1920s and 1930s. Being such a key text in the history of representation, it inevitably also foregrounds the larger theme of representation itself.

A host of other mimetic paradigms are used in the chapter. Terms from film and stage abound. "Stagemanager's prompt" (558.36), "Chamber scene," "Ordinary bedroom set," and the idea of a "dumbshow" precede the main action and, as in Shakespeare's *Hamlet*, suggest the theater. At the same time, "Closeup. Leads" (559.17–19), followed by "Closeup. Play!" "Callboy," "Footage" (559.29–31), and "Replay!" (560.06) mix terms from theater and film direction. The positioning of the male and female "leads" and the marking of their emotions—"exhibits rage," "exhibits fear" (559.24, 559.27–28)—suggest the evolving acting styles and pragmatics of direction from the era of silent cinema. Further cinematic terms scattered through the episode include "soundpicture" (570.14), "projector" (576.18), and "Regies Producer with screendoll Vedette" (577.15–16), as *regisseur* can be a French term for producer and *vedette* one for star.

The years between the drafting of the episode in 1925 and its publication in *transition 18* in 1929 were important in the rapidly developing technology and art of the cinema. The freestanding term "Close up" may remind us of the title of a contemporary magazine started by millionaires Kenneth Macpherson, Bryher, and poet H.D., which ran from 1927 to 1933 and was one of the first to take cinema seriously as an art form.[11] For Walter Benjamin, the growth of cinematic devices such as "close up" and "slow motion" represented profound changes in the modern mass-consciousness of seeing and knowing, changes which are not hard to see also at work in *Finnegans Wake*.[12]

Discussions about the development of early cinema in relation to avantgarde theater and the visual arts were clearly in play, from Futurism to modernist literary writers such as Virginia Woolf.[13] Jean Cocteau, for example, complained about cinema's "wrong turning" when it tried to "photograph theatre" and claimed that the 1919 expressionist classic *The Cabinet of Dr Caligari*, "which consists in flatly photographing eccentric sets," was an "even more serious mistake."[14] Joyce, on the other hand, in III.4 relishes the confusion of the theatrical, cinematic, and visual arts. This helps him to develop an exploration of the theatricality of identity which had been a feature of his writing at least since the "Scylla and Charybdis" episode of *Ulysses*. Their languages help him to formulate an expression of the plural and polymorphous nature of identity in which each person may be "another like that alter but not quite such anander and stillandbut one not all the selfsame" (581.32–33).

It is fundamental then that the chapter should be so determined to proliferate paradigms of represented action. A cluster of terms from the game of chess surrounds the instruction to "Play" (559.29): "Discovered . . . Check" (559.21–22), "nanny's gambit," "eight and eight sixty four," "knight" (559.34–36), "queen's lead," "His move," "Two pieces," "pawn," "castle," "chequered," "one square," and "stalemating" (560.01–11). We then have terms from the board game backgammon (where the players can "double") and the card game whist (560.11–12), by which time the language of games seems to have taken over that of film and stage. Specialist vocabularies from games of many kinds, familiar and more abstruse, are woven in. These include horse racing and betting odds, "One to one bore one" (583.10), "tyddlesly wink" or tiddlywinks (583.35), "Polo," "Pelouta," the favorite Basque sport *pelota* (567.35), and the English public school game fives (589.27).

One of the best known, densest, and most prolonged verbal clusters uses terms from the game of cricket to describe the parents in bed in their "Third position of concord" (582.29–583.25). Cricket is played on a "pitch," which has a marked "crease," and two stands of three wooden "wickets," which are topped by "bails," making them resemble HCE's three-pronged siglum in its upright form. There are two teams: one presents a "batter" who has an "innings," and the other one bowls various types of "bowling" ("yorkers," "bouncers," and "googlie") and has fielders who stand in various fixed field positions that have such unmistakable names such as "cover point," and square leg ("square to leg") or the wicket keeper who fields "behind the stumps." If he can "break his duck" (i.e., score beyond zero), the batsman scores runs, while he is still "not out." These are recorded as a number, although in a real game they never reach a score as high as the Noah-like "nine hundred and dirty two not out," which we find here. If no runs are scored from an "over" of six balls, the bowler is said to have "bowled a maiden over." It is easy to see how Joyce could choose cricket terms, with their "wickedy" levels of meaning, to help evoke the Porters' love-making scene.

A bewildering array of other paradigms and mixtures of them also come into play. During the account of the "second position of discordance" (564.01–02), the exterior Phoenix Park scene is described at first in the voice of a tourist guide: "much the admiration of all the stranger ones, grekish and romanos, who arrive to here" (564.08–10). The passage recalls one of the most familiar and significant historical events to appear in Joyce's writing: the murders of British Chief Secretary Cavendish and Permanent Undersecretary Burke that took place in the year of his birth, 1882 (564.29–30). In Joyce's earlier works ("A Little Cloud" and the "Aeolus" episode of *Ulysses*) we are introduced to the legendary Dublin journalist Ignatius Gallaher, who made his name by a coded geometrical description of the route of the murderers' getaway for the American press. The geometrical flavor of the description here (564.10–11) may well owe much to that feat.

A more celebratory historical-political scene from an earlier period of the Union is also recalled (568.16–569.03): the Royal Visit to Dublin by King George IV in 1821 at which the then proud mayor, Abraham Bradley King, was instantly knighted, causing all the church bells to ring (569.04–16). For this scene Porter becomes "Sir Pournter" and "Lord Pournterfamilias," perhaps in recognition of his pub landlord's pouring skills.

Sex crimes and political crimes coalesce in Joyce's Phoenix Park. The park is the location of a mysterious incident involving Joyce's father, often recalled in the *Wake*. In "A Painful Case," James Duffy walks home through the park at night and witnesses a couple making love, which makes him feel "alone" and "outcast from life's feast" (*D* 117). Darker and more polymorphous sex scenes are suggested here with indications of flagellation (564.23–24) and Sodom and Gomorrah, "the pities of the plain." There may be a scarlet woman and a pimp lurking alongside Parnell in the formulation "scarlet pimparnell" (564.28).

The Phoenix Park scene collates the Freudian "primal scene" of the parents' love-making, witnessed if not fully understood by the child, with scenes of political union and disunion and may indeed at times recall the political nightmare world of the Macbeths. Unlike the murderous Macbeths, though, the parenting Porters probably stick to legal activities in their daytime world, even if it is legal language which provides one of the strangest paradigms for representing their dream world by night.

In one of the longest and most distinctive set pieces in the chapter, a full-blown "casus" in Jesuit casuistical style is presented. In it the Porters appear as Honuphrius and Anita (572.21–573.32), the lead actors in a surreal comedy of sexual infidelity in which everyone becomes implicated when their thoughts and actions are examined in such microscopic detail. Confessional culture and the legalistic gaze of the clerisy into the intimacy of the marital bedroom fascinated Joyce throughout his work from *Stephen Hero*, *Dubliners*, and *A Portrait* to the "Oxen of the Sun" and "Penelope" episodes of *Ulysses*. For Michel Foucault the policing and defining of sexual practices from the counter-reformation to twentieth-century modernity defines the boundaries of subjectivity, freedom, and power.[15] Even Foucault might have been astounded by the fantastical clerical legalism of this passage. In his Paris library Joyce held a book of such matrimonial cases in Latin compiled by M.-M. Matharan. According to Thomas Connolly, this item was "the most heavily marked of all the books in the Joyce library and obviously should be the subject of an independent study."[16] Connolly reproduces a number of the marked passages whose tone, language, and subject matter (such as prohibited degrees of relatedness or "consanguinuity") clearly connect to this one, though Joyce's version is much more fun to read than the original.

The passage may be understood as an extrapolation of all the various possible sexual ramifications of the dream scene between the parents, the children, and other characters: a coded debate about how a married couple make love legally when everyone else seems to be making love with everybody else. Michael the priest has "debauched" Anita, so his role as judge is far from being a disinterested one. In context the "case" may connect to the father's request to commence or resume the couple's interrupted love-making to which they are "Legalentitled," he says (571.28). In the second part of the case a financial debt is discussed which plays on the metaphor of conjugal duty or "conjugal debt" that describes marital sex in some casuistical writing.

After such a lengthy and complex passage as this one, it is a relief to recall that *Finnegans Wake* also contains refreshingly brief and almost realistic snatches of dialogue. Here the parents decide to go back to bed:

—He sighed in sleep.
—Let us go back.
—Lest he forewaken.
—Hide ourselves.

Then with a hint of Pepys:

—To bed. (576.10–17)

The final two words recall the direct narrative style and selfhood of Samuel Pepys's diary, which Joyce reinforces as the couple continue, in its often quoted line, "On to bed!" (577.36). Though the name Pepys does not appear in its full form, it is typical to find a punning trace of it in a chapter about watching, when the mother is described as her husband's "peepingpartner" (580.26). As in Pepys, there is a certain realistic groundedness in this chapter's narrative of returning to bed.

Labyrinthine Pseudoselves

It is, no doubt, worth paying special attention to the passage which follows, where the parents begin their return voyage to bed, this being the passage with which Joyce began the composition of the chapter (576.18–577.35). A heading in the surviving manuscript "First Draft" version confirms that in Joyce's mind it was built out of the discursive paradigm of a "Prayer" (*JJA* 60, 21). No doubt one reason why genetic study is popular in contemporary

Wake studies is because it appears to offer a way to the core, the essential or original basic sense of a passage. In this aspect, genetic study corresponds with one of the most pragmatic reading strategies for new readers and group readers of the book who, as Fritz Senn advises, should "[t]ry to find if there is a basic, continuous or a dominant sense."[17]

The paragraph in question here typically is a single elongated sentence expanded by accumulations of appositional phrases that exfoliate paradigms. The core elements in the syntax usually remain, however obscured or deferred they may have become.[18]

If the reader were to reassemble the base syntax, they might extract a prayer that is addressed to the "giant builder of all causeways" (576.18–19), who is variously addressed in the first nine lines. He is asked to assist the main couple, "our forced payrents" (576.27), down the ladder or staircase ("laddercase" [576.30]). He is to guide them through "the labyrinth of their samilikes" (576.32–33), forty or so of which are then listed, in order that they might "recoup themselves" (577.20) in some other times and places (again elaborated) until they reach their destination. In simplest form the passage is a request to the god of roads to deliver the couple from a "loss of bearings" (576.34–35) on their way back to bed.

Finnegans Wake is definitively polyvocal, and all of these terms are polysemantic. Different readings may well seize upon different syntactic cores and emphasize different aspects of the polysemy, and the best readings of this or any other passage will attempt to take account of more than one level at a time. However, given some such basic structure as the above, the passage begins to yield up its sense or senses. The accumulating lists of potentially substitutable elements, whether or not a reader can ever hope to put more than a few of them into place at any one time, at least have a place to fall into.

In III.4, as elsewhere, words can complicate or resist the core syntax. The "main verb" in the main part of this sentence is an example, since the request to "prick this man and tittup this woman" (576.26–27) is rather surprising as the content of a prayer, somewhat shocking and somewhat obscure. Tracking back through the genetic record in the *Archives*, we can locate the manuscript drafts on which Joyce revises his main verbs, starting with *prick* and *bob*, then replacing *bob* with *twot* (*JJA* 62, 11) and, having changed that to *coign*, replacing it in turn with *thwait* before settling on *tittup* (*JJA* 62, 21). While *prick* and *tittup* reinforce the suggestion that this is a prayer for the resumption of the parents' happy sexual union, and *tittup* legitimately appears in the OED meaning "canter" and may recall the many onomatopoeic "tips" and "tups" of the "Sirens" episode of *Ulysses*, none of the substituted words seem especially appropriate as terms to convey the action of helping someone down a staircase, even on a horse or in a nightmare.

Around its syntactic core, deeper senses of the passage articulate complex Wakean models of composite identity in a language that is inflected by modern psychology and richly capable of expressing complex psychological states. The prayer is for the couple to progress on a journey of selfhood and identity "through the labyrinth of their samilikes and the alteregoases of their pseudoselves" (576.32–33). The journey back to bed is therefore a journey through past or alternative identities and possible worlds. It extends for several paragraphs in which parallels proliferate until the narrator concludes with a rueful conceptual clarity (which may apply to the situation of the characters or to that of the reader): "Scant hope theirs or ours to escape life's high carnage of semperidentity by subsisting peasemeal upon variables" (582.14–16). The reader and the couple must try to avoid "subsisting" on "variables," potentially resulting in "carnage" to their fixed identity, and yet there is "scant hope" that they will be able to do so.

If the bedroom scene-setting suggests the mimetic illustration of a Raphael, then the movement of the Porters through these shifting states of selfhood here suggests a more modernistic intertext from the visual arts. Marcel Duchamp's *Nude Descending a Staircase(2)*, first shown at the Armory Exhibition in New York in 1913, plays with representation to the extent that it was renamed "a staircase descending a nude" by one witty journalist at the time. In it Duchamp depicts motion in successive superimposed images of a human figure, suggesting the montage of still frames into motion that fascinated photography and cinematography at the time. In the nineteenth century, science had made use of early moving picture photography to observe the detail of animal and human movement, and Duchamp's work is glossed as being in dialogue with these experiments on the borders of art and science. One such example is the chronophotography or "stop-motion photography" of Étienne-Jules Marey (1830–1904) and Eadweard Muybridge (1830–1904), whose "Woman Walking Downstairs" from his 1887 picture series *The Human Figure in Motion* directly parallels Duchamp's scene.[19]

Joyce's replacement of static mimesis with a form of representation that captures the passage of the Porters through their alter egos and pseudo-selves reveals a suggestive contemporaneity with Duchamp. It may also recall the "planes and volumes" that Futurist sculptor Umberto Boccioni proposed as an alternative to the routine recourse to representing the nude in sculpture and suggests that the cinematic staging of the chapter may have these other forms of resonance, which are connected to the conceptual aspect of montage.[20] Boccioni himself formed a part of Joyce's conversation with Frank Budgen on their first meeting in Zurich in 1915.[21]

As the couple return on a "diamond wedding tour" (578.32–33) of their past selves, "down the scales, the way they went up" (579.02), the language may suggest the allotropic states by which carbon becomes diamond (fascinating to D. H. Lawrence in a famous letter to Edward Garnett about *Women in Love*)[22] or the chromatic scale of musical notes from which melody may be formed. In his drafts of the descent passage, Joyce's use of the words *degrade* and *degradation* in their root Latinate sense may suggestively recall the hero's obsession with the lightly stepping female figure on a *bas relief* from the repressed classical past in Wilhelm Jensen's novel *La Gradiva*, which was the subject of an important literary dream analysis by Sigmund Freud.[23]

No doubt such shifting states of identity might also have connected to Joyce's interest in a new and more complex version of Irish national and cultural identity, transformed by the conditions of diaspora and an emerging postcolonial identity at the time of the Irish Free State, which he voiced in a letter he wrote to Valéry Larbaud in July 1924 (*LettersI* 217). His Porters are "champion ethnicist[s]" and "the dibble's own doges for doublin existents" (578.12–14).

As we have seen, place in this chapter is localized or "Lucalised" (565.33) in Lucan and Chapelizod on the southwest corner of Phoenix Park. Yet the prayer passage invokes Finn, the mythic builder of the Giant's Causeway in Northern Ireland and a host of other mythic, hybridized, multileveled, and globalized locations, roads, and polydirectional journeyings or "corkscrewn perambulaups" (576.20). Many of these sites are associated with the British-Celtic Archipelago, as befits a chapter in which an "act of union" (585.25) takes place. Many go beyond it. They include "York from Leeds" (576.22), the Phoenicians (576.28), the "via mala, hyber pass" (Via Mala and Khyber Pass, 577.23), the road to "mandelays" (577.24), the Appian Way of "happyass cloudious" or Appius Claudius (581.22–23), Edinburgh's "long sizzleroads neath arthruseat" (577.28), the alpine track or country road (*land weg* in German, 577.23–24), and the Rainbow Bridge to Valhalla that concludes Wagner's "rhaincold," *Das Rheingold* (578.23). Any place can become all places and any journey any kind of journeying whether through place, time, or the unconscious. Berlin's *Unter den Linden* becomes a woman's "unterlinnen" (577.29–30), and there are a Septuagesima calendar puzzle and a jazzy stepping ma with her *cul* under her bustle in "steptojazyma's culunder buzztle" (578.22). The journey of the chapter is the hallucinatory journey of Swift's Gulliver, "Bigrob dignagging his lylyputtana" (583.09), through imaginary lands which in the *Wake* may also be the "*Gorotsky Gollovar's Troubles*" (294.18–19)—travels in the head (*golova* in Russian) or troubles of the head of the city-state.

The question of "Which route are they going?" (578.29) gives rise to a suitably digressive accumulation of alternatives, scattered, especially, with London place-names: "martial sin with peccadilly" (Marshalsea and Piccadilly, 577.04–05), Stepney (578.36), Chelsea (587.26), Cheapside and Covent Garden (577.30); the cluster of the Angel, Amen Corner, Norwood, Southwark, Euston, and the West End in "Angell sitter or Amen Corner, Norwood's Southwalk or Euston Waste" (578.29–30); or Cripplegate, Longacre, Seven Sisters, and Wormwood Scrubs (579.32–34).

Various Positions

We arrive at the "fourth position" in the final paragraph of a chapter whose narrative has in part been structured—like a range of bodily practices from cricket to theater, film, classical ballet, modern dance, and sexual intercourse—as a series of more or less defined "positions," according to which bodies may be arranged or a scene may be observed.

Developing the idea that people make love in such set postures or "positions" may still, of course, cause some shock in certain circles, but this notion is probably as old as human intercourse. A comparatively modern point of reference might be found in the early sixteenth-century Italian Renaissance erotic illustrations sometimes known as *Aretino's Postures*, painted by Giulio Romano, engraved by Marcantonio Raimondi, and subsequently accompanied by descriptive sonnets by Pietro Aretino. Romano was a pupil of Raphael and is quite probably named in the "romanos" already mentioned as appearing in the episode (564.09). This slight connection between Raphael and the suppressed tradition of the pornographic may not be quite sufficient to implicate the whole modern history of mimetic realism in the visual arts with the desire to represent the human body, especially the female body, in an erotic pose as some might be tempted to do. It is nevertheless fascinating to see the emergence of the representation of the unrepresentable in the form of a stylized series of "positions" in this example and to note its suggestive relevance to this section of the *Wake*.

The nearest things to sex manuals that the Victorian age produced were translations of the *Kama Sutra of Vatsayana* (1883) and *The Perfumed Garden of Sheyk Nefwazi* (1886) by Richard Burton who, like Joyce, had lived in Trieste. Various different postures in sexual intercourse whether for sexual pleasure, spiritual elevation, or reproduction are important in these texts, where they are described and named sometimes by analogies with animals. It is also the animalistic sexual posture of the partners which Freud particularly seizes on in building his interpretation of the "Wolf Man," a case history on which Joyce drew in composing the episode: "I mean the postures which he saw his parents adopt—the man upright and the woman bent down like an animal."[24] The turn-of-the-century pioneer sexologist Henry Havelock Ellis was another well known contemporary who was keen to apply his encyclopedic research on sexual practices and representations throughout world cultures and history to improving the sexual happiness of the late-Victorian married couple, proposing the then-radical suggestion that sexual pleasure might be increased by the variation of positions adopted by the couple during intercourse. His name is surely present in the "Wachtman Havelook seequeerscenes" (556.23–24) in which a man both "wakes" and "watches" the outline of the couple on the blind.

In the love letters which Joyce wrote to Nora when he was staying in Dublin in 1909 he declares: "I dream of you in filthy poses sometimes," and their correspondence explores the erotic potential of several such "filthy poses" (*SL* 184). In the contemporary world of free sex advice and freely available pornography, the advantages of various sexual postures for fun and fantasy—and for the maximal exposure of the sexual organs and body fluids to the camera for the excitement of the voyeur—can hardly be overlooked. But there is much surreal comic potential in sexual postures, too. In Ian McEwan's short story "Solid Geometry," the protagonist finds a section of his great-grandfather's diary which deals with the sexual positions. It describes a bodily position, on the absurd borderline of science and magic, into which the man can fold his partner in order to make her disappear, and he proceeds to put this strange idea into practice.[25]

In such contexts it is interesting to note that the fifty-something Porters are unlike most other Joycean married couples in their bedroom scenes, in that we actually do see them making love. They are seen in their four positions of marital "fornicolopulation" (557.17): "harmony" (559.21), "discordance" (564.02), "concord" (582.30), and "solution" (590.22–23). A quasi-musical structure or tonic *sol fa* of comic-surreal sexual gymnastics and voyeurism is woven into the narrative frame. The second position suggests seeing as much as doing: "meseedo" (564.04). The third position includes the word *Sidome* (582.30). Joyce's notebooks reveal his recognition of a cute synchronicity: the sequence of the fifth, first, and third notes in the scale, which would be named *si do me* in the English *sol fa*, is written in German in the letters *H*, *C*, and *E*, thus reinforcing the obvious homophone with sodomy. The "fourth position of solution" refers to "Two me see" (590.24), although it is not finally clear how much this "me" "johnny" is able to see of the "two" before they disappear. It is one of the delightful paradoxes of the physics of visibility (developed in the modern technology of photography) that, if the couple have been visible to an exterior voyeur at night as a silhouette projected onto a blind by an interior light, they will become invisible to such a viewer just as it gets light in the morning.

To one kind of Freudianism it is the truth of sex that provides the best grounding of the true and real. Yet there is, in the end, no more a literal mimetic *tetraptych* of sexual positions in this chapter than there is simple mimesis anywhere else in the *Wake*. The four "positions" to different extents and in different ways may just as well imply the different points of view of a fourfold polyvocal kind of narration, which we have seen throughout the *Wake*, at least since the 1923 draft when Joyce merged his story of Tristan and Isolde with the characters of the four New Testament Gospel writers or the voyeuristic old men, who also represent the four provinces of Ireland. An early reader such as William York Tindall, for example, confidently referred to "Mark's monologue" as if coherently delivered by a knowable character, although his being named "Mark!" (564.02) might just as easily be an address to someone called Mark or an invitation to an unnamed person to pay attention.[26] Joseph Campbell and Henry Morton Robinson soon noted that the four positions are directly connected to the narrative points of view of the four gospellers of New Testament narrative.[27] Yet the narrative voicing is not so easy to comprehend in this way either, as its polyvocal quality transgresses this fourfold scheme, making it as hard to say who the narrative is spoken by at any one point as it is to say what it is about.

Take, for example, the closing picture of the parental couple as Humperfeldt and Anunska "wedded now evermore in anastomoses," presumably both to each other and to every other potentially analogous couple with the same or even with different names (585.22–23). What unites and/or separates them may be a moment of satisfactory sexual "Closure" or else one of frustration. The final line of the nursery song "Polly Put the Kettle On" is recast here as "You never wet the tea" (585.31), and to some readers this phrase, or "Never Again" (590.10), represent some kind of sexual failure for the couple or else a decision on their part to give up on love-making forever. Do the Porters "wake" in the sense that they are in mourning, like the Blooms, for a lost child?

Any such interpretation would evidently depend upon fixing a stable narrative point of view. An overly hasty interpretation apparently related to a misunderstanding of contemporary sex and birth control contributed to the widespread belief that the Blooms in *Ulysses* do not have sex after the death of Rudy, even though we know that Bloom practices a "withdrawal method" of contraception by ejaculating on Molly's arse. In that context the phrase "Withdraw your member" in III.4 (585.26) may have significant family planning (as well as maybe also legal and parliamentary) connotations. It is hard to say whether in the closing paragraphs the patriarch is described as being bankrupt or "bankrump" (590.03) partly, like Joyce's father, as a result of the "explosium of his distilleries" (589.36), or if he is a receiver of the divine covenant, rainbow, and mythic pot of gold as "formast of the firm" (590.15–16). If, as the references to "McKenna's insurance" (589.18) and "Lloyd's" (590.05) suggest, the economic theme here is focused on the paradoxical workings of the modern personal insurance business, the two states may not in fact be separate after all.

A negative ending to III.4 would at any rate be hard to reconcile with the joyful resurrection themes of Book IV that follow and the vindication of her husband offered by ALP in the form of the letter there. The ending leaves such narrative mimesis irresolvable, and the chapter dissolves like a dream.

In III.4 the Porters are awake at night, and/or waking up in ways that reflect the process of reading a book whose "pragmatic impossibilities," to quote Fritz Senn, "help to define the unnameable in pursuit of the undefinable" (78). We have the ghost or promise of mimesis which is supported but ultimately dissipated by a range of associated intertextual paradigms. As elsewhere in the *Wake*, in III.4 we have a wealth of such moments when the "whole concreation" becomes "a complex matter of pure form" (581.28–30) or when, in one of the book's many travel metaphors for being half awake, "It's only the wind on the road outside for to wake all shivering shanks from snorring" (577.36–578.02).

Notes

1. Anthony Burgess, in "What It's All About," the opening chapter of his *Shorter "Finnegans Wake"* (London: Faber, 1939), suggests that "Mr Porter and his family are asleep throughout much of the book" (7). See also Edmund Wilson, "The Dream of H. C. Earwicker," in *The Wound and the Bow* (London: Methuen, 1961), 218–43, and John Gordon, *"Finnegans Wake": A Plot Summary* (Dublin: Gill and Macmillan, 1986).

2. Mikhail Bakhtin, *Problems in Dostoievsky's Poetics* (Minneapolis: University of Minnesota Press, 1984).

3. Margaret Solomon, "The Porters: A Square Performance of Three Tiers in the Round," in *A Conceptual Guide to "Finnegans Wake,"* ed. Michael H. Begnal and Fritz Senn (University Park: Pennsylvania State University Press, 1974), 201.

4. Finn Fordham offers a sevenfold reading model in *Lots of Fun at "Finnegans Wake"* (Oxford: Oxford University Press, 2010), 7–36.

5. Thomas Hofheinz, *James Joyce and the Invention of Irish History* (Cambridge: Cambridge University Press, 2012). For Joyce's father's years in the Chapelizod distillery (1873–76), see John Wyse Jackson with Peter Costello, *John Stanislaus Joyce* (London: Fourth Estate, 1997), 67–72.

6. For a full annotation of Eliot's intertexts, see *The Annotated Waste Land with Eliot's Contemporary Prose*, ed. Lawrence Rainey (New Haven, Conn.: Yale University Press, 2005). Polypragmus is the name of a character in Day's *Parliament of Bees*.

7. Joseph Sheridan Le Fanu, *The House by the Churchyard* (London: Macmillan, 1899). Parodied in *Ulysses* and reputed to have been one of Joyce's father's four favorite books, Joyce requested details from it from Frank Budgen in letters of September 1933 and 1937 (*LettersI* 337, 396).

8. These references were added to the proofs in 1937: see *JJA* 62: 454 and 484.

9. Daniel Ferrer demonstrates this Freudian connection in *How Joyce Wrote "Finnegans Wake": A Chapter-by-Chapter Genetic Guide*, ed. Luca Crispi and Sam Slote (Madison: University of Wisconsin Press, 2007), 410–35.

10. To gloss "soorcelossness" for Harriet Shaw Weaver, Joyce wrote on May 13, 1927: "the source is not to be found any more than that of the Nile" (*SL* 322).

11. See Laura Marcus in Peter Brooker and Andrew Thacker's *Oxford History Critical and Cultural of Modernist Magazines: Volume 1* (Oxford: Oxford University Press, 2009).

12. Walter Benjamin, "The Work of Art in the Age of Its Mechanical Reproduction," in *Illuminations* (London: Fontana, 1973), 219–53.

13. Virginia Woolf, "The Cinema," in *Selected Essays* (Oxford: Oxford University Press, 2008), 172–76. See also Laura Marcus, *The Tenth Muse: Writing about Cinema in the Modernist Period* (Oxford: Oxford University Press, 2007), 99–178.

14. Jean Cocteau, quoted in Rene Clair, *Reflections on the Cinema* (London: William Komber, 1935), 15.

15. Michel Foucault, *The History of Sexuality* (London: Penguin Books, 1979).

16. Thomas Connolly, "The Personal Library of James Joyce," *University of Buffalo Studies* 22.1 (April 1955): 25–28.

17. Fritz Senn, "Vexations of Group Reading," in *"Finnegans Wake": Fifty Years*, European Joyce Studies 2, ed. Geert Lernout (Amsterdam: Rodopi, 1990), 70. I am grateful to the 2011–13 University of Leeds, School of English *Finnegans Wake* reading group who shared the re-exploration of this chapter with me.

18. Clive Hart's *Structure and Motif in "Finnegans Wake"* (Evanston, Ill.: North-

western University Press, 1962), 40–41, contains an important early description of *Wake* syntax in a brilliant parody of a *Wake* sentence.

19. See William Anastasi, "Joyce and Marcel Duchamp," in *tout-fait: The Marcel Duchamp Studies Online Journal* 2.5 (April 2003). Online at http://www.toutfait.com/issues/volume2/issue_5/articles/anastasi/anastasi1.html.

20. See Umberto Boccioni, "Technical Manifesto of Futurist Sculpture" (1912), in *Modern Sculpture Reader*, ed. Jon Wood, David Hulks, and Alex Potts (Leeds: Henry Moore Institute; Los Angeles: Getty Publications, 2012), 33–40.

21. Frank Budgen, *James Joyce and the Making of "Ulysses"* (Oxford: Oxford University Press, 1972), 198–99.

22. D. H. Lawrence, letter to Edward Garnett, 5 June 1914, in *The Letters of D. H. Lawrence: Volume Two, 1913–1916*, ed. George J. Zytaruk and James T. Boulton (Cambridge: Cambridge University Press, 1981), 183.

23. Wilhelm Jensen, *Gradiva*, with Sigmund Freud, *Delusion and Dream in Wilhelm Jensen's "Gravida*,*"* trans. Helen M. Downey (Los Angeles: Sun and Moon Press, 1993). The word is highlighted in David Hayman's transcription in *A First-Draft Version of "Finnegans Wake"* (Austin: University of Texas Press, 1963).

24. Sigmund Freud, "From the History of an Infantile Neurosis (The Wolf Man)" (1918), in *Pelican Freud Library: Volume 9*, trans. James Strachey (London: Penguin, 1979), 270–71.

25. Ian McEwan, "Solid Geometry," in *First Love, Last Rites* (London: Picador, 1976), 25–40.

26. William York Tindall, *A Reader's Guide to "Finnegans Wake"* (Syracuse: Syracuse University Press, 1969), 293.

27. Joseph Campbell and Henry Morton Robinson, *A Skeleton Key to "Finnegans Wake"* (London: Faber, 1947), 266, 267, 273, 275.

17

"Ricorso"

The Flaming Door of IV

VICKI MAHAFFEY

The final book of Joyce's carefully inscribed book of life and death, light and darkness, both embraces and defies conclusion. As the ticks of a clock mark the loss and continuation of time in the same moment, in Book IV of *Finnegans Wake* (the "Ricorso") the passage from night to day marks a simultaneous annihilation and rejuvenation of the book's two parental protagonists, HCE and ALP. Their "awakening" from sleep is also, counterintuitively, a kind of dying, as they pass the baton of life to the son and daughter who will replace them. Joyce depicts their "essence" as continuing not only in the bodies of their progeny but also in nature, specifically light and water, the rising of the sun and the falling of the rain. As he does throughout the book, Joyce treats these two requirements for natural life as male and female, respectively. But like all opposites in a world governed by the coincidence of contraries, male and female are not only opposed but also identical and reversible, like the twins they produced.

The "Ricorso," then, is not unlike the poem by Yeats that both Joyce and Stephen Dedalus sang to their dying mothers, "Who Goes with Fergus?" The speaker urges a young man and woman to look beyond and above the narrow confines of their love for one another and to see the whole of nature with the eyes of a poet, as embodied and eroticized in a continual, gigantic play of opposites. The main sexual opposition is between light and dark, represented in the contrast between the "brazen cars" of the sun and the shadows of the wood, as well as the connection between the "white breast of the dim sea" and the night sky, bejeweled with "all disheveled wandering stars."[1] In the

"Ricorso," Joyce extends the list of sexualized opposites from light and dark and male and female to life and death, soul and body, beginning and ending.

In the "Circe" episode of *Ulysses,* Lynch's cap ridicules Stephen's insistence that "Extremes meet. Death is the highest form of life. Ba!" (*U* 15.2098). When the cap says "ba," without the final "h," it not only looks back at the "bat" in "Nausicaa" ("ba" in Bloom's inner narrative) but it also looks forward to the "Ricorso," Joyce's most extensive exploration of the idea that "Death is the highest form of life." In this section, Joyce addresses death-life through the meeting of the extremes of light and darkness at sunrise, that time when the opposites of beginning and ending are also conjoined, recalling the image of the *uroboros,* the unending snake with his tail in his mouth. Annexing references to a range of sun gods (the Egyptian Ra; the Irish/Celtic Lugh; Jesus as the rising "sun" of God; Agni, the Hindu god of fire; and the Irish hero Diarmaid, to name only a few), Joyce explores what happens to the spirit or "personality"—what the Egyptians called the "ba"—in its journey through the afterlife. In some versions of Egyptian myth, the ba, often depicted as a bird with the head of a human, roams forth from the corpse by day but must return to it at night, a pattern that Joyce applies in *Finnegans Wake* to the living body in sleep (the ba flies forth from the body and returns upon waking). When the ba leaves the body, its goal is to be released from it and reunite with its "ka" or life force (which departed from the body at the moment of death) in order to form "akh." In the solar vision of the afterlife, the akh could choose to travel with Amen-Ra, the sun god, on his daily journey of death and rebirth.[2]

The best overview of Joyce's engagement with the Book of the Dead in *Finnegans Wake* is John Bishop's chapter, "Inside the Coffin," in *Joyce's Book of the Dark.*[3] Bishop beautifully describes how the Egyptian texts portray the heavenly journey of the sun through day and night as the movement of Ra (or Amen-Ra) in a sun boat that passes at evening into the kingdom of the dead, which was understood as "the domain and body of Osiris." Osiris became lord of the dead when, after the pieces of his body had been scattered over the landscape, he was re-membered and returned to life. In one account, it was Isis who reassembled him, but Bishop emphasizes the fact that Osiris's son Horus, another sun god, was also instrumental in reviving his father. Bishop concludes that in *Finnegans Wake,* Tim Finnegan (who fell) and Finn MacCool (who cannot be killed and therefore arises again and again) function much like the "team" of Amen-Ra (or Horus) and Osiris in the Egyptian mortuary texts. Joyce, like the Egyptians, uses scraps of a "hieroglyphic" story to connect the phenomenological experience of an individual living (and dying) in a body with the experience of a country (here Ireland) and with the cosmology of the heavens. What Bishop emphasizes less strongly is the generational dimension of the sun's navigation first through daylight and then through the darkness of Amenti (Bishop argues that Joyce preferred to call it "amentia," the loss of mind and consciousness), the world of concealment: the darkness actively gives life to the day, much as Osiris fathered Horus.[4] The father fathers the son (sun), and the sun in turn revives the father: this is the human generational story of how day follows night and vice versa.

The Coffin Books (usually inscribed on coffins) and the Book of the Dead (usually written on papyrus and placed in tombs) were designed as guides for the dead to help them find reanimation through the union of ba and ka and to avoid dying again in the afterlife. These books consisted of spells to help the dead navigate the Duat, the afterworld, which is also a world of the dark. By implication, Joyce is presenting *Finnegans Wake* as such a book, a "bokes of tomb" (597.06).

If we imagine *Finnegans Wake* against the backdrop of ancient Egyptian solar religion and its funerary literature, it allows us to recapture a vision of words as magical "spells" that are not readily comprehensible. Moreover, these spells are closely related to material existence: sometimes they were written on cloths used to wrap the bodies of the dead, and at other times they marked the coffin that contained the body. Moreover, the primary purpose of these spells was to preserve the "life" of the dead, even after death. The living also sometimes wrote to the dead to request their help. The fragments of strange writing inscribed on coffins or papyri are "letters" written to the dead and also for the dead to guide them toward continued life.

I propose a reading of *Finnegans Wake* as a book of enchanting (literally "musical") spells for the sleeping body and the wandering spirit. At the very end of the book, readers reach the point where rebirth and death converge. This is the time when the dead awaken and the living croak ("the quick quoke" [595.02]), a "magic moning" (608.19) when everything turns "rolywholyover" (597.03). The jackdaw (a songless bird) "still stilleth" (597.31) and "the torporature is returning to mornal" (597.32–33). "Into the wikeawades warld from sleep we are passing" (608.34). And it is a time when letters are written from the living to the dead and the dying to the living, cryptic letters of love, rebellion, hope, and despair. Everything tries to converse or conflict with its opposite as the condition of its continuation. The Ricorso falls roughly into four parts (Dirk van Hulle divides it into five):[5] the first concerns the rising of the sun and the "passing" of life and light from father to son, HCE to Shaun, and the last concerns the passing of the river of life (Liffey) into the ocean and the beginning of the rain (reign) of ALP's daughter in her stead (as ALP says to HCE in her final monologue, "He's for thee what she's for me" [620.33]). Light and water bookend the section: the two interior scenes concern Saint Kevin and his relation to water, and Saint Patrick (along with the druid Laoghaire) and his relation to fire.

Fire and Water

The episode begins in Fireland, an island, at sunrise. The punning link between Ireland and Fireland is underscored when the narrator riffs to the rhythm of the song, "God Save Ireland": "Good safe firelamp! hailed the heliots" (613.01). As the sun/son rises, the river Liffey is emptying herself into the ocean, experiencing a diffusion that is both a death and a rejuvenation as she returns to being a child borne by her father to a toy fair (628.08–09). But even the island of Ireland is conjoined with its opposite and counterpart: it is twinned with a "dark" Ireland, the island of New Ireland in the Southern Hemisphere (in Papua New Guinea), which along with New Britain is part of the Bismarck archipelago in Melanesia ("Milenesia waits. Be smark" [601.36]). The name Melanesia comes from the Greek words for dark and island, and it is one of three groups of islands in the Pacific in the southwest part of Oceania).[6] Like Ireland, New Ireland at the time Joyce was writing was agricultural and poor, with a population that was primarily black, speaking several local languages (an online Travel Guide numbers them at 715). The several references to local places in New Ireland (towns, such as Lamusong, 595.04, mountains, such as Lambel, 595.06, and bays, such as Fangelava Bay, "Fangaluvu Bight" [594.23–24]) serve as highly specific reminders that everything is completed by its opposite.

The main theme of the Ricorso is reformation (and succession: history repeats itself with a difference).[7] As Anna Livia Plurabelle says to her husband HCE in her final letter, "One of these fine days, lewdy culler [lady killer], you must redoform again" (624.19–20; she also says that according to his brother, he was brought up in "Brostal," or a borstal reformatory, 624.31–33). The motto of the MacCowell family was "[g]reat sinner, good sonner" (607.04, sun: *Sonne* in German), an abbreviated formula for reformation in which the son is also a rising sun. But language is also constantly being reformed (and deformed) in ways that obscure old meanings and license new ones, as *Finnegans Wake* itself testifies.

The chapter begins with the "eversower of the seeds of light," "lord of risings," "Pu Nuseht" ("the sun up" written backwards), speaking "to the cowld owld sowls that are in the domnatory of Defmut" (593.20–23). These cold souls to which the rising sun speaks are in a "domnatory," which is both a dormitory for sleeping and a place of damnation. "Defmut" is not only deaf-mute (an apt description of those who are sleeping) but also Tefnut, the Egyptian goddess of moisture who sat in judgment of the dead in the underworld, usually depicted with the head of a lion on which she carries the sun. She was born—with her brother Shu—when her father Atum masturbated. Through Tefnut, or sun-carrying moisture, fire and water are identified as versions of the twin principles of creation.

As the sun rises, and "an inedible yellowmeat turns out the invasable blackth" (594.32–33), the narrative makes sport with the east, yeast, breakfast, cocks and roosters, rainbows, Guinness, and the phoenix. "[Y]easterloaves" (598.20–21), for example, combines yesterday's loaves with Easter and its rising of the Son in the east. In the previous chapter HCE was described as "king of the yeast" (578.04). These disparate things all bear some relation to rising: the sun, bread, sleepers, the dead, and the rooster-penis-phoenix all rise or help others arise. Even Guinness is seen not only in relation to genesis but as a drink in which light rises to the top of the darkness after it is poured ("genghis is ghoon for you" [593.17–18], which combines the slogan "Guinness is good for you" with Genghis [Kahn] is going/goon for you; the promise of nurture and the threat of massive destruction are intertwined). The comic parallel between the cock crowing at sunrise, the re-erection of the penis, and the resurrection of the dead is given a homey familiarity through the prospect of breakfast—especially a breakfast of hen's eggs, tea, bacon, and freshly baked bread. But the east is not only the place where the sun rises. It is also associated with Easter, the time when the son/sun of God arose from the dead (associated in popular culture with eggs and Spring, the rebirth of the year). "Our shades of minglings mengle them and help help horizons. A flasch and, rasch, it shall come to pasch, as hearth by hearth leaps live" (594.15–17). Paschal time is associated as well with the rise of an independent Ireland, sparked by the deliberately timed Easter Rising of 1916. The connection between the long-desired resurgence of Ireland, sunshine, and the succession of generations is humorously apparent in the rendering of Sinn Fein as "Sonne feine" (fine son/fine sun, 593.08).

Perhaps the most overdetermined image of HCE in relation to sunrise (the rising of his son Shaun to replace him) is that of the phoenix. Joyce writes, "In the wake of the blackshape, *Nattenden Sorte* [dark coming on]; ... tamtam, the

Phoenican wakes" (608.28–32).[8] The phoenix is associated with Phoenix Park, and especially the obelisk of the Wellington Monument that serves as the giant HCE's penis. The phoenix is also a breed of rooster (another "cock") whose rising (and crowing) awakens others: "Conk a dook he'll doo" (595.30). The phoenix is associated with Phoenicians, Egypt (through Heliopolis), Jesus, and a resurrection that is also a finish (or "phoenish" [322.20]). The mythology of the phoenix (Indian, Egyptian, and later Phoenician and Greek) treats death and birth as coterminous, and it also suggests a mode of parthenogenetic reproduction from father to son (human repetition with a difference).

The sacred version of the phoenix in the Book of the Dead is a *benu*, a stork, heron, or egret associated with the god Ra and worshiped at Heliopolis. According to the 11th edition of the *Encyclopedia Brittanica*, which Joyce regularly consulted, the *benu* was a symbol of the rising sun; it was called "the soul of Ra (the sun)" and the Sun's renewed "heart." According to an ancient poem on the phoenix attributed to Lactantius, the bird sings a sweet song to accompany the rising sun, which the sun god Helios would stop his chariot to hear.[9] The encyclopedia entry posits that the myth of the phoenix arose as a way of explaining how the sun rises.

The *Encyclopedia Brittanica* account includes additional details about the father-son relationship:

> According to the story told to Herodotus (ii.73), the bird came from Arabia every 500 years, bearing his father embalmed in a ball of myrrh, and buried him in the temple of the sun. . . . According to Pliny (*Nat. hist.* x. 2), there is only one phoenix at a time, and he, at the close of his long life, builds himself a nest with twigs of cassia and frankincense, on which he dies; from his corpse is generated a worm which grows into the young phoenix. Tacitus (*Ann.* Vi. 28) says that the young bird lays his father on the altar in the city of the sun, or burns him there; but the most familiar form of the legend is that in the *Physiologus* (*q.v.*), where the phoenix is described as an Indian bird which subsists on air for 500 years, after which, lading his wings with spices, he flies to Heliopolis, enters the temple there, and is burned to ashes on the altar. Next day the young phoenix is already feathered; on the third day his pinions are full grown, he salutes the priest and flies away. . . . [B]oth Horapollon and Tacitus speak of the phoenix as a symbol of the sun. (*Encyclopedia Brittanica*, 11th ed., s.v. "phoenix")

This history clarifies the way Joyce connects the diurnal fall and rise of the sun with the succession of the father by the son, as well as with sleep and waking, death and resurrection. References throughout the book to the color heliotrope (usually in relation to Issy, as in "Heliotrope leads from Harem" [610.36–611.01]) highlight the kinship between Issy as Isis and HCE as the phoenix ("phoenix" is also a reddish-purple color associated with the city of Heliopolis and sun worship). The image of the phoenix was important in early Christian art and exegesis because of the way it narrates the succession of the father by the son through autogenesis. The rising of God's son out of death becomes a pattern for the way generations of men succeed one another more generally. The rising of the sun is "supernoctural" (598.17)—that supernatural energy that rises again and again over the night. *Dominus* (Lord in Latin) is also "dorminus" (sleep) who commands the darkness ("Dies is Dorminus master and commandant illy tonobrass" [609.28–29], *tenebras*: darkness in Latin]).

The world is rejuvenated not only through the diurnal reappearance of light and heat, a movement replicated at the human level in a man's self-renewal through his "son," but also through the washing or cleansing of water through rain and baptism, a process Joyce genders as female. These two modes of renewal overlap in the playful depiction of soap as "sunlight"—a device Joyce first developed in the "Circe" episode of *Ulysses* when the lemon soap rises and becomes a talking sun. To see how the sun that represents male resurgence becomes the laundry soap whereby women clean up the dirt of the world, we must focus on a particular brand of soap, "sunlike sylp" (594.11–12): Sunlight Soap, manufactured by the Lever brothers ("Lever hulme!" [594.13]) from 1885 to 1930. The play on soap's relation to sunrise through the removal of (dark) dirt through the morning ritual of washing is also apparent in Joyce's riff on the catch phrase coined by Thomas Barratt, "Good morning, have you used Pears' soap?" The line was parodied in *Punch*, where a soap certificate is being filled out by a poorly washed tramp: he writes, "I used your soap two years ago and have not used any other since." This language is echoed in "Guld modning, have yous viewsed Piers' aube? Thane yaars agon we have used yoors up since when we have fused now orther" (593.09–11). (Lever Brothers took over Pears' Soap after Barratt's death in 1914; the takeover was completed in 1920.)

Kevin, Hydrophilic Woman-Hater

Anna Livia lives, laves (washes), and finally leaves ("leaves" here fluctuates in its meaning between noun and verb); a fragmented signature to a letter by her occurs early in the episode as "wassing seoosoon [washing see you soon, wishing to see you soon] liv" (595.08).[10] Her "son" Kevin, an avatar of Shaun, is not only sunlike ("His face is the face of a son" [602.12]); he also shares his mother's commitment to renewal through water. "Hydrophilos" (606.05), he sits in his "sate of wisdom, that handbathtub" (606.06–07) and meditates "continuously with seraphic ardour the primal sacrament of baptism or the regeneration of all man by affusion of water" (606.10–12). Ironically, Kevin's love of water—his mother, ALP, and "his holy sister" (605.36)—and cleanliness makes him not only "perpetually chaste" (606.01) but also misogynistic. In his fear of a sexual fall he throws Kathleen out of his rocky "bed" to her death in Lake Glendalough (the story is the subject of Thomas Moore's "By that Lake whose Gloomy Shore," an Irish melody that Joyce alludes to as "by that look whose glaum is sure" [600.36–601.01]). Kevin, with his propensity to "celibrate the holy mystery" (600.35) in a celibate manner, "exorcised his holy sister" (605.36), whom the narrator then describes as a lost city under the lake, "our lake lemanted, that greyt lack, the citye of Is is issuant (atlanst!) urban and orbal" (601.04–06).[11]

As HCE is being supplanted by his rising son, so ALP will be replaced by Issy, the cloud Nuvoletta, who is about to "fall" in the form of life-giving rain. "And she is coming. Swimming in my hindmoist. Diveltaking on me tail. . . . It's something fails us. First we feel. Then we fall. And let her rain [reign] now if she likes. Gently or strongly as she likes. Anyway let her rain for my time is come" (627.03–13).[12] ALP is "passing," and Issy is coming into her own not by rising but by falling out of her "great blue bedroom," the sky (627.09). As the sun dispels the darkness, the falling rain condenses from the cloud, an obscuring formation that Joyce associates with his difficult book, his "wolk [cloud in Dutch] in process" (609.31, "Work in Progress").

Men and women, then, are equally committed to renewal, to "[c]ontinuarration" (205.14), but by different—even opposite—movements. The new man rises, the new woman falls, but both do so playfully, "in ludubility learned" (607.03), even joyfully. HCE as Finn is also "Funn" (600.10), and ALP is a "Lough!" or lake that is also a laugh (601.07), like Minnehaha ("minnyhahing here from hiarwather" [600.07–08]). Although a poignant one, shot through with the losses and misperceptions of mortality, *Finnegans Wake* is still a comedy in the largest sense: it is an affirmation of reality in all of its painful and risible transience—"Nought is nulled" (613.14). In several respects the ending of *Finnegans Wake* is plotted in diametrical opposition to that of "The Dead": instead of discovering, like Gabriel, that it is time to set out on his journey "westward," the characters of *Finnegans Wake* are moving eastward, toward renewal (through death). Instead of moving to an intimation of mortality and sleep accompanied by the rhythm of an unusual snowfall, in *Finnegans Wake* the stress is on waking and resurrection, although the inevitability of death is neither forgotten nor denied. Instead, death is simply a "punct," part of the rhythm of an ongoing cyclical pattern of beginnings and endings. Darkness and snow are receding as the new day dawns: "Hail, regn of durknass, snowly receassing, thund lightening thund, into the dimbelowstard departamenty" (607.25–26). Joyce's position in *Finnegans Wake* approximates that of Wallace Stevens's poetic narrator in "Sunday Morning," in its paradoxical insistence that nothing is more eternal than that which is ephemeral: nothing "has endured / As April's green endures."[13]

Saint and Sage: Patrick and Laoghaire (608–15)

In *The Golden Bough,* Sir James Frazer includes an account of fire festivals throughout Europe. He calls one of the two main theories that have been used to explain these festivals "the solar theory," which argues that they were designed to be "sun-charms or magical ceremonies intended, on the principle of imitative magic, to ensure a needful supply of sunshine for men, animals, and plants by kindling fires which mimic on earth the great source of light and heat in the sky."[14] The phenomenon of sunrise acts as a subtext that unifies light, the east, Christianity, the lust for gold ("Goldselforelump! Halled they. Awed" [613.01–02]—to the rhythm of "God save Ireland"), the resurrection of the phoenix ("from ennemerable Aschias unto fierce force fuming"), the cockcrow, the anticipation of a breakfast of ham, eggs, and tea, the discoveries of day-*élèves*/tea leaves, and the motif of converting darkness to light, or ignorance to knowledge (otherwise figured as an act of conquering one's opposite). Even the Christian trinity is reconfigured in relation to the sun: father, son, and holy ghost appears as "the firethere the sun in his halo cast. Onmen" (612.29–30). It is later revised in the language of eggs, which contain little yolk "suns": "the farmer, his son and their homely codes, known as eggburst, eggblend, eggburial and hatch-as-hatch can" (614.31–33).

The sun is construed as a great fire on a hilltop, metonymically associated with smoke—the smoke of the Pascal fire lit by St. Patrick at Slane when he challenged the druids (and especially King Laoghaire) at Tara. What Muta calls "fumiste" (*fumus*: smoke in Latin) that rolls out of the Lord, "Domoyno" (609.24), is also the smoke that arises from peat fires in the morning. The hidden verbal links that support the God-home parallel are 1) the proximity of "Dominus" (lord) and domicile and 2) the pun on Patrick's name as "peatrick" or peat rick (as well as pea trick: "thuartpeatrick" [3.10]). Patrick's association with peat takes on a new (if buried) significance near the end of the passage, where peat is silently replaced with a synonym, sod (which rhymes with God), and Patrick is visited with sodomy (sod in me) while praying. (Laoghaire, or "Bilkilly-Belkelly-Balkally" [612.32], sticks his four fingers and thumb up Patrick's ass. Compare Buckley shooting the Russian general.)

The rising of the sun heralds the return of color to the phenomenal world, a fact emphasized by the reference to light shining through stained glass—the windows of the village church: what Joyce describes as a triptych depicting the progressive isolation of St. Kevin in one panel, the meeting of St. Patrick and the druid in the other, and a dimly illuminated St. Lawrence O'Toole, patron saint of Dublin, in the middle.[15] The emphasis on color is further enhanced by the many references to prismatic refractions of light, the seven-hued spectrum of the rainbow. In the background is the legend that King Laoghaire's druid blotted out the sun, which Patrick caused to reappear, whereupon the onlookers glorified Patrick's god. Laoghaire-Berkeley is described as being "for shouting [shutting] down the shatton [shadow/shutter/shat on] on the lamp of Jeeshees" ([612.33], the sun). Berkeley's championship of darkness here is not only a denial of Christ (as the son/sun) but also a rejection of women (Jesus is Jee *shees*) similar to that of Kevin and earlier the Jarl van Hoother when he shut the shutter upon the prankquean. It also plays with the inversion between anal penetration and the emergence of feces: he would have shat on the lamb/lamp of Jesus. The gesture of "up yours" is literally acted out on Patrick, aggressively mimicking in reverse the movement of darkness through the body.

Joyce wrote to Harriet Shaw Weaver that the first version of the "Saint Patrick and the Druid" sketch (written in 1923) describes "the conversion of S. Patrick by Ireland" (*LettersIII* 79), not the reverse. In the Ricorso, Joyce suggests that Patrick is "converted" by gaining a different understanding of light from his encounter with the druid. He grows more cognizant of the prismatic variety of color hidden in what seems to be invisible. He has learned that "divine" variation is internal, as he uses the shamrock to illustrate (what seems to be one God is actually three).

Part of what makes the encounter so difficult is that it is simultaneously several different encounters. Not only does St. Patrick compete with the druid over whose god is most powerful; Bishop Berkeley is also disputing with someone (Allan Sanson identifies the figure behind Patrick here as Sir Isaac Newton) about the nature of light and optics.[16] The episode is at the same time a retelling of the conflict between generations encoded in the story of how Buckley (here Berkeley) shot the Russian general (here Patrick) and how Napoleon (here Berkeley) shot Wellington's "big white arse" (here Patrick's). Sage (native) faces off against saint (invader) in a contest likened to a horse race, but what seems to happen is that it is not the older man who is "shot" or penetrated in the arse but the younger, Patrick. It is by being sodomized (an act here of violence, not love) that Patrick is "converted" to a more colorful and varied view of what enlightenment means.

Patrick (who was Roman British by birth, literally a *Roman* catholic named Sucat) is clearly both the saint and the foreigner; furthermore, through his denomination as Paddrock and his association with the shamrock, he becomes another incarnation of St. Peter, rock of the church, which recalls the Tree-stone (Tristan) dichotomy used to designate the twins, Shem and Shaun. Patrick is represented as drinking and fasting; he wears white and hums with his greyfriars; and he is subject to "eruberuption" (612.23, turning red, which underscores his Englishness).

Patrick's opponent, the druid, is not only King Laoghaire but also Berkeley (and Buckley). He is a sage whose "fiery grassbelonghead all show colour of sorrelwood herbgreen" (611.33–34), and he is elsewhere associated with thyme, parsley, spinach, cabbage, olives, and lentils. Not only do these references identify him with food (as Patrick was linked with drink); they also make him *green* (accented by a little fiery orange)—he is the Irishman; as a sage he is also literally a green herb. Like the Cyclops', the druid's vision tends to reduce everything—including orange—to green. As a druid, he is associated with both tree worship (as opposed to stones or the rock on which the Church was founded) and snakes—some scholars believe that when St. Patrick is credited with driving the snakes out of Ireland it is a reference to his victory over the druids. As Bishop Berkeley, of course, he is an Irish idealist philosopher who believes in the true inwardness of reality, but against the background of the rest of the book he reveals new identities: he is the three lipoleum boys who shot Wellington's harse/arse, and he is also Buckley, the Irish soldier in the Crimean war who shot the Russian general after seeing him defecate and wipe himself with a sod of turf (an evocation of *sod*omy combined with *ass-ass*-ination). The Russian general, avatar of HCE, by being Russian, gets associated with Bobrikoff, the Russian governor of *Finn*land who was assassinated on June 16, 1904.[17] When Berkeley puts his hand up Patrick's ass, he is acting out the metaphor buried in the word *assassination*. Moreover, although we know Wellington and Patrick as the "victors," Joyce represents them as assassinated—by their enemy and by history, represented by the four fingers (Mamalujo, the anal annalists) and the thumb, their "ass" who follows after them.

The revolution that is *Finnegans Wake* frees and constrains readers to experience revolutions of their own: upheavals that are at the same time historical returns. Instead of repeating the refrain "Teems of times and happy returns," the narrative warns that "Themes have thimes and habit reburns. To flame in you" (614.08–09). The return of the sun marks the rekindling of habit, the temptation to "Haven money on stablecert," or to bet even money on stable certainties in an effort to ensure a haven (or heaven). Against the haven of habit, *Finnegans Wake* pits liberty of perusiveness, a renewed awareness that "nought that is has bane" (614.07–08), and a multiplication of "increasing, livivorous, feelful thinkamalinks" (613.19). The hope is for chiaroscuro *and* color, for a bigger and more varied world: "let every crisscouple be so crosscomplimentary [white and black], little eggons, youlk and meelk, in a farbiger [colored in German/far bigger] pancosmos" (613.10–12). Saint Patrick has been converted by his "assassination" in Ireland to understand light as more than one thing; although it seems transparent and white, it is inwardly a rainbow, that arc of color and sign of promise that appears when moisture acts as a natural prism for sunshine.

Letters and a Farewell

Finnegans Wake is, above all, "Acomedy of letters" (425.24), and it ends with the longest version of ALP's letter (615.12–619.19),[18] followed by the voice of the woman/river itself: "Lsp! I am leafy speafing." Liffey has become "leafy," suggesting both the leaves of a tree and those of a book (619.20). The letter is Joyce's main metaphor for both book and life. With its salutation (ave) and closing (salve) the letter replicates in miniature the course of a human life, its beginning and ending, seen as one individual's private message to another. Life and literature converge in the letter, "That letter selfpenned to one's other, that neverperfect everplanned" (489.33–34). The letter that is *Finnegans Wake* is "a letter to last a lifetime" (211.22), a letter about yearning, defiance, love, misdeeds, loss, and renewal. It is perhaps because of the way the letter serves as a kind of fetish, a miniature version of both book and life, that Joyce moved ALP's letter from the letter chapter to the end of the book, which is also its beginning.[19] At the end, ALP is described as putting (or "pitting") "hen to paper and there's scribings scrawled on eggs" (615.10).

The eggs on which the hen scribbles a letter of hail and farewell to her husband and "cock" are her children as well as the white pages of a book. Her errors are the kinds of errors characteristic of letters by women who had been only sporadically educated (like Molly Bloom). They are also meaningful because they portray an attentiveness to the way sound creates subterranean connections among disparate words, as Molly does when she refers to Ben Dollard as a "base barreltone" (*U* 8.120). "Extremes meet" in the misprint, which results from listening to as well as seeing (or spelling) words. As Joyce writes, "In that earopean end meets Ind" (598.15–16). East meets west not only in Europe but also in an open ear and an open heart.

ALP understands that her letter is not only erroneous but anonymous, a form of self-erasure: "here's lettering you erronymously" (617.30). She also knows that letters are a form of mediation that are a substitute for copulation: her letter is not only anonymous and erronymous but "onanymous" (435.31): there is something masturbatory in the expression of a sentiment addressed to someone else that may not ever be received or reciprocated (this is also true of publishing a book). "[I]s there one who understands me?" (627.15) ALP asks. She imagines her letter as something potentially social, like tea or spirits, that has not yet been shared: it is "Carried in a caddy or screwed and corked" (624.01). It is like a letter in a mailbag ("On his mugiss-tosst surface" [624.02]) that may or may not be delivered to its designated recipient; it is in transit, or bobbing on the ocean, or buried in the earth: "With a bob, bob, bottledby. Blob. When the waves give up yours the soil may for me. Sometime then, somewhere there, I wrote me hopes and buried the page when I heard Thy voice" (624.02–05). The man to whom she writes is not only her husband and lover but also, as the capital *T* of *Thy* suggests, her God. "Thi is mi" (607.19): "This is my body" and "thee is me." She experiences not only a growing isolation ("Loonely in me loneness" [627.34]) and revulsion to her former life ("I thought you the great in all things, in guilt and in glory. You're but a puny" [627.23–24]) but also an apprehension of herself as connected with everything else, that bridge "Where you meet I" (626.07–08). Finn MacCool has become "*Find Me Colours*" (626.17); she has searched for him on the hilltops of Wicklow. His invasion (of her, of Ireland) unexpectedly produced an "invision" (626.28) not unlike that of Patrick after his meeting with Berkeley.

The most surprising aspect of ALP's final monologue is the way she grows younger as she passes out and away into her "salvocean" (623.29). As *Finnegans Wake* reaches the point where it will roll over into its beginning, taking on the characteristics of "Tobecontinued's tale" (626.18), ALP's speech begins to devolve into that of a child. The book ends almost as a reversal of how *A Portrait of the Artist as a Young Man* begins, with a fairy tale ("Once upon a time and a very good time it was" [*P* 7]). Her monologue is peppered with allusions to fairy tales and the "nonsery reams" that she's "about fetted up" with (619.17–18).[20] Although she is expecting to be replaced by her daughter, she is also devolving into that daughter and remembering how her young beau was "like to me fad" (626.10, or dad). Although references to fairy tales abound (Cinderella appears as "Saltarella" [627.05] and her prince is a "bumpkin" or pumpkin [627.23]), ALP emerges most appropriately as "Sleeping Beauty," pricked into dreaming: "That was the prick of a spindle to me that gave me the keys to dreamland" (615.27–28). Her lover, as befits a phallic mason modeled on Ibsen's Master Builder, is Jack of "Jack and the Beanstalk," or "jerk of a beamstark" (615.25). The "happy" ending is bittersweet: it is designed both to "hide away the tear, the parted" (625.30–31) and to show how all will "begin again in a jiffey" (625.32–33, or Liffey). HCE is again "singing" or sucking his thumb (like Finn and an infant, 625.16), and ALP begins using baby talk, first to a little pea and caraway seed ("Pretty mites, my sweetthings, was they poorloves abandoned by wholawidey world?" [625.24–25]) and finally to her father in which she will simultaneously die and begin again: "Carry me along, taddy, like you done through the toy fair!" (628.08–09).

Finally, when ALP speaks she is opening her mouth, which is a bodily enactment of river water reaching *its* mouth and emptying itself into the sea. The opening of ALP's mouth has affinities with the ancient Egyptian ritual described in the Pyramid Texts as the "opening of the mouth," in which the mouth of a statue or mummy is magically opened by Ptah so that it can breathe and eat in the afterlife.[21] The mouth of the Liffey, "our turfbrown mummy" (194.22), is in the east. Unlike Gabriel in "The Dead," Anna Liffey has set out on her journey eastward, toward the rising sun. The places (east and west) where the sun rises and sets, which Yeats referred to as "the flaming door,"[22] were also considered doors through which Ra's sun boat passed on its way to and from Amenti, the world of darkness, by the Egyptians. These portals between worlds recall the other name of the Earwicker-Plurabelle family, the Porters, a name that evokes not only the lightheadedness of dark stout (a potable form of spirits), and characters who are carrying something (as in the French verb *porter*, to carry) such as a mailbag or a bag of Christmas presents or children or a humpback, but also doorkeepers. HCE and ALP are the keepers of the "flaming door" that separates life from death, darkness from light, as well as the keepers of bodily portals (especially the ear, the mouth, and the anus that all bodies share). If HCE as an earwig is thought to enter the brain through the always-open ear (or "earopean"),

ALP carries the reader toward "salvocean" by opening her mouth. When the dying river of life opens her mouth (a bodily portal) as she flows eastward out to sea, it is a form of reanimation that will bring her (and perhaps her readers as well) back to the beginning, to genesis (or Guinness) and the garden of Eden: "riverrun, past Eve and Adam's, from swerve of shore to bend of bay," bringing us "by a commodius vicus of recirculation back to Howth Castle and Environs" (3.01–03).

Notes

1. W. B. Yeats, "Who Goes with Fergus?" in *William Butler Yeats: Selected Poems and Three Plays*, ed. M. L. Rosenthal (New York: Collier, 1986), 15.

2. John Bishop argues that Egyptians could hope to avoid a "second death" in two ways: by attaining a place in Amen-Ra's "sun-boat," or by reenacting Osiris's death and resurrection in order to live eternally in a region of Amenti called Sekhet Hetep. *Joyce's Book of the Dark: "Finnegans Wake"* (Madison: University of Wisconsin Press, 1986), 104.

3. The first critic to write extensively about the Book of the Dead was James Atherton, in *The Books at the Wake* (Carbondale: Southern Illinois University Press, 1959). As Bishop recounts, Joyce wanted to have someone write a long essay on the relation between *Finnegans Wake* and the Book of the Dead (87). See also Danis Rose, *Chapters of Coming Forth by Day*, A Wake Newslitter Monograph, no. 6 (Colchester: A Wake Newslitter Press, 1982).

4. Bishop, *Joyce's Book of the Dark*, 98, 99, 102.

5. Dirk van Hulle, "The Lost Word: Book IV," in *How Joyce Wrote "Finnegans Wake": A Chapter-by-Chapter Genetic Guide*, ed. Luca Crispi and Sam Slote (Madison: University of Wisconsin Press, 2007), 436. I follow his division with one exception: I include ALP's letter (his section four) with her soliloquy (his section five).

6. Finn Fordham points out that Joyce's reformation of the word *Melanesia* to *Milenesia* makes a connection between the islands in the Southern Hemisphere and the Milesians who inhabited Ireland during its prehistory. See his excellent section on "The Archipelago" in "The End': 'Zee End': Chapter I.1," in *How Joyce Wrote "Finnegans Wake,"* 474–75.

7. In this respect I part company from Philip Kitcher, who argues that the Ricorso shows "there is nothing new"—*Joyce's Kaleidoscope* (New York: Oxford University Press, 2007), 242–50: "the self-deceptive faith in a new beginning is the real subject of the vignettes that succeed one another in rapid succession through the opening section of Part IV" (243); ALP "understands completely that there will be no renewal" (250).

8. See Finn Fordham's comments on the phoenix in "The End: 'Zee End," 475–76.

9. *Encyclopedia Brittanica*, 11th ed., 457. In book 15 of the *Metamorphoses*, Ovid characterizes Pythagoras's teachings on the phoenix: "They say that, from the father's body, a young phoenix is reborn, destined to live the same number of years. When age has given it strength, and it can carry burdens, it lightens the branches of the tall palm of the heavy nest, and piously carries its own cradle, that was its father's tomb, and, reaching the city of Hyperion, the sun god, through the clear air, lays it down in front of the sacred doors of Hyperion's temple" (trans. A. S. Kline, Borders Classics, 2004).

10. ALP's function as that which washes away the dirt of the world is complicated by the references to the Magdalene laundries for fallen women, especially the Manor Mill steam laundry in Dublin ("mannormillor" [614.13]) and a washing house, "Wishwashwhose" [614.03]). These references serve as reminders that women were forced to be "clean," and if they disobeyed, they were punished by being made to clean up the dirt of others. For the importance of the Magdalene laundries in Joyce's short story "Clay," see Martha Stallman and Margot Backus, "The Woman Who Did: Maria's Maternal Misdirection in 'Clay,'" *Joyce Studies Annual* 2013, 129–50.

11. See Margot Norris on Kevin's relation to water, "The Last Chapter of *Finnegans Wake*: Stephen Finds His Mother," in *Critical Essays on James Joyce's "Finnegans Wake*," ed. Patrick A. McCarthy (New York: G. K. Hall, 1992), 212–30.

12. The raining/reigning of young women who gain power over men through "wetting" is also represented as urination, a word in which Joyce accents the syllable "rin" as "rain." One version of HCE's sin in the park is that he watched two girls urinate.

13. Wallace Stevens, "Sunday Morning," in *The Palm at the End of the Mind*, ed. Holly Stevens (New York: Vintage Books, 1972), 6.

14. Sir James Frazer, *The Golden Bough: A Study in Magic and Religion*, vol. 1, abridged (1922; New York: Macmillan, 1958), 744.

15. Grace Eckley is particularly helpful on Lawrence O'Toole (as well as Egyptian mythology and Saint Kevin), in "Looking Forward to a Brightening Day: Book IV, chapter i," in *A Conceptual Guide to Finnegans Wake*, ed. Michael H. Begnal and Fritz Senn (University Park: Pennsylvania State University Press, 1974), 211–36. See especially 226.

16. Allan Sanson, "Thirty-Two May Days for *Finnegans Wake*," PhD diss., Massey University, New Zealand, 2012. Sanson reads these two figures from the Age of Enlightenment as contesting the physical (as well as the spiritual) nature of light, contrasting Berkeley's theory of light as immaterialist (and divine) in *A New Theory of Vision* with Newton's discovery of the rainbow in *Optiks*, in which Newton demonstrates that light is not only material but "corpuscular" (75–76).

17. See Spurgeon Thompson's essay on the assassination of Bobrikoff, "The Subaltern *Finnegans Wake*," *Internationalist Review of Irish Culture* 1.1 Rome (2007).

18. See Patrick A. McCarthy, "The Last Epistle of *Finnegans Wake*," in his *Critical Essays on James Joyce's "Finnegans Wake*," 96–103, and also Van Hulle, "The Lost Word," 447–53.

19. Both Dirk Van Hulle and Finn Fordham discuss this in their essays in *How Joyce Wrote "Finnegans Wake."*

20. Eckley has a useful list of many of these allusions in "Looking Forward to a Brightening Day," 228.

21. "Amen; ptah! His hungry will be done!" (411.11).

22. "The Valley of the Black Pig," in Yeats, *Selected Poems*, 25–26.

Contributors

Sheldon Brivic of Temple University has written six books, five of them on Joyce. The last two of these were *Joyce's Waking Women: An Introduction to "Finnegans Wake"* and *Joyce through Lacan and Zizek: Explorations*. His non-Joycean book is *Tears of Rage: The Racial Interface of Modern American Fiction: Faulkner, Wright, Pynchon, Morrison*. He is working on a novel called "Stealing."

Richard Brown is reader in modern literature in the School of English at the University of Leeds. He is the author of *James Joyce and Sexuality* and *James Joyce: A Postculturalist Perspective*. He is the editor of *Joyce, "Penelope," and the Body* and the Wiley-Blackwell *Companion to James Joyce* and founding coeditor of the *James Joyce Broadsheet*. He has recently completed a monograph on *Joyce and the Modernity of Literature*.

Tim Conley is professor of English and comparative literature at Brock University in St. Catharines, Ontario. He is the author of *Joyce's Mistakes: Problems of Intention, Irony, and Interpretation*, editor of *Joyce's Disciples Disciplined: A Re-Exagmination of the "Exagmination" of "Work in Progress,"* and coeditor (with Jed Rasula) of the anthology *Burning City: Poems of Metropolitan Modernity*.

Kimberly J. Devlin is professor of English at the University of California, Riverside. She is the author of *Wandering and Return in* Finnegans Wake and *James Joyce's "Fraudstuff."* Her articles on Joyce have appeared in *PMLA, Novel, James Joyce Quarterly*, and several essay collections. She has coedited *Joycean Cultures/Culturing Joyces* and *"Ulysses"—Engendered Perspectives*.

Jeffrey Drouin is assistant professor of English and codirector of the Modernist Journals Project at the University of Tulsa. He is the author of *James Joyce, Science, and Modernist Print Culture: "The Einstein of English Fiction,"* as well as several articles on periodical studies, digital humanities, and World War I. He is also the creator of the Ecclesiastical Proust Archive http://proustarchive.org.

Enda Duffy is professor of English at the University of California, Santa Barbara. He is the author of *The Subaltern Ulysses* and *The Speed Handbook: Velocity, Pleasure, Modernism* and coeditor of *Joyce, Benjamin, and Magical Urbanism*. He is currently working on a cultural history of modern Ireland and a book on energy in modernist culture.

Colleen Jaurretche teaches at the University of California, Los Angeles. She is the author of *"The Sensual Philosophy": Joyce and the Aesthetics of Mysticism* and numerous essays on Joyce, as well as the editor of *Joyce, Beckett, and the Art of the Negative*. She is cofounder and codirector of Libros Schmibros Lending Library, a public humanities project based in Los Angeles.

Sean Latham is the Pauline Walter McFarlin Professor of English and Comparative Literature at the University of Tulsa, where he serves as editor of the *James Joyce Quarterly*, coeditor of the *Journal of Modern Periodical Studies*, and codirector of the NEH-sponsored Modernist Journals Project. He is the author or editor of seven books, including *Am I a Snob? Modernism and the Novel*; *The Art of Scandal: Modernism, Libel Law, and the Roman à Clef*; and *Cambridge Companion to "Ulysses."*

Jim LeBlanc holds a PhD in French literature from Cornell University, and he is director of library technical services at Cornell. He has written on various topics from backroom library workflows and metadata management to existential phenomenology, popular music, and twentieth-century European literature, including a number of essays on Joyce.

Vicki Mahaffey is professor at the University of Illinois at Urbana-Champaign. She is the author of *Reauthorizing Joyce*; *States of Desire: Wilde, Yeats, Joyce, and the Irish Experience*; and *Modernist Literature: Challenging Fictions*. She also edited *Collaborative Dubliners: Joyce in Dialogue*. She is finishing two books: *Literary Modernism: An Introduction* and *The Joyce of Everyday Life*.

Patrick A. McCarthy is professor of English at the University of Miami at Coral Gables and editor of the *James Joyce Literary Supplement*. He is the author of several books on *Finnegans Wake* including *Joyce, Family, "Finnegans Wake"* and *The Riddles of "Finnegans Wake,"* and editor of *Critical Essays on James Joyce's "Finnegans Wake."* Other books on Joyce include *"Ulysses": Portals of Discovery* and *Joyce/Lowry: Critical Perspectives*, coedited with Paul Tiessen.

Mia L. McIver writes on literature, philosophy, and art from the nineteenth century to the present. She has taught at Boston University, University of California, Irvine, Loyola Marymount University, and UCLA. She also writes fiction and drama and edits the literary journal *Unstuck*.

Margot Norris is Chancellor's Professor Emerita at the University of California, Irvine. She is the author of five books on the works of James Joyce: *The Decentered Universe of "Finnegans Wake," Joyce's Web, Suspicious Readings of Joyce's "Dubliners,"* a monograph on the 1967 Joseph Strick film of *Ulysses*, and *Virgin and Veteran Readings of "Ulysses."* She is working on a book titled *The Value of Joyce*.

Carol Loeb Shloss is consulting professor of English at Stanford University. She has written the Pulitzer Prize–nominated biography of James Joyce's daughter, Lucia Joyce: *To Dance in the Wake*. She is the author of four other books and many essays on Joyce, literary modernism, and the arts. She is completing *Treason's Child: Mary de Rachewiltz and Ezra Pound*.

Christine Smedley is lecturer in English at the University of California, Riverside. Her work focuses on modernism and experimental writing, specifically James Joyce and Mina Loy. She is working on a book entitled *Joyce and America* that explores the writer's lifelong, though critically neglected, engagement with American literature and culture.

David Spurr is professor of modern English and comparative literature at the University of Geneva. He is the author of *Joyce and the Scene of Modernity*, *The Rhetoric of Empire*, and *Conflicts in Consciousness* on T. S. Eliot, as well as coeditor of *The Space of English*. He has published widely on modern English and French literature and on literary theory and has most recently completed *Architecture and Modern Literature*.

John Terrill is a PhD candidate at the University of California, Riverside. His research interests include the intersection of developing technologies and modernist theories of subjectivity. His dissertation is entitled "'A Life of Telegrams and Anger': Forging the Subject in the Mechanisms of Modernity."

Index

Abel, 117–18, 140, 169, 178
Absalom, Absalom! (Faulkner), 260
Acts of the Apostles, 209
Adam, 14, 21, 31–32, 38–39, 48
Adorno, Theodor, 56
"Aeolus" (Joyce, J.), 224, 278
Affect, 45
Affordance: defined, 111n24; in game theory, 99–103, 105, 108–9, 111n24
Africa, 104, 124, 235n2, 259
Agnomen, 30–33
Allmaziful, 2, 77, 262
ALP (fictional character), 221, 233, 235; as African, 235n2, 259; awakening of, 290; clothes of, 79–80; as deity, 262; ecocriticism and, 9, 133–47; Famine and, 125–26; fluidity of, 133–35, 137, 140–41, 147; food and, 138–39; habeas corpus and, 62, 71; HCE and, 137–39, 140–42, 146, 190, 195, 199, 222, 263; as hen, 24–25, 71, 301–2; as Isis, 172, 174, 183; letter and, 12, 25, 71, 87n3, 174–75, 179–80, 293, 301–4; Liffey and, 9, 133–34, 138–45, 147n6, 169, 172, 293, 301–4; Mamafesta and, 77–78; as mother, 126, 140, 172, 177, 245, 262, 301–2; as prophetess, 25–26, 28n16; rebellion of, 269; in "Ricorso," 290, 293, 296–97, 301–4, 304n7, 305n10; washerwomen and, 136–46, 148n15
Alphabet, 8, 16–17, 20–21; *The Book of Kells* and, 75–76, 82–87; language as material and, 24–25
Ambient poetics, 53, 56
Amen-Ra, 291, 304n2
Analog: defined, 184n2; hearing as, 170–71, 184n3; mutuomorphomutation of, 175, 178, 183
Angels, 154–55, 161–62, 167

Anna Livia Plurabelle. *See* ALP
Annotations to "Finnegans Wake" (McHugh), 3–4
Annunciation, 22
Anticolonial revolution, 186–87
Anti-music, 52–53, 57
Apertio aurium (opening of the ears), 83
Apologia Pro Vita Sua (Newman), 114
Aquinas, Thomas, 212
Arabian Nights, 33
Aretino's Postures (Romano), 284
Armenians, 124–25
Arrah-na-Pogue (Boucicault), 204, 208
Art, 11, 133
Artists, 114, 120, 244
The Art of Being Ruled (Lewis), 245–46
Atherton, James, 136, 304n3
Atmosphere: affect and, 45; character and, 45–48; climate in, 46–49, 55; in "The Dead," 46–47; defined, 44; of detective fiction, 54; ecocriticism and, 53; in *Finnegans Wake*, 7–8, 44–57; in genres, 44–45, 54–55; HCE undone by, 57n9; identity and, 56; obsolescence of, 44–45; pathetic fallacy in, 47–48; personification and, 8, 49–50; reader and, 55; as temporal, 55–56; in *Ulysses*, 17, 47; weather in, 46–47, 49–50, 53, 56
Atom splitting, 199
Attridge, Derek, 3–4
Austen, Jane, 157, 164, 166
Autobiography, 114, 126

Badiou, Alain, 256, 262–63
"The Ballad of Persse O'Reilly," 39
Barnacle, Nora, 285
Beckett, Samuel, 95, 108, 254n26

Bédier, Joseph, 207, 210
Begnal, Michael, 6, 87n2
Being and Nothingness (*L'être et le néant*) (Sartre), 7, 29, 31, 37, 41
Bel and the Dragon episode, 27n6
Belshazzar's feast, 7, 16
Benjamin, Roy, 218n8
Benjamin, Walter, 277
Benstock, Bernard, 87n2
Benstock, Shari, 25
Berkeley, Bishop, 299–300, 302, 305n16
The Best Foot Forward (Finn), 247–48
Bible: Cain and Abel in, 117–18, 140, 169, 178; Deuteronomy, 27n9; Famine and, 117–19, 121, 130n23, 130n29; Genesis, 17, 145, 206, 217; Habakkuk, 19–20, 25–26, 27nn7–8; Jacob and Esau in, 117, 227, 265, 274; New Testament, 201–5, 209–10, 213; Old Testament, 204; prodigal son in, 118–20; Wheat and Tares parable, 22, 120, 130n29. See also *The Book of Kells*; Daniel; Gospels
Biddy (fictional character), 80–82, 84
Biopolitics, 67–69
Bishop, John: on Book of the Dead, 291–92, 304n2; on *Finnegans Wake*, 38, 60, 127, 136, 148n10, 158–59, 174, 192, 265, 271n37
Blake, William, 201, 255–57, 259–60, 270n7
Blanchette Brewster (fictional character), 259–60
Bloom, Harold, 1
Bloomsday, 106, 108
Boccioni, Umberto, 282–83
Bodies That Matter (Butler), 68–69
Body: ambiguous status of, 8, 59–60, 63; of Christ, 67, 179, 212; dance and, 162; nature and, 143, 145; sovereign, 60–61, 63, 69; words related to, 59, 201–2, 210. See also Flesh; Habeas corpus
Böhme, Gernot, 55
Book burning, 248–49
The Book of Kells: Christ in, 82; *Finnegans Wake* and, 8, 75–76, 82–87, 87nn2–3, 88n5; letters and, 8, 75–76, 82–87, 87n2; Sullivan and, 83–86
Book of the Dead, 173, 262, 291–92, 295, 304nn2–3
Boss fight, 105–8
Boucicault, Dion, 204, 208
Boustrophedon, 16, 18
Brady, Joseph, 39
Brivic, Sheldon, 235n2, 258, 269

"The Bruno Philosophy" (Joyce, J.), 264
Buckley (fictional character), 188–90, 195, 197, 199, 299–300
Budge, E. A. Wallis, 172–74, 178
Budgen, Frank, 110n11, 283
Buell, Lawrence, 134
Burial, 61, 71, 132n49
Burke, Thomas Henry, 38–39, 278
Burtt, Edwin Arthur, 180
Butler, Judith, 68–69
Butt (fictional character), 188, 190–92, 195–98
Byron, Lord, 11, 241–45, 251, 253n12

Cain, 117–18, 140, 169, 178
"Calypso" (Joyce, J.), 272, 276
Campbell, Joseph, 5, 95, 257, 286
Cannibalism, 63, 118
Carroll, Lewis, 3, 15, 101
Castration, 266
Catholic Church: Famine and, 231, 237n29; Finn and, 11, 247–49, 253n21; priests, 141–42, 226, 267, 280
Cavendish, Frederick, 38–39, 278
Chapelizod, 273–76, 283
Characters: atmosphere and, 45–48; chunking and, 98; as figures of change, 256; as location, 150–51, 166; minor, 150, 152–55; political dimension of, 152–53, 167; system of, 9–10, 149–68; as topography, 47
Cheng, Vincent, 26n4
Chiasm, 18, 27n8
Childe Harold's Pilgrimage (Byron), 244–45
Children: competition among, 156–57; copybook of, 169; culture of, 155–56; guessing game of, 154–61, 165; performance by, 149–50, 153–56; sexual awareness of, 154–55, 160, 163–67; waking of, 273
Christ, 22, 258; body of, 67, 179, 212; in *The Book of Kells*, 82; HCE as, 17–18; rising of, 214–16; Shaun as, 223, 225–26, 229; sovereign representation and, 60
Chuff (fictional character): as angel, 155, 161–62, 167; in "The Mime of Nick, Mick and the Maggies," 151, 154–55, 157, 160, 162–64, 166–67
Chunking: defined, 97–98; in game theory, 95–102, 104–5, 111n21
Cinema, 182–83, 198, 277
"Circe" (Joyce, J.), 112n25, 187, 291, 296
Circumpictified, 151
Citizen (fictional character), 121

312 Index

Clarke, Bruce, 102
Claybook, 16, 20–21
Climate, 46–49, 55
Closing-time republicanism, 187
Clothes, 79–80
Cocteau, Jean, 277
Coercion Acts, 64, 123, 131n41
Coherence, game theory and, 106–8
Collideorscape, 6, 97–98, 108
Colonialism, 259–61
Common reader: defined, 8, 86; *Finnegans Wake* as, 8, 75–87
Communal feasting, 122
Competition, 150, 156–57
Conceptual Guide to "Finnegans Wake" (Begnal and Senn), 6, 87n2
Conflict: historical, 10, 193–96; media and, 188–93, 197–200
Confrontation, 190–91
Confucius, 18, 22
Connolly, Thomas, 279–80
Conrad, Joseph, 75, 82
Constraints: in game theory, 99–101, 104–9, 111n24; in modernism, 112n25
Countergospel: Eucharist and, 212; evangelists in, 203–7, 213–16, 286; faith and, 217; joysis crisis in, 201, 207, 210–11, 215, 221; "Mamalujo" sketch and, 202–3; New Testament and, 201–5, 209–10, 213; origins of, 201–2; Tristan and Isolde myth in, 201–4, 207–10, 213–15, 221, 286
Courage, cowardice vs., 192–93, 195, 198
Courtship: in Austen novels, 157, 164, 166; "The Mime of Nick, Mick and the Maggies" and, 9–10, 157–58, 161, 166
Cowardice, courage vs., 192–93, 195, 198
Creation story, 24, 47–48
Creativity: of prophecy, 19; women and, 22–23, 25–26
Cricket, 278
Crispi, Luca, 13
Criteria accessibility relations, 112n33
Cross of quaternity, 96–97
Culture: of children, 155–56; nature and, 9, 142–44
Cyclical time, 17, 71
"Cyclops" (Joyce, J.), 109n4, 121

Dali, Salvador, 261, 271n24
Dancing, 161–62, 165–66, 242
Daniel: dreams interpreted by, 18–19, 24; Habakkuk connected with, 27n7; as prophet, 7, 16–19, 24–25
Danto, Arthur C., 56–57
Dark, in "Ricorso," 290–94, 296–99, 303
Daughter: in father, 257–60, 269; sale of, 261
Dave the Dancekerl (fictional character), 11, 241, 243–44, 249–52, 254n29
Davis, Thomas, 194–95
Davitt, Michael, 116, 120, 130n28, 231, 237n29
"The Dead" (Joyce, J.), 46–47, 193, 276, 297, 303
The Decentered Universe of "Finnegans Wake" (Norris), 29
Deleuze, Gilles, 71
Deliverance, 220, 225
De Profundis (Wilde), 114
Derrida, Jacques, 109, 217
Desire: language and, 201–2; mother as object of, 222; of women, 9–10
Detective fiction: atmosphere of, 54; *Finnegans Wake* as, 7, 15–17
Deuteronomy, 27n9
De Valera, Eamon, 188, 193
Devils, 154–56, 167
Devlin, Kimberly J., 33, 139
Dialogue, media and, 199
Digital: defined, 184n2; games, 95–96, 112n25; mutuomorphomutation of, 175, 178, 183; vision as, 170–71, 184n3
Divinity, as contradiction, 264–66
Dolph (fictional character), 175–76, 178, 182–83
Don Juan/Don Giovanni (fictional character), 241–43, 247, 251
Donnelly, James S., 121
Doors, 65–66
Double-talk, 3
Dreams: dream within, 222; habeas corpus and, 69; interpretation of, 18–19, 24, 86, 283; of married couples, 274; Other and, 31, 37–41; self in, 159; Yawn and, 256–57, 259–60
Drunken text, 192
Dublin, 260–61; as Finn MacCool, 27n6; motto of, 68, 94; porters of, 273–74
Dubliners (Joyce, J.), 94, 234; "The Dead," 46–47, 193, 276, 297, 303; "An Encounter," 92; "Eveline," 154; game theory and, 92, 95; "Grace," 225; "A Little Cloud," 278; "A Painful Case," 279; taverns in, 187; urban setting of, 134

Duchamp, Marcel, 282
Dufrenne, Mikel, 55

Earwicker (fictional character), 10, 26, 32, 36, 49, 78–80
Earwicker family (fictional characters), 10, 169, 172–73, 273. *See also* Porter family
Earwigs, 32, 42n6, 303
Eco, Umberto, 45
Ecocriticism: ALP and, 9, 133–47; atmosphere and, 53
Ecological imaginary, 133, 136
Eddington, Sir Arthur, 185n23
Education, in Ireland, 267
Egyptian mythology, 10, 12, 294; Amen-Ra, 291, 304n2; in Book of the Dead, 173, 262, 291–92, 295, 304nn2–3; Horus in, 169, 171–75, 178–79, 181–83, 185n22, 292–93; Isis in, 172–74, 183, 292; Osiris in, 172–74, 178–79, 181, 183, 185n18, 292–93; Papyrus of Ani and, 178; Ra in, 291, 295, 303; Set in, 169, 171–76, 178–79, 181–83, 185n22; Thoth in, 172–75, 178, 181, 185n15
Einstein, Albert, 180, 185n23, 199
Electric media, 170–71, 181–83
Eliot, T. S., 50–51, 103, 204, 274
Ellis, Henry Havelock, 285
Ellmann, Richard, 135, 267
Emerald Green: An Ecocritical Study of Irish Literature (Wenzell), 134
Emergence: defined, 102; in game theory, 8, 93–97, 100, 102–6, 108–9
Empson, William, 50–52
"An Encounter" (Joyce, J.), 92
Engels, Friedrich, 130n23
England: Famine and, 117–23, 227, 231, 237n29; O'Conor and, 192–96
Enright, Anne, 262
Epiphany: defined, 67; habeas corpus and, 59–60, 66, 67, 69–72
Epstein, Edmund, 92, 95–96, 98, 170, 242, 257
Esau and Jacob story, 117, 227, 265, 274
L'être et le néant (*Being and Nothingness*) (Sartre), 7, 29, 31, 37, 41
Eucharist, 212
"Eumaeus" (Joyce, J.), 202
Evangelists: in countergospel, 203–7, 213–16, 286; Yawn interrogated by, 255–57, 267–68, 271n25
Eve, 14, 31–32, 38–39, 140, 266; made of Adam, 48; Mary and, 210

"Eveline" (Joyce, J.), 154
The Expanding Universe (Eddington), 185n23
Explosion, 223
Eyesight. *See* Vision

Failure, modernism as, 92
Fairhall, James, 116
Faith, 217
Faith and knowledge (*Foi et savoir*) (Derrida), 217
Fall, 14, 24, 38, 141; of HCE, 33–41, 142, 265–67, 305n12; shame and, 30–32
Famine: ALP and, 125–26; Bible and, 117–19, 121, 130n23, 130n29; Catholic Church and, 231, 237n29; England and, 117–23, 227, 231, 237n29; export during, 120, 122, 226; imagery, 63, 117; memory of, 116–17, 121–22, 124–25, 129n10, 132n50; nationalism and, 115–16, 120–25, 128n6; pigs and, 63, 119, 130n23; souperism in, 117, 129n15; spalpeens and, 125, 131n48; split vision of, 9, 116–28; in *Ulysses*, 121, 123
"Fare Thee Well" (Byron), 243, 245, 253n12
Father: daughter in, 257–60, 269; HCE, 170, 174–75, 180, 221–22, 226–28, 257, 261, 265; Issy and, 10, 97, 170, 175–77, 180, 257, 261; mother controlled by, 262; Oedipus and, 10, 170, 174, 177, 180, 183, 248; as Other, 227; sun and, 292–95
Faulkner, William, 260
Feenichts Playhouse, 149
Festy King (fictional character), 62–67, 70, 72
Finn, Francis J., 11, 247–49, 253n21
Finnegans Wake (Joyce, J.): as Allmaziful, 2, 77, 262; atmosphere in, 7–8, 44–57; as aural book, 148n9; Beckett on, 95, 108, 254n26; Bishop on, 38, 60, 127, 136, 148n10, 158–59, 174, 192, 265, 271n37; catalogue of, 91–92, 102–4, 109; center of, 10; as common reader, 8, 75–87; condensations in, 3; critical reception of, 1; as detective fiction, 7, 15–17; excesses of, 1–5; experimentalism of, 2–5; fire in, 12, 293–96, 298; frameworks, 6–7; game theory and, 8, 90–109; habeas corpus in, 8, 59–73; handbooks to, 5–6; "Haveth Childers Everywhere" in, 263, 268–69; homophones in, 11, 220–35, 235n2; interrogations in, 227, 236n6, 252, 255–57, 267–68, 271n25; Mamafesta in, 77–78, 80, 82, 91; "Mamalujo" sketch and, 202–3;

maps of, 56; McHugh on, 3–4, 6, 16, 22, 28n16, 46, 49, 104, 118, 123–24, 144–45, 180, 205, 241, 246, 253n12, 257–61, 265; metaphors, viii–ix, 3–4, 97; mimesis in, 12, 272–87; music and, vii–viii, 52–53, 57; nesting structure of, 11–12, 256, 263; object library of, 96; Ondt and Gracehoper in, 16, 229–31, 245; plurabilities of, 4, 9, 26, 77–78, 262; politics of, 2–3, 10–11, 59–60, 186–87; positions in, 273, 278, 284–87; prophecy in, 7, 14–26; pub in, 187–99; revision of, 246–48, 264; spells in, 292; as strabismal apologia, 8–9, 114–28; title of, 90–91; in *transition*, 11, 241, 244–48, 251, 277; water in, 12, 14, 293–96; *Work in Progress* and, 50, 90, 95, 186–87. *See also* Countergospel; "The Mime of Nick, Mick and the Maggies"; Polyvocality; "Ricorso"

Finn MacCool, 59, 68, 103, 193–94, 221, 292; Dublin as, 27n6; invasion by, 302

Fire, 12, 293–96, 298

First-Draft Version of "Finnegans Wake" (Hayman), 202

Flaming door, 303

Flesh: spirit made, 211–13; words and, 59–62, 201–3, 211

Floras, 157, 161–64, 166–68

Fog, 46

Foi et savoir (Faith and knowledge) (Derrida), 217

Food: ALP and, 138–39; iconography of, 122–23; Shaun eating, 226–27

Fordham, Finn, 47, 115–16, 133, 141, 256, 304n6

Foucault, Michel, 279

Four Masters of Ireland, 203, 205, 213

Fratricide, 117–18

Frazer, James, 298

French kiss, 10–11, 208–9, 211, 213

Freud, Sigmund: Joyce, James, and, 3, 38, 124, 148n19, 256–57, 275, 285; Wolf Man of, 275, 285

Fuger, Wilhelm, 87n3

Gabriel Conroy (fictional character), 46, 297, 303

Games: digital, 95–96, 112n25; guessing, 154–61, 165; ladder, 101; mimesis and, 277–78; modernity as, 110n10; Stephen Dedalus and, 92–94; video, 99–100, 106, 108, 113n34; word ladder, 101

Game theory: affordance in, 99–103, 105, 108–9, 111n24; boss fight in, 105–8; chunking in, 95–102, 104–5, 111n21; coherence and, 106–8; constraints in, 99–101, 104–9, 111n24; *Dubliners* and, 92, 95; emergence in, 8, 93–97, 100, 102–6, 108–9; *Finnegans Wake* and, 8, 90–109; magic circle in, 99–101, 108, 111n23; *A Portrait of the Artist as a Young Man* and, 92–95; progression in, 93–94, 96; rules in, 99–100; titles and, 90–91; tutorial, 92–95; *Ulysses* and, 92, 94, 101, 106–7

The gaze (*le regard*): Lacan and, 41nn1–2; of Other, 29–31, 33–36, 40, 41n1; Sartre on, 29–30, 35–36, 40, 41nn1–2

Genesis, 17, 145, 206, 217

Genetic criticism, 6, 11, 102, 263, 280–81

Genocide, 124–25

Genre, 44–45, 54–55

Geometry lesson, 169–70, 174–75, 177, 178–82

Gibson, James, 100

Gilbert, Stuart, 241

Glasheen, Adaline, 66, 241, 246

Glotfelty, Cheryll, 134

Glugg (fictional character): as devil, 155, 167; HCE and, 158–59; in "The Mime of Nick, Mick and the Maggies," 151, 154–61, 163–67

God: discourse of, 265; HCE as, 17–18; as multiplicity, 255–57; prophets and, 16–22, 25–26, 27n7, 27n9

Gods of the Egyptians (Budge), 173–74

The Golden Bough (Frazer), 298

Gordon, John, 257

Gospels: Ireland and, 205–6, 213–14; John, 215–16; order of, 204–7; Pauline doctrine of, 211; rewritten, 201–5, 209–10, 213, 216–17; universality in, 218n8. *See also* Countergospel

Gottfried, Roy K., 127

"Grace" (Joyce, J.), 225

Guessing game, 154–61, 165

Guilt, Other and, 29–31, 33, 35, 37, 41

Habakkuk, 19–20, 25–26, 27nn7–8

Habeas corpus: ALP and, 62, 71; defined, 59–60; dreams and, 69; epiphany and, 59–60, 66, 67, 69–72; fantasy of, 72; in *Finnegans Wake*, 8, 59–73; HCE and, 59, 61–63, 67–69, 71–73; pigs and, 62–64, 66–67; politics and, 59–60; trial and, 8, 61–67, 70–72

Index 315

Hansen, Mark, 102
Hart, Clive, 57n6, 96–98
"Haveth Childers Everywhere" (Joyce, J.), 263, 268–69
Hayles, N. Katherine, 102
Hayman, David, 190, 202
HCE (fictional character), 65, 81, 276, 278, 286; agnomen of, 30–33; ALP and, 137–39, 140–42, 146, 190, 195, 199, 222, 263; atmosphere undoing, 57n9; awakening of, 290; as Christ, 17–18; fall of, 33–41, 142, 265–67, 305n12; as father, 170, 174–75, 180, 221–22, 226–28, 257, 261, 265; game theory and, 98, 102–5; Glugg and, 158–59; as God, 17–18; habeas corpus and, 59, 61–63, 67–69, 71–73; in "Haveth Childers Everywhere," 263, 268–69; as "Here Comes Everybody," 4, 31, 33, 37, 39–41; identity of, 4, 31–33, 35–36, 40–41, 116, 256, 268, 300; king and, 31–34; letter and, 175, 179–80; as O'Conor, 183, 189, 193–94, 196, 198; as Osiris, 174, 178, 181, 183, 185n18; Others and, 29–41; as phallus, 266, 295; as prophet, 15, 17–20, 25, 28n16; in pub, 187–99; in "Ricorso," 290, 293–95, 297, 303; savaging of, 235; women's writing and, 25–26; Yawn and, 256–63
Healy, Timothy Michael, 64
Hearing: as analog sense modality, 170–71, 184n3; *Apertio aurium* and, 83; media and, 191, 198; Shem as, 10, 169–71, 265
Hegel, Georg, 36
Heidegger, Martin, 56
Hen: ALP as, 24–25, 71, 301–2; Biddy, 80–82, 84
Henke, Suzette, 148n19
Henry II, 260
Henry IV (Shakespeare), 227
Historical conflicts, 10, 193–96
History: discourse of, 265; distorted, 121; media and, 190–91, 193, 196–200; nature and, 56–57; voices of, 257
Hitler, Adolf, 131n39, 244
Hogg, Reverend, 38–39
Homophones: in *Finnegans Wake*, 11, 220–35, 235n2; salvage, 11, 220–21, 235; salvation, 11, 222–23, 235; salves, 11, 220–22, 225, 231–32, 234; savage, 235n2; savaging, 234–35, 235n2; saving, 11, 220, 230–32, 235
Homosexuality, 242, 252n7, 265–68
Horkheimer, Max, 156
Horus: in Egyptian mythology, 169, 171–75, 178–79, 181–83, 185n22, 292–93; Shaun as, 169, 171–75, 178–79, 181–83
The House by the Churchyard (Sheridan Le Fanu), 274, 288n7
How Joyce Wrote "Finnegans Wake" (Crispi and Slote), 6

Identity: atmosphere and, 56; character system and, 150; of HCE, 4, 31–33, 35–36, 40–41, 116, 256, 268, 300; Irish, 115–19, 283; memory and, 124; Others mediating, 39; of Shaun, 11, 129n19, 220–21, 223–28, 257; shifting states of, 282–83; of Stephen Dedalus, 93
Ignatius Gallaher (fictional character), 278
Image: letter as, 75–76, 82, 85–86; in modernism, 75
Impure Sound, 53
Incest, 11, 177, 236n17, 242–44, 258
Injustice, 257, 263–64
Interrogations: in *Finnegans Wake*, 227, 236n6, 252, 255–57, 267–68, 271n25; of Yawn, 252, 255–57, 267–68, 271n25
Ireland: artists in, 114, 120; as cannibal, 63; education in, 267; fire and, 293; foreign invaders of, 38; Four Masters of, 203, 205, 213; Gospels and, 205–6, 213–14; historical conflicts in, 10, 193–96; identity of, 115–19, 283; media and, 190–91, 193, 196–200; as mother, 245; national sin of, 117, 120–21; new, 194; proletariat of, 186–87, 200; resurgence of, 294; revolution in, 124, 186–87, 194; Wellington from, 26n4
Irigaray, Luce, 258–59, 266
Irish Sketch Book (Thackeray), 119, 123
Irish stew, 122–24
Isis, 172–74, 183, 292, 296
Issy (fictional character), 25, 100, 108, 267, 297; father and, 10, 97, 170, 175–77, 180, 257, 261; as Isis, 172–73, 296; Jaun and, 239–40, 242–43; Lenten lecture and, 239–40, 242–43, 245–50; names of, 151. *See also* Izod
"Ithaca" (Joyce, J.), 101, 109n4, 136, 272
Izod (fictional character): in Floras, 157, 161–63; in "The Mime of Nick, Mick and the Maggies," 151, 154–55, 157–63, 165–67

Jacob and Esau story, 117, 227, 265, 274
Jade, 22
Jail Journal (Mitchel), 116–17

Janitor, 23
Janus, 66
Jaun (fictional character), 222, 227, 234; Byron and, 11, 241–45; Dave the Dancekerl and, 11, 241, 243–44, 249–52, 254n29; Issy and, 239–40, 242–43; Lenten lecture of, 239–50; Shem and, 241
John, gospel of, 215–16
Jolas, Eugene, 91
Jolas, Maria, 187
Jouissance, 11, 211–14
Joyce, James: allusive technique of, 241–42; anti-music of, 52–53; autobiography, 114, 126; "The Bruno Philosophy" by, 264; Empson and, 50–52; Eucharist preoccupying, 212; Freud and, 3, 38, 124, 148n19, 256–57, 275, 285; metafictional gestures of, 16; nature and, 134; politics of, 186, 260; reader addressed by, 16; "Realism and Idealism in English Literature" by, 255; Sartre and, 7, 29–31; *Stephen Hero* by, 67, 279; Thoth important to, 185n15; Vico influencing, 17, 19, 48, 76–79, 96, 189, 194; vision of, 126–27, 132n55; Weaver and, 2, 52, 90, 92, 109n5, 110n7, 127, 134, 154, 156, 205, 229, 239, 250, 273, 275, 288n10, 299; *Work in Progress* by, 50, 90, 95, 186–87. *See also Dubliners; Finnegans Wake; A Portrait of the Artist as a Young Man; Ulysses*
Joyce, Stanislaus, 9, 115, 186, 234
Joyce's Waking Women (Brivic), 235n2, 258, 269
Joysis crisis, 201, 207, 210–11, 215, 221
Just memory, 124
Juul, Jesper, 93, 106, 108

Kate (fictional character), 199
Kelleher, Margaret, 126
Kelly, Timothy, 39
Kenner, Hugh, 75
Kersse (fictional character), 188–91, 194–97, 199
Kevin (fictional character), 12, 296–98
Kinealy, Christine, 118
King (fictional character), 31–34
Kiss: in *Arrah-na-Pogue*, 204, 208; jouissance of, 11, 211–14; shout and, 208–9; tongue and, 10–11, 208–9, 211, 213; in Tristan and Isolde myth, 10–11, 202, 204, 207–10, 213; in *Ulysses*, 208–9, 211, 213
Kitcher, Philip, 230, 304n7

Lacan, Jacques, 41nn1–2, 71, 213, 266
Land War, 64
Language: as being, 40, 43n23; as bodily utterance, 201; desire and, 201–2; dramatized, 153–54; as event, 211; fusion of, 212–13; injustice and, 264; materiality of, 24–25, 232; mysterious, 15–16, 19–20; nature as, 144; in prayer, 76–77, 82, 88n4; reformation of, 293; sexuality and, 21–22, 24; system, Weaver criticizing, 2; vitality of, 76. *See also* Words
The Language of New Media (Manovich), 95
Laoghaire (king), 298–301
Lawrence, D. H., 251–52, 283
Legitimacy, 260–64
Lenten lecture: Issy and, 239–40, 242–43, 245–50; Jaun giving, 239–50
Leopold Bloom (fictional character): kiss of, 208–9, 211; in *Ulysses*, 17, 47, 121–23, 136–37, 144, 202, 208–9, 211, 223–24, 245, 276, 287
"Lestrygonians" (Joyce, J.), 208
Letters: ALP and, 12, 25, 71, 87n3, 174–75, 179–80, 293, 301–4; *The Book of Kells* and, 8, 75–76, 82–87, 87n2; Earwicker and, 79–80; HCE and, 175, 179–80; as image, 75–76, 82, 85–86; interpretation of, 78–82; introduction of, 12, 71–72; multidimensional, 5–6; Nightletter, 174, 179, 181; prayer and, 76–77; as proteiform graph, 5, 20, 78–79, 83; Shaun carrying, 231–35, 257; Shem and, 234; in *Ulysses*, 17
Lévy, Bernard-Henri, 43n23
Lewis, Wyndham, 113n36, 227, 245–46, 249
Liffey. *See* River Liffey
Light: media and, 197–200; in "Ricorso," 201, 290–94, 296, 298–99, 305n16
Lily Miskinguette (fictional character), 33–35
Literature: philosophy and, 56–57; in revolutions, 174–78
"A Little Cloud" (Joyce, J.), 278
Liu, Lydia, 109, 111n17
Lloyd, David, 116
Logos, 23–24, 215
London, 284
Lowe-Evans, Mary, 225

Maamtrasna murders, 64
Macbeth (Shakespeare), 166, 168n13, 274, 279

MacCarthy, Fiona, 242
Magic circle, in game theory, 99–101, 108, 111n23
"Maid of Athens" (Byron), 242
Mamafesta, 77–78, 80, 82, 91
"Mamalujo" sketch (Joyce, J.), 202–3
Manganiello, Dominic, 186, 260
Manovich, Lev, 95
Married couples: dreams of, 274; sexuality of, 279–81, 285–87
Mary, 22, 210
Mary Jane (fictional character), 46
Masculinity, 23, 93, 258–59, 263, 266
Matharan, M.-M., 279–80
Maurice Behan (fictional character), 52
McCarthy, Patrick A., 230
McCormack, John, 224, 246–47
McHugh, Roland: *Annotations to "Finnegans Wake"* by, 3–4; on *Finnegans Wake*, 3–4, 6, 16, 22, 28n16, 46, 49, 104, 118, 123–24, 144–45, 180, 205, 241, 246, 253n12, 257–61, 265
McLuhan, Marshall, 49, 109, 191
Media: conflict and, 188–93, 197–200; dialogue and, 199; electric, 170–71, 181–83; hearing and, 191, 198; Irish history and, 190–91, 193, 196–200; light and, 197–200; new, 95–96, 191, 197–98; polyvocality and, 10, 170–71, 181–83; radio, 188–89, 195–97, 199; revolution, 181–83; vision and, 191, 198. *See also* Television
Memory: exchange, 128; Famine, 116–17, 121–22, 124–25, 129n10, 132n50; identity and, 124
Men: masculinity of, 23, 93, 258–59, 263, 266; renewal and, 297
Metafictional gestures, 16
Metaphors: *Finnegans Wake*, viii–ix, 3–4, 97; reversal of, 3–4
"The Mime of Nick, Mick and the Maggies" (Joyce, J.): character system in, 9–10, 149–68; Chuff in, 151, 154–55, 157, 160, 162–64, 166–67; courtship ritual and, 9–10, 157–58, 161, 166; dance in, 161–62, 165–66; Floras in, 157, 161–64, 166–68; Glugg in, 151, 154–61, 163–67; guessing game in, 154–61, 165; Izod in, 151, 154–55, 157–63, 165–67; *A Portrait of the Artist as a Young Man* and, 155–56, 158
Mimesis: in *Finnegans Wake*, 12, 272–87; games and, 277–78; paradigms, 276–80;

polyvocality and, 272–73, 281, 286; Porter family and, 12, 272–73, 276, 278–79
Minor characters, 150, 152–55
Mistress Kathe (fictional character), 23–26
Mitchel, John, 114, 116–17, 120, 131n41
Modernism: constraints in, 112n25; as failure, 92; image in, 75
Modernity, as game, 110n10
Molly Bloom (fictional character): kiss of, 208–9, 211, 213; nature and, 134, 139–40, 144, 147; in *Ulysses*, 134, 139–40, 144, 147, 208–9, 211, 213, 262, 276, 287, 302
Molony, Senan, 38
Mookse and Gripes parable, 107–8, 245
Moore, Thomas, 244
Morash, Christopher, 117, 121, 124, 130n29, 130n31
Morton, Timothy, 53, 55–56, 133, 144
Mother: ALP, 126, 140, 172, 177, 245, 262, 301–2; father controlling, 262; Ireland as, 245; as object of desire, 222; Oedipus and, 10, 170, 174, 177, 180, 183, 248
Murphies, 122–23
Music, vii–viii, 52–53, 57
Mutuomorphomutation, of digital and analog, 175, 178, 183
My Mother Was a Computer (Hayles), 102

Nation, self as, 115–16
Nationalism, 143–44; Famine and, 115–16, 120–25, 128n6; incest and, 243–44
National sin, 117, 120–21
Nature: art and, 133; body as product of, 143, 145; culture and, 9, 142–44; history and, 56–57; Joyce, James, and, 134; as language, 144; Molly Bloom and, 134, 139–40, 144, 147; as process, 48–50; romanticized, 146–47; women identified with, 134–36. *See also* Ecocriticism
"Nausicaa" (Joyce, J.), 202, 224, 245, 291
Nazis, 131n39, 244, 248
Nebuchadnezzar, 18–19, 27n6
Nesting structure, 11–12, 256, 263
"Nestor" (Joyce, J.), 94, 209
Newell, Allen, 98
Newman, John Henry, 114
New media, 95–96, 191, 197–98
New Science (*Scienza Nuovo*) (Vico), 17, 76–77, 88n4
New Testament, 201–5, 209–10, 213. *See also* Gospels

Newton, Isaac, 180–81, 299, 305n16
Nightletter, 174, 179, 181
Noah, 274
Norris, Margot, 25–26, 222, 226, 232; *The Decentered Universe of "Finnegans Wake"* by, 29; "The Politics of Childhood in 'The Mime of Mick, Nick and the Maggies'" by, 155–57
Norwegian sea captain (fictional character), 18, 188, 190, 194
Nude Descending a Staircase (Duchamp), 282
Nude exposure, 34, 37–38

Object library, 96
Obligation world, 227, 236n17
O'Conor, Roderick, 187; England and, 192–96; HCE as, 183, 189, 193–94, 196, 198
Oedipus, 10, 170, 174, 177, 180, 183, 248
Ogden, C. K., 144–45
O'Grada, Cormac, 125, 132n50
O'Hanlon, John, 5, 87n2, 128, 135, 137, 227
Old Testament, 204
Ondt and Gracehoper fable, 16, 229–31, 245
The One vs. the Many: Minor Characters and the Space of the Protagonist in the Novel (Woloch), 152
Opening of the ears (*Apertio aurium*), 83
Ordination, 150
Original sin, 30, 33–39
O'Shea divorce trial, 63–65, 70, 120
Osiris: in Egyptian mythology, 172–74, 178–79, 181, 183, 185n18, 292–93; HCE as, 174, 178, 181, 183, 185n18
Others: dreams and, 31, 37–41; gaze of, 29–31, 33–36, 40, 41n1; guilt and, 29–31, 33, 35, 37, 41; HCE and, 29–41; identity mediated by, 39; paternal, 227; self's relationship with, 29–30, 36–37, 40; shame and, 30–31, 33, 35–36
Oulipo movement, 100, 112n25
"Oxen of the Sun" (Joyce, J.), 23, 279

"A Painful Case" (Joyce, J.), 279
Papyrus of Ani, 178
Paris Funds, 120, 130n28
Parnell, Charles Stewart, 60, 62–65, 70, 120
Pathetic fallacy, 47–48
Patrick (saint), 298–302
Pauline doctrine, of Gospels, 211
Peat, 196

Peel, Robert, 123, 131n41
"Penelope" (Joyce, J.), 180, 279
Pepys, Samuel, 280
Personification, 4, 8, 49–50
Pethers, Caroline, 65, 70
Phallus, 266, 295
Philosophy, 56–57, 266
Phoenix, 181, 294–96, 298, 305n9
Phoenix Park, 7, 24, 35–37, 279, 295; Feenichts Playhouse in, 149; murders, 38–39, 63, 250, 278
Pigott, Richard, 63
Pigs: Famine and, 63, 119, 130n23; habeas corpus and, 62–64, 66–67; Set as, 178; women and, 62–63, 73n6
Platt, Len, 243
Playthrough, 109
Plot, 45
Pluralities, 4, 9, 26, 77–78, 262
Poetographies, 151
Poetry, 50–51
Politics: biopolitics, 67–69; characters and, 152–53, 167; of *Finnegans Wake*, 2–3, 10–11, 59–60, 186–87; habeas corpus and, 59–60; of Joyce, James, 186, 260
"The Politics of Childhood in 'The Mime of Mick, Nick and the Maggies'" (Norris), 155–57
Polyvocality: explorations of, vii–ix; in family of voices, 256–57; media and, 10, 170–71, 181–83; mimesis and, 272–73, 281, 286; mysteries of, 4–5; nesting structure of, 11–12; pronouns and, 47; prophecy and, 15, 20; in spatial regions of page, 10, 169; of words, 3, 17, 264
Porter family (fictional characters): awakening of, 287; bedroom scenes of, 279–81, 285–87; in Chapelizod, 273–75; mimesis and, 12, 272–73, 276, 278–79; name of, 273–74; pseudoselves of, 280–84
Porters, of Dublin, 273–74
Portmanteaux, 3, 15–16
A Portrait of the Artist as a Young Man (Joyce, J.), 120, 186, 211, 229, 279, 302; Byron and, 244; epiphany in, 67, 70; game theory and, 92–95; "The Mime of Mick, Nick and the Maggies" and, 155–56, 158; Stephen Dedalus in, 24, 70, 92–96, 107, 156, 158, 196, 209–11, 223, 225, 227, 244, 266–68; tongue in, 209; urban setting of, 134

Index 319

Possible worlds theory, 105–6, 236n17
Pound, Ezra, 1–2, 101, 112n26, 239
The Pound Era (Kenner), 75
Prayer, 76–77, 82, 87, 88n4
Pride, 42n10
Priests, 141–42, 226, 267, 280
Prodigal son, 118–20
Programmers, 96, 98, 111n21
Progression, in game theory, 93–94, 96
Proletariat, Irish, 186–87, 200
Pronouns, 46–47
Prophecy: as creative act, 19; in *Finnegans Wake*, 7, 14–26; polyvocality and, 15, 20
Prophets: ALP, 25–26, 28n16; Daniel, 7, 16–19, 24–25; female, 23–26; God and, 16–22, 25–26, 27n7, 27n9; HCE, 15, 17–20, 25, 28n16; reader as, 19; role of, 7, 21; sexual context and, 21–22; as spokesperson, 27n9
Protection of Person and Property Act of 1881, 64
Proteiform graph, letter as, 5, 20, 78–79, 83
"Proteus" (Joyce, J.), 232
Pseudoselves, 280–84
Pubs: HCE in, 187–99; television in, 188, 191, 193, 196–99
Pure Sound, 50, 52–53

Quran, 23, 27n11

Ra, 291, 295, 303
Rabaté, Jean-Michel, 88n5, 263–64
Radio, 188–89, 195–97, 199
Rain, 46, 53, 57, 296–97, 305n12
Rainbow, 299, 301, 305n16
Rainbow Girls. *See* Floras
Rape, 258
Rasula, Jed, 87n3
Reader: atmosphere and, 55; carnal knowledge of, 84–85; chunking by, 96–99, 101; idealization of, 80; Joyce, James, addressing, 16; as prophet, 19; women's writing and, 26. *See also* Common reader
"Realism and Idealism in English Literature" (Joyce, J.), 255
Reformation, 293
Le regard. *See* The gaze
Relay metaphor, viii–ix
Renaissance polyphony, vii
Renewal, 12, 296–98, 301
Revenge, writing associated with, 159–60

Revolution, 173, 301; anticolonial, 186–87; drinking and, 192; injustice and, 257; in Ireland, 124, 186–87, 194; literature in, 174–78; media, 181–83; scientific, 180
Richard III (Shakespeare), 228
Ricoeur, Paul, 116, 121, 124–25, 128
"Ricorso" (Joyce, J.): ALP in, 290, 293, 296–97, 301–4, 304n7, 305n10; Book of the Dead and, 291–92, 295, 304nn2–3; dark in, 290–94, 296–99, 303; HCE in, 290, 293–95, 297, 303; Laoghaire in, 298–301; light in, 12, 201, 290–94, 296, 298–99, 305n16; Patrick in, 298–302; reformation in, 293; renewal in, 12, 296–98, 301; succession in, 293–96; sun in, 291–99, 301, 303
River Liffey: ALP and, 9, 133–34, 138–45, 147n6, 169, 172, 293, 301–4; source of, 140, 148n17
Rivers, 14–15; names of, 136, 148n10; women inseparable from, 9
Robinson, Henry Morton, 5, 95, 257, 286
Le roman de Tristan et Iseut (Bédier), 207, 210
Romano, Giulio, 284
Rosa Miskinguette (fictional character), 33–35
Rose, Danis, 5, 87n2, 127–28, 135, 137, 227
Rosenbloom, Paul S., 98
Rossa, Jeremiah O'Donovan, 116, 120
Russian general (fictional character), 188–90, 195–96, 299–300
Ryan, Marie-Laure, 106, 112n33

Said, Edward W., 260
Salen, Katie, 99, 111n23
Salvage, 11, 220–21, 235
Salvation, 11, 222–23, 235
Salves, 11, 220–22, 225, 231–32, 234
Santner, Eric, 60–61, 67, 69
Sartre, Jean-Paul: *Being and Nothingness*, 7, 29, 31, 37, 41; on the gaze, 29–30, 35–36, 40, 41nn1–2; Joyce, James, and, 7, 29–31; on language as being, 40, 43n23; on pride, 42n10
Savage, 235n2
Savaging, 234–35, 235n2
Saving, 11, 220, 230–32, 235
Scientific revolution, 180
Scienza Nuovo (*New Science*) (Vico), 17, 76–77, 88n4

"Scylla and Charybdis" (Joyce, J.), 264, 277
Self: in dreams, 159; as nation, 115–18; Other's relationship with, 29–30, 36–37, 40
Senn, Fritz, 6, 87n2, 281, 287
Set: in Egyptian mythology, 169, 171–76, 178–79, 181–83, 185n22; Shem as, 169, 171–76, 178–79, 181–83
Setting, 45
Seven Types of Ambiguity (Empson), 50–51
Sexuality: children and, 154–55, 160, 163–67; in geometry lesson, 170, 177, 180–82; homosexuality, 242, 252n7, 265–68; incest, 11, 177, 236n17, 242–44, 258; language and, 21–22, 24; in marriage, 279–81, 285–87; positions in, 284–87; prophets and, 21–22
Shakespeare, William, 166, 168n13, 227–28, 274, 279
Shame: fall and, 30–32; Others and, 30–31, 33, 35–36; pride and, 42n10
Shaun (fictional character), 97–98, 113n36, 146; in boss fight, 105–8; as Christ, 223, 225–26, 229; food eaten by, 226–27; geometry lesson of, 169–70, 174–75, 177, 178–82; as Horus, 169, 171–75, 178–79, 181–83; identities of, 11, 129n19, 220–21, 223–28, 257; as Kevin, 12, 296–98; letter carried by, 231–35, 257; as new Ireland, 194; Ondt and Gracehoper fable and, 229–31; as salve, 220–22; Shem merging with, 92, 116, 127, 169–71, 173, 175, 178, 254n31, 265; Shem's rivalry with, 9, 105–8, 241, 245–46, 250, 264–65; Shem's strabismal apologia and, 9, 114–28, 131n39; as son, 222, 294–95; Stephen Dedalus similar to, 227; as vision, 10, 169–71, 265; watching of, 273. *See also* Jaun; Yawn
Shelton, Jen, 258
Shem (fictional character), 62, 87, 91, 97–98, 146, 227; art created by, 11; in boss fight, 105–8; Dave the Dancekerl and, 11, 241, 243; as Dolph, 175–76, 178, 182–83; as hearing, 10, 169–71, 265; Jaun and, 241; letter and, 234; as new Ireland, 194; Ondt and Gracehoper fable and, 230, 245; as savage, 235n2; savaging of, 235; as Set, 169, 171–76, 178–79, 181–83; Shaun merging with, 92, 116, 127, 169–71, 173, 175, 178, 254n31, 265; Shaun's rivalry with, 9, 105–8, 241, 245–46, 250, 264–65; strabismal

apologia of, 9, 114–28, 131n39; vision and, 178–79
Sheridan Le Fanu, Joseph, 274, 288n7
Shout, kiss and, 208–9
Sigla, 88n5, 91, 96, 99, 110nn7–8, 278
Signifiers, 4, 15–16, 24
Sinn Fein, 11, 194–95, 243, 294
"Sirens" (Joyce, J.), 101, 225, 281
A Skeleton Key to "Finnegans Wake" (Campbell and Robinson), 5, 95
Sleep, 271n37. *See also* Dreams
Slote, Sam, 6, 203
Snow, 46–47
Soap, 296
Soccer, 99, 102
Social imaginary, 116
Solar theory, 298
Sollers, Phillippe, 2–3
Solomon, Margaret, 273
Soorcelossness, 275, 288n10
Souperism, 117, 129n15
Sovereign body, 60–61, 63, 69
Sovereign representation, 60–61
Spalpeens, 125, 131n48
Spells, 292
Spem in Alium (Tallis), vii
Spirit, 211–13, 218n11
Stephen Dedalus (fictional character), 217, 262, 290; epiphany of, 67, 70; games and, 92–94; identity of, 93; in *A Portrait of the Artist as a Young Man*, 24, 70, 92–96, 107, 156, 158, 196, 209–11, 223, 225, 227, 244, 266–68; Shaun similar to, 227; in *Ulysses*, 22–23, 78, 94, 140, 209, 216, 232, 291
Stephen Hero (Joyce, J.), 67, 279
Stew, 122–24
Stories, competition and, 150
St. Patrick, 63
Strabismal apologia: defined, 114; *Finnegans Wake* as, 8–9, 114–28; of Shem, 9, 114–28, 131n39
Subjectivity, 160–61, 257–58, 264
Subordination, 150
Succession, 173, 177–78, 227, 293–96
Sullivan, Sir Edward, 83–86
Sun: flaming door of, 303; in "Ricorso," 12, 291–99, 301, 303
Sylvia Silence (fictional character), 54
Symbols, lack of, 48, 57n6
Synaesthesia, 51, 53
Synge, John Millington, 63

Index 321

Taff (fictional character), 188, 190–91, 195–97
Tallis, Thomas, vii
Taverns. *See* Pubs
Television, 169, 182–83, 185n24; dialogue and, 199; in media conflict, 197; in pub, 188, 191, 193, 196–99
Tenors, 224–25, 246–47
Text machine, 191–93, 198
Thackeray, William Makepeace, 119, 123
Theall, Donald, 109, 191, 198
Thoth, 172–75, 178, 181, 185n15
Thunder, 48, 53
Tim Finnegan (fictional character), 14, 17, 59, 194, 292
Tindall, William York, 37, 87n2, 230, 233, 286
Tone, atmosphere and, 44
Tongue: kiss and, 10–11, 208–9, 211, 213; in *A Portrait of the Artist as a Young Man*, 209; words and, 10, 201, 208–9, 211
Tower of Babel, 4, 52, 209
Transition, 11, 241, 244–48, 251, 277
Trevelyan, Sir Charles, 118
Trial: habeas corpus and, 8, 61–67, 70–72; O'Shea divorce, 63–65, 70, 120
Tristan and Isolde myth: Bédier telling, 207, 210; in countergospel, 201–4, 207–10, 213–15, 221, 286; kiss in, 10–11, 202, 204, 207–10, 213

Ulysses (Joyce, J.), 78, 81, 103, 127, 185n15, 246; "Aeolus," 224, 278; Annunciation in, 22; atmosphere in, 17, 47; "Calypso," 272, 276; catalogue in, 109n4; "Circe," 112n25, 187, 291, 296; condemnation of, 234; "Cyclops," 109n4, 121; "Eumaeus," 202; Famine in, 121, 123; game theory and, 92, 94, 101, 106–7; "Ithaca," 101, 109n4, 136, 272; kiss in, 208–9, 211, 213; Leopold Bloom in, 17, 47, 121–23, 136–37, 144, 202, 208–9, 211, 223–24, 245, 276, 287; "Lestrygonians," 208; letter in, 17; Molly Bloom in, 134, 139–40, 144, 147, 208–9, 211, 213, 262, 276, 287, 302; "Nausicaa," 202, 224, 245, 291; "Nestor," 94, 209; "Oxen of the Sun," 23, 279; "Penelope," 180, 279; "Proteus," 232; "Scylla and Charybdis," 264, 277; "Sirens," 101, 225, 281; Stephen Dedalus in, 22–23, 78, 94, 140, 209, 216, 232, 291; title of, 90;

urban setting of, 134; "Wandering Rocks," 91, 106, 110n11
Understanding "Finnegans Wake" (Rose and O'Hanlon), 5
Urination, 305n12

Valentino, Rudolph, 182
Van Hulle, Dirk, 245
Vico, Giambattista: Joyce, James, inspired by, 17, 19, 48, 76–79, 96, 189, 194; *New Science* by, 17, 76–77, 88n4
Video games, 99–100, 106, 108, 113n34
Vision: as digital sense modality, 170–71, 184n3; of Joyce, James, 126–27, 132n55; media and, 191, 198; Shaun as, 10, 169–71, 265; Shem and, 178–79

"The Waltz" (Byron), 242
"Wandering Rocks" (Joyce, J.), 91, 106, 110n11
Warner, Marina, 54
War of Independence, 194
Washerwomen: ALP and, 136–46, 148n15; voices of, 9, 134–36, 147, 199–200
The Waste Land (Eliot), 204
Water, 12, 14, 293–96
Waves, 206
Weather, 46–47, 49–50, 53, 56
Weaver, Harriet Shaw: Joyce, James, and, 2, 52, 90, 92, 109n5, 110n7, 127, 134, 154, 156, 205, 229, 239, 250, 273, 275, 288n10, 299; language system criticized by, 2
Wellington, Duke of, 18, 24, 26n4, 295, 300
Wenzell, Tim, 134
"The West's Awake" (Davis), 194–95
Wheat and Tares parable, 22, 120, 130n29
Wilde, Oscar, 114, 125, 234, 252n7
Winds, 206
Wolf Man, 275, 285
Woloch, Alex, 152
Womb, 21–24
Women: creativity and, 22–23, 25–26; desire of, 9–10; freedom of, 262, 266; Kevin hating, 12, 296–98; as mechanical object, 261; nature identified with, 134–36; pigs and, 62–63, 73n6; prophetesses, 23–26; renewal and, 297; river inseparable from, 9; writing by, 7, 21–26
"Women on the Market" (Irigaray), 258–59
Words: as air, 57; body related to, 59, 201–2,

210; dance of, 162; as divine, 77–79; flesh and, 59–62, 201–3, 211; ladder game, 101; as logos, 215; polyvocality of, 3, 17, 264; tongue and, 10, 201, 208–9, 211; in womb, 21–24

Work in Progress (Joyce, J.), 50, 90, 95, 186–87

Writer complexus, 76

Writing: as carnal knowledge, 84; iconic space of, 88n5; revenge associated with, 159–60; Thoth associated with, 178; on wall, 16–20; by women, 7, 21–26

Yawn (fictional character), 252; dreams and, 256–57, 259–60; HCE and, 256–63; interrogation of, 255–57, 267–68, 271n25

Yeats, W. B., 2, 142, 290

Ziarek, Ewa, 23

Zimmerman, Eric, 99, 111n23

The Florida James Joyce Series

EDITED BY SEBASTIAN D. G. KNOWLES

The Autobiographical Novel of Co-Consciousness: Goncharov, Woolf, and Joyce, by Galya Diment (1994)
Bloom's Old Sweet Song: Essays on Joyce and Music, by Zack Bowen (1995)
Joyce's Iritis and the Irritated Text: The Dis-lexic Ulysses, by Roy Gottfried (1995)
Joyce, Milton, and the Theory of Influence, by Patrick Colm Hogan (1995)
Reauthorizing Joyce, by Vicki Mahaffey (paperback edition, 1995)
Shaw and Joyce: "The Last Word in Stolentelling," by Martha Fodaski Black (1995)
Bely, Joyce, and Döblin: Peripatetics in the City Novel, by Peter I. Barta (1996)
Jocoserious Joyce: The Fate of Folly in Ulysses, by Robert H. Bell (paperback edition, 1996)
Joyce and Popular Culture, edited by R. B. Kershner (1996)
Joyce and the Jews: Culture and Texts, by Ira B. Nadel (paperback edition, 1996)
Narrative Design in Finnegans Wake*: The Wake Lock Picked,* by Harry Burrell (1996)
Gender in Joyce, edited by Jolanta W. Wawrzycka and Marlena G. Corcoran (1997)
Latin and Roman Culture in Joyce, by R. J. Schork (1997)
Reading Joyce Politically, by Trevor L. Williams (1997)
Advertising and Commodity Culture in Joyce, by Garry Leonard (1998)
Greek and Hellenic Culture in Joyce, by R. J. Schork (1998)
Joyce, Joyceans, and the Rhetoric of Citation, by Eloise Knowlton (1998)
Joyce's Music and Noise: Theme and Variation in His Writings, by Jack W. Weaver (1998)
Reading Derrida Reading Joyce, by Alan Roughley (1999)
Joyce through the Ages: A Nonlinear View, edited by Michael Patrick Gillespie (1999)
Chaos Theory and James Joyce's Everyman, by Peter Francis Mackey (1999)
Joyce's Comic Portrait, by Roy Gottfried (2000)
Joyce and Hagiography: Saints Above!, by R. J. Schork (2000)
Voices and Values in Joyce's Ulysses, by Weldon Thornton (2000)
The Dublin Helix: The Life of Language in Joyce's Ulysses, by Sebastian D. G. Knowles (2001)

Joyce Beyond Marx: History and Desire in Ulysses *and* Finnegans Wake, by Patrick McGee (2001)

Joyce's Metamorphosis, by Stanley Sultan (2001)

Joycean Temporalities: Debts, Promises, and Countersignatures, by Tony Thwaites (2001)

Joyce and the Victorians, by Tracey Teets Schwarze (2002)

Joyce's Ulysses *as National Epic: Epic Mimesis and the Political History of the Nation State,* by Andras Ungar (2002)

James Joyce's "Fraudstuff," by Kimberly J. Devlin (2002)

Rite of Passage in the Narratives of Dante and Joyce, by Jennifer Margaret Fraser (2002)

Joyce and the Scene of Modernity, by David Spurr (2002)

Joyce and the Early Freudians: A Synchronic Dialogue of Texts, by Jean Kimball (2003)

Twenty-first Joyce, edited by Ellen Carol Jones and Morris Beja (2004)

Joyce on the Threshold, edited by Anne Fogarty and Timothy Martin (2005)

Wake Rites: The Ancient Irish Rituals of Finnegans Wake, by George Cinclair Gibson (2005)

Ulysses *in Critical Perspective,* edited by Michael Patrick Gillespie and A. Nicholas Fargnoli (2006)

Joyce and the Narrative Structure of Incest, by Jen Shelton (2006)

Joyce, Ireland, Britain, edited by Andrew Gibson and Len Platt (2006)

Joyce in Trieste: An Album of Risky Readings, edited by Sebastian D. G. Knowles, Geert Lernout, and John McCourt (2007)

Joyce's Rare View: The Nature of Things in Finnegans Wake, by Richard Beckman (2007)

Joyce's Misbelief, by Roy Gottfried (2007)

James Joyce's Painful Case, by Cóilín Owens (2008; first paperback edition, 2017)

Cannibal Joyce, by Thomas Jackson Rice (2008)

Manuscript Genetics, Joyce's Know-How, Beckett's Nohow, by Dirk Van Hulle (2008)

Catholic Nostalgia in Joyce and Company, by Mary Lowe-Evans (2008)

A Guide through Finnegans Wake, by Edmund Lloyd Epstein (2009)

Bloomsday 100: Essays on Ulysses, edited by Morris Beja and Anne Fogarty (2009)

Joyce, Medicine, and Modernity, by Vike Martina Plock (2010; first paperback edition, 2012)

Who's Afraid of James Joyce?, by Karen R. Lawrence (2010; first paperback edition, 2012)

Ulysses *in Focus: Genetic, Textual, and Personal Views*, by Michael Groden (2010; first paperback edition, 2012)

Foundational Essays in James Joyce Studies, edited by Michael Patrick Gillespie (2011; first paperback edition, 2017)

Empire and Pilgrimage in Conrad and Joyce, by Agata Szczeszak-Brewer (2011; first paperback edition, 2017)

The Poetry of James Joyce Reconsidered, edited by Marc C. Conner (2012; first paperback edition, 2015)

The German Joyce, by Robert K. Weninger (2012; first paperback edition 2016)

Joyce and Militarism, by Greg Winston (2012; first paperback edition, 2015)

Renascent Joyce, edited by Daniel Ferrer, Sam Slote, and André Topia (2013; first paperback edition, 2014)

Before Daybreak: "After the Race" and the Origins of Joyce's Art, by Cóilín Owens (2013; first paperback edition, 2014)

Modernists at Odds: Reconsidering Joyce and Lawrence, edited by Matthew J. Kochis and Heather L. Lusty (2015)

James Joyce and the Exilic Imagination, by Michael Patrick Gillespie (2015)

The Ecology of Finnegans Wake, by Alison Lacivita (2015)

Joyce's Allmaziful Plurabilities: Polyvocal Explorations of Finnegans Wake, edited by Kimberly J. Devlin and Christine Smedley (2015; first paperback edition, 2018)

Exiles: A Critical Edition, by James Joyce, edited by A. Nicholas Fargnoli and Michael Patrick Gillespie (2016)

Up to Maughty London: Joyce's Cultural Capital in the Imperial Metropolis, by Eleni Loukopoulou (2017)

Joyce and the Law, edited by Jonathan Goldman (2017)

At Fault: Joyce and the Crisis of the Modern University, by Sebastian D. G. Knowles (2018)

Ulysses *Unbound: A Reader's Companion to James Joyce's* Ulysses, *Third Edition*, by Terence Killeen (2018)

www.ingramcontent.com/pod-product-compliance
Lightning Source LLC
Chambersburg PA
CBHW031427160426
43195CB00010BB/647